HOMEPAGE
USABILITY
50 WEBSITES DECONSTRUCTED

JAKOB NIELSEN & MARIE TAHIR

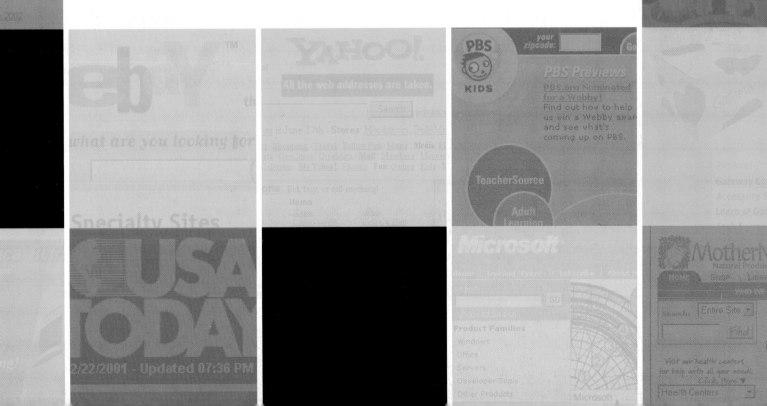

New Riders

International Standard Book Number: 0-7357-1102-X

Library of Congress Catalog Card Number: 00-111648

Printed in the United States of America

First Printing: October 2001

06   7 6

Trademarks

Warning and Disclaimer

Credits

Publisher   David Dwyer

Associate Publisher   Stephanie Wall

Executive Editor   Steve Weiss

Senior Development Editor   Jennifer Eberhardt

Managing Editor   Sarah Kearns

Copy Editor   Jake McFarland

Technical Editor   Steven Sanchez

Product Marketing Manager   Kathy Malmloff

Publicist   Susan Nixon

Cover Designer   Aren Howell

Interior Designer   Allison Cecil

Compositor   Suzanne Pettypiece

Proofreader   Linda Seifert

Indexer   Lisa Stumpf

Table of Contents

SITES

About the Authors

Dr. Jakob Nielsen

Jakob is principal of Nielsen Norman Group; he was previously a Sun Microsystems Distinguished Engineer. Nielsen's Alertbox column about web usability has been published on the Internet since 1995 (www.useit.com). Nielsen has been called "the world's leading expert on web usability" (*U.S. News & World Report*), "the guru of Web page usability" (*The New York Times*), and he "knows more about what makes web sites work than anyone else on the planet" (*Chicago Tribune*).

Marie Tahir

Marie is Director of Strategy at Nielsen Norman Group, where she has focused on B2B and B2C user experience redesign. She previously managed the Human Factors group at Intuit, Inc., where she introduced and taught user centered design methodology and oversaw the user experience of the TurboTax, ProSeries, and QuickenLoans product lines. Prior to Intuit, Marie was at Lotus Development Corp., where she pioneered field research and user profiling methodology and was responsible for the usability of the SmartSuite product line. She is the co-author of "Bringing the Users' Work to Us: Usability Roundtables at Lotus Development" in Wixon and Ramey's *Field Methods Casebook for Software Design*.

About the Tech Editor

Steve Sanchez

is the founder and CEO of iNexus.com, a Los Angeles-based firm that consults, builds, and promotes Internet solutions for business. Over the past 10 years, he has worked with leading companies in industries such as travel, medical, and publications, creating sites that work for both owners and users. A long-time evangelist for strengthening the online user's experience, Steve is a "Raving Fan" of database-driven web sites, web communities for business, and technologies such as dynamic Flash, VR tours, Active Server Pages, and Microsoft's upcoming .NET. He enjoys photography, travel, sailing, and scuba diving. He lives in Los Angeles with his wife and four children.

Dedication

For Faran Tahir, with great appreciation

Marie Tahir

For my parents, Dr. Helle H. Nielsen and Dr. Gerhard Nielsen

Jakob Nielsen

Acknowledgments

We would like to thank the following members of Nielsen Norman Group for substantial help with many aspects of this book project, including selecting the sites, collecting the screenshots, defining the page metrics, measuring the page metrics, and improving the guidelines:

Brenda Brozinick
Kara Pernice Coyne
Susan Farrell
Shuli Gilutz
Luice Hwang
Hoa Loranger

We also thank Rolf Molich and Gia Rozells for insightful comments on the guidelines.

The New Riders editorial team provided substantial assistance, enabling us to complete this project on time. We particularly thank Jennifer Eberhardt for help with many aspects of the manuscript and the mapping of the screen space used by different categories of page elements.

A Message from New Riders

As the reader of this book, you are our most important critic and commentator. We value your opinion and want to know what we're doing right, what we could do better, in what areas you'd like to see us publish, and any other words of wisdom you're willing to pass our way.

When you contact us, please be sure to include this book's title, ISBN, and author, as well as your name and email address. We will carefully review your comments and share them with the authors and editors who worked on the book.

Email: errata@newriders.com

Visit Our Web Site: www.newriders.com

On our Web site, you'll find information about our other books, the authors we partner with, book updates and file downloads, promotions, discussion boards for online interaction with other users and with technology experts, and a calendar of trade shows and other professional events with which we'll be involved. We hope to see you around.

Email Us from Our Web Site

Go to www.newriders.com and click on the Customer Support link if you

- Have comments or questions about this book.
- Want to report errors that you have found in this book.
- Have a book proposal or are interested in writing for New Riders.
- Would like us to send you one of our author kits.
- Are an expert in a computer topic or technology and are interested in being a reviewer or technical editor.
- Want to find a distributor for our titles in your area.
- Are an educator/instructor who wants to preview New Riders books for classroom use. In the body/comments area, include your name, school, department, address, phone number, office days/hours, text currently in use, and enrollment in your department, along with your request for either desk/examination copies or additional information.

Preface

Homepages are the most valuable real estate in the world. Millions of dollars are funneled through a space that's not even a square foot in size. The homepage's impact on a company's bottom line is far greater than simple measures of e-commerce revenues: the homepage is also your company's face to the world. Increasingly, potential customers will look at your company's online presence before doing any business with you—regardless of whether the actual sale is closed online.

The homepage is the most important page on any website, getting more page views than any other page. Of course, users don't always enter a website from the homepage. A website is like a house in which every single window is also a door: People may follow links from search engines and other websites that reach deep inside your site. However, one of the first actions these users will take after arriving at a new site is to go to the homepage. Deep linking is very useful, but it doesn't give users the overview of a site that they can get from the homepage—if the homepage design follows strong usability guidelines, that is.

That's why we've written a book specifically about homepage usability.

Other aspects of web usability are important as well, and this book is certainly not the only usability book you should read or own. But, the homepage is the most important page on your site and we feel it warrants extra attention and its own book.

In the initial years of commercial web projects, we user advocates were kept busy fighting against design excess and fashion-driven sites that contradicted everything we knew about user behavior. Our first battle was to defeat the horrible, user-hostile designs promoted by glamour agencies and people who wanted to make the Web into television. We have partly won this battle, but we have not yet succeeded in making the Web into a truly usable environment that supports users' goals and maximizes companies' returns on investments. Stopping *bad* design doesn't guarantee *good* design; it just eliminates the worst flops that nobody would be using anyway.

The field of web usability has now matured sufficiently that we can develop specialized guidelines to codify the best design practices for specific components of a website. This book is the frontline of our second campaign for a usable Web: After defeating bad design, we are now fighting for good design. Here we present 113 homepage usability guidelines for moving forward. These guidelines are a solid foundation on which you can build a homepage that will work for you and your customers.

The Role of the Homepage

The most critical role of the homepage is to communicate what the company is, the value the site offers over the competition and the physical world, and the products or services offered. This sounds simple and obvious, but many design teams struggle and fail to create a usable homepage design because they don't share this common understanding of what the homepage needs to do, or they get locked into a narrow or misguided vision of its purpose.

There are many metaphors for the role of homepages in the user experience. All have some relevance because the homepage does play many roles. Not all metaphors are equally valid, however, and some of them can be misleading if they dominate your thinking.

These are some of the more common metaphors for homepages:

Magazine cover. The primary business goal of a cover is to make you pick up the magazine from a sea of hundreds of them at the newsstand. In contrast, users don't see the homepage until they have already decided to single out the website and visit it. Thus, homepages don't need to stand out and grab the user's attention because the user will already be looking at them. A secondary job of a magazine cover is to define by example the content, style, and so forth inside the magazine. This area is where you can learn the most lessons for web design.

Your face to the world. The old saying goes that you get only one chance to make a first impression. On the Web you really get only one chance to make any impression. When the first impression isn't good, you don't get a second chance because the user will never return. At the same time, web design is interaction design, and the experience that follows after users enter the site is key. Contrary to a beauty contest, you can't be too superficial on a homepage; you need to deliver on the promises.

Artwork. People look at artwork in two steps: They first give the piece a quick once-over to see whether it interests them at all. Then they take the time to really look at the piece and appreciate or analyze it. Many design teams think of their homepage as artwork and invest only in the visual rather than the interaction design of the page. Your homepage's visual design should, of course, be clean and professional since customers do take a first impression from this design. Unlike artwork, however, they're not going to just to sit and enjoy the homepage after they've decided it's worth checking out. The homepage is just a stepping stone to their true destination inside your site. Therefore, always invest more in the interaction design of your site.

Building lobby. A lobby is not a destination in itself; you just pass through it. The homepage too is the entrance point and funnels traffic in different directions. Thus every homepage needs good signage like the signs in a hospital lobby for the different wards and departments. Hospital signage gives due priority for urgent destinations like the emergency room or labor and delivery, and your website should prioritize users' destinations, too.

Company receptionist/concierge. Related to the lobby metaphor is the idea of a human being who directs visitors to the right place, welcomes returning customers, provides friendly and helpful guidance, and makes people feel cared for. These are all valuable qualities for a homepage but can result in annoying and interruptive "assistants" if taken too literally.

Book table of contents. The design for the table of contents for a book focuses on getting you to one place and provides a hierarchical overview. By giving you a list of choices, the table of contents gets you directly to your choice through the convention of page numbers. This metaphor is the one that comes closest to the mechanics of the hypertext link, which is the foundation of web use.

Newspaper front page. The front page of a newspaper presents a short, prioritized overview of most important news. Front pages have the advantage of being edited by an authority who selects the content from many contributors. Because of their regular publishing schedule, newspapers have time to craft the front page and get it right. This metaphor should not be taken literally since a printed newspaper is a once-per-day product that is updated on a 24-hour schedule. Websites might need to be updated many times a day or just a few times a month. A newspaper also might have many other elements besides the news, but it doesn't have to represent them all on the front page, because the standard format for a newspaper is so recognizable and navigation is as simple as just flipping to a page or major section. Websites need to represent many more services on the homepage because the genre is less established than newspapers.

Brochure. The original approach to web marketing was to treat the website as the company's brochure with the homepage serving as the lead-in to the brochure. A homepage does have to entice people to follow through and read further, but that's where the similarity stops. Brochures have very straightforward goals, mainly to get people to contact the company and follow up. Brochure can be driven by marketing messages and have great bandwidth for glossy design. Readers also more readily accept that the brochure has a glib spin on the company and its products and services. Web users, in contrast, are much more goal-driven—they have decided to go there for some reason, not just to page through the content. Users only care how well the site is serving their specific purpose for visiting that day and get very annoyed when corporate messages get in their way.

All these metaphors have some truth to them, but each has ways in which it differs from the true nature of homepages. Websites are not artwork, newspapers, buildings, or people. It is dangerous to take a single metaphor and use only that. Not only that, it is hard to design a homepage because it must have aspects of all the metaphors. Most designs go overboard in one direction.

The homepage has multiple goals and the users also have multiple goals. Sometimes a user arrives at a homepage to find out what the company does—maybe to invest in it or perhaps to place it on a shortlist of possible vendors. Sometimes a user is researching a specific purchase, and sometimes a user needs to get service and support for products he or she already owns. Trouble is, it's often the same person who flits between goals from one visit to the next. It's not possible to simply segment the users, fit them into neat little boxes, and provide a narrow range of choices to each type of user.

Inexperienced users often feel overwhelmed by homepages that don't clearly help them understand their options. When they can't understand a website, users may become embarrassed and blame themselves; you will rarely hear from them. They will just leave the site and turn to places that feel more welcoming. More savvy users are often very unforgiving. If their current specific need isn't met on any given trip to the website, they will remember that and hold it against the website. Such users will sometimes be very vocal and send email asking, "Why don't you put feature X on the homepage?" Remember that such user comments don't imply that X needs its own homepage button; it just means that X is hard to find with the current design for that user.

The challenge is to design a homepage that allows access to all important features without cramming them onto the page itself, too often overwhelming new users. Focus and clarity are key, as is an understanding of users' goals.

The Organization of This Book

In our consulting practice, we are often asked to review homepage designs for usability. After many such reviews, several general patterns and issues became apparent. We typically charge $10,000 for a usability review of a homepage. Knowing that many companies cannot afford the consulting fee, we decided to share our knowledge in this book.

This book has two parts: The first part is general analysis of guidelines and statistics, and the second part is 50 concrete examples of individual homepages and their usability issues.

The first chapter in the book presents the guidelines we observed in our practice. When reading the chapter, you may be tempted to dismiss the guidelines as obvious. "*Of course,* homepages should follow these rules," you say. Yes, indeed, but even the best sites often overlook usability guidelines in their design. That's why it is helpful to have the guidelines combined into a single chapter and that's why we start the book with that chapter.

In the second chapter of the book, we compile a statistical analysis of the 50 sites reviewed in this book. Theory often seems dry and unapproachable. It's tough, but we highly recommend that you slug through it. It's the part that will help you the most in improving your own homepage.

We didn't just want to be theoretical in this book; we also wanted to help you by collecting examples of how others are solving design challenges. Many people learn best from specific examples, and there is no doubt that the second part of the book—the reviews of the 50 home-pages—constitutes the most approachable and intriguing aspect. We hope that the book will reach a broader audience than many usability texts because this part is so colorful and lively. This broad overview lets you learn from both the good and bad.

Although many of the site reviews focus on negative aspects of what's wrong with each individual design, the guidelines give a constructive view of how to build a usable homepage from the beginning. The two parts of the book complement each other well because the many examples illustrate how hard it is to comply with all the usability guidelines.

Flip through the pages; mark examples that apply to your work; show the book to your colleagues; immerse yourself in the details. Details matter for usability, and the book design is intended to make it easy to understand both the parts and the whole in a manner that is still best supported by the printed page—especially *big*, nicely printed pages.

Because this book contains 50 reviews, we've been joking that its value is half-million dollars for the readers. Makes the cover price seem cheap, wouldn't you say? Of course, the book isn't really worth $500,000. First, a list of recommended changes to your own site is obviously worth more than a list of usability issues for a third-party site. Second, a review for one of our clients includes not only the specific types of presentation-level comments you see in this book, but also the more strategic side of how to serve their particular customers and their tasks. This analysis wouldn't be interesting for anyone but the particular company, so we don't cover it here. This is truly not a half-million dollar book, but if you take its advice, you can increase the business impact of your homepage by a very substantial amount, making the book a bargain.

Your Action Items

After you finish reading the book, don't just put it on the shelf. That's the one place where it's not going to do any good for your bottom line. Instead, follow this plan of action.

First, assess how well your current homepage complies with the usability guidelines. Don't spend too much time on this project, but simply step through the 113 guidelines and decide whether your site follows or violates each guideline. You can give half-credit for partial compliance, but don't get too fancy with your scoring scheme. Count 0, 1/2, or 1 point for each guideline. If a guideline doesn't apply because of the nature of your site, then don't score it.

Second, divide the final count by the number of guidelines you did score to arrive at your usability compliance rate.

- If you're above 80%, consider yourself in good shape, though you might want to make a few minor fixes to areas where you have violated guidelines.

- If you're between 50 to 80%, start a redesign project to produce a new homepage. Your current homepage is definitely not a disaster, but it is bad enough that isolated modifications to individual areas will not suffice.

- If you're below 50%, you are probably not serving your customers well with your current approach to web design. Most likely, you should abandon the entire current site and start over from scratch. Rethink your Internet strategy and base your new approach on studies of your customers and their real needs.

For any given site, there are always reasons why a few of the usability guidelines don't apply and may be broken. The perfect website will probably follow around 90 to 95% of the usability guidelines that apply to that particular site and do something different, but appropriate, in the remaining cases. It is important, though, to know the guidelines before you can break them because the guidelines really do describe the design approach that works best for most users most of the time.

The Companion Web Pages

We are maintaining an online presence to supplement this book at
http://www.useit.com/homepageusability.

We will be posting corrections of any substantive errors that may be discovered after the printing of this volume. We won't bother with minor typos or misspellings, but if any major mistake has survived the many rounds of editing and proofreading, we will provide a fix online.

The companion web page also contains a study guide to support instructional use of the book. The study guide will be helpful for reading groups in companies and other organizations—for example, your company's web team may read the book and then meet to discuss its implications for your own homepage.

Jakob Nielsen and Marie Tahir
October 2001

Homepage Guidelines

This chapter summarizes our major design guidelines to ensure homepage usability. While many of these guidelines can apply to web design in general, they are especially critical to follow when designing your homepage, because the stakes are so high. Your homepage is often your first—and possibly your last—chance to attract and retain each customer, rather like the front page of a newspaper. One of the biggest values of a newspaper's front page is the priority given to top news items. All homepages would benefit from being treated like a front page of a major newspaper, with editors who determine the high-priority content and ensure continuity and style consistency.

Even small changes to homepages can have drastic effects. Consider the homepage for *The New York Times*. If you kept all design and writing exactly the same on this site but decided to show only local New York content on the homepage and link to all national and international news, it would inexorably alter the entire site. On closer examination, this change doesn't seem small at all.

While we encourage you to use these guidelines as a checklist when designing your homepage, recognize that they are written in an abbreviated manner here. You'll need to look at the individual site examples to see these guidelines used properly or, more often, overlooked. This is an extensively illustrated book, and it is only in the context of a visual example that you can fully appreciate the negative impact of ignoring these guidelines.

All said, these are just guidelines, not axioms. For all sites, there are surely exceptions. However, we've developed these guidelines from our combined 14 years of experience, running user tests on homepages and observing what makes them pass or fail user scrutiny. Although you can greatly improve the usability of your homepage by following these guidelines, you also need to involve your own users in the process through methods such as field studies and usability testing and incorporate iterative feedback into your development cycle. If you make a decision not to follow a guideline, do so based on customer information in the context of your homepage.

What's Not in These Guidelines

In an effort to limit the focus of this book specifically to homepage guidelines, there are several important issues we do not address. Most of these topics deserve a level of detail that we feel is best left to separate books and reports, many of which exist already and are listed here.

Determining Homepage Content

One of the most important design decisions for any homepage is determining what content merits homepage coverage. We don't address this issue in these guidelines because it depends on each site's users and tasks, as well as the company's business goals. Unfortunately, many companies' corporate politics drive homepage design more than users' needs do. Often many departments are lobbying for homepage real estate, and the best lobbyists win. We encourage you to champion users' needs as the key factor in design decisions and to involve users throughout your design process.

There are several usability methods that can identify and prioritize users' needs based on real data and observation. This is not the place to go into details about user testing, task analysis, field studies, or usability engineering methodology and process in general. These topics each require their own book, and indeed several such books have been written and continue to be written. We maintain a set of web pages at **http://www.useit.com/books,** with references and links to those books that we recommend the most at any given time.

General Web Design

We have limited our guidelines to those that are critical for successful homepage usability, although many would improve the usability of other web pages as well. Similarly, many, if not most, of the guidelines for the design of general web pages, web content, and web navigation would increase the usability of homepages. After all, a homepage is a web page, and thus home-page designers should consider all of the guidelines for web usability, not just those that are specific to homepages. For detailed information on general web design, see *Designing Web Usability: The Practice of Simplicity*, by Jakob Nielsen.

Vertical Industry Segments

We don't address special design considerations for vertical industry segments, such as homepages for software companies, conferences, or dentists. For every industry or type of company, there will be many detailed guidelines that address the ways customers of such companies expect to interact with websites and the best ways to serve those users' needs.

We cannot provide a set of generic vertical guidelines. That would be a contradiction in terms. The only way to generate vertical design guidelines is to study each industry's users and their tasks. Our preferred approach for doing so is the comparative usability test, which generalizes findings across a broad variety of sites within a given vertical segment. This is not the place for a discussion of how to run a comparative study; instead we refer you to a report that details the methodology used to derive 207 guidelines for e-commerce usability from a test of 20 websites. This 44-page methodology report is available from **http://www.NNgroup.com/reports/ecommerce/methodology.html**.

Accessibility

While some of our individual site reviews point out major design issues that would impede people using assistive technology, accessibility is too large a topic to do due diligence in these guidelines. We refer you instead to our detailed guidelines for accessibility at **http://www.NNgroup.com/reports/accessibility**.

Children

The emphasis in this book is on designing homepages for use by adult users. Some of the guidelines also apply when designing for children, but there are many big differences that would be beyond the scope of this book to discuss. Detailed findings from our testing of websites with children and the resulting list of 70 special usability guidelines for kids can be found at **http://www.nngroup.com/reports/kids**.

International Users

While we point out a few guidelines for serving international users in this book, we refer you to our detailed guidelines at **http://www.NNgroup.com/reports/ecommerce/international.html**. See also *International User Interfaces*, by Elisa del Galdo and Jakob Nielsen.

Intranet Homepages

These guidelines focus on websites that are publicly available on the Internet and thus target external users. Intranet designs target the organization's own employees and sometimes require different guidelines. Many of the guidelines in this book are still useful for intranet designers if they are adapted appropriately. For a targeted list of 111 intranet guidelines based on usability studies of intranet designs, please see **http://www.nngroup.com/reports/intranet/guidelines**.

The Guidelines

The following sections contain our 113 guidelines for ensuring homepage usability. The guidelines are categorized by topic area, and most give examples from the homepage reviews, which you can find in alphabetical order beginning on page 56.

Communicating the Site's Purpose

Imagine how disorienting it would be to walk into a store and not be able to tell immediately what services or goods were available there. The same is true of your homepage. It must communicate in one short glance where users are, what your company does, and what users can do at your site. If your site misses the mark here, it's nearly impossible to recover. Why should users do anything at a site if they can't figure out what there is to do there? And yet in countless user studies, we've seen users staring right at the homepage, unable to satisfactorily answer the question "What is the purpose of this site?" In order to communicate well, homepages must give appropriate emphasis to both branding and high-priority tasks. The homepage must also have a memorable and distinct look, so that users can recognize it as their starting place when coming from any other part of the site.

1 **Show the company name and/or logo in a reasonable size and noticeable location.** This identity area doesn't need to be huge, but it should be larger and more prominent than the items around it so it gets first attention when users enter the site. The upper-left corner is usually the best placement for languages that read from left to right.

2 **Include a tag line that explicitly summarizes what the site or company does.** Tag lines should be brief, simple, and to the point. For example, Global Sources' tag line, "Product and Trade Information for Volume Buyers," is a good, straightforward summary of what the site offers (we did, however, offer minor suggestions for improvement in the homepage review). Vague or jargonistic tag lines only confuse users, or worse, make them mistrust the site, especially if users perceive them as marketing hype. For example, Ford's tag line, "Striving to Make the World a Better Place," while pluckily optimistic, doesn't describe Ford's automotive business in any way.

Tag lines might not be necessary when the company name itself explains what the company does, such as the Federal Highway Administration, or if the company is extremely famous, such as Microsoft. If your company has many sites or services, the tag line for the main company homepage should summarize what the company is all about, and the subsites should have their own tag lines explaining the purpose of that particular site or service.

3 **Emphasize what your site does that's valuable from the user's point of view, as well as how you differ from key competitors.** The tag line is a great place to do this, if you can do it succinctly. For example, Wal-Mart frequently differentiates itself from competitors in advertising media by claiming that it offers the lowest prices, but doesn't say so anywhere on its homepage except for a brief mention in the title bar. A simple tag line that stated this differentiator would give users unfamiliar with the company an instant sense of what the site can offer them.

4 **Emphasize the highest priority tasks so that users have a clear starting point on the homepage.** Give these tasks a prominent location, such as the upper-middle of the page, and don't give them a lot of visual competition. In other words, if you emphasize everything, nothing gets focus. Keep the number of core tasks small (1–4) and the area around them clear. For example, a financial news website, like CNNfn, should devote prime real estate to high-priority tasks like checking a stock quote, getting the current summary of the major U.S. stock markets, and getting a summary of the current financial news headlines. The most challenging, yet most critical, aspect of this guideline is actually determining *what* the highest priority tasks are from the user's perspective. You must have a deep understanding of your users' needs, which is best acquired by studying your users in the context in which they will use your website before you begin the homepage design.

While the Philip Morris website lists its subsidiaries, you can't tell that each logo in the list is a link.

Global Sources' tag line is short, straightforward, and gives a good description of what the site is all about.

5 Clearly designate one page per site as the official homepage. Within the site, restrict the use of the terms "Home" and "Home Page" to refer to this one main homepage and use a different term for the front pages of departments or subsites. Users should never face multiple "Home" buttons or links that go to different places. Of course, if your company is a conglomerate, the main homepage will likely link to other separate sites that have a clear identity and unique homepage apart from the parent company. For example, Philip Morris has a separate homepage for Miller Brewing Company (a subsidiary) that is linked to from the Philip Morris homepage.

6 On your main company website, don't use the word "website" to refer to anything but the totality of the company's web presence. Specifically, don't use it to refer to subsites or departments. Using "website" to refer to parts of the site separates, rather than unites, your company's total offerings and it can confuse users, who naturally think that a different website means that they are going to a different company. For example, Ford's homepage uses an icon to mark links to external websites. However, Ford only uses this icon next to the link for its dealer finder, making it seem like it isn't part of the company. From the user's' perspective, of course, getting information about the cars and getting information about where to buy the cars are all parts of the same task.

If you offer web applications or services on separate websites, some users might go straight to a service website without going through the corporate homepage. It's fine to refer to those subsites as websites on the specific sites themselves, but from the corporate homepage it's better to present them as major categories. This portrays them as part of your total offering, rather than separate from it. For example, the Philip Morris website lists its subsidiaries, such as Kraft Foods International Inc., as part of its "Family of Companies," but doesn't label them as websites.

7 Design the homepage to be clearly different from all the other pages on the site. Either use a slightly different visual design (that still fits with the look and feel of the site) or have a prominent location designator in the navigational apparatus. This visual distinction and navigational signposting ensures that users can recognize their starting point when they return from exploring a new part of the site.

Communicating Information About Your Company

In addition to the homepage tag line, all business websites need to provide a clear way to find information about the company, no matter how big or small the company is, or how simple or complex the range of products or services are. People like to know with whom they are doing business, and details about the company give credibility to the site. For some websites, such as those for large conglomerates, getting company information might be the sole reason that users come to the site. Yet even for sites that deliver a simple web service, many users still want to know who is behind the service.

These guidelines also apply to government sites and to sites for many other types of not-for-profit organizations, although some of the details may vary. For example, a government agency would not need an Investor Relations link. It is a common mistake, especially on government homepages, to play up the wrong kinds of information about the agency. People need to be able to find out how the organization is structured and who runs it, but they do not need to have an interface that's designed to emphasize internal bureaucratic structure or one that promotes the current minister or department head at the expense of granting citizens fast access to the services and information they need.

8 **Group corporate information, such as About Us, Investor Relations, Press Room, Employment and other information about the company, in one distinct area.** This grouping gives people who want the information a clear and memorable place to go. It also helps users who don't care about this information by separating it from the rest of the homepage content. For more information on the usability of the investor relations area of websites, see **http://www.nngroup.com/reports/ir**.

9 **Include a homepage link to an "About Us" section that gives users an overview about the company and links to any relevant details about your products, services, company values, business proposition, management team, and so forth.** The recommended name for this link is "About <name of company>."

10 **If you want to get press coverage for your company, include a "Press Room" or "News Room" link on your homepage.** Journalists appreciate and rely on sections like these when trying to cover a particular company. For more information on optimizing web design for press relations, see **http://www.NNgroup.com/reports/pr**.

11 **Present a unified face to the customer, in which the website is one of the touchpoints rather than an entity unto itself.** Don't separate your web presence from the rest of your company by referring to "Company.com" as different from "Company." Your customers should feel they are dealing with one indivisible, consistent company. It is important, however, to make distinctions between web-only services and services listed on the site that are available only through a different medium. For example, a television station might offer webcasts that are available only on the website as well as list information for programs that are available only on television. Users need to understand where to go for which service.

12 **Include a "Contact Us" link on the homepage that goes to a page with all contact information for your company.** If you want to encourage site visitors to contact your company directly, instead of seeking information on the website first, include contact information such as the primary address, phone number, and email directly on the homepage.

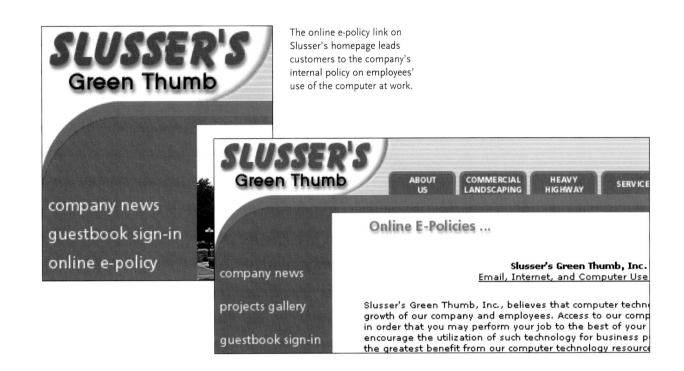

The online e-policy link on Slusser's homepage leads customers to the company's internal policy on employees' use of the computer at work.

13 If you provide a "feedback" mechanism, specify the purpose of the link and whether it will be read by customer service or the webmaster, and so forth.

14 Don't include internal company information (which is targeted for employees and should go on the intranet) on the public website. Not only does this internal information clutter the public website, it can actually be misleading if users think that internal policies are directed toward them. For example, Slusser's homepage links to its company's internal policy for computer resources, including guidelines for appropriate web usage, which could worry some users that Slusser's knows more about their web surfing habits than is actually the case. Job postings are an example of largely company-focused content that might be beneficial on both intranet and public sites, however, because they are chiefly targeted at potential employees, not current ones.

15 If your site gathers any customer information, include a "Privacy Policy" link on the homepage.

16 Explain how the website makes money if it's not self-evident. If users cannot easily discover a business model (such as selling stuff or carrying advertising), their trust in the site will be lowered because they will fear that it has some hidden way of "getting" at them. People know that there is no such thing as a free lunch.

Content Writing

Effective content writing is one of the most critical aspects of all web design. Most users scan online content, rather than carefully reading, so you must optimize content for scannability and craft it to convey maximum information in few words. Although this is a general web guideline, we're offering content writing guidelines here that are especially important for homepages, where you must work hardest to capture and hold your users' interest, and where you often have the least amount of space to represent the greatest number of topics.

A skilled editor is an essential part of effective content creation. The editor should not only set style standards but must also ensure that the site follows them consistently. The editor should develop or revise content specifically for web use—it's not enough to repurpose content from other mediums and post it to the homepage. Of course, the design team must also involve real users in this process, both when gathering initial requirements and when revising the design as the site evolves.

17 **Use customer-focused language. Label sections and categories according to the value they hold for the customer, not according to what they do for your company.** For example, on a heating oil site, what should you call a category of home energy tips? On **www.jamesdevaney.com**, it's called "Consumer Information." This company-focused phrase is based solely on how the fuel company values this customer (as a consumer, not a business). Instead, think of how the customer would view the information, such as "Home Energy Tips." Ask customers what they look for when they need such information. Use the words they use.

18 **Avoid redundant content.** Repeating identical items, such as categories or links, on the homepage in order to emphasize their importance actually reduces their impact. Redundant items also clutter the page; all items lose impact because they are competing with so many elements. In order to feature something prominently, feature it clearly in one place. On the other hand, redundant content can help people if you repeat items that belong in multiple categories or you include links to the same page but offer synonyms that represent words your users use to describe the content.

19 **Don't use clever phrases and marketing lingo that make people work too hard to figure out what you're saying.** For example, the "Dream, Plan, & Go" category on Travelocity might sound catchy to a marketing person, but it's not as straightforward as "Vacation Planning." Every time you make users ponder the meaning behind vague and cutesy phrases, you risk alienating or losing them altogether. Users quickly lose patience when they must click on a link just to figure out what it means. This isn't to say that homepage text should be bland, but it must be informative and should be unambiguous.

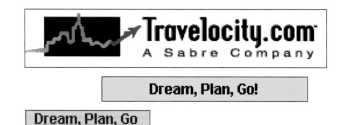

"Dream, Plan, Go" doesn't explain anything about what makes this feature different from all its other travel planning features.

20 **Use consistent capitalization and other style standards.** Otherwise users read meaning into things when they shouldn't. For example, if some items in a list follow sentence-style capitalization, but one item uses initial uppercase letters, the inconsistency gives that one item undue emphasis over the other items. Usually this kind of inconsistency happens not by design, but because the content comes from different sources and isn't appropriately edited for consistency. Although these small mistakes might seem nitpicky, they can cause users to feel that the site is unprofessional or untrustworthy. We also advise against the popular style of using all lowercase letters for titles, categories, and other links. Not only is it not as scannable as mixed case, but also invariably you'll need to break with the style standard for a proper name, which will look inconsistent.

21 **Don't label a clearly defined area of the page if the content is sufficiently self-explanatory.** For example, it is usually not necessary to label the main news headline of the day because the size and placement indicate its role. Similarly, if you have a boxed area where you feature a product, it's probably not necessary to give it a generic title such as "Featured Product." Titles often are meaningless space wasters.

22 **Avoid single-item categories and single-item bulleted lists.** It's overkill to categorize one item, and things that don't fit into existing categories can signify a need to rewrite or reorganize the content. See Asia Cuisine for an example.

23 **Use non-breaking spaces between words in phrases that need to go together in order to be scannable and understood.** Most homepages use multicolumn layouts, and text must fit into narrow spaces. Because there are many possibilities for where text breaks depending on the user's screen resolution, monitor size, window size, browser version, and so forth, forcing certain phrases to stay together can maintain the integrity and logic of the content.

24 **Only use imperative language such as "Enter a City or Zip Code" for mandatory tasks, or qualify the statement appropriately.** For example, you might say, "To See Your Local Weather, Enter a City or Zip Code." People are naturally drawn to text that tells them what to do on a site, especially if it is next to a recognized widget, such as an input box or a dropdown menu, and often dutifully follow instructions because they think that they *must* do what the instructions say.

25 **Spell out abbreviations, initialisms, and acronyms, and immediately follow them by the abbreviation, in the first instance.** This is helpful for all users, especially for anyone using a screen reader. For example, the Federal Highway Administration's homepage refers several times to the "MUTCD" but fails to explain on the homepage that this is short for "Manual on Uniform Traffic Control Devices." Abbreviations that have become widely used words, such as DVD, are exceptions to this guideline. Especially avoid using unexplained abbreviations as navigation links.

26 **Avoid exclamation marks.** Exclamation marks don't belong in professional writing, and they especially don't belong on a homepage. Exclamation marks look chaotic and loud—don't yell at users. If you break this guideline once, you're likely to start breaking it all over the homepage, because all items on the homepage should be of high importance.

27 **Use all uppercase letters sparingly or not at all as a formatting style.** All uppercase words are not as easy to read as mixed case words, and they can make the page look busy and loud. For example, "PSYCHOLOGY OF WORDS" is not as readable as "Psychology of Words."

28 **Avoid using spaces and punctuation inappropriately, for emphasis.** For example, L O B S T E R S or L.O.B.S.T.E.R.S. might look interesting to you but would foil a user who was searching for "lobsters." Unusual punctuation also reduces scannability and would be annoying to visually impaired users whose audio browsers spell out the word instead of reading it as a word.

Revealing Content Through Examples

Showing examples of your site's content on the homepage helps users in many ways. First, example content can help instantly communicate what the site is all about, so users know whether they are on the right site for their needs. Second, examples can reveal the breadth of products or content offered at your site. Third, specifics are more interesting than generalities. You stand a better chance of piquing user interest if you provide something concrete to read or look at instead of just abstract category names. Last, and probably most important, examples can help users successfully navigate, because they show what lies beneath the abstract category names. Examples help differentiate categories, saving users from clicking through categories just to see what's there.

29 **Use examples to reveal the site's content, rather than just describing it.** Well-chosen examples of content can convey much more than words alone. For instance, a category called "Breaking News" with a description that says "Get All of Today's Top Stories Here" is not nearly as interesting or informative as showing the top five news headlines, followed by a link to all breaking news. Or, on an e-commerce site, a simple category called "Sale Items" is not as compelling as seeing a few actual products that are on sale, complete with their prices. Often it takes more words and space to describe a category than it does to show some of that category's contents and link to more information. In brick-and-mortar stores, customers rely on examples to orient themselves and find the items they need. Similarly, homepages should show small pictures of the products or other content in each department, so users can do a quick visual sweep to see if they are in the right place. Examples also help users who don't read your site's language very well.

30 **For each example, have a link that goes directly to the detailed page for that example, rather than to a general category page of which that item is a part.** Don't put the burden on the user to find the item they're interested in once again on the second page. For instance, if your homepage features news coverage of a film festival, and you show a photo and caption for a specific film, those items should link directly to information about that particular film, not a general page for the festival. The exception is examples that are so short and self-contained that there is no more information about them deeper within the site.

31 **Provide a link to the broader category next to the specific example.** If you prominently feature a single product, service, or article on the homepage, make sure that the rest of the page clearly communicates the full breadth of products, services, or content supported by the site (unless you are a one-product company), because people sometimes believe that the main feature is all there is. For example, if a job-listing site prominently features three listings in the medical industry with no adjacent link to "Listings in Other Industries," users might easily think that the site lists jobs only for medical personnel.

32 **Make sure it's obvious which links lead to follow-up information about each example and which links lead to general information about the category as a whole.** Do this both by wording and placement of the links. The link for the example should be directly next to the information about the example, while the link to the category should be offset with a small amount of whitespace. For example, if Amazon.com features a specific mystery novel on its homepage, it should have a link at the end of the description of the novel to "Complete Description and Reviews," as well as a link a bit lower in the section to "Complete Listing of Mystery Novels."

Archives and Accessing Past Content

Often, you have users who return to your site often or new users who are interested in what you've done before they found you. It's helpful to include archives to content that has recently moved off the homepage.

㉝ Make it easy to access anything that has been recently featured on your homepage, for example, in the last two weeks or month, by providing a list of recent features as well as putting recent items into the permanent archives. If you rotate content of featured stories or products, make sure to include a link to the other featured stories or products. If the featured story will be moved to another URL after it rotates off the homepage, make a link to the URL for the permanent location right away so people can bookmark the permanent link instead of the temporary link.

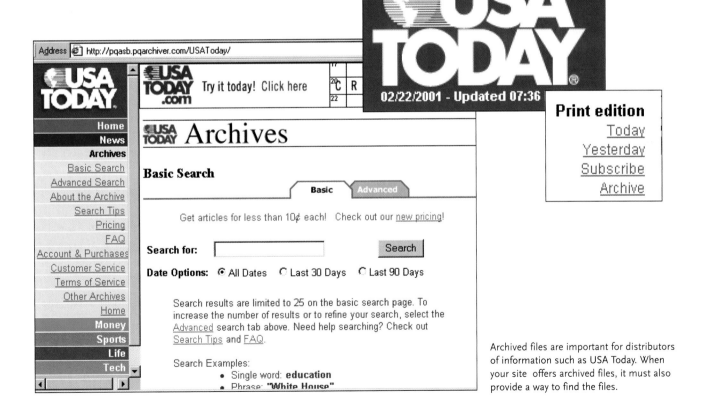

Archived files are important for distributors of information such as USA Today. When your site offers archived files, it must also provide a way to find the files.

Links

Links are obviously not unique to homepages, but because homepages serve as the portal to the site and thus tend to have more links than typical site pages, following design guidelines for homepage links is especially crucial to user success.

34 **Differentiate links and make them scannable.** Begin links with the information-carrying word, because users often scan through the first word or two of links to compare them. Keep links as specific and brief as possible. Don't include obvious or redundant information in every link—adding non-differentiating words makes users work harder to find the important words. For example, if you list press releases for your company and every one of them begins with the company name, it's difficult to quickly get the gist of each press release by scanning through the list. Or, if the proper names of your subsidiaries include the company name, such as "FedEx Express," "FedEx Ground," "FedEx Home Delivery," listing them as such presents users with a column of identical words ("FedEx"), and they must read through all of the links carefully to glean the difference.

35 **Don't use generic instructions, such as "Click Here" as a link name.** Instead, use meaningful text in the link names to tell users what they'll get when they click. This helps users to quickly differentiate between links when they are scanning through them. For example, instead of saying "Click Here for Layette Items" just say "Layette Items."

36 **Don't use generic links, such as "More..." at the end of a list of items.** Instead, tell users specifically what they will get *more of*, such as "More New Fiction" or "Archived Book Reviews." Generic "More..." links are especially problematic when the page has several of them, since users can't easily differentiate between them when scanning the page.

37 **Allow link colors to show visited and unvisited states.** Reserve blue for unvisited links and use a clearly discernable and less saturated color for visited links. Although some sites are now using gray for visited links, we recommend against doing so because it is difficult to read and has been widely used in user interfaces to mean that something is unavailable. Similarly, it is unhelpful to use black for visited links when the text color is black, because it can cause people to have trouble finding the links they visited before.

38 **Don't use the word "Links" to indicate links on the page. Show that things are links by underlining them and coloring them blue.** Never name a category "Links" by itself—this is akin to labeling a category of information "Words" in a print medium. Name the category after what the links are pointing to.

39 **If a link does anything other than go to another web page, such as linking to a PDF file or launching an audio or video player, email message, or another application, make sure the link explicitly indicates what will happen.** For example, CNNfn uses icons quite effectively to indicate audio and video files as such. Being thrust into a new medium without warning is startling for any user, but is especially agonizing for users with slow connections, who often have to wait for the new application to load just so they can exit out of it. Worse, in a limited memory situation, launching a helper application or memory-intensive plug-in can crash the browser or computer.

CNNfn.com uses icons to identify audio and video files.

Verisign locks in 'dot.com'
3Q hires slowest in decade 🔊
Senate expected to pass tax bill

(full story) 🎥

Navigation

Because the primary purpose of a homepage is to facilitate navigation elsewhere on the site, it's critical that users be able to find the appropriate navigation area effortlessly, differentiate between the choices, and have a good sense of what lies beneath the links. Users should not have to click on things just to find out what they are. The navigation area should also reveal the most important content of the site so that users have a good sense of what's there by looking at the top-level categories.

40 **Locate the primary navigation area in a highly noticeable place, preferably directly adjacent to the main body of the page.** Avoid putting any top horizontal navigation (primary or otherwise) above graphical treatments such as horizontal rules or banner areas—users often ignore anything within or above a rectangular shape at the top of the screen. We call this behavior "banner blindness," and we have seen it in numerous tests. See Microsoft's top navigation area, which begins with "All Products" for an example of navigation that many users will likely miss.

41 **Group items in the navigation area so that similar items are next to each other.** Grouping helps users differentiate among similar or related categories and see the breadth of products or content you offer. For example, group product categories for prescription medications and over-the-counter medications. Similarly, on an e-commerce site, all items related to shopping, such as the shopping cart, account information, and customer service should be in the same area.

42 **Don't provide multiple navigation areas for the same type of links.** For example, don't have multiple areas for categories or multiple areas for news. Groups that are too similar can fragment and complicate the interface, making the user work too hard to create order and meaning.

43 **Don't include an active link to the homepage on the homepage.** For example, if you include a "Home" link as part of your regular navigation bar, it shouldn't be clickable on the homepage. If you use components, create a special component that is used only on the homepage with an inactive Home link. If it's clickable, some users will inevitably click it and wonder if the

page has indeed changed. Similarly, if you link your logo to the homepage from other pages on the site, the logo shouldn't be clickable from the homepage. All other pages on the site do need a link to the homepage.

44 **Don't use made-up words for category navigation choices. Categories need to be immediately differentiable from each other—if users don't understand your made-up terminology, it will be impossible for them to differentiate categories.** For example, although Accenture uses the made-up word "uCommerce" for its flavor of e-commerce, they appropriately use the more familiar term "eCommerce" in the navigation bar. On the other hand, Disney's mysteriously named "Zeether" category will likely give both kids and adults an undesirable pause in the navigation area.

45 **If you have a shopping cart feature on your site, include a link to it on the homepage.** This allows users to immediately see what they've selected, without having to navigate through any product screens or go through checkout before they are ready to do so. This is especially important if your site saves shopping cart selections from prior visits.

46 **Use icons in navigation only if they help users to recognize a class of items immediately, such as new items, sale items, or video content.** Don't use icons when simple text links are clearly differentiable from each other, such as in category names. If you find that you need to ponder to come up with an icon for navigation, chances are it's not going to be easily recognizable or intuitive for users. For example, the icons for "Links" and "Forum" on Asia Cuisine don't help to further explain these categories or make them more immediately recognizable; they just clutter the page.

Search

Search is one of the most important elements of the homepage, and it's essential that users be able to find it easily and use it effortlessly. Our recommendations for the homepage treatment of search are fairly straightforward: make it visible, make it wide, and keep it simple. Of course, the real power of search is all in the implementation. For 29 in-depth search implementation guidelines, see **http://www.NNgroup.com/reports/ecommerce/search.html**.

47 **Give users an input box on the homepage to enter search queries, instead of just giving them a link to a search page.** Users now expect and look for an input box with a button next to it—if they don't see it, they often assume the site doesn't have a search feature. Try to find search on Boeing's, Coles', or Southwest's homepages, for examples of how difficult it is without input boxes as the visual cue to search.

48 **Input boxes should be wide enough for users to see and edit standard queries on the site.** Allow enough space for at least 25 characters in the font size used by most of the users—even better to allow for 30 characters.

49 **Don't label the search area with a heading; instead use a "Search" button to the right of the box.** This design is preferred because it is the simplest. "Go" is also acceptable as the action button for search, but requires that you label the area "Search." Place search at the top of the main body of the page, but below any banner area. This gives people the greatest chance of finding search when they need it. Even if you follow the other guidelines for search, it doesn't help if you place it in a low-priority position on the page. See ExxonMobil for an example of a poorly placed search input box.

50 **Unless advanced searches are the norm on your site, provide simple search on the homepage, with a link to advanced search or search tips if you have them.** If you have advanced search, but it is used infrequently, don't include a link to it on the homepage. Instead, offer users the option to do an advanced search when you present the search results.

51 **Search on the homepage should search the entire site by default.** Never hide search scope from users if you narrow their search in any way. Users nearly always assume that they've searched the entire site, unless you tell them otherwise, and assume the site doesn't have what they're looking for if they don't find it with search.

52 **Don't offer a feature to "Search the Web" from the site's search function.** Users will use their favorite search engine to do that, and this option makes search more complex and error prone.

Tools and Task Shortcuts

Homepage tools, or shortcuts to certain tasks, can be a great way to give prominence to popular features of your site and meet your users' needs more quickly. The key is to choose carefully *which* tasks to feature as tools on the homepage.

53 **Offer users direct access to high-priority tasks on the homepage.** These homepage tools should let users enter any required data directly on the homepage. If possible, consider giving users zero-click access to the answers, meaning that the homepage displays the most-needed information automatically. This kind of feature is typically possible only for sites that recognize the user and personalize the page to display information that user is likely to request as a first task, such as "Current Balance of Your Bank Account: $xx." More commonly, you can offer users one-click access to the answers, meaning that you load a separate page to display the results. For example, the Travelocity "Book Your Flight Now" feature is an effective one-click tool, which allows users to enter criteria for a desired flight directly on the homepage and then see the results on a separate page.

54 **Don't include tools unrelated to tasks users come to your site to do.** Some sites seem compelled to include tools simply because they are available, not because they are appropriate. For example, you don't need to offer users a tool to get their weather forecast if you have a non-news or non-weather site, such as James Devaney Fuel Company. Tools are one of the first things users look at on homepages because they often contain input boxes and dropdown menus, which users recognize and are attracted to, so don't show them unless they are truly essential and facilitate top-priority tasks.

55 **Don't provide tools that reproduce browser functionality, such as setting a page as the browser's default starting page or bookmarking the site.**

Graphics and Animation

When you use graphics to purposefully illustrate content, you can greatly enhance a homepage. On the other hand, graphics can weigh down the design in visual clutter and slow download times, so it's important to use them judiciously and edit them for the Web. Similarly, animation with a purpose can enhance online content—but it typically is best suited for more complex content than appears at the homepage level.

56 **Use graphics to show real content, not just to decorate your homepage.** For example, use photos of identifiable people who have a connection to the content as opposed to models or generic stock photos. People are naturally drawn to pictures, so gratuitous graphics can distract users from critical content.

57 **Label graphics and photos if their meaning is not clear from the context of the story they accompany.** If the level of specificity between the picture and the story differ, it's a good idea to label the picture. For example, if you have a story about a film festival and show a still photo from one of the films, label it to clarify both what it is and how it relates to the more general category. On the other hand, if you're using a picture in an iconic way to help users quickly identify what a story is about when scanning the page, you probably don't need to label it. For example, if you use a close-up of a medicine bottle with pills in it next to an article on a new drug approved by the FDA, you don't need to label it. It's usually a good idea to label any photos of people—it doesn't hurt people who recognize the person and can help people who can't match the face with the name.

58 **Edit photos and diagrams appropriately for the display size.** Overly detailed photos and drawings don't convey information and look cluttered. It's often unhelpful just to shrink a big photo—it's usually better to crop it. See ESPN for examples of well-cropped photos; see CNNfn's photo of the market floor for an example of a poorly cropped photo.

59 **Avoid watermark graphics (background images with text on top of them).** They add clutter and often decrease visibility. If the graphic is interesting and relevant, users won't be able to see it clearly; if it's not, it's unnecessary. Often, watermark graphics are purely decorative and add no value. For example, Ford's busy watermark graphic nearly disguises the only car photo.

60 **Don't use animation for the sole purpose of drawing attention to an item on the homepage. Animation rarely has a place on the homepage because it distracts from other elements.** Animation requires a user's attention and should be shown by itself, whereas homepages have multiple elements requiring attention. For example, animation could be very helpful to show how to do a procedure that is easier seen than described, like swaddling a baby, but it wouldn't be appropriate to show it on a homepage, where it would draw attention from all other elements on the page.

61 **Never animate critical elements of the page, such as the logo, tag line, or main headline.** Not only do users tend to ignore animated areas because they look like ads, they're also difficult to read. Animation tends to have a hypnotic effect on viewers, so even if you get people to stare at animated elements, they're less likely to absorb and retain the information than if they'd seen it in a simpler format. For example, Asia Cuisine's logo is difficult to read because it is still only for a few seconds at a time—the rest of the time (no joke) it is being drawn onto the screen by a lobster.

62 **Let users choose whether they want to see an animated intro to your site—don't make it the default.** If you do ever automatically launch an animation without the user's request, provide an easy and noticeable way to turn it off.

Graphic Design

Graphic design most often hurts usability when it's used as a starting point for the homepage design, rather than as a final step to draw appropriate focus to a customer-centered interaction design. Graphic design should help lend a sense of priority to the interaction design by drawing the user's attention to the most important elements on the page.

63 **Limit font styles and other text formatting, such as sizes, colors, and so forth on the page because over-designed text can actually detract from the meaning of the words.** If text elements look too much like graphics, users tend to overlook them, mistaking them for ads.

64 **Use high-contrast text and background colors so that type is as legible as possible.**

65 **Avoid horizontal scrolling at 800x600.** Horizontal scrolling invariably causes usability issues—the biggest being that users don't notice the scrollbar and miss seeing content that is scrolled off of the screen.

66 **The most critical page elements should be visible "above the fold" (in the first screen of content, without scrolling) at the most prevalent window size (800x600 at the time of this writing).** If you have critical content that appears "below the fold" (requiring that the user scroll down), add visual clues so users know it is there. For example, don't include large amounts of whitespace between items that are above and below the fold—it's better if the items are closer together, since even seeing the top of a line gives users a good hint that there is more content below the visible portion of the screen.

67 **Use a liquid layout so the homepage size adjusts to different screen resolutions.**

68 **Use logos judiciously.** Aside from the logo for the site, use other logos only if your users know them well and you want to draw users' attention to them. Don't use a logo just because one exists for a particular product or program. For example, many government agencies design logos for each new initiative or program. Keep such logos for internal use—users don't need to see all of them. See the Coles image on this page for an example of how logos can clog up the interface.

To some users, these logos on the JobMagic site may look more like ads than links.

In Coles' case, the entire bottom navigation area ends up looking like ads, because there is a logo for each choice.

UI Widgets

UI widgets, such as dropdown menus, selection lists, and text boxes, invariably draw users' attention. As we recommend you do with any graphical addition to your homepage, use them sparingly and only when they are necessary for the task.

69 Never use widgets for parts of the screen that you don't want people to click. Make sure widgets *are* clickable. For example, if you use graphical bullets next to text, make them clickable as well as the text. In countless studies, we've seen users carefully try to click bullets, and if they're not clickable, they assume the whole line isn't a link, even when the bullet text is clickable.

70 Avoid using multiple text entry boxes on the homepage, especially in the upper part of the page where people tend to look for the search feature. Users sometimes confuse text entry boxes with search boxes, and often type search queries in the wrong place. This is especially problematic if you don't offer an input box for search but do have input boxes for other features. See Victoria's Secret and PBS for examples.

71 Use drop-down menus sparingly, especially if the items in them are not self-explanatory. Users are attracted to them, and they're often the least effective navigation devices. If you have very few items in a dropdown list, it's often better to list them directly on the homepage. Similarly, avoid long dropdowns—they are difficult for users to operate effectively, and users often struggle to differentiate between the items in the list. It's often better to take users to a separate page for the selection, where you can explain the different items or at least organize them into more meaningful categories than a single list.

Because these homepages don't have input boxes for their search features, users could easily mistake these input boxes for search, even though they're labeled otherwise.

Window Titles

Each homepage needs a simple, straightforward window title (determined by the TITLE tag of each HTML document). Although many people might not notice window titles while they are using websites, titles play a critical role in bookmarking and finding the site with search engines. When users bookmark a site, the window title becomes the default bookmark name, so the title should begin with the word that users will most likely associate with the site when they are scanning through a bookmark list. Similarly, search engines display the window title in search results and use it to determine relevancy to the search terms, so the title must be scannable and identifiable in long results lists. In order to be scannable, window titles should convey the most information possible in the fewest words.

72 **Begin the window title with the information-carrying word—usually the company name.** Users scan, rather than read, text on screens, so if you don't catch them with the first word, you risk losing their attention. If you start the window title with anything but the most important word, the company name gets lost in bookmark lists and search results. For example, many window titles begin with "Welcome" or "Homepage," which might look okay in isolation, but convey no differentiating site information in the first word. Similarly, if your company name begins with an article, such as "the" or "a," don't include the article in the window title. For example, the window title for "The New York Times" should be "New York Times."

73 **Don't include the top-level domain name, such as ".com" in the window title unless it is actually part of the company name, such as "Amazon.com."** Suffixes such as ".com" add an unnecessary word to the window title and create an artificial distinction between a company's presence on and off the Web. Users already know that they are on the Web when they go to a website, so they don't need the ".com" to tell them so.

74 **Don't include "homepage" in the title. This adds verbiage without value.** As long as you have a simple URL for the homepage of the site, it's not necessary to specify the homepage as such in the window title. Of course, each page in your site should have a unique window title, so that no other page can be confused with the homepage in history lists and bookmarks.

75 **Include a short description of the site in the window title.** This description is especially important for sites that are not yet widely known, so users can easily remember or understand what the site's purpose is if they've previously bookmarked it or get it as a search result. Consider using the tag line for the site, if you have one, but only if it is short, meaningful, and in straightforward language instead of vague marketese. For example, Slusser's window title, "Slusser's Commercial Landscaping and Heavy Highway," works well because it lists the company name first, followed by an understandable description (although we suggest moving "Landscaping" to the end).

76 **Limit window titles to no more than seven or eight words and fewer than 64 total characters.** Longer titles are less scannable, especially in bookmark lists, and will not display correctly in many applications. See JobMagic's window title for an example of an overly long, truncated window title.

URLs

It's critical to keep homepage URLs as simple and memorable as possible. Users not only need to be able to remember the URLs for sites they've visited, but they also need to be able to succeed quickly when they are guessing a company's domain name, as people often must do. Once users locate a website, a simple homepage URL helps them quickly understand that they are in the right place, whereas complex URLs can make them wonder if they're indeed on the correct page.

77 Homepages for commercial websites should have the URL http://www.company.com (or an equivalent for your country or non-commercial top-level domain). Do not append complex codes or even "index.html" after the domain name. It is especially startling when users enter a simple URL and get to a site, only to have the URL they typed replaced by a long, scary-looking URL. Make sure your site responds to both "www.company.com" and "company.com."

78 For any website that has an identity closely connected to a specific country other than the United States, use that country's top-level domain. A country-specific domain is appropriate either for localized sites that feature a particular country's language and/or content, or for sites that are differentiated because they are located in that country. If the site also has customers outside of its country, and especially if it has customers in the United States, it's good to also register the name with ".com" as the top-level domain. For example, Asia Cuisine is a Singapore-based company, but it appeals to an international audience. Users can reach the site by either the Singapore URL, **http://www.asiacuisine.com.sg** or **http://www.asiacuisine.com**.

79 If available, register domain names for alternative spellings, abbreviations, or common misspellings of the site name. This is especially true if you have any punctuation in the company name, such as Wal-Mart, or names made from several words, such as Victoria's Secret. Both of these sites allow for common misspellings—you can reach Wal-Mart's website at **http://www.wal-mart.com** or **http://www.walmart.com** and Victoria's Secret through **http://www.victoriassecret.com** or **http://www.victoriasecret.com**.

80 If you have alternative domain name spellings, choose one as the authorized version and redirect users to it from all the other spellings. Use this correct spelling in all instances on the site and in any offline promotions.

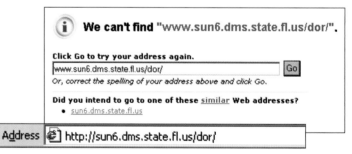

Finding the Florida Department of Revenue homepage can be challenging. If users don't enter the URL exactly the way it appears when the page displays, they'll get an error message. Note the uncommon absence of "www."

News and Press Releases

In order for news stories and press releases to be effective on your homepage, you need to craft effective headlines and *decks* (the summary of the story below the headline). This applies to either the company news that you show on your homepage, or any news that your site delivers as content. Headlines and decks should actually give users information, rather than merely trying to tantalize them into clicking through to the real information. It's just as important to help users know when not to click something, if they're truly not interested. You can only get so many wasted clicks from users before they give up.

81 **Headlines should be succinct, yet descriptive, to give maximum information in as few words as possible.** For example, the headline "Ben Affleck Recovering" gives more information in fewer words than "Doctors Report on Ben Affleck's Progress," which promises content in the article that follows, but doesn't really tell users anything. Headlines should relate to the deck below them, rather than to the whole story that follows.

82 **Write and edit specific summaries for press releases and news stories that you feature on your homepage.** Don't just repurpose the first paragraph of the full article, which was likely not written to be a stand-alone piece. Give users content in the deck—don't just describe the content that follows. Trying to hold out on the details in order to entice users to click through can backfire; generalities aren't as captivating as specifics. For example, "Getting more sleep and spending time with loved ones are two of the five ways you can increase your life span by five years, says Surgeon General Satcher" is more intriguing and informative than "Surgeon general describes ways that people can increase their life span."

83 **Link headlines, rather than the deck, to the full news story.** If your headline style doesn't have a perceived affordance for clickability, such as blue underlined text, include a "Full Story" link at the end of the deck. A perceived affordance is what you think you can do with a UI element based on looking at it. For example, the pseudo-3D appearance of a button suggests that you can click it. For more information about the use of affordances in user interface design, see Don Norman's classic book *The Design of Everyday Things* (Currency/Doubleday: New York, NY, 1990).

84 **As long as all news stories on the homepage occurred within the week, there's no need to list the date and time in the deck of each story, unless it is truly a breaking news item that has frequent updates.** The time and date at the top of the homepage are enough to show a user that content is current. For example, Red Herring uses a good deal of space unnecessarily listing dates that all occur within the same week. It is essential, however, to list the date prominently on the page for the full article, because articles can be found and cached (for example by search engines) much later in time, and old content can be mistaken for current news unless items are dated with a full date, including the year. For the same reason, articles should not refer to relative times, such as "today" or "next week."

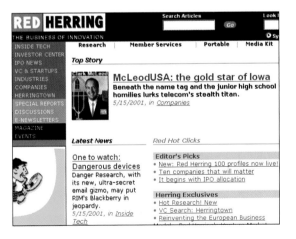

Notice that Red Herring includes the date at the end of each news summary. Because users can safely assume these summaries on the homepage are current, the dates aren't necessary here. The date should be included, however, on the page for the full article.

Popup Windows and Staging Pages

In general, it's best to show site content immediately. Intermediary screens are rarely necessary and keep users from getting to the main site content. What may be amusing once is often extremely annoying the 3rd or 30th time. Worse, the intermediate pages might confuse some users into not recognizing the "real" homepage.

85 **Take users to your "real" homepage when they type your main URL or click a link to your site.** Splash screens must die. An exception: If your site has material that is inappropriate for minors or that is likely to offend some users, it is appropriate to have a splash screen warning about the content.

86 **Avoid popup windows.** Extra windows keep users from getting to your site content, and even if such windows contain valuable information, users are likely to dismiss them immediately as ads. Instead, put critical information in a highly noticeable area of the homepage. The other drawback to popup windows is that they go away—once the user gets rid of them, they're gone, so users often can't find the information again even if they want to. It's better to design your homepage to give high priority to critical content.

87 **Don't use routing pages for users to choose their geographical location unless you have versions of your site in many different languages, with no single dominant language.** If you have very few language choices, it's best to provide homepage links to those languages in the native language. If you have a dominant language for your site with multiple other languages, take users directly to the homepage in that language, and include a single link to "International Versions of Site." It's best not to use dropdown menus for this purpose because they're difficult for users to navigate when long, and they often don't show users all the options at once.

Popup windows such as the one at Barnes & Noble obscure the user's view of the homepage and are usually dismissed as ads.

Advertising

Warning: users have grown savvier about ads on websites. Users have learned to ignore ads.Unfortunately, they often also ignore anything resembling an ad or next to an ad. If you use advertising from outside companies, you must ensure that you preserve the integrity of your content. The cost of lost customers might quickly outweigh the benefits of advertising revenue.

88 **Keep ads for outside companies on the periphery of the page.** Never place ads next to high-priority items; they will cause such items to be ignored. Especially avoid placing any important items above an ad, because users will often exhibit banner blindness, ignoring anything above the banner area.

89 **Keep external ads (ads for companies other than your own) as small and discreet as possible relative to your core homepage content.** When you have users evaluate your homepage, ask them to tell you the first three things that come to mind when they open the page. If any of the three comments are about ads, the ads are attracting too much attention.

90 **If you place ads outside the standard banner area at the top of the page, label them as advertising so that users don't confuse them with your site's content.** See CNNfn for an example of how to label an advertisement in the middle of the page, and see USA Today for an example of how easily an unlabeled ad in the middle of the page can look like actual content.

91 **Avoid using ad conventions to showcase regular features of the site.** The more you make content look like an ad, the less likely users will read it. For example, GE describes its acquisition of Honeywell on the homepage in a box that looks very much like an ad, rather than a press release or news item.

Welcomes

Many sites seem compelled to include welcome messages on their homepages. Cheerful "welcomes" on homepages are nostalgic remnants of the early days of the Web, when getting to one of the few available sites was a feat worth acknowledging.

92 **Don't literally welcome users to your site. Before you give up prime homepage real estate to a salutation, consider using it for a tag line instead.** The best welcome you can give users is a concrete definition of what they can do on the site and a clear starting point from which to begin. An exception to this guideline is the more appropriate use of "welcome" in a phrase that confirms that the site has recognized a registered user.

Communicating Technical Problems and Handling Emergencies

Unfortunately, sometimes you encounter problems on your site or your company is affected by an emergency. It's important to update your homepage with relevant information that your users need.

93 **If the website is down or important parts of the website are not operational, show it clearly on the homepage.** Provide an estimate of how long it will take to correct the problem—not just "Try again later," but "We expect that we'll be ready to serve you again at 4:00 p.m. Eastern time." Inform the user about alternatives that might be available while the website is down, for example, "Our customer service department is ready to serve you at 1-800-456-7890." Reserve such messages for critical information that already exists on your site—don't give users "under construction" messages for parts of the site that are yet to come or are getting a redesign.

94 **Have a plan for handling critical content on your website in the event of an emergency.** In an actual emergency, there won't be time to come up with alternative versions of your homepage. For example, prepare an alternative homepage design that has a main feature area to notify users of the emergency, as well as a simplified navigation scheme that offers a few cross-references and a way to get back to your site's regular homepage. Emergencies are often characterized by flash crowds in which many times the normal number of users want to get information about the emergency. To serve this increased load, the alternative design should be more lightweight than the normal design: fewer graphics and other embedded objects, simplified HTML, and no dynamically computed elements.

Credits

Users come to your site for content. Avoid cluttering your homepage with useless credits or telling users how great your site is.

95 **Don't waste space crediting the search engine, design firm, favorite browser company, or the technology behind the scenes.** Users really don't care, and each item you add to a page adds to its overall complexity and steals focus from the actual content. If these items are links to other sites, they can also cause users to get lost on those sites when looking for something on yours. For technology-oriented sites, it might be appropriate to include a "How We Run This Website" section under "About Us," but keep the specifics off the homepage.

96 **Exercise restraint in displaying awards won by your website.** Most users don't really care that you have been appointed "Hot Site of the Day" by somebody.

At the same time, awards, recognition, and favorable reviews from independent authorities can be one way to enhance credibility. Awards for the quality of products or services are usually more helpful in building trust than awards for "cool design" or other aspects of the website itself. Thus, awards for customer-oriented issues may be mentioned on the homepage, whereas awards for the web team's efforts should be relegated to an "About This Site" area. In either case, don't let awards overstay their welcome. Featuring a stale award from last year undermines credibility since it communicates that you haven't done anything good lately (except if it's included in a history section).

Page Reload and Refresh

When users reload or refresh your homepage, changes can be jarring. Try to keep the transition as smooth as possible and maintain continuity with their previous experience of your page.

(97) Don't automatically refresh the homepage to push updates to users. Automatic reloading feels intrusive— it's like pulling the rug out from under your users, particularly if they are using a part of the page that disappears or changes position during the refresh. For example, NewsNow automatically updates the page every five minutes, which means many of the headlines move off of the homepage and get replaced by new ones. This forced reloading can also lead to technical problems for users on dialup connections, whose computers might try to dial up at unexpected times (such as when the user is on the telephone on a line shared by a modem), or when the previous version of the page is replaced with an error message stating that the page could not be loaded. On slow connections you're taking up the user's bandwidth and time without asking if it's okay. For site features that require real-time updates, like sports scores, chat rooms, and stock tickers,

consider providing a tool that enables users to get a live data feed. Such tools might potentially utilize an audio signal to attract the user's attention in case of breaking news. If you do so, it will be important to exercise restraint and only "ring the bell" for something truly important, as determined by an editorial decision or by a user-defined alert preference setting.

(98) When doing a refresh, update only content that has actually changed, such as news updates. For example, don't rotate through a set of photos, because users will waste their time trying to figure out what has happened and why the change has happened instead of focusing on useful tasks. Meaningless change is especially bad when sites randomly rotate through content—users waste time trying to figure out the pattern when there is none.

NewsNow automatically refreshes its homepage every five minutes. Although these screenshots were taken more than 15 minutes apart, it appears that the only thing being updated is the advertising. Is the refresh really worth the potential risk of disconnecting users?

Customization

Homepage customization can work well if it gives users value without requiring much or any setup effort from them. If it is possible to make intelligent and relevant recommendations based on a user's past behavior on your site, or if you can offer users specialized content based on criteria such as their geographical location, then users might indeed benefit.

(99) If your homepage has areas that will provide customized information once you know something about the user, don't provide a generic version of the content to first-time users—craft different content for that space. For example, if you have a customized welcome message that shows a registered user's name, don't display any of the text if you don't know the user's name. See MotherNature's homepage for an example of how silly such welcomes look when you don't have user information yet. Generic welcomes are akin to Dear Sir letters—they don't make anyone feel special. Similarly, don't offer users recommendations that purport to be tailored just for them, when in fact they are generic for all users. So, if you have a UK site

that has an area for local weather, don't choose a city, such as London, for your users—if you don't know their city, offer users an area to enter it and a rationale for doing so. For example, "Enter Your City Name or Postal Code to See Your Local Weather Report."

(100) Don't offer users features to customize the basic look of the homepage UI, such as color schemes. It's better to focus resources on coming up with the best design that will be the most readable for the greatest number of users. You should respect users' browser preferences, however, such as font size, by using relative rather than absolute sizes.

Gathering Customer Data

Many websites, including several of the ones in this book, begin asking for user data, such as email addresses, right on the homepage. Most do not explain why users should give up their privacy. In general, many web users, even experienced ones, are justifiably wary about giving away their personal information because they know now that fulfilling these requests often results in unsolicited commercial email and clogged inboxes.

(101) Don't provide plain links to registration on the homepage; instead explain (or at least link to) the customer benefits of registration. For example, Amazon explains the benefit by simply saying "Sign in to get recommendation." Users don't come to sites to register, but they might do so if the reasons are compelling enough. Thankfully, more websites seem to be allowing users to explore the site without mandatory registration—none of the sites in this book required users to register. Yet many sites offer homepage links to registration without any explanation of why users might want to do so.

(102) Explain the benefits and frequency of publication to users before asking them for their email addresses. Don't ask users to give their email addresses to get an unspecified newsletter or other item of unknown content or frequency. Also, link to a sample newsletter and explain the privacy policy next to the place where you ask for the user's email address. For more information on the usability of email newsletters, see **http://www.nngroup.com/reports/newsletters**.

Fostering Community

The best thing you can do at the homepage level to foster a community of users is to reveal what resources the site has to bring people together. Of course, the deeper issue is whether a user community is appropriate for your site, but if so, it's good to give people specific examples of what they can get from community features you provide.

103 **If you support user communities with chat or other discussion features, don't show generic links to them.** Instead list actual discussion topics and provide any schedules on the homepage.

104 **Don't offer a "Guestbook" sign in for business sites.** Guestbooks make a site look amateurish and give no customer benefit. Sites that cater to clubs or subcultures, where users might enjoy some benefit from just getting their names in the book or seeing who else visited the site, are excepted from this guideline.

PlanetRx has a tab for Community but leaves users in the dark about what it means.

Dates and Times

Users need to know that information they see on your homepage is current, but they don't necessarily need to see dates and times next to each item. When you do show dates and times, it's important to format them so that all users will be able to translate them to their local time. During major holidays it can be appropriate to add a small decoration to make the homepage feel more current and connected to users' non-Internet experience. For more on how to celebrate holidays on websites, see **http://www.nngroup.com/reports/holidays**.

105 **Show dates and times for time-sensitive information only, such as news items, live chats, stock quotes, and so forth.** Don't show dates and times on e-commerce or other transaction sites that don't have time-sensitive material. It's not necessary to show the day of the week, but if you do, only do so if it is from the current week.

106 **Show users the time that content was last updated, not the computer-generated current time.** Clearly indicate this distinction, with a phrase such as "Updated <date, time>."

107 **Include the time zone you are using whenever you reference a time.** If your site has international users, show the time in the most common time zone, as well as relative to GMT, for example, "9:00 a.m. EDT or (GMT −4)." Any localized homepages should show that location's local time, as well as the time relative to GMT.

108 **Use standard abbreviations, such as p.m. or P.M.** Don't abbreviate further, such as "p."

109 **Spell out the month or use month abbreviations, not numbers.** "Jan. 2, 2003" is much less ambiguous than "01/02/03," which could mean either the 2nd of January, or the 1st of February, since many countries conventionally mention the date, rather than the month, first.

Stock Quotes and Displaying Numbers

Because many homepages include stock quotes now, we've included a few guidelines to make them more readable and understandable. Although you can display stock quotes and numbers on any web page (and use these guidelines to optimize their display), it's especially important to follow these guidelines when displaying such information on the homepage, where even minute optimizations can reduce distracting clutter.

110 **Give the percentage of change, not just the points gained or lost in stock quotes.**

111 **Spell out stock abbreviations unless the abbreviation is completely clear, such as "IBM."** Many stock symbols are unintuitive, such as "C" for Citigroup, or "HWP" for Hewlett Packard ("HP" is taken by Helmerich & Payne).

112 **Use a thousands separator appropriate to your locale for numbers that have five or more digits.** For example, in the United States, fifty-three thousand should be written "53,000."

113 **Align decimal points when showing columns of numbers.** This makes it much easier for users to compare or mentally add and subtract numbers.

These are the varied ways stock quotes are displayed by CNNfn, Philip Morris, USA Today, and ExxonMobil.

Homepage Design Conventions

In addition to the guidelines presented in this chapter, the next chapter presents design conventions that have evolved and are continuing to evolve on the Web based on our analysis of the homepages in this book. The chapter ends with our "Recommended Homepage Design" (page 52), which we suggest that you use, along with the guidelines in this chapter, to evaluate your existing homepage design and inform future designs.

Homepage Design Statistics

Jakob's Law of the Internet User Experience states that "users spend most of their time on *other* sites than your site." This is true no matter how big your site is, because no site accounts for more than 50% of a user's time. In fact, most websites account for only a few percent of their users' time online. This law implies the need for websites to be easy to use and to follow design conventions—users will be hard pressed to remember any special interaction tricks from one visit to the next, given the amount of time they'll spend on other sites between the two visits. In this chapter we measure the extent to which such conventions exist on the Web today. Over time, we expect even more design conventions to emerge. As this happens, we recommend that you employ these new conventions for your next website redesign, if not before.

Homepage design goes beyond the dictates of Jakob's Law because of the importance of the first-time visitor's experience. By the time a user arrives at your homepage for the first time, that user will already be carrying a large load of mental baggage, accumulated from prior visits to thousands of other homepages. The one exception to this rule are services like AOL and MSN, which are frequent first stops for novice Internet users. A few of the Web's very biggest websites, such as Amazon or Yahoo, might count themselves among the first 10 or 20 sites visited by new users, but even these huge sites have many users who don't discover them until they've visited a large number of other sites first.

In general, though, the fact remains that users will have seen a very large number of homepages by the time they arrive at your site for the first time. And by this time, users have accumulated a generic mental model of the way homepages are supposed to work, based on their experiences on these other sites.

Two conclusions follow from the dominance of other websites in forming the user's mental model:

First, the vast majority of other sites have horrible usability and aren't worth using—users quickly discover this and abandon them. The average user expectation upon encountering a site for the first time is that the site is probably going to be a disappointment. Users invest very little time (often on the order of 10 seconds) looking over a new site in the hope it will be one of the rare good ones. But if the site seems too strange or too difficult, or if it's not apparent how the site applies to their immediate concerns, they'll be out of there as fast as they can click their mouse.

Because the decision to linger or leave is often made at the homepage, or after looking at one or two pages linked from the homepage, the homepage needs to communicate immediate value and enable visitors to find good, relevant "stuff" within seconds. Both of these requirements imply that the homepage has to follow standard user interface design conventions, because users won't have time to learn anything new. Instead, they'll spend all of their brainpower during the limited judgment period on extracting goal-directed value. If you divert their attention—to even the smallest degree—from finding content to having to learn something new, you lose.

The second conclusion is that the average first-time visitor to your site won't be a novice user in the true sense of the term. The user will typically have a good deal of experience with other homepages and will be acquainted with the way most other pages work. To the extent your homepage works similarly, users will feel welcome and will understand the familiar design conventions.

Enemies of usability sometimes complain that design conventions stifle creativity and that it would be boring if all homepages looked the same. Both of these complaints are misguided. First, the very concept of design is problem-solving under constraints. Design doesn't mean "make any random thing," it means "make something that works in the real world." Designers have always needed to work within such constraints as, say, the limited resolution of newsprint or the size of the printed page. Accepting that web design is interaction design and that it's necessary to accommodate human behavior is simply one more design constraint, but it's one that should encourage creativity, not dampen it. Second, the design conventions don't at all mean that all homepages will look the same. Almost all magazines follow the convention of placing page numbers in the corner of the pages, displaying headlines in type larger than that of the body text, having the table of contents at the beginning, and many, many more principles that are common for the simple reason that they make magazines easy to read. This doesn't mean *Vogue* looks the same as *Sports Illustrated* or the *Far Eastern Economic Review*. Similarly, homepages that address different audiences or represent different companies will look different, even if they all promote ease of use by sticking to the conventions.

This chapter presents our assessment of homepage design conventions based on an analysis of the 50 homepages in this book. We often present the statistics in terms of the average value or the most prevalent value of a design element. In some cases, it's also interesting to discuss the range of values that are used, which we often do by listing three different numbers: the first quartile, the median, and the third quartile. The first quartile (Q1) is the number for which 25% of the sites have a lower value and 75% of the sites have a higher value. Similarly, the third quartile (Q3) is the value for which 75% of the sites have a lower value and 25% of the sites have a higher value. That being the case, half of the sites fall between the first and the third quartile. The median indicates the midpoint where half of the sites have a lower value and half of the sites have a higher value.

Download Time

Using a regular analog modem like those used by the majority of home users, these homepages required an average download time of 26 seconds—almost three times the recommended maximum response time delay of 10 seconds. Only 28% of the sites met this goal, which is actually quite modest. For true optimum usability, pages need to download in less than one second, and not a single one of these homepages was that fast. Even when using a cable modem or a DSL line, most of the sites were slower than the 10-second limit.

Unfortunately, 26% of the homepages took more than half a minute to load. Most users would be long gone—unless they happened to be collecting screen snaps for their own book on homepage design. In many cases, these incredibly slow sites may have been hurt by delays beyond the simple download of their page contents. Servers can be slow, as can the Internet, and no one has control over that. From the user's perspective, however, all that matters is whether the site seems responsive or sluggish. These facts of life on the Web are all the more reason to keep your page size down.

If the homepage is slow, users quite reasonably conclude that the rest of the site will be slow and painful to use as well, and they are likely to abandon the site completely.

Basic Page Layout

We looked at the size of the page on the screen and the extent to which it accommodated different window sizes and was divided into frames.

Page Width

Most homepages in the sample were clearly designed for an 800-pixel-wide browser window, corresponding to the 800x600 monitor resolution—still the most common for home users. The following numbers refer to the width of the web page itself, not including the browser chrome such as scrollbars.

Value	Page Width
Q1	768 pixels
Median	770 pixels
Q3	774 pixels

We recommend that pages be designed for optimal display at around 770 pixels, because that is the area available for content in an 800-pixel-wide window. As discussed in the following section, we also recommend that the layout be "liquid" so that it will stretch to accommodate as many different window sizes as possible, both wider and narrower than the "standard" window.

Liquid Versus Frozen Layout

Of the 50 homepages, 18% used a liquid layout that automatically adapted to the size of the user's browser window. Most sites used a frozen layout that stayed the same in big and small windows. Frozen pages were cut off in a small windows, and they displayed huge amounts of wasted whitespace in large windows.

Even though frozen layouts are the norm, we recommend using a liquid layout. Users with big monitors will appreciate seeing more content by making the window as large as they want—not to mention getting use out of the money they spent on the large screen. Users with small monitors will also benefit by a page that re-wraps to suit their smaller windows. Finally, liquid layouts will print equally well on both 8.5x11 and A4 paper.

Page Length

Page length varied widely, although most homepages fell between one and three full screens on the 800x600 monitors. We caution against excessively scrolling homepages: if your design goes beyond four full screens in the size of window most common among your user base, you probably should simplify the homepage and move some features to secondary pages. On the other hand, there's no need to cram everything onto a single screen as long as the most important features are visible above the fold.

Value	Page Length
Q1	634 pixels, or about one full screen
Median	1,018 pixels, or about two full screens
Q3	1,334 pixels, or about three full screens

Frames

Only 4% of the sites used frames on the homepage. Because frames cause usability problems, it's best to avoid them. Most designers made the right choice regarding this design element and didn't use them.

Fundamental Page Design Elements

Two things users often look for first on a homepage are the logo and the search feature. People need to know where they are and they often want to search. Thus, these two elements need to be particularly easy to find. For sure, one should not have to search for search.

Logo

All sites had a logo of some form. The placement of the logo on the page was as follows:

Logo Placement	Value
Upper left	84%
Upper right	6%
Upper center	6%
Other position	4%

We recommend that your site include a logo on the home-page placed in the upper-left corner of the page. On all other pages, except for the homepage itself, the logo should be a link that leads to the homepage.

The sizes of the logos were about as different as the logos themselves. Because logos are two-dimensional graphics, we are stating the size in terms of the total number of screen pixels consumed by the logo and also as the size of a square image that would take up the same number of pixels. Most logos are rectangular, so they typically have a greater width and lower height than the size of the square listed here.

Value	Logo Size
Q1	3,365 pixels (a square 58 pixels wide & tall)
Median	5,485 pixels (a square 74 pixels wide & tall)
Q3	12,286 pixels (a square 111 pixels wide & tall)

Search

Unbelievably, 14% of the homepages didn't have a search feature, and so they have been excluded from this analysis. The following percentages refer to those homepages that did have search capabilities.

In 81% of the sites, search was represented as a box in which users could type a query. Because this is also the design that we have found to work best in our user testing of many other sites, we strongly recommend using a search box. Only 20% of the sites used a less-usable search design where users had to click a link that took them to a separate search page. (Note that the percentages add up to more than 100% because one site had two locations for search.)

The placement of the search feature (whether a box or a link) on the homepages was as follows:

Search Placement	Value
Upper right	35%
Upper left	30%
Upper center	14%
Middle left	12%
Other position	12%

We recommend placing search in the upper part of the page, so that it's noticeable. Although the exact placement depends on the other items at the top of your page, we recommend placing it in either of the top corners. Although upper-right may be marginally better than upper-left, the difference is so small that it's acceptable to place search in the upper-left if that works better with the overall design.

Furthermore, several different terms were used as labels on the search button or the search link. The most common labels were as follows:

Search Label	Value
Search	42%
Go	40%
Find	9%
Find It	5%

These statistics suggest a toss-up between "Search" and "Go," but we have a preference for "Search" from a usability perspective because it seems to better define the feature and saves on overall word count because it doubles as a label for search.

In terms of color, the search box itself was white in 97% of the cases, and white almost seems to be a defining characteristic of a user-input field. Therefore, we recommend sticking to a white text field in the search box.

The width of the search boxes was as follows:

Value	Width of Search Box
Q1	85 pixels, or 14 characters
Median	110 pixels, or 18 characters
Q3	171 pixels, or 28 characters

For the best usability of search, users should be able to enter fairly long queries, seeing all of their text without having to scroll the search box. The average search boxes on the Web today are far too small for anything but the shortest queries. Even the larger search boxes in our sample would be too small to contain the query "search usability guidelines" which is 29 characters, including the quotation marks.

We recommend making the search box at least 25 characters wide in the prevalent font used by most of the users. 30 characters would be better.

Simple searches made up 70% of the homepage search features in our sample, meaning that the search engine looked for the user's query in all pages on the site. Scoped searches accounted for 30% of the searches, meaning that the search engine considered only a smaller part of the site (the so-called search scope). Usability is almost always best with simple search because scoped search offers too many opportunities for users to make errors and search the wrong scope.

Links to an advanced search feature were offered on 21% of the sites. Whether advanced search is necessary depends on the complexity of the site, but it's definitely better to defer any fancy search options to a separate "advanced search" page. This protects all users from the intricacies of advanced search, but allows users who want to enter other criteria a place to do so. In most cases, advanced search is also the only place we recommend to offer a scoped search. People who enter advanced search do so at their own risk, and many novice users stay on safer turf, confining themselves to simple search where they are less likely to get into trouble.

A complete set of individual site search areas can be found in the Appendix.

Navigation

The dominant navigation scheme on each homepage was distributed as follows. (Note that the numbers add up to more than 100% because a few sites offered two equally prominent navigation schemes.)

Navigation Scheme	Value
Left-hand navigation rail	30%
Tabs	30%
Links across top of page	18%
Categories in middle of page	12%
Pull-down menus	10%
Other (right, bottom, upper center)	6%

There is no clear winner, but there are four different navigation schemes that all seem to have good usability and that are found sufficiently often on the Web to be considered commonly known:

- **Left navigation rail.** This design was originally made popular by CNET as the so-called "yellow fever" design (a prominent yellow stripe running down the left of all its pages). In a 1999 redesign, CNET abandoned this style although, as the data shows, it's still found on many sites, including BBC Online.

- **Tabs.** Currently used by many sites, including Wal-Mart. Originally popularized by Amazon.com, although it's no longer Amazon's primary navigation scheme.

- **Links across the top.** The style currently used by Accenture.

- **Categories in the middle of the page.** Popularized (and still used) by Yahoo!.

Even though pull-down menus are also fairly frequently used, we don't recommend them for main navigation because they hide the choices most of the time.

Footer Navigation

Of the homepages in our sample, 80% included a list of navigation links across the bottom of the page. As indicated by this high percentage, it's a common design convention to feature certain options at the end of the page. Unfortunately, there is no agreement about what to include in this navigation list. Some sites list the main areas of the site under the theory that doing so provides users with a second chance at using these important links if they missed them while scrolling down the page. Other sites take the opposite approach and reserve the bottom of the page for links that could best be called footnotes, such as copyright info and contact information.

Because of the lack of a standard, users don't know what to expect in the footer, and this makes the area less useful than it could be. Because bottom-of-the-page navigation is less than optimal, we recommend that you not use it for primary navigation features. Also, it's a general usability principle to minimize duplication: if the same choice appears twice, users have to wonder whether the two links are different or identical. Finally, of course, homepage pixels are precious, so it's better to conserve them and not spend them twice on the same feature, no matter how important.

As a conclusion, we recommend that you use the footer for footnote-style navigation and not repeat the primary segments of your site's information architecture.

The median number of links in the footer area was 7.5, keeping quite close to the general advice for menus and similar lists to be around 7±2.

We recommend keeping the list of footnote links short. The number of links should be at most seven, and the words chosen should be sufficiently terse to keep the entire list on a single line of text when displayed in the most common size of window.

Site Map

Although we didn't comment on it in many of the site critiques, 48% of homepages provided a link to a site map. Because it's not currently clear whether sitemaps really help users navigate, we recommend including a site map only if substantial resources are allocated to its design and if it's been extensively tested with real users performing real navigation tasks.

We have a separate report that provides guidelines for the design of the site map itself (**http://www.NNgroup.com/ reports/sitemaps**). The present section only concerns the way users would navigate from the homepage to the site map.

Among those homepages that included a site map link, this feature was named as follows:

Site Map Label	Value
Site Map	63%
Site Index	13%
Site Guide	8%

Other terms included "Map," "See All Categories," "Site Contents," and "Sitemap" (one word).

We recommend calling the site map link "Site Map."

Routing Pages

A routing page is a page that is displayed to users before they get to the real homepage. Such pages are similar to splash pages (covered in the following section) in that they are an initial hurdle that users have to clear before seeing the homepage. But contrary to splash pages, routing pages serve a useful function in the design by allowing users to take some action instead of simply having to wait and suffer. The typical goal of a routing page is to route users to the correct destination for companies that provide multiple homepages. The two most common uses of routing pages are to warn under-age users away from "adult" content and to guide international users to the appropriate country site.

Because there were no pornography sites among the sample we chose for this book, we didn't come across routing pages that were trying to screen out minors. Routing pages for international users were found in 2% of our sample.

In general, we recommend against routing pages except for sites that carry pornography or other potentially offensive content on the homepage. While a routing page can't guarantee that minors won't see pornography, it might protect people who stumble across pornographic sites by mistake.

Splash Pages

Splash pages are a curse on the Web and should be eliminated in almost all circumstances. Not only are splash pages an annoyance, but given how rarely they occur on the Web these days, they also violate users' expectations. Just allow users immediate access to the homepage and make sure that this page provides a sufficiently clear introduction to your site.

Only 6% of the sites in our sample had a splash page. In other words, 94% of the sites took users straight to the homepage.

Frequent Features

Common features exist on many or even most sites. Sometimes it's inherent in the very concept of a website that the homepage should contain certain features, such as information about the company or organization behind the site as well as how to contact the company. Other shared elements have emerged over the history of the Web. For example, most corporate websites include a section for job seekers, and most websites collect some form of customer information, so that privacy policies have become widespread as well.

As the Web evolves, it's likely that even more conventional features will become established, especially for sites in specific genres such as corporate sites and government sites. We recommend that you keep an eye on other major sites in your category and add features to your site if they become so commonplace that users will start to expect them.

Frequent features should have familiar names. This makes it easier for users to find these features and it allows them to focus most of their attention on those features that are unique to each site. The less you have to wonder about the meaning of shared features, the more you can think about the new features.

Sign In

At 52%, slightly more than half of the sites offered registered users the opportunity to sign in on the homepage, but none of the sites went so far as to require users to sign in before letting them use the site's basic features. While we recommend that you offer the option to sign in on the homepage if your site supports registration, we recommend against imposing a sign-in screen that prevents users from progressing beyond the homepage. Your site should treat users so well that they'll be motivated to sign in as soon as possible, but if users don't want to sign in, it's highly counterproductive require this, except at the last moment—say, when users want to review their account information.

There are almost no conventions for what to call the sign-in feature on the homepage. The following labels were used:

In all, 46% used the word "account" in some part of the name for their sign-in feature (including 3% that used the phrase "customer account").

The vocabulary is too scattered for a firm recommendation. Unfortunately, the concept of user registration is still sufficiently unsettled for great conventions to have developed. We recommend choosing the specific labels for your site based on the main benefit users will gain from registering and signing in. Often, this will be an account, but there will be many cases where it wouldn't be appropriate to refer to personalization features as an "account." Because there is no standard terminology in this area, we recommend subjecting your site's labels to additional scrutiny in user testing.

Sign-In Label	Value
Your Account	19%
Login	19% (including one site that actually used the word "logon")
Sign In	15%
My Account	12%
Account	12%

About Us

Of the homepages sampled, 84% included a navigation link to get information about the company. We highly recommend including such a feature. Even though you might think users care only about what your site can do for them and not about your company itself, experience shows that providing information about the company is one of the most trust-enhancing elements you can add.

On the Web, all companies are equal: nothing more than content in a window on a screen. On the one hand, this equality is a great democratizing aspect of the Internet. Truly, the Web provides boundless opportunity for new companies to gather customers world-wide, and it's possible to promote innovative services and specialized products that would be denied shelf space and airtime in the traditional world. On the other hand, this very openness makes the Web a playground for both scam artists and spammers. Most Internet users receive several daily e-mails about hot babes and get-rich-quick schemes. In this environment, users quickly develop thick skin and a healthy skepticism—if not, they will have been mercilessly separated from their money and won't be in your customer base.

To establish credentials as a bona fide company, you must give users an easy way to discover your company's background information from the homepage. In any case, providing information about your company or the organization is one of the basic purposes of your website. This information may not be among the most useful or the most frequently requested, but it has to be there.

Among those homepages that provided company information, this link had the following names:

Company Information Label	Value
About <name-of-company>	55%
About Us	21%
Company Information (or Company Info)	7%
Who We Are	5%

Other choices included "Inside the Company," "Learn About Us," "Our Company," "Our Story," and simply "About."

We recommend including the name of the company in the About link, as well as shortening or abbreviating lengthy company names in this link. For example, the website for Acme Products should have a link called "About Acme."

Contact Info

In our sample, 90% of the sites provided a way for users to discover contact information for the company—typically a mailing address, a telephone number, and an email address.

Among sites that provided contact information, the way to get it was as follows:

Placement of Contact Information	Value
Listed directly on the homepage	4%
Explicit Contact Us link	60%
Available through About Us link	22%
Available through other links such as Help and Customer Service	14%

Among homepages that used a Contact Us link to provide contact information, this feature was named as follows:

Company Contact Label	Value
Contact Us	89%
Contact <name-of-company>	4%
Contact Numbers	4%
Contact	4%

We recommend you include a contact link on the homepage and that you call it "Contact Us."

For companies that want to discourage customer contacts, it may be possible to avoid an explicit contact link if the contact information is provided as the first element seen when users follow the "About <company name>" link. This approach still allows customers to contact the company if they're determined to do so, but encourages them to first try other avenues for solving their problem. Regardless, we recommended that you always include a link to the contact information from the About Us page. It's critical that people who are interested in your company be able to find the location of its headquarters or a real telephone number that will be answered by a live human being.

Privacy Policy

A total of 86% of the homepages included a link to the site's privacy policy. Even though many users won't read this policy under normal conditions, having it prominently available is another way to encourage them to trust the site—an explicit policy communicates that their privacy is taken seriously. We strongly recommend that all sites that collect information from users feature a privacy link on the homepage.

If your site is intended for anonymous use, you can avoid a privacy policy on the homepage, but you should include a link in each location at which you ask for information from users anyway (when collecting email addresses for newsletter subscriptions, for example).

Among homepages that included a privacy policy link, this feature was named as follows:

Privacy Policy Label	Value
Privacy Policy	47%
Privacy	19%
Privacy Statement	12%
Privacy Notice	5%
Privacy & Security	5%

Other terms included "Privacy Guarantee," "SafeHarbor," "Security & Privacy," as well as more vague terms such as "Site Policies" and "Terms and Conditions."

We recommend calling the link "Privacy Policy." If another name is used, we strongly recommend using the word "privacy" as the first word in the link.

Job Openings

Of the homepages sampled, 74% featured an explicit link for job seekers. An additional 8% of sites provided employment information in their About Us area.

If the company doesn't have any job openings or if recruiting is a low priority, it's acceptable to relegate information about job openings to the About Us area, where most (but not all) job seekers will look for it if they don't find an explicit link on the homepage. Moving jobs off the homepage minimizes the salience of the recruiting effort, because only people who are actively looking for jobs have a chance to see that the company is hiring.

Among homepages that included a link for job seekers, this feature was named as follows:

Employment Label	Value
Careers	18%
Jobs at <name-of-company>	16%
Jobs	13%
<name-of-company> Jobs	13%
Employment	11%
Employment Opportunities	5%
Jobs & Careers	5%
Join Our Staff	5%

Other terms used included "Careers at <name-of-company>," "Career Opportunities," "Job Opportunities," "Job Search," "Opportunities," and "Work at <name-of-company>."

Use of the various name elements were as follows:

Use of Employment Labels	Value
Jobs (or Job)	53%
<name-of-company>	34%
Careers (or Career)	29%
Employment	16%
Opportunities	11%

Based on this analysis, we recommend including the word "jobs" in the name of the employment feature. Not only is it the most frequently used word, it's also the shortest and most straightforward. It's possible to combine the word "jobs" with the name of the company, but this doesn't seem necessary on most homepages because it's implied that all features on the page relate to the company unless they are labeled otherwise. An example of an exception would be a newspaper site where you would expect the "jobs" link to lead to a general section about jobs at other companies, possibly including classified ads. Thus, a newspaper site should use a link called "Jobs at <name-of-newspaper>." If using a longer name, the word "jobs" should be the first word in the link.

Help

Over half, 54%, of the homepages had a help feature, and based on this, help is currently not common enough on the Web for users to absolutely expect to find it. Also, users often avoid help even when it's offered because of previous bad experiences with useless help on other sites. Thus, we don't recommend including help just for the sake of having it. Only offer help if your site has a substantial number of advanced and complex features that cannot be simplified enough to be self-explanatory. Also offer help only if you are willing to devote sufficient technical writing resources to producing good and helpful content.

Among homepages that offered help, the placement on the page was as follows:

Placement of Help	Value
Upper right	41%
Upper center	11%
Upper left	4%
Middle left	11%
Lower right	7%
Lower center	11%
Lower left	19%

There is no true consensus as to where to put help, and that's one of the problems in getting users to use help. Because they don't know where to look for it, they are less likely to notice it and less likely to click on it.

Although it doesn't have the true majority, the upper-right placement of help is much more common than the other choices. We recommend placing help in the upper-right part of the page. This is also the place help is found in most desktop applications and dialog boxes.

Graphics and Multimedia

Plain text is the foundation of most web information, especially on homepages, which are dominated by navigation and news, both of which usually require words. Other media types are usually best used in conjunction with words, but they do have their place on many homepages.

Pictures

The median number of illustrations per homepage was 3. Even so, the days of the bloated homepage design seems to be past, because the median proportion of the homepages allocated to pictures was no more than 8%.

As a general rule of thumb, we recommend allocating somewhere between 5% and 15% of the homepage to images. Some sites may need more if their content is highly visual. Other sites might work best with no graphics at all. This question cannot be decided in the abstract because it depends on the nature of the site and its content. However, if your homepage creeps beyond spending more than 15% of the pixels on graphics, you've encountered a warning sign of possible design bloat. In such cases it's best to double-check whether the images are truly informative and helpful to users.

ALT Text

Among those homepages that included graphics ALT texts would have been beneficial for visually impaired users, only 42% included ALT texts. Including ALT text for images is the oldest and easiest of the guidelines for making websites accessible to users with disabilities, so it's a disgrace that the majority of homepages don't provide them.

We didn't assess whether the ALT texts were helpful or well-written, only whether they were there. Because this book is not the place for an in-depth discussion of how to improve usability for users with disabilities, we refer the interested reader to our extensive accessibility guidelines, which are available as a separate report (**http://www.NNgroup.com/reports/accessibility**).

Music

Only 4% of the sites played music as soon as the user entered the homepage. Considering that 96% of the sites provide a quiet user experience, this is what we currently recommend. In the future, it may be possible to use audio effects to increase usability and communicate better with users. However, even when better audio design becomes possible, it's still most likely that your website should avoid automatically playing audio on the homepage, instead restricting it to areas where it makes more sense and doesn't startle users.

Animation

Of the sites studied, 30% included some form of animation on the homepage. This is a sufficiently high percentage to suggest that animation might no longer startle or surprise users just because it's there. However, it's rare to see animation used well. Quite often, things seem to be moving just because the designers had the ability to make them move—not because the user experience was enhanced by the movement. In user testing, we often find that animation is too aggressive and intrusive. It not only annoys users but also distracts them from their intended tasks. For this reason, and because 70% of sites sampled avoid animation on the homepage, we advise your mainstream site to avoid animation on the homepage unless you have very good reasons for making something move.

Advertising

Nearly half, 46%, of the homepages carried advertising in the traditional sense, that is, promotions for other companies and their products. Among those sites that carried ads on the homepage, the median number of ads was 3, which seems to be an absolute upper limit from a usability perspective. Any more, and users aren't likely to pay attention to the individual ads, and the page feels busy and disjointed.

We don't believe advertising has a great role as a business model for websites, and we have been saying so since 1997 (for more information, please see our write-up at **www.useit.com/ alertbox/9709a.html**). Even so, many websites still rely on external ads for some part of their income, and it's hard to recommend that such sites eliminate advertising even though it hurts usability.

In all, 84% of the homepages carried internal advertising, which we defined as specific advertising-shaped or advertising-looking areas that promoted the site's own products or services. Of course, there is a fine line between having a navigation option for a product or featuring a product as an example of a product line and actually advertising it, but the promotional nature of the content and the advertising-looking nature of the graphic usually made the distinction clear. In general, if the text focused more on the deal than on the product itself, we counted it as internal advertising. Among those sites that carried internal advertising on their homepages, the median number was 4.5.

In other words, sites bombard users more with internal ads than with external ads, even though the external ads usually have the guaranteed benefit of generating advertising income. We recommend somewhat less internal advertising than we see on current pages—two or three are fine, but not four or five. Typically, the space used for internal ads can be used more productively, enhancing other elements of the homepage. While it's true that anything promoted on the homepage sells more, the increased sales of that product may come at the cost of reduced sales of everything else because users gain less understanding of the homepage's general function and the user experience is degraded relative to most of the goals users have when arriving on the homepage.

Typography

In designing the appearance of online text, readability is key because users will be viewing the text on a display screen with fairly low resolution. All computer screens are bad from a typographical perspective, and that will not change for many years to come because high-resolution screens are so expensive.

Body Text and Background Colors

Of the homepages in our sample, 72% used black for their body text. Almost all of these sites used white as the background color, thereby achieving the maximum possible contrast and the highest possible readability.

A meager 8% used blue text (mainly on white backgrounds), and 8% of sites used gray text (always on white backgrounds). Because these color schemes are less readable than black on white, they are also less recommended. However, they aren't necessarily horrible as long as the text is fairly dark relative to the white background.

Only 4% of the sites used white text on a black background. Even though this combination also provides the maximum possible contrast, it has slightly lower readability for most people than black text on a white background, which is more standard and looks more like print.

On the other hand, 84% of the homepages used a white background. This is the simplest and usually the best, especially when coupled with black or very dark text.

The median font size was 12 points. Virtually all text appeared in a sans serif font, although 4% used a serif typeface (with little horizontal lines protruding from the bottom of the characters). Even though serif fonts are usually easier to read in print, the thin serifs don't render as well on the current generation of low-resolution computer screens, so readability is higher for sans-serif typefaces like Verdana and Arial. Our current recommendation is to use sans-serif type for body text. Once high-resolution screens become common, this advice may change.

Link Formatting

Next to the use of colored text, the underline is the second-most important cue to users that text is clickable, and 80% of the homepages underlined the links. We continue to recommend that links be underlined, except possibly in navigation bars that use a design that makes it more than commonly obvious where users can click.

Of the homepages in our sample, 60% used the traditional standard for link colors: blue. This is a fairly small majority, but still large enough that we continue to recommend blue as the color for unvisited links. If links are blue, users know what to do. End of story.

Only 12% of sites used black links. This is less recommended, except for cases where one deliberately wants to downplay the links. In general, people look for colored text when trying to find out what they can do on a page.

In our study, 74% of the homepages changed the color on links leading to pages that the user had already visited. We highly recommend changing the color on visited links because this is one of the primary ways users understand where they have been on the site and also a helpful way to avoid having them go repeatedly to the same place by mistake.

Of those sites that used a different color for visited links, 54% made the visited links purple. Light blue and gray were the runner-ups with 16% and 11%, respectively. Most sites used some form of lighter or less saturated color for their visited links than for the unvisited links that lead to places where the user had not been yet.

Recommended Homepage Design

The following table shows our recommendations for the values you should choose for your homepage for each of the criteria discussed in this chapter. The recommendations are based on two considerations:

What user testing has shown to work best with the way people behave online.

What this chapter has shown to be the prevalent design decisions on other homepages.

One of the main findings from *many* usability studies is that sites work best when they follow the conventions users know from other sites. So the more sites do things a certain way, the more usability will usually increase by complying with that convention. Even when a convention may be suboptimal from a theoretical perspective, in practice it will work well because users will *know* how it works.

Each of the recommendations is annotated with a star rating to indicate how critical this guideline is to a satisfactory user experience:

★ ★ ★   **Essential Recommendation**: Should be followed by virtually all projects; violate only if you have test data to prove something different works better for your specific circumstances.

★ ★   **Strong Recommendation**: Should be followed by most projects; deviate only if you have a good reason to believe your site has different needs.

★   **Default Recommendation**: Safe default to follow, unless you can think of something better.

Homepage Issues	Strength of Recommendation	Recommended Design
Download time	★ ★ ★	At most 10 seconds at the prevalent connection speed for your customers. For modem users, this means a file size of less than 50 KB. Faster is better.
Page width	★ ★	Optimized for 770 pixels, but with a liquid layout that works at anything from 620 to 1024 pixels.
Liquid versus frozen layout	★ ★	Liquid.
Page length	★ ★	One or two full screens is best. No more than three full screens (currently 1000 to 1600 pixels).
Frames	★ ★ ★	No.
Logo placement	★ ★ ★	Upper left.
Logo size	★ ★	80x68 pixels.
Search	★ ★ ★	Provide search. Have it on the homepage. Make it a box.
Search placement	★ ★ ★	Upper part of the page, preferably in right or left corner.
Search box color	★ ★ ★	White.
Search button	★ ★	Call it "Search" ("Go" also acceptable).
Width of search box	★ ★	At least 25 characters, but 30 characters is better.
Type of search	★ ★	Simple search. (Advanced or scoped search relegated to secondary search interface—not shown on homepage.)

Homepage Issues	Strength of Recommendation	Recommended Design
Navigation	★★	One of the four main types: left-hand rail, tabs, links across the top, or categories in the middle of the page.
Footer navigation links	★	Use for "footnote style" links such as copyright and contact info. At most, 7 links across the bottom of the page. A single line when displayed in the common size of window.
Sitemap link	★★	"Site Map," if you have one.
Routing page	★★	No.
Splash page	★★★	No.
Sign-in	★	If providing protected content, either include the word "account" in the name of this feature or call it "Sign In."
About the company	★★★	Always include this feature.
About link	★★	Call the link "About <name-of-company>."
Contact information	★★	Provide a link to contact info and call it "Contact Us."
Privacy policy	★★★	Include one if the site collects data from users and link to it from the homepage.
Name of privacy link	★★	Call it "Privacy Policy."
Job openings	★★	Include an explicit link on the homepage if recruiting is important to the company. (Otherwise, list jobs under "About Us"). Call the link "Jobs."
Help	★	Don't offer it unless the site's complexity makes help unavoidable.
Help placement	★★	Upper right.
Auto-playing music	★★★	No.
Animation	★★	No.
Graphics/Illustrations	★	Somewhere between 5-15% of the space on the homepage.
Advertising	★★	At most, 3 ads (whether external or internal).
Body text color	★★	Black.
Body text size	★	12 points.
Body text size frozen	★★★	No. Always use relative sizes that make it possible for users to make the text larger or smaller as desired.
Body text typeface	★	Sans-serif.
Background color	★★	White.
Link color, unvisited links	★★	Blue.
Link color, visited links	★	Purple.
Link colors, different for visited and unvisited links	★★★	Yes. Unvisited links should be the most saturated color. Visited links should be a desaturated or less prominent color, but not light gray.
Link underlining	★★	Yes, except possibly in lists in navigation bars.

Introduction
to the Homepages

The following pages contain usability reviews of 50 homepages. All the sites were chosen because they were prominent in some way: Most sites came from top-10 lists of most-visited sites in the U.S. and other countries, as well as lists of the world's largest companies. We also included the sites of a few prominent government agencies and some well-run small companies and non-profit institutions.

Because the sites are among the best on the Internet, it is interesting to note how many usability problems we found on these homepages. The mistakes are not indications of bad designs or incompetent site managers. Rather they are indications of the sorry state of today's Web when it comes to usability and user support: Even the best sites are riddled with design elements that hurt users.

Some of our comments might seem picky; we have tried to comment on everything big and small. In terms of sheer volume, the smaller usability issues dominate the reviews. Most of these minor problems will not prevent a determined user from using the site, so they are not true usability catastrophes like the ones we often find when we study people trying to complete an entire task on the Web. Even so, the smaller usability problems are worth highlighting and they are worth fixing. The homepage must protect the company's image. Users do notice small things; inconsistencies and weaknesses impact trust and lower your company's reputation in the user's eyes. Users may simply think your company is sloppy. Finally, the cumulative effect of many small problems can be confusing and will make it difficult for users to find what they need on your site. Even a typo can make it harder to understand the available choices.

If you go to any of these homepages on the Web today, they will probably look different than the screenshots on the following pages. Most likely, many of the usability problems we describe will be long gone by the time you visit the sites. That's okay—these homepage analyses are intended as a varied set of examples of different styles of homepage designs and not critiques of specific companies and their websites. We are not out to advise you what website to use for your daily news or personal finance needs. We want to help you understand the usability impact of homepage design decisions.

Each screenshot represents the best efforts of a talented design team at a certain point in time during 2001. You can learn from their efforts and from their mistakes. The usability analysis of the individual design elements remains equally valid and helpful as a learning resource even after the sites that featured those elements have removed them.

www.about.com

About - The Human Internet - Microsoft Internet Explorer

File   Edit   View   Favorites   Tools   Help

← Back • → • ⊗ ⬙ ⌂ | ⌕ Search ⭐ Favorites ⬀ History | 🔖• ⬐ ⬒ ⬚ ⬛

Address ⬙ http://about.com/   ▼   ⭧ Go

AB⬤ut ®The Human Internet™

BargainDog The Best Bargains *from* The Best Sites

Monday, June 11, 2001

| **Guide of the Day** | **Riven** | **Pill Shill** | **Adventure Travel** |
| Kelly Rivera -- Your Guide to Health for Kids | Why did Hemingway and F. Scott Fitzgerald say farewell to friendship? Guide Esther Lombardi knows. | Some publications won't run ads for abortion pill RU-486. Advertising Guide Apryl Duncan has the story. | Head to Foot and Mouth Disease country for a vacation bargain, says Guide Mark Kahler. |

Find It Now: [   ] GO

Resources: Baseball | Cards | Horoscopes | How To | Kids' Privacy | Quizzes
Sex and the City | **Soap Awards** | Summer Travel | Timothy McVeigh

Partners: Auctions | Delta | Eddie Bauer | Free Downloads | **Insurance Quotes**
Jobs | **Make Cash** | **Music Radio** | Play Games | Sweepstakes | Travel

Site Index: # A B C D E F G H I J K L M N O P Q R S T U V W X Y Z

Arts & Humanities Books, writing, fine arts...	**Home & Garden** Decorating, design, repair...	**Pets** Dogs, cats, horses, birds...
Autos Cars, motorcycles, racing...	**Homework Help** History, languages, science...	**Real Estate** Buy, sell, rent...
Citysearch Cities/Towns U.S., Canada...	**Industry** News, research, commerce...	**Recreation & Outdoors** Gear, advice, training tips...
Comedy Jokes, cartoons, multimedia...	**Internet & Online** Help, tips, tutorials...	**Religion & Spirituality** Beliefs, scriptures...
Computing & Technology Hardware, software...	**Jobs & Careers** Resumes, interviews, tips...	**Science** Biology, space, geography...
Cultures Traditions, languages, int'l news...	**Kids** Fun sites, safe chat...	**Shopping** Online/offline, bargains...
Education Adult ed, teachers, college...	**Money** Stocks, credit, banking...	**Small Business** Small B2B resources, start-ups...
Food & Drink	**Movies**	**Sports**

Newsletter Signup
Subscribe to **About Today**. Enter email below!
[   ] Go!

Magazine Center
Subscribe Now!

Stock Quotes
Enter ticker/keyword
[   ] Go!

Member Center
Log in or Register!
Community and more.

About Shortcuts
Customize this site

News Center
Today's Best
Today's Weather

Hot Forum Topics
Giving Up
U.S. Government
"The death penalty represents society's

About.com, originally known as The Mining Company, is a collection of more than 700 special-interest subsites, each run by an expert guide in that field.

Ironically, there is no way to find out what the About.com site is about from its homepage, or what special value this site adds relative to the millions of Yahoo rip-offs. Edited overviews and navigation guides are a great feature, especially since each area is run by an enthusiast who cares deeply about his or her specialty. This key differentiator is not communicated except by the picture of the **Guide of the Day** and is only explained well by following the **Our Story** link at the bottom of the page. In fact, About.com does a good job organizing a lot of information—with the exception of the rather useless alphabetical site index, it's easier to scan this page and get to the various services than it is at Yahoo.

Window Title

It's good that the window title lists the site name first so it will bookmark alphabetically. It's also a good idea to repeat a meaningful tag line in the window title—in this case, however, the tag line doesn't help to explain the site name.

Tag Line

This odd tag line doesn't tell users what About.com is about or tell them what they can do on the site. This site isn't human; it's a collection of links and articles. A better tag line might be "Your Guide to the Best of the Internet."

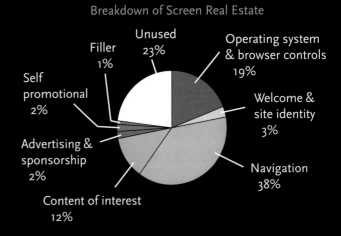

Breakdown of Screen Real Estate

- Unused 23%
- Filler 1%
- Self promotional 2%
- Advertising & sponsorship 2%
- Content of interest 12%
- Navigation 38%
- Welcome & site identity 3%
- Operating system & browser controls 19%

www.about.com

1. This rather understated advertising format doesn't interfere with use of the page as much as larger banner ads do.

2. For once, a real person in the obligatory "smiling lady" picture. It's especially good that About.com shows one of its real guides, because that's a major advantage of the site.

3. This obscure headline doesn't tell enough about the content. Don't write just for insiders when placing stories on a general-interest page.

4. Avoid "clever" headlines like this one. Users need straightforward headlines that tell them what the story is about. Dare to believe in the strength of your content. Saying that the story is about the abortion pill probably attracts more attention anyway.

5. This cutesy word play isn't only hard to parse (head, foot, mouth), it's downright unappealing. Who wants to travel to experience a disease?

6. **Find It Now** is a non-standard and long-winded label for the search feature. Simplify and make it recognizable. Call it "Search."

7. Good that this search box allows ample space for entering and reviewing words or phrases.

8. These **Go** buttons are inconsistently formatted, which adds clutter to the page.

9. You cannot expect people to disclose their email addresses without first giving them a sample of the newsletter. What do they get? Not a very attractive option, since most people are getting too much email already and want to sign up only for newsletters they find extremely valuable. Also, every time a site asks for a user's email, it needs a privacy statement that the address won't be sold or given out, as well as a way to opt in or out of any promotional mailings.

10. **Go** isn't the proper command verb for taking out a subscription to a newsletter—"Subscribe" would be more appropriate. Also, better to specify "Enter **your** email below." Otherwise, users sometimes mistakenly think they need to know the email to send their request to, such as the **About Today** email used here.

11. The differences between **Resources** and **Partners** are unclear. For example, **Play Games** sounds like a resource, because it's a special-interest category.

12. **Timothy McVeigh** isn't really a resource; it's a news category.

13. This link to a magazine site should be in the **Partners** area.

14. **Make Cash** is just too crass. At least mention what types of work or business you are trying to sell.

15. An alphabetical index isn't as efficient as a search or as comprehensive as the categories. For example, "online brokerage" can be found under **O** but not under **B**. If users look under **S**, they find a link to stocks (general stock information) but not to stock trading, which could be another name for brokerage services. So depending on how users think about their question, they might never find the appropriate services by diving into the alphabetical index.

16. No need for the enthusiastic exclamation point—it's enough to command "Go" without yelling.

17. Because this site is all about searching for information, it works to have the search feature in the center of the page like this. If it were in the more standard position in the upper-right or left corner, it would less optimal. It's nicely grouped here with all the other ways of finding information.

    Too, the background shading in these rows simplifies the appearance of this complex category area.

18. Most of these category names are clear and differentiated. There is no doubt what users will find under **Pets**, versus **Money**, for example.

19. The subcategories in this area should be links for two reasons: first, the standard "Yahoo design" for a taxonomy has taught users to *expect* links here. Second, having direct links to the most popular subcategories will save many users an extra page view and thus make them more likely to use the service.

20. What would motivate anybody to register? There needs to be a link to a page that explains the benefits of joining.

21. **Community** doesn't make sense on a general-purpose page. It's better to have communities deeper within the site, where users share common interests.

22. This category should be named "Cities/Towns" and *should not* include the name of another website (**Citysearch**).

23. The name of the site causes trouble in several places, particularly here. **About Shortcuts** sounds like the place to find information about shortcuts. It's dangerous to use a frequently occurring natural-language word as the name of a website because of this exact problem—it reads strangely when combined with the names of features. In any case, there is no need for this headline because customization actually fits well in the **Member Center** category above it.

24. The **News Center** needs to show some of the content right here instead of giving the generic link to **Today's Best**. You can't expect users to just randomly click in case there might be something interesting.

25. International news fits better in the **News Center**.

www.accenture.com

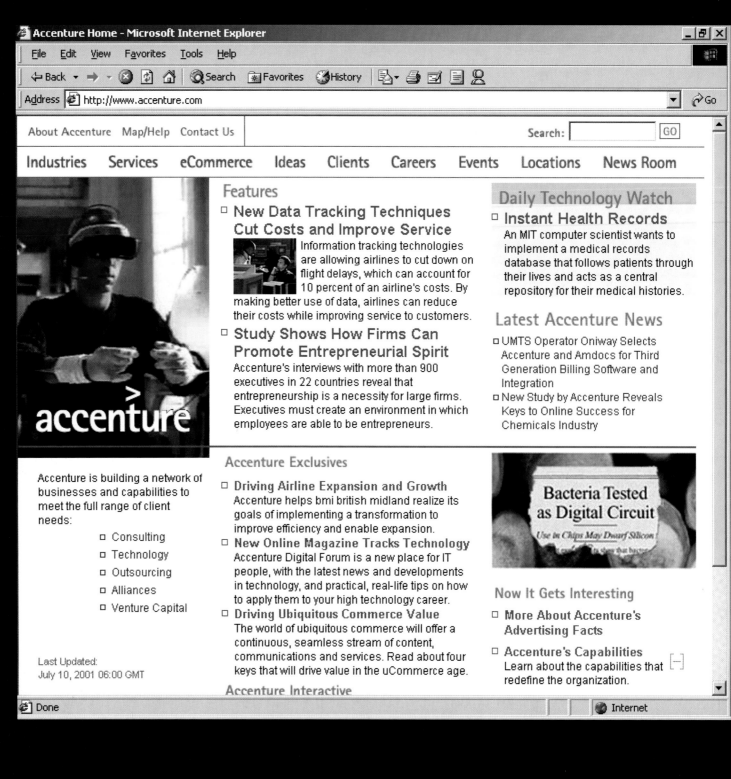

Accenture is the new company name for Andersen Consulting, formed after a nasty divorce from the parent company, Andersen Worldwide and Arthur Andersen. Accenture won the rights to be independent, but lost the company name in the process. Accenture is the world's largest consulting services company. Accenture's goal, as stated in the **About Accenture** section of the website, is to be a "global market maker, architect and builder of the new marketplace, developing innovations to improve the way the world works and lives." As if that explained things. Accenture emphasizes that it helps its clients leverage technology to achieve their goals. Accenture's clients include 84 of the Fortune Global 100 and more than half of the Fortune Global 500.

Accenture's homepage is full of words, but it fails to adequately answer the basic questions, "Who is Accenture?" and "What do they do?" Accenture is likely not allowed to use its ex-name, "Andersen Consulting," anywhere on the site, which presents real challenges. It takes the stance of a well-established, famous company, but can't really tell users about its history. Instead, Accenture focuses on what makes it cool and different now. Unfortunately, this doesn't really help to differentiate it from any other startup out there. Like many startups, Accenture's stilted copy writing focuses on how *technology* solves its clients' problems, rather than on the human expertise and experience of an established, worldwide consulting firm. The layout is dense and needs an information architecture overhaul.

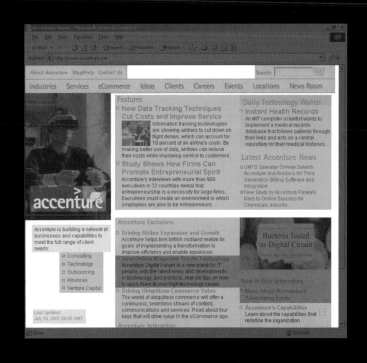

Breakdown of Screen Real Estate

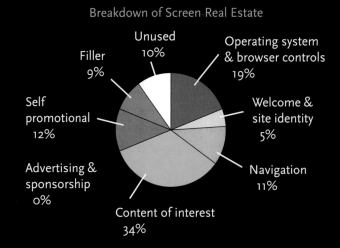

- Unused 10%
- Operating system & browser controls 19%
- Filler 9%
- Self promotional 12%
- Welcome & site identity 5%
- Advertising & sponsorship 0%
- Navigation 11%
- Content of interest 34%

Window Title
> This window title will bookmark appropriately by company name. No need to include the word **Home**, though.

Tag Line
> Accenture's tag line, which it has used in advertising since 2001, is **Now It Gets Interesting**. Although this tag line does appear on the page, it's not readily apparent—it's down in the bottom-right corner. This tag line doesn't help explain the newly named company or what it does, let alone the purpose of the website.

www.accenture.com

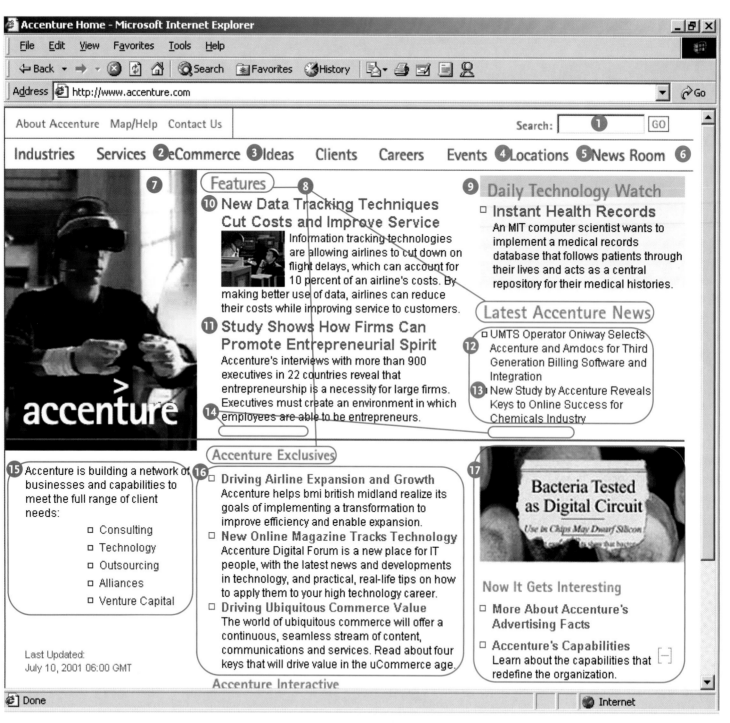

(1) Good to have a search input box on the homepage. Better if it were wider so that users could more easily edit and review their entries.

(2) Thankfully, Accenture used the common term **eCommerce**, even though this link goes to a section that describes Accenture's "uCommerce" solutions. If you must make up words, it's critical to define them, as Accenture does on its **uCommerce** page, and refrain from using them (undefined) as navigation links.

(3) **Ideas** is a rather puzzling category name. This link goes to a list of Accenture's latest research and would be clearer if it were named "Research."

(4) Good to have an obvious link to **Locations** on the homepage.* Such a link is one of the two most important factors to user success in finding a company's physical locations.

(5) Good to have a homepage link to an area with news and press releases, so that journalists can quickly find company information.

(6) There's no homepage link for investor relations—a standard link for a corporate site.

(7) This photo is initially intriguing, but without a caption to explain a clever shot, users sometimes get frustrated or are misled about the site's overall purpose. It just happens that we caught Accenture's homepage in our screenshot at a time when the photo seemed somewhat relevant to the company (clearly some "technology" is happening here). This photo updates every time the screen refreshes and randomly cycles through a collection of photos, most of which have no apparent connection to Accenture. Photos include bunnies, orchids, bacteria, boats, and even the United States Constitution. In fact, these all were featured in different Accenture ads, but they don't link to the explanation of the ad campaign that appears elsewhere on the site. Best to avoid purely decorative, gratuitous graphics and stick to pictures that illustrate relevant content on your homepage.

(8) What is the difference between **Features**, **Accenture Exclusives**, and **Latest Accenture News**? All of these categories contain a mix of articles about Accenture research and its clients, with a few articles about new technology sprinkled in. It would be clearer to structure the content into these three categories: "Latest Research," "Case Studies," and "Technology News."

(9) This boxed feature area, which focuses on one new technological advancement per day, is an interesting addition to the site. Better, though, to connect it to the overall theme of the site, by emphasizing the business impact of the technology rather than offering a rote report of "what it is."

* *Making It Easy For Users to Find Physical Locations*, Nielsen Norman Group, 2001.
See http://nngroup.com/reports/locators/.

(10) The headline for this area is fine, but the deck doesn't give much more detail. Better to give an example of one thing that airlines gleaned from the data and then express the benefit in the new bottom line.

(11) It's ironic that the copy for a study about encouraging risk and innovation sounds so pedantic and dry. This deck would be much better (and the study would sound more interesting) if it gave one clear example of how to promote entrepreneurial spirit in your company and what the payoff can be.

(12) Why are these links gray—the color used elsewhere on the page to show visited links? This color makes the "latest news" the lowest priority on the page.

(13) Why can't this headline tell what at least one of the keys to online success is? Give users information—don't keep them in suspense with a cliffhanger headline.

(14) All of the feature areas should have a link to archives of the past stories for the area. Currently, not even the headings, such as **Features**, link to an archives list. If users have seen an article on an earlier visit to the homepage, they need an easy way to find it again. It is possible to find some past stories elsewhere on the site, but it takes a good deal of digging.

(15) Although it's good to devote an area of the homepage to defining what the company does, these categories are too broad to be helpful. Any company comprising other companies can say that it is "a network of businesses and capabilities." Because Accenture's offerings are complex, better to make this definition even shorter and explain in more detail elsewhere. It would be more meaningful to simply introduce the bullets with "Learn about all of Accenture's core offerings."

(16) This text area, like the **Features** and **News** areas, is too dense and wordy. It's very difficult to get the gist of these articles by scanning them, but that's exactly what users need from online content. The articles are also too close together. Once users visit a link, this problem gets worse—the title changes from blue to gray, which de-emphasizes the title and makes the articles even less.

(17) Bad enough to bug people with ads, worse to devote a large corner of your homepage to rehashing the ads all over again. Most people don't like ads. Ads keep people from the real thing that they want to do (read a magazine, watch a television show). Repeating the ads here, and providing links to learn more about them, arrogantly assumes that users want to *enjoy* the interruption all over again, rather than do what they came to the website to do. Worse, when users click on the bacteria photo, they go to a general page about Accenture's advertising campaign, instead of straight to the bacteria story. When you feature a specific item, link it to specific content—don't take users back to a more general level.

continues

www.accenture.com

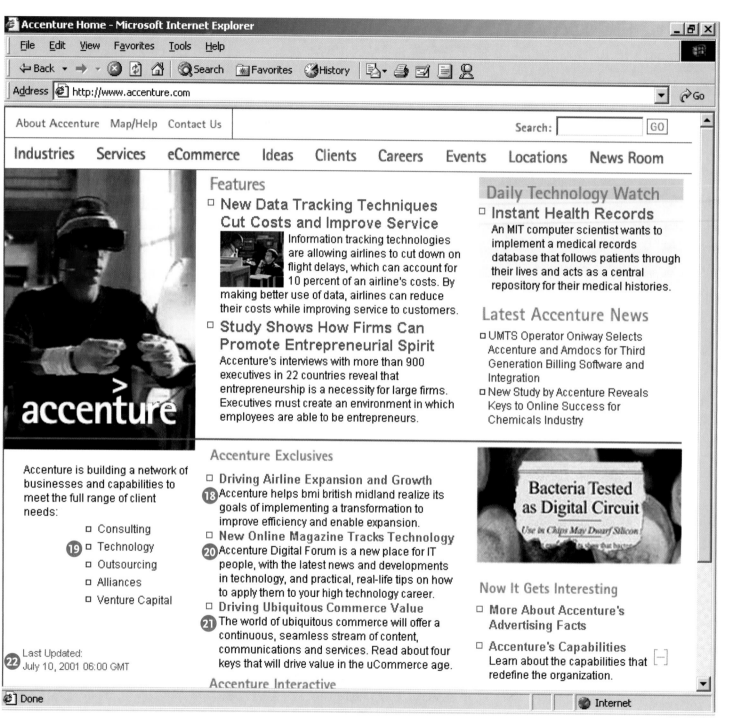

About Accenture   Map/Help   Contact Us

Search: [   ] GO

Industries   Services   eCommerce   Ideas   Clients   Careers   Events   Locations   News Room

Features

□ **New Data Tracking Techniques Cut Costs and Improve Service**
Information tracking technologies are allowing airlines to cut down on flight delays, which can account for 10 percent of an airline's costs. By making better use of data, airlines can reduce their costs while improving service to customers.

□ **Study Shows How Firms Can Promote Entrepreneurial Spirit**
Accenture's interviews with more than 900 executives in 22 countries reveal that entrepreneurship is a necessity for large firms. Executives must create an environment in which employees are able to be entrepreneurs.

Daily Technology Watch

□ **Instant Health Records**
An MIT computer scientist wants to implement a medical records database that follows patients through their lives and acts as a central repository for their medical histories.

Latest Accenture News

□ UMTS Operator Oniway Selects Accenture and Amdocs for Third Generation Billing Software and Integration
□ New Study by Accenture Reveals Keys to Online Success for Chemicals Industry

Accenture is building a network of businesses and capabilities to meet the full range of client needs:

□ Consulting
(19) □ Technology
□ Outsourcing
□ Alliances
□ Venture Capital

(22) Last Updated:
July 10, 2001 06:00 GMT

Accenture Exclusives

□ **Driving Airline Expansion and Growth**
(18) Accenture helps bmi british midland realize its goals of implementing a transformation to improve efficiency and enable expansion.

□ **New Online Magazine Tracks Technology**
(20) Accenture Digital Forum is a new place for IT people, with the latest news and developments in technology, and practical, real-life tips on how to apply them to your high technology career.

□ **Driving Ubiquitous Commerce Value**
(21) The world of ubiquitous commerce will offer a continuous, seamless stream of content, communications and services. Read about four keys that will drive value in the uCommerce age.

Accenture Interactive

Bacteria Tested as Digital Circuit
Use in Chips May Dwarf Silicon!

Now It Gets Interesting

□ **More About Accenture's Advertising Facts**

□ **Accenture's Capabilities**
Learn about the capabilities that redefine the organization.

18 This deck skirts the real issues with unexciting pronouncements, but includes no relevant detail. Don't waste space on wordy phrases like "implementing a transformation to improve efficiency and enable expansion." Instead, briefly state what Accenture helped change to make the airline faster and bigger. It's also difficult to scan for the client's name here—it should be in uppercase letters.

19 It's not clear that these bullets link to descriptions of Accenture's different business units, especially since they are a faded gray color. And except for **Venture Capital**, these categories are too general to be helpful. If you wanted help setting up an IS department in your company, would you go to **Consulting**, **Technology**, or **Outsourcing**? Better to promote the "Services" link to a main page area and then list the core business services with a brief description of each one. That would let users see what Accenture does on the homepage and give them a way to drill down quickly to their area of interest.

20 This description of the online magazine isn't as compelling as it would be to actually feature a blurb from the lead article. The current description is too general and a bit confusing. Is this a magazine or an online forum? The name of the publication combined with the reference to it as a "place" make it seem like an interactive forum, rather than a static publication.

21 This headline and deck don't properly introduce and define the concept of uCommerce. The abbreviation **uCommerce** and spelled-out phrase **Ubiquitous Commerce** need to be together and lead off the deck, followed by a quick list of the four keys that drive value. The "continuous, seamless stream" phrase doesn't help and should be deleted.

22 Because Accenture's homepage doesn't really have time-critical content, it's overkill to show the time last updated and subject all users to the task of calculating their time relative to GMT. Showing the date last updated would suffice and avoid this complexity altogether.

In the bottom-right corner of Accenture's homepage lurks a little gray minus sign. If you click it, this rating scale by OnlineOpinion appears. As if self-reported user data isn't misleading enough, this collection method is especially bad. Not only is access to it fairly well hidden, it doesn't give users any criteria for rating the page, making it impossible to interpret the resulting data. What exactly are users rating here? Aesthetics? Ease of use? Content? Last, in order to see what each symbol means, you must keep your mouse pointer still on it for about three seconds— this requires too much patience and mousing precision.

www.amazon.com

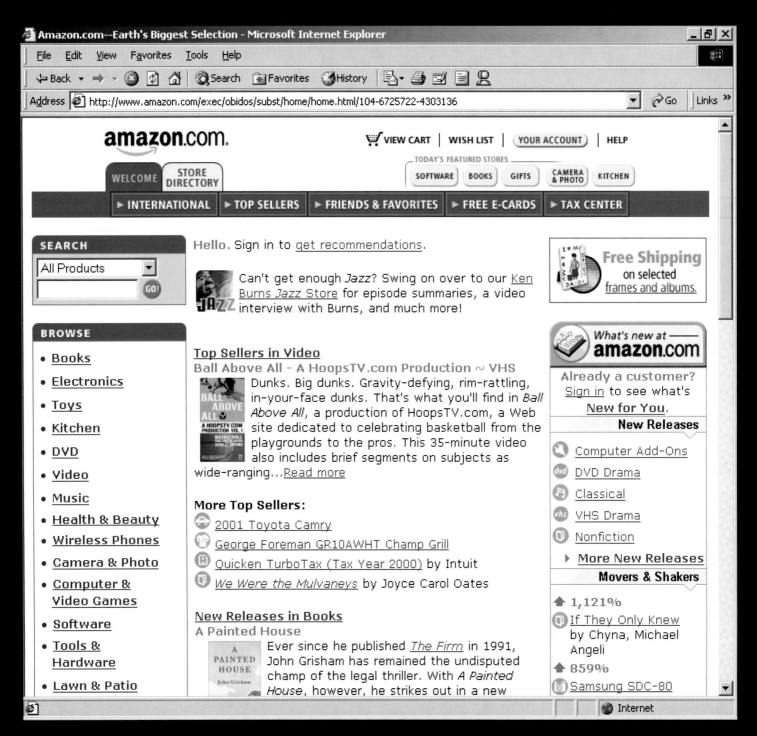

Amazon.com offers a wide variety of products, from books, music, and software to cars, electronic goods, and appliances. Amazon augments its product descriptions with information and recommendations from both Amazon staff and customer reviews.

Amazon successfully categorizes a vast selection of products while maintaining an uncluttered appearance on its homepage. It uses color sparingly and effectively for emphasis. Amazon also does a very good job of revealing content on the homepage and proving by example what the site is selling. A downside to this homepage for new users, however, is that it's optimized for personalization. Amazon would probably be better off designing a separate homepage for first-time users. Although this homepage is better than most other homepages, it pales in comparison to Amazon's overall site usability and great shopping support.

Window Title

Earth's Biggest Selection doesn't tell what the site offers. Better to say, "Earth's Biggest Store."

URL

This complex URL looks confusing and doesn't let users know where they are. The numbers at the end make it seem as if it contains personal information, or that bookmarking and emailing it could violate your privacy.

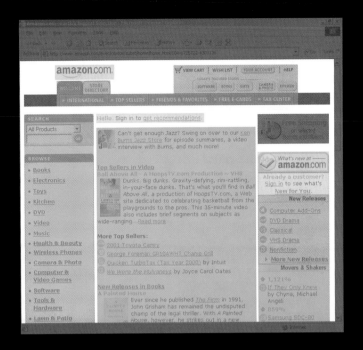

Breakdown of Screen Real Estate

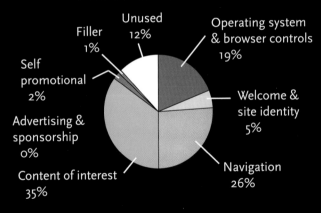

www.amazon.com

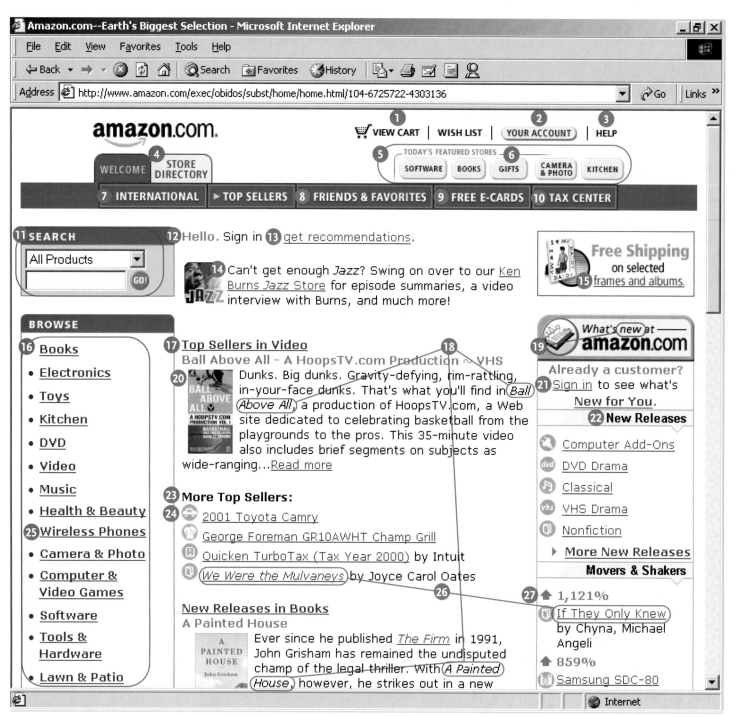

1 "Shopping Cart" would be more explicit than **View Cart**, although the site makes good use of the highly recognized icon.

2 No reason to present **Your Account** differently from the other items in this section.

3 Good to have **Help** in the increasingly standard upper-right corner.

4 **Store Directory** duplicates the **Browse** area and is an unnecessary secondary homepage. If it were eliminated, there would be no need for these tabs, which add complexity to the top of the page.

5 **Today's Featured Stores** tabs waste space and offer no value to the user. Users can better see what's in these stores through the featured examples in the main body of the page, and can use the left navigation area if they want to link to the general category.

6 **Gifts** is an odd category next to **Software** and **Books**—any of these items could be gifts.

7 The **International** section isn't descriptive enough to be immediately recognizable as a way to choose another country's site. It's easy to misinterpret this as an area featuring international books or music. Better to use a more informative link, such as "International versions of site."

8 **Friends & Favorites** is a meaningless category name.

9 **Free E-Cards** offers a better way to deal with gifts because it is a specific tool to help you with gift giving, rather than a general gift store.

10 Promoting seasonally appropriate content is good, but this should get more prominence and show more products. After all, taxes are relevant to nearly all users.

11 Good to default scoped search to an option that searches everything so that users have to explicitly limit their search, if they want to. The **Search** box should be wider so that users can more easily review and edit their queries.

12 **Hello** is an unnecessary level of friendliness before you know the user's name and feels more like a typical bad form letter than a personal touch.

13 Very good to sell the benefit of signing in rather than to just promote registration as a user task.

14 This description uses good highlighting that emphasizes what the described item is about. Even if a reader is scanning quickly, the italicized "Jazz" and the informative hyperlink convey the gist.

15 **Photo albums and Photo frames** is an odd and seemingly random combination of items.

16 These items should be grouped next to each other according to relevancy. **Kitchen** and **Lawn & Patio** should be together, as should **Toys** and **Computer & Video Games**, and **Electronics**, **Wireless Phones**, and **Camera & Photo**.

17 Judicious use of highlighting color makes headlines like this one stand out on the page without taking up too much space.

18 These descriptions were not written for online reading. It's nearly impossible to tell that the *Ball Above All* description is talking about basketball. The description of *A Painted House* is similarly verbose. At the least, the site could highlight the key words to make them scannable.

19 It's hard to tell what this graphic is or how it relates to what's new. More helpful to emphasize the word "*new.*"

20 The graphic for the video would be easier to see and wouldn't look as crowded if the text didn't wrap below it.

21 It's confusing to offer two locations for **Sign in**, since new or returning customers can use the sign in at the top of the page. This location is too buried—better to have one prominent place for sign in and then customize the page accordingly.

22 What's the value of these **New Releases**, if they're just general categories? Better to not feature them this way on a site that's not yet personalized. It would be better to actually show some of the big sellers from each of these categories or only from the most popular categories.

23 These **Top Sellers** include a random selection of items and require the user to understand the icons, which are difficult to see and comprehend.

24 The **Top Sellers** section uses an inconsistent manufacturer/author credit. If "Quicken TurboTax by Intuit," why not "Camry by Toyota"?

25 Why call this category **Wireless Phones**? If this includes cell phones and cordless phones, why not just call it "Telephones," which would be more scannable in the list?

26 Why are book titles in italics here but not in **Movers & Shakers**? Also, why are software titles not in italics?

27 In **Movers & Shakers**, this percentage increase information doesn't really give meaningful data or help users in any way. Better to tell users which items have reached a significant, understandable landmark, such as a "Top 10" list, so that it's relative to other sales.

www.artic.edu

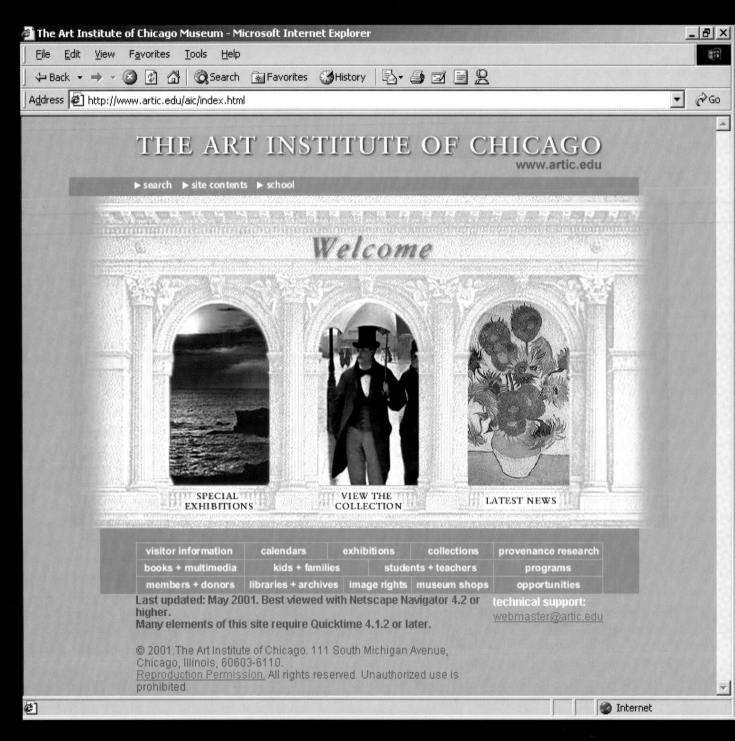

This homepage is the virtual home to The Art Institute of Chicago's museum. The museum is one of the world's greatest, hosting more than 300,000 pieces in its collections. From the museum's website, users can learn about its collections, special exhibitions, and programs.

Overall, this homepage presents a fairly clean and attractive front for the museum. Beauty often comes at a price, however, and several elements that make this page attractive cause usability problems as well. This isn't to suggest that usability must compromise beauty. In fact, if the Art Institute implemented the changes we suggest to its homepage, it would have more room to showcase the true beauty of its collections and would give due prominence to key user tasks.

Window Title
Don't put "The" at the beginning of a window title—it will alphabetize under "T" instead of "A." Although the Art Institute includes "The" in its name, users will still most likely think to look for it alphabetically under "A."

URL
This URL is too complex and will be difficult for users to remember. Also, although the museum is affiliated with an educational institution, a museum's domain name should end with ".org, " not ".edu. " It would be much simpler and easier to remember if the museum had the domain name **www.artic.org** and the school had **www.artic.edu**.

Tag Line
This site doesn't have a tag line, but it should have a simple one to explain what The Art Institute of Chicago is. Nowhere on the homepage does it explicitly say that it is a museum.

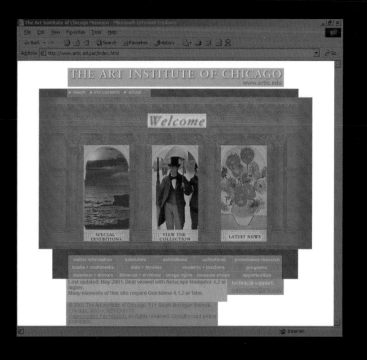

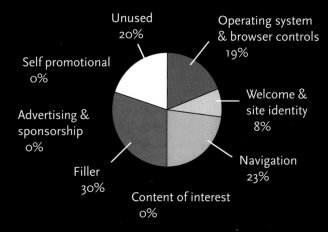

Breakdown of Screen Real Estate

Unused 20%
Operating system & browser controls 19%
Self promotional 0%
Welcome & site identity 8%
Advertising & sponsorship 0%
Navigation 23%
Filler 30%
Content of interest 0%

www.artic.edu

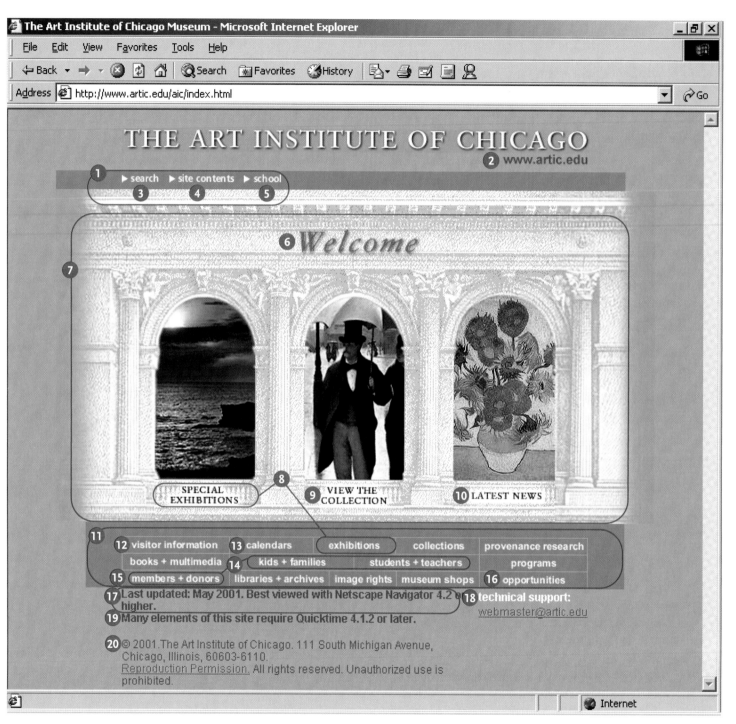

1. Not only are these little arrows before each choice unnecessary, they also falsely suggest a hierarchy among these items, as if this were a breadcrumb trail navigation. Better to use simple links.

2. It's odd to give this URL here. First, this URL doesn't go to the current page, it goes to a splash screen where users choose whether to go to the museum or school homepages. Second, it's not an active link, so users don't go anywhere if they click it, which some users surely will. It's likely that the museum lists it here because the real URL isn't memorable. Better to fix the URL instead.

3. **Search** should have an input box on the homepage. Users expect to see an input box at the top of the screen and often overlook links to search.

4. "Site Map" is the more common name of links to overviews of the site. **Contents** implies that users need to go there to get any content, when in fact the top-level categories on the **site contents** page are about the same as the links at the bottom of the homepage.

5. This link should be "School of The Art Institute of Chicago." Uppercase letters make it clear it is a proper name, and spelling out the school name removes the ambiguity of **School**.

6. Although this looks like just another unessential, hokey welcome, this area actually has important information in it, which users are likely to miss. When you roll your mouse over the pictures beneath the **Welcome** area, it tells you what exhibit the items are from. It's not good to hide information like this and separate it from the content to which it refers.

7. This bold choice for a central graphic area has positive and negative aspects. The upside is that it clearly connects the site to artwork and looks attractive. The designers made imaginative use of the building's windows by having them frame the selected pieces. The downside is that, with only three windows, the selected pieces can't show more of the breadth of the museum's collections—all the pieces shown here were done within roughly a 100-year timeframe, while the museum's collection includes pieces from thousands of years BC. The space used by the large graphic could instead be used to show more art pieces, or to chunk the navigation area into more meaningful segments.

8. The difference between **Special Exhibitions** and **Exhibitions** is unclear. At first it seems that these are redundant options. In fact, **Special Exhibitions** goes to just the featured *exhibition* (no plural) and should be indicated as such with the name of what the exhibition is (Edward Weston photos, in this case).

9. The site needs to consistently use singular or plural for the museum's collections. We suggest plural, because the museum, in fact, has many different collections.

10. There's no immediately apparent connection between Van Gogh's *Sunflowers* and the museum's **Latest News**, but the proximity of these items to one another implies a connection. Better to feature a couple of interesting news stories and a link to more news or have a clear caption area that explains the connection.

11. It's difficult to tell what the ordering scheme is for these items. It's hard to believe they're organized by popularity— do more users come for **provenance research** (currently on the first line) than for **members + donors?**

12. It would be nice to list the museum's operating hours right on the homepage, because looking up this information is likely a common task for users of this site.

13. Why is **calendars** plural here? This link should be the more precise "Calendar of Events," which is what the page beneath uses as a heading.

14. These different audience groups should be grouped next to each other.

15. **Members + donors** implies that this area is reserved for those who already have that status. In fact, this link goes to membership information, so it should be named "Membership and Donors." A clearly labeled link is especially important because there is no other apparent way to join the museum from the homepage.

16. **Opportunities** is a euphemistic and indirect way of saying "Jobs" or "Employment," either of which would make better link names.

17. If you're going to include a date on a homepage, it's good to make it the date last updated, as this site does, because that gives user meaningful information, instead of a stamp of the current date.

    Too, the unhelpful **Best viewed with** message doesn't tell users how to get a higher version of Netscape, and it leaves Internet Explorer users out completely.

18. **Technical support** is a rather misleading term, because only a link to email the webmaster is provided. Does the webmaster of this site actually provide technical support or just gather user's feedback? Better to just include this address in a "Contact Us" area.

19. Telling users that they need QuickTime at this point doesn't help at all. First, it's better to inform users in context, when they actually need it. Second, this message doesn't help users fix the problem in any way, such as by telling them how to check whether they have QuickTime already or by linking to the website where they can get it.

20. Good to have the address of the museum right on the homepage. It would be better if it included a phone number and a link to additional "Contact Us" information.

www.asiacuisine.com.sg

Asiacuisine.com.sg is a site about the Asian food scene, with a focus on Singapore. The site reviews restaurants and wine and includes recipes from famous chefs.

This homepage reveals the site's split focus on two rather disparate user groups: the food service professional and the food enthusiast. The site's advertisements and event listings clearly cater to the insiders, while much of the content caters to the food lover. This page provides too much detail in the verbose text blocks, but not enough detail in the listings, which would best support users in likely tasks such as choosing a good restaurant or bottle of wine. The site claims to be a portal for Asian cuisine, but it's not—it focuses narrowly on one location, and it doesn't provide enough breadth for visitors to regularly use the site to find a variety of goods and services. For example, it should group recommendations by type of Asian cuisine and location. The top five restaurants on the homepage, however, span the globe from Singapore to Australia.

Window Title

Don't include the word "website" in a window title—it wastes words stating the obvious. Also, no need to add the title of the print magazine (*New Asia Cuisine*), since it's so close to the website title.

Tag Line

Asia's Leading Food and Beverage Portal would be an appropriate tag line if the site actually covered all of Asia. In fact, the site mainly covers Singapore businesses. Also, the tag line appears in an animated area of the screen and is visible for less than two seconds at a time, so it is easily overlooked (in our picture, a small portion of it bisects the logo).

URL

Good that this URL has the .sg, because it verifies that this is a Singapore site. It's also good that users can just type **www.asiacuisine.com** and get to the site.

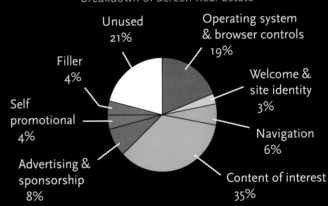

Breakdown of Screen Real Estate

Unused 21%

Operating system & browser controls 19%

Filler 4%

Welcome & site identity 3%

Self promotional 4%

Navigation 6%

Advertising & sponsorship 8%

Content of interest 35%

www.asiacuisine.com.sg

1 This logo area is not only animated, it's drawn onto the screen by a big lobster every few seconds (no joke). This distracts users' attention away from the real content of the site, and it makes the logo less memorable, because users can't see it long enough to remember what it looks like.

2 These tabs bury the site's offerings. Better to use the homepage as the portal it claims to be and include these categories right on the homepage with a featured link for each one.

3 **Links** is about as generic and unhelpful a name as you can get on the Web. This actually goes to URLs for many different food and beverage sites—just say so, and lose the globe icon.

4 **Forum** has some potentially interesting features, such as "Ask the Chef" and "Chat," but they're hidden behind this generic name and meaningless icon. Better to reveal more of the content on the homepage—link directly to "Ask the Chef" and feature one or two discussion topics with a link to more.

5 The **Home** tab should not be clickable on the homepage.

6 The difference between **Magazine** and **Ezine** is not clear. In fact, **Magazine** refers to Asia Cuisine's hardcopy magazine, while **Ezine** is a newsletter. Fine to link to the magazine; better for the newsletter to explain the value to users so they are compelled to subscribe, for example, "Get weekly recipes emailed to you."

7 Online videos should be integrated into the site by topic area, rather than separated as they are here. This makes it look like the site sells video products.

8 Good to have a search input box at the top of the homepage. No need to label it with **Search for**—the **Search** button does that. Also, the **Search** button is not properly aligned with the input box.

9 **Zoom In** has nothing to do with this category of links. Links to **About Us** and webmaster feedback are common enough that they can stand on their own without a category name.

Also, all the links in this section go to information about the holding company that owns the Asia Cuisine website, rather than to specific information about Asiacuisine.com. Users will be first interested in learning about *this* website, rather than the hierarchy a step above.

10 Emphasizing **biased** puts a negative spin on sharing your tastes, which is what this article is trying to encourage users to do. Also, "bias" is a negative message to promote on the homepage of a site that relies so heavily on compiling opinion data. Finally, this text is indirect, verbose, and requires too much close reading to figure out the main message.

11 Good that the text wraps and adjusts to the user's preferred font size settings—bad that the phrase **Wine Scene** breaks at this common setting (medium fonts). If a phrase needs to be together to be understood, put a non-breaking space between the words.

12 Need to tell where these restaurants and chefs are located. Many of these are in Singapore, but one is in Australia.

Give users more information to motivate them to click through. This list should include the ratings that the restaurants and the wines received, to show that these are top selections.

13 Need to include captions for pictures that don't directly relate to the text next to them. In this case, it's not clear from the photo that this is a food made from durians—it needs a caption like "durian pastry."

Too, these feature areas (**News**, **events**, and **video**) are not sufficiently separated from one another and should be labeled, to make them more scannable. Currently they all run together, and the useful links to the archives blend in and look like part of the story.

14 Don't have multiple links to the same thing in one area. In any case, **here** is the least helpful sort of link—always tell users what they are going to get from the link, so that users scanning the links on the page can quickly get the gist of the content.

15 Need to include links to past featured restaurants, wines, and chefs.

16 It's difficult to wade through this verbose paragraph to get the meaning. Have confidence in and be direct about the content—the readers' voyeuristic pleasure in finding out what celebrities like to eat surely stands on its own and needs only a simple title. Intrigue them more with a photo of one of the featured celebrities slurping noodles. Content aside, there's no reason to format one item as a bullet—it makes the paragraph too narrow.

17 Both the diagram and the photos are too detailed for this small display size. Better to crop the image and just show one durian pastry at a time.

18 Why waste so much space here? This page has a great deal of content below the fold—better to move it up.

19 This **Monthly Contest** is really a thinly veiled ploy for one of the site's advertisers (if users have paid attention to the ads on the site, they'll be able to easily answer the question). Sites that recommend and rate services need to build readers' trust and shouldn't jeopardize that trust with an inappropriate blend of advertising and content.

20 Great to feature one chef every month, but it would be good to list the restaurant name as well.

www.bn.com

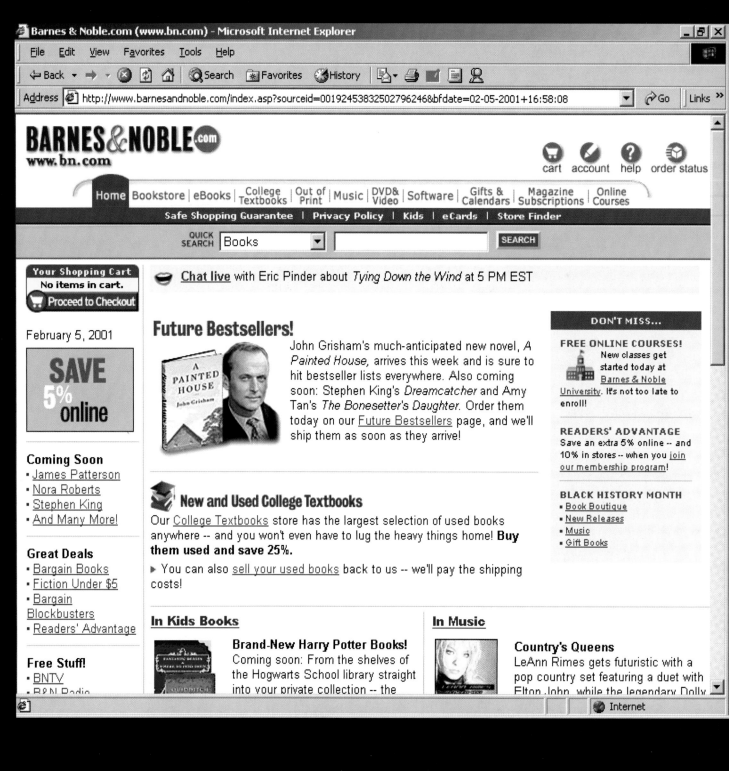

BN.com, the online component to the brick-and-mortar store, is a book, music, and software site.

BN.com's biggest weakness is that its homepage doesn't facilitate browsing because it's not well organized and doesn't showcase its content well. It appears that as Barnes & Noble expanded its business, it added departments in random places on the homepage without a clear plan for information architecture. Not only does this homepage lack meaningful content groupings, but it also shows a selection of content that's too narrow—for example, one fiction writer and one music artist. Content this limited reduces the chance that any one user will like a choice enough to explore further.

Window Title
    This window title will bookmark well, but would be better if it included a brief description of the site. Also, no need to include the URL.

URL
    Bad URL—looks confusing and doesn't let users know where they are. It makes it seem as if bookmarking and emailing it will reveal personal information.

Breakdown of Screen Real Estate

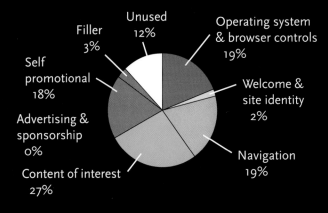

Unused 12%

Filler 3%

Self promotional 18%

Advertising & sponsorship 0%

Content of interest 27%

Operating system & browser controls 19%

Welcome & site identity 2%

Navigation 19%

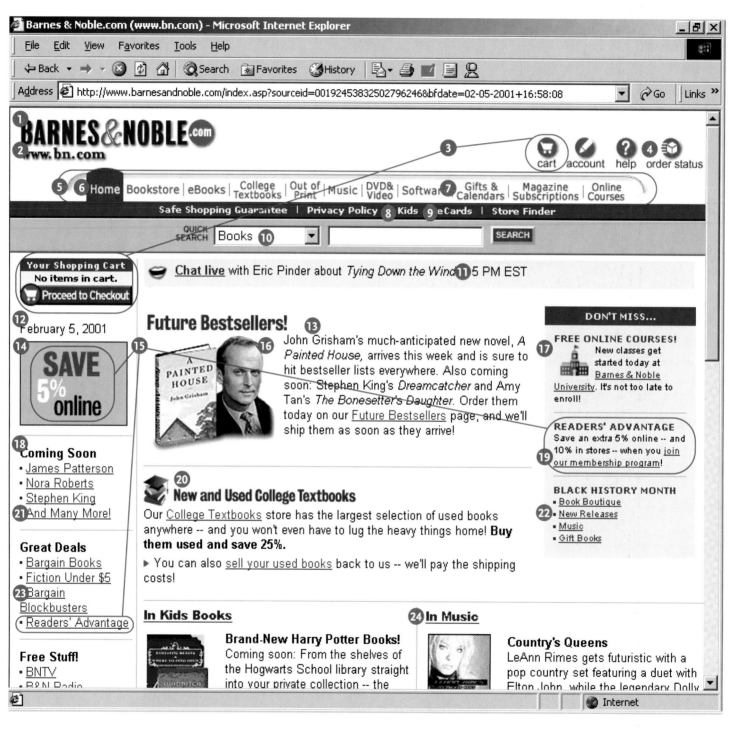

1 It's good that the logo associates the site with the brand identity of the brick-and-mortar store.

2 The dual identity (**Barnes & Noble** and **BN**) is confusing and is used inconsistently on the site. While it's good that the site registered both domain names, there should be one official domain name for the site.

3 Using two shopping carts is confusing. The other cart says it takes you to checkout—does the top cart do the same, or something else?

Too, it's strange to offer **Proceed to Checkout** when there is nothing in the cart. Also, **No items in cart** is not quite as clear as "Your cart is empty."

4 Website support should be simplified to one navigation area with items such as a shopping cart, help, shopping guarantees, and a privacy policy in one place.

5 Having so many tab choices diminishes their value. The tabs don't appear to be grouped in logical order from a user's perspective (books next to textbooks, etc.), although they probably reflect organizational chronology of the company.

6 This **Home** tab shouldn't be clickable when you are already on the homepage.

7 **Gifts & Calendars** is an odd grouping—any of the categories could be gifts and there's no immediately apparent connection between gifts and calendars.

8 This link to **Kids** seems especially vague in this context—placed next to **Privacy Policy** and **Safe Shopping Guarantee** under **Home**. It should be next to other product categories in order to make sense.

9 **eCards** should be listed with **Gifts & Calendars** rather than with these administrative options.

10 When you pull down the **Quick Search** menu, the categories don't map to what's on the tabs or follow the same order. The categories also include the item **Prints & Posters**, which doesn't appear elsewhere on the site. In addition, they don't show all the categories, such as **Out of Print**, **Gifts**, and **Courses**.

11 It's important to list the date as well as the time for live events like this. **EST** will confuse international users. Better to also list the time relative to GMT, or link EST to an explanation.

12 It's not necessary to list the current date on this site, since there isn't time critical content aside from the chat, which should list the time it's scheduled.

13 It looks like this entire area is devoted to John Grisham's *A Painted House* rather than to three upcoming books. It would be better to bold the author names to facilitate online scanning.

14 This ad might be effective if it appeared as it does here; however, on the live site it's animated and flashes multiple messages. Users tend to block out banner-like ads, especially if they are animated.

15 These redundant links to **Readers' Advantage** reduce rather than increase their impact. Bombarding users with redundant marketing tends to make them ignore it, rather than give it serious attention.

16 John Grisham's photo should be labeled in a caption and as ALT text.

17 Because it's a stretch to think of coming to Barnes & Noble for a university course, the site really should give more information on the types of courses offered, to entice people to click the link.

18 This section would be more helpful if it gave more detail about what is coming soon. Does this mean that these authors have new books coming out? Or does this mean that the authors are going to be featured in an interview or an online chat on the site?

19 The link shouldn't be to joining a program, but should highlight the benefit to the user, as in "Save 5%..."

20 The **New and Used College Textbooks** area should have links to buying used books, with explanations of how this works. This area also should enable users to search for used texts.

21 **And Many More!** isn't a helpful link. Better to say "More New Releases." Also, it would be better to use a slightly different visual treatment for this link to more—a simple indent would differentiate this link from the links to specific content.

22 These generic links under **Black History Month** force users to dig for content. Better to provide a link to a main page for this topic and then use this screen space to show some of the actual content to draw in customers.

23 It's hard to differentiate among these categories. What is the difference between **Bargain Books**, **Bargain Blockbusters**, and **Readers' Advantage**?

24 While it's great to feature example content for a category, one link to country music is probably too narrowly focused for the entire music category. Better to show a little more breadth.

www.bbc.co.uk

BBC Online Homepage - Welcome - Microsoft Internet Explorer

File   Edit   View   Favorites   Tools   Help

Back ▾ → ▾ ⊗ ⮂ ⌂ | ⚲Search ▒Favorites ⟳History | ▨▾ ⮾ ✉ ▤ ⚇

Address ⬚ http://www.bbc.co.uk ▾ ⮡Go

Text only

BBC ONLINE HOMEPAGE
Welcome to the UK's favourite website

➡ **A-Z Index**
➡ **Search BBC**

[ ] Go

MONDAY
6th August 2001

Make the BBC my Homepage

my BBC   What's On TV & Radio   Audio-Video

CATEGORIES
News
Sport
Weather
Arts
Education
Entertainment
Food
Gardening
Health
History
Homes
Kids
Live Chat
Music
Nature
Radio
Religion
Science
Teens
What's On
World Service

Essential info
Waiting for exam results? Relax, we've got all the help and advice you need. Also find out more about the clearing process, re-sits and gap years.

CATEGORY: RADIO

Star talk
All the news and gossip about your favourite stars and the chance to tell us about your star spotting.

CATEGORY: TEENS

Feel the music
Get details about the CBBC Prom in the Park. Find out what's in store and who's going to be there.

CATEGORY: KIDS

▶**NEWS**

Latest bulletins 🎥 🔊

IRA weapons 'breakthrough'
Macedonia talks hit snag
Police probe India asylum blaze

▶**SPORT**

Sports bulletins 🎥 🔊

Stewart: Hand Ashes over
Live: World Athletics

▶**YOUR WEATHER**

London
max 25°C
min 14°C

Type a UK town or postcode
[ ] Go

▶**Where you live**
Choose a site ▾ Go

▶**Live Radio**
🔊➡ R1 R2 R3 R4 R5
World Service

UK HOMEPAGES
England
N Ireland
Scotland
Wales

[TV and Radio websites... ▾] Go

Get more from the Web...

▶**beeb.com**
Your online shopping guide

AT THE BBC
About the BBC
BBC Talent
BBC Jobs

WebGuide
The best of the web!
Get reviews and links.

Newsletter **Don't Miss This**
Subscribe now to our free weekly newsletter.

WebWise
Master the Internet

E-cards
Get access to the best

Internet

BBC.co.uk is the online home to the British radio and television giant, BBC. From this site, users can check programming information, listen to radio broadcasts, and get news updates of all kinds, ranging from weather, sports, and celebrity gossip to a wealth of special interest topics. Users can also get financial and organizational information about the BBC from the website.

BBC's homepage is a clean, well-categorized page overall. It offers a good combination of categories for browsing and featured content. Its weaknesses include poor archiving of past content and insufficient priority given to online programming guides. Also, this page is guilty of trying to cram too much general web content onto the site, rather than just focusing on its specialty area.

Window Title
Although ist's good that the window title begins with the site name, it's not necessary to include **Homepage** or **Welcome**. It would be better to include a brief phrase that tells what the site is all about.

Tag Line
Welcome to the UK's favourite website is as much of a tag line as this homepage has. The welcome is unnecessary. The favorite website ranking is pertinent and could be part of a useful tag line if it also included a brief bit about the site's purpose.

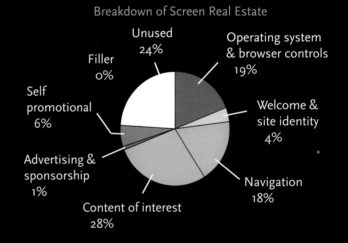

Breakdown of Screen Real Estate

- Unused 24%
- Filler 0%
- Operating system & browser controls 19%
- Self promotional 6%
- Welcome & site identity 4%
- Advertising & sponsorship 1%
- Navigation 18%
- Content of interest 28%

www.bbc.co.uk

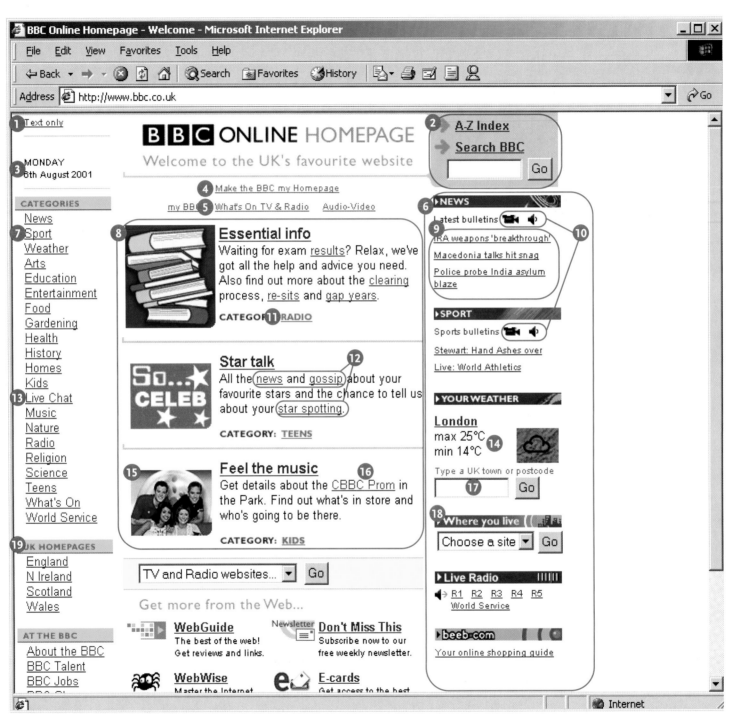

1. Good to offer users a text-only option for viewing the site. The placement in the upper-left corner is uncommonly considerate toward blind users who will hear this link as the first option when accessing this page through their screen readers. If you do offer a text-only version of the site, it's important to test it with target users, to ensure that the design is effective for their needs.

2. This search area is too complicated and confusing. First, move the **A-Z Index** out of this area and call it "Site Map." Next, don't include both a link to **Search BBC** and an input box—what's the difference between these two options? If anything, include a link to "Search Tips" or "Advanced Search."

3. The date area should specify that this is the date for the time the content was last updated.

4. Don't waste space repeating browser functionality. Especially since BBC already has a customizable option for the home-page, **My BBC**, there's no need to give this link that just updates browser preferences.

5. No need to have two links to online programming guides for BBC television and radio. Because this is likely a high-priority task for the site, though, it would be better to have one highly visible link to this in the main body of the page.

6. The background graphics on these headings detract from the text, look busy, and don't add any value. The graphics are so small that they are virtually unrecognizable.

   These headings use inconsistent capitalization schemes. The top three use all capitals—**Where you live** is sentence style, and **Live Radio** is initial capitals. The headings should have the same general style, and should follow the same style rules.

7. Although it's good to take these three top-priority categories out of the alphabetical ordering that follows them and give them top billing, it would be better to leave a little space before starting the alphabetical list. Right now it's too difficult to see where the new order begins, and it looks like the categories might be in random order. It's also questionable whether these three items need to be in the category list on the homepage at all, since they all have a special section with featured content on the right.

8. Good to feature specific items in the main body of the page. There should be a link to archives of past features, however, especially since these update frequently. If a user sees something of interest, it's difficult to find it later if it's no longer featured.

9. It's hard to write headlines that communicate a story in three to five words, but the BBC seems to have a good writer on this important job.

10. The way these video and audio icons work isn't consistent with the audio icon under the **Live Radio** heading. These are clickable—under **Live Radio** they are not. There is no way to listen to or watch the individual clip for one bulletin. Instead you must listen to or watch all the latest bulletins. Better to let users control what headlines they see or hear. The audio icon is animated, which is distracting and makes it appear to have higher priority than the static video icon.

11. **Radio** seems like an odd category for this item. Radio is just the medium to tell the story, so if anything, the story should have a speaker icon to show it's available in audio format.

12. It's not necessary to give three separate links to **news**, **gossip**, and **star spotting**. All go to one **So Celeb** page, where it's tough to differentiate gossip from news. It would be more compelling to actually feature gossip, news, or star spotting on the home-page and use the graphic to show the star, rather than the So Celeb page name, and then link to more celebrity news.

13. A generic link to **Live Chat** is not as interesting as featuring the content of current and upcoming chat sessions, or just providing chat links within relevant content areas. However, this link goes to a well-categorized chat page that outlines the chat programs nicely. It's good to provide such a page so that chat lovers can browse for topics that interest them.

14. It would be nice to show users the current weather, not just the high and low forecasts.

15. This photo should have a caption to identify the people in it. Kids probably know them well, but there is no need to make older people feel even more out of it.

16. Rather than teasing, it would be better to tell what the **CBBC Prom in the Park** is in the deck and then link to the roster of performers. Better still to feature one performer and link to a complete lineup.

17. Good that this search box allows the flexibility of searching by both name and postcode within a single field. Too many other geographically oriented tools use complex designs that require the user to understand multiple fields and use each one appropriately. Computers are perfectly capable of differentiating between a city name and a code.

18. **Where you live** doesn't clearly explain this feature, and **Choose a site** is too general for users to know what to expect here. Users can choose their city (if available) and go to a special local BBC site. It would be more straightforward to call this area "Local BBC Sites" and tell users to "Choose your city" in the dropdown.

19. Because the BBC offers a small number of country home-pages, nice to just list them here and not make users go through an intricate geographical selection process.

continues

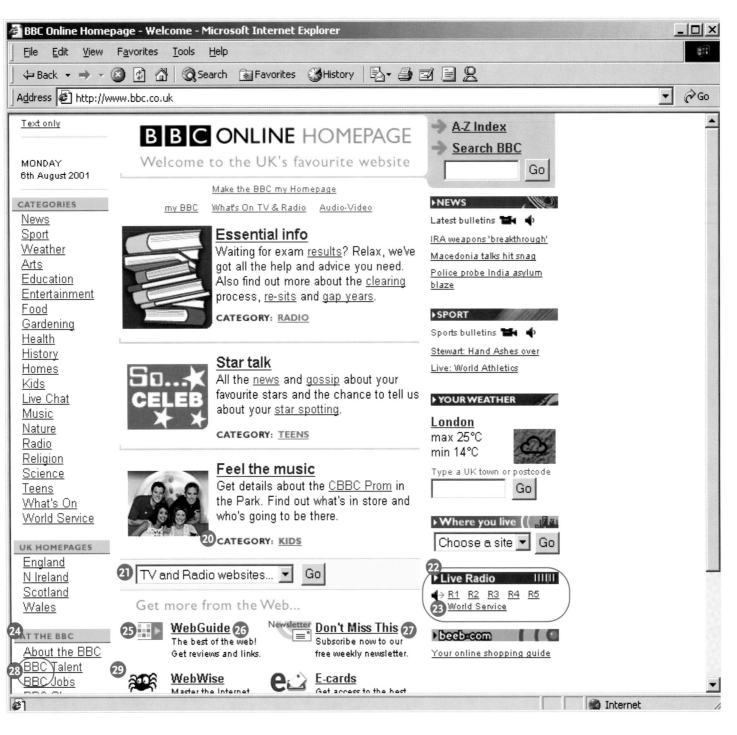

(20) Giving users the category for these features on the homepage doesn't help them understand the feature and takes up space. Once users go to a particular feature, they can always explore further in that category, or go to the category list from the homepage if they want to explore broad categories. Some features fall into multiple categories, which make this single category listing even more confusing—here the category **Kids** doesn't seem as appropriate as **Music**. Later links to prom news on the site did categorize it as **Music**.

(21) This menu contains links to different sections of the BBC site, but this wording makes them seem like links to external radio and TV websites. Don't use the word "website" to refer to anything but the totality of a website. Next, why have this drop-down at all? Most of the menu items are repeated elsewhere on the page. Dropdowns are difficult for users to manipulate and don't allow users to see all available choices at once.

(22) Here's a missed opportunity to leverage the Web to be a better medium than regular radio. One of the most frustrating parts of listening to radio is waiting to find out on a break what it is that you've been listening to. Here it's actually worse. You have to click each station link, wait for the download, listen, and then wait for the break to find out what you were listening to. Much better if this area showed users what was currently playing on each station, so they could choose what they prefer up front and learn the artists' names for music. BBC could even do some useful cross selling and link to a partner who sells that artist's material. These options are much more valuable and applicable to the user's task than random products heaping together and trying to pawn them off in **Beeb.com**. Last, unlike a simple dial, if you play one of these stations and continue to web surf, it's tricky to remember how to turn it off. You can't do it from here, although that would be preferable—you have to go out to the Real Player window and do it.

(23) Good to show the speaker icon to indicate that these are audio links. Because there is only one icon for the six links, however, users might mistake it for some kind of global control and try clicking it to control the volume or turn off sound for the stations. If there were a separate link and listing for each station, it would be good to repeat the audio icon next to each row.

(24) Good to have a separate section for the BBC company information. The heading **At the BBC** is a little vague—users might consider that they are "at the BBC" when they are on this page.

(25) What's this graphic? It doesn't explain the **WebGuide**—it just provides a redundant link to it.

(26) It's an interesting idea to have BBC-endorsed and reviewed links to different content categories. This could be explained better here, though. The overly enthusiastic **Best of the Web!** seems suspiciously positive—as if this might go to advertisers' sites. Better to simply say: "BBC's Categorized Website Reviews."

(27) Don't miss *what*? Don't try to sell users on a generic **Weekly Newsletter**. Most sites have one of these, and users are getting weary of cluttered inboxes. Sell the specific value, not the delivery vehicle—tell users what content and benefits they'll get from the email.

(28) The **BBC** in these links makes them less differentiable and scannable, because they don't start with information-carrying words, such as **Jobs**. Also, **Talent** is a well-known term for performers in the entertainment industry, but might not be as widely known by all users. If it's not known, it puts a rather gloomy cast on **Jobs**—are they for people without talent?

(29) "Bruce the spider," shown here, is the mascot for BBC's WebWise program, which is intended to simplify the Internet for beginners. WebWise links to online education programs that teach new users Internet skills. A well-intentioned goal by BBC. This link to **WebWise** doesn't really communicate this, though, and it's located below the fold and requires scrolling—something that is probably *only* challenging for beginner Internet users. Also, it's not clear if this program is intended for children or for all beginning users. For adults, it's rather patronizing to use a cartoon guide for beginners—the Microsoft paperclip is more popular in parodies than in serious business use.

www.boeing.com

Boeing is the world's largest manufacturer of commercial airliners and military aircraft, as well as NASA's largest contractor. Boeing has yearly revenues of 51 billion dollars and employs nearly 200,000 people.

This homepage does an adequate job of separating Boeing's main product lines. For a site with so few links from the homepage, however, the items are not sorted optimally. It would be better if there were three major areas: "Corporate Information" (such as investor relations and employment), "Product Information" (such as commercial airplanes and business jets), and "Programs" (such as technological innovation, like Connexion by Boeing). It would also be nice if the site communicated more about what's newsworthy at Boeing. One large photo of a satellite communicates the general idea, but it doesn't give any specific information.

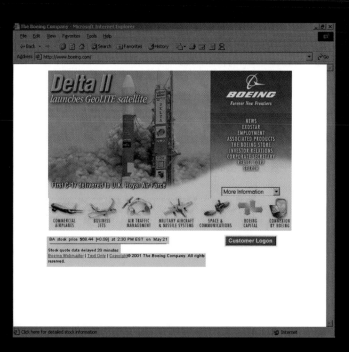

Window Title
: This page will bookmark under "T" instead of "B"—never begin a window title with "the."

Tag Line
: **Forever New Frontiers** might be appropriate for the space part of the business, but not for the jumbo jets. Also, this font is not very readable.

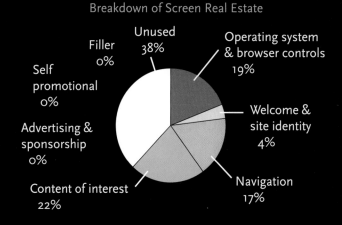

Breakdown of Screen Real Estate

- Unused 38%
- Filler 0%
- Self promotional 0%
- Advertising & sponsorship 0%
- Content of interest 22%
- Operating system & browser controls 19%
- Welcome & site identity 4%
- Navigation 17%

www.boeing.com

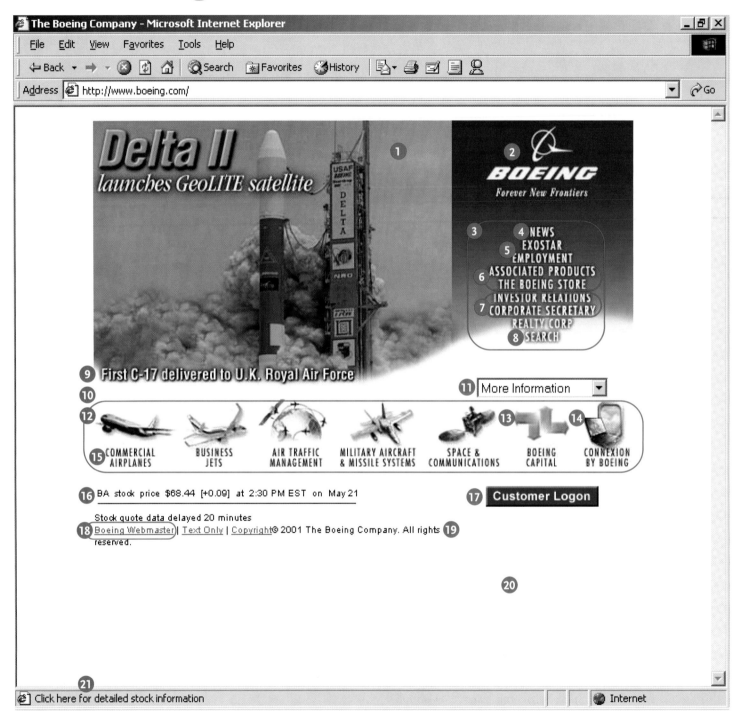

1. This photograph immediately associates the site with the aerospace industry, and the action in the photo adds excitement and interest.

2. Not only does this logo's placement deviate from the standard upper-left corner, it is smaller than the logo that is in the standard place, making this look more like the Delta II homepage than Boeing.

3. This navigation area should be left justified, not centered. Also, the obscure link names tend to overshadow the useful and standard links such as **Employment** and **Investor Relations**.

4. It would be better to show a few news stories, so that users can immediately see what's going on at the company, rather than offer a generic news link.

5. It's impossible to figure out what **Exostar** means—even if you follow the link.

6. The difference between **Associated Products** and **The Boeing Store** isn't immediately apparent.

7. **Corporate Secretary** is an oddly named link to material that closely mirrors that found under **Investor Relations**. What's the difference?

8. **Search** should be an input box at the top of the page—users will rarely, if ever, find it here.

9. This looks like a caption for the photo, but it's actually a separate headline.

10. This area should have a link to past featured stories and photos, so that users returning to the site can find items of interest they remember from their last visit.

11. This unimportant-looking miscellaneous dropdown actually leads to—and effectively buries—core homepage elements like **About Boeing**. This is equivalent to having a trash can on your homepage to hold all the links you couldn't figure out where to place in your information architecture.

12. It's a good concept to show a picture of the different product families; however, it doesn't really work for **Boeing Capital** and **Connexion by Boeing**. Also, these graphics have too much depth and detail to be easily differentiated from each other— we suspect these pictures probably were once larger, and Boeing had to reduce their size as it added product lines to the homepage. In any event, these items now seem forced into this visual navigation model. Better to include **Capital** and **Connexion** in the other navigation bar and show simpler line drawings of the different product lines.

13. This icon doesn't communicate money. Worse, **Boeing Capital**, which leads to leasing programs, is separated from the product information. It's more likely that users will want the leasing information *after* they find out that the Boeing Business Jet will cost them a cool 38 million dollars, plus possible "escalation charges."

14. The meaning of **Connexion by Boeing** is impossible to figure out without following the link. In fact, it's an interesting feature of their planes, but it would be better to feature this in a small news item than in the static navigation area.

15. All uppercase is not as readable as mixed case. Also, this font is not very readable, especially the white version on the graphical background. Better to use a simple font rather than use a graphic to display text.

16. Good that this links to a more detailed stock quote; however, it doesn't look clickable. Also good that Boeing uses the international date format.

17. **Logon** is not as standard a term as "Sign in" or "Login."

18. Better to tell users the purpose of this link (which is to send feedback on this website) than to personalize it. In any case, this link actually goes to general contact information, and should be named "Contact Us."

19. Why break the line here? This could easily fit on one line.

20. It's amazing that a site with offices in 60 countries and customers in 145 countries worldwide has no way for users to access *any* international information, not even office locations or options for non-English speakers.

21. If you ever pass your mouse over the stock information area, the status bar retains this message except when you hover over a link—surely a bug, but potentially confusing for the few users who notice the status bar.

www.cdnow.com

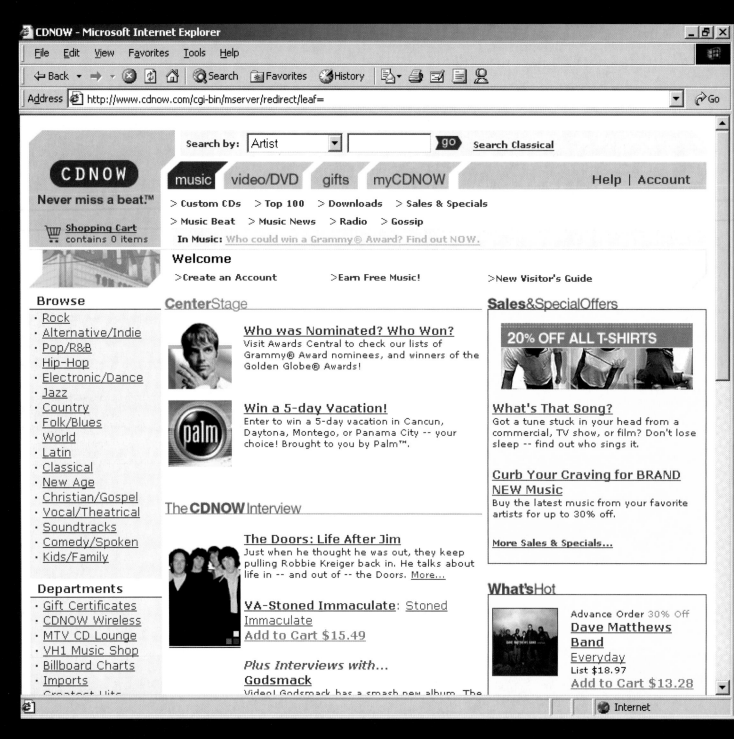

CDNOW sells music, movies, and promotional items, such as T-shirts, based on music and movie themes. CDNOW claims that it offers 10 times the inventory of a brick-and-mortar music and video store.

CDNOW's homepage shares a common problem with many homepages: It doesn't give enough information about the site to allow a user to quickly understand and assess the site's value and advantage over the competition. This site begs for a clear, descriptive tag line, but instead it offers only a vaguely clever but nondescript phrase: **Never miss a beat**. Because the site name focuses specifically on music and, for that matter, CDs, it's easy for users to overlook the other offerings, such as movies. CDNOW wastes a good deal of prime homepage real estate on navigation links that reveal nothing of the site's true value, which is its self-purported comprehensive inventory. CDNOW would be much more helpful if it included more specific links to its diverse inventory.

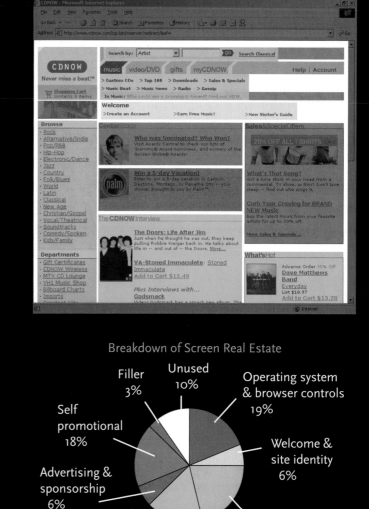

Window Title
Although this title's use of the company name first is good for bookmarking, it would be better if it also included a quick list of the other items sold, such as videos and DVDs.

URL
This URL is too complex.

Tag Line
Never miss a beat might sound catchy, but it tells users nothing about what CDNOW has to offer them.

Breakdown of Screen Real Estate

- Filler 3%
- Unused 10%
- Operating system & browser controls 19%
- Self promotional 18%
- Welcome & site identity 6%
- Advertising & sponsorship 6%
- Navigation 21%
- Content of interest 17%

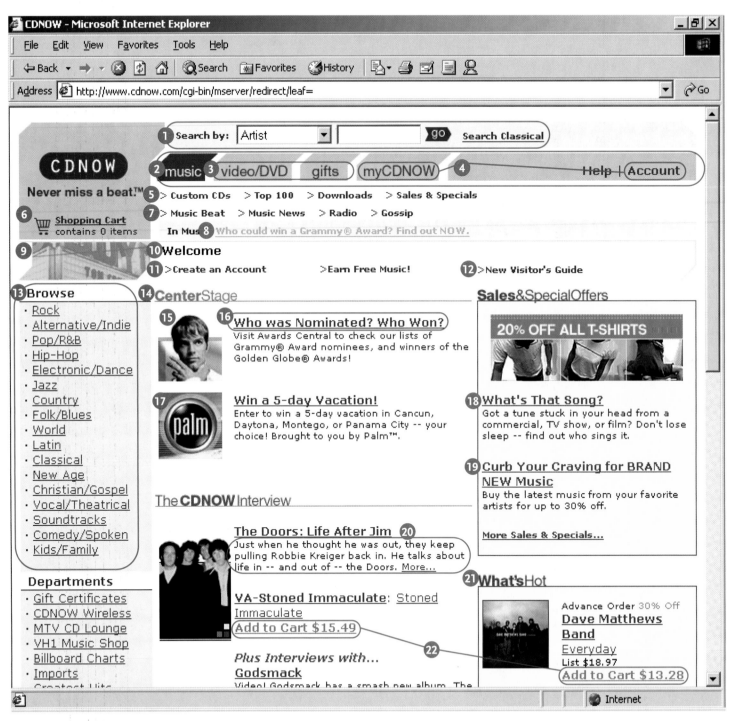

1. This search area looks too complicated. Better to have a simple "Go" button, instead of the arrow-shaped one. The **Search Classical** link compounds this confusion. It's not clear why classical music gets this special treatment.

2. These tabs don't look particularly clickable, and they are oddly shaped in a way that subtly (and mistakenly) implies a hierarchy. The dark blue coloring of the **music** tab doesn't work very well to show the current selection, both because it's hard to read and because it looks too flat to look like it's selected.

3. Both of these tabs come as a surprise because it's not at all clear from the homepage or the site name that you can get anything here but CDs. What is the site selling? Is it music, T-shirts, and movies? What are **gifts** on this site? Are they the same sales items, but gift-wrapped?

4. What's the difference between **myCDNOW** and **Account**?

5. These > characters imply a hierarchy and are commonly used for breadcrumb-style navigation schemes. It would be better to eliminate them and just use separate links for the navigation choices.

6. It's good that the shopping cart clearly describes its empty status, but the way this works once users add items to the cart isn't. The cart should list the items it contains after the user adds them. Instead, it lists only the number of items, which is quite unhelpful because a mere count of items doesn't necessarily correlate to having the correct items.

7. What's the difference between **Music Beat** and **Music News**?

8. What's the relationship between this link on who could win the Grammy Awards and the main story below it? This seems redundant, and the tiny yellow font is easy to overlook.

9. This graphic has no apparent connection to the site and wastes precious space that could have been used on a better UI for the shopping cart above it.

10. No need to have a generic "Welcome" on the site. Better to give users some meaningful information about the site as a welcome.

11. This link isn't compelling from a user's perspective because it doesn't make clear whether this is a mandatory or optional task, or communicate any value that the user will get by creating an account.

12. This **New Visitor's Guide** links to a good description of CDNOW but an unwieldy site tour. It would be much more effective to move the useful site description to the homepage and delete this visitor's guide (and the tour).

13. Although it's good that this navigation list appears on the standard left side of the page, the list of musical categories is somewhat difficult to scan because the order is unclear. The categories could be better organized into groups with a bit of space between them.

14. The **CenterStage** title could easily be eliminated because it's not very descriptive. If the content in this section is truly exciting and draws people in, a title isn't necessary.

15. Why alienate users who might not recognize this artist? Better to include the artist's name on all photographs.

16. This is one of the few good examples of a relevant news story on an e-commerce site. All too often, sites post news stories or press releases about their companies that fail to interest users. Users of this site likely will be quite interested in Grammy Award coverage. Because of this, "Grammy Awards" should be part of the title or should be highlighted in the description, to make it more noticeable.

17. This logo for Palm is one of the most visible and identifiable elements on the page, and it's potentially quite problematic because users could think this site sells Palm Pilots instead of music. Unless sites are trying to promote explicit co-branding, it's better to avoid promoting unrelated products, especially in such a hot real estate zone.

18. Although this feature sounds intriguing, it doesn't fit in a **Sales&Special Offers** category. Most likely, "Sales & Specials" was an internal name that CDNOW used to refer to the screen area reserved for dynamic content, and no one ever rethought this section title.

19. This vague and cutesy title obscures information that users likely would care about, such as the **30%** savings—nearly unnoticeable here. Also, **Curb Your Craving** implies that users should *not* buy brand-new music. Because users don't read every word, it's important to make every word count and to give them more content here. Better to use a simple title that tells users about the 30% savings and to list some of the artists, with a New icon next to the recording title.

20. This text doesn't leverage the interview content. It would be more compelling and informative to include a quote from the artist here.

21. It's odd that **What'sHot** is below the fold at 800×600. Also, how does this category differ from **CenterStage**?

22. Great to list the price and facilitate shopping from the homepage. Users don't like having to hunt for prices.

www.citigroup.com

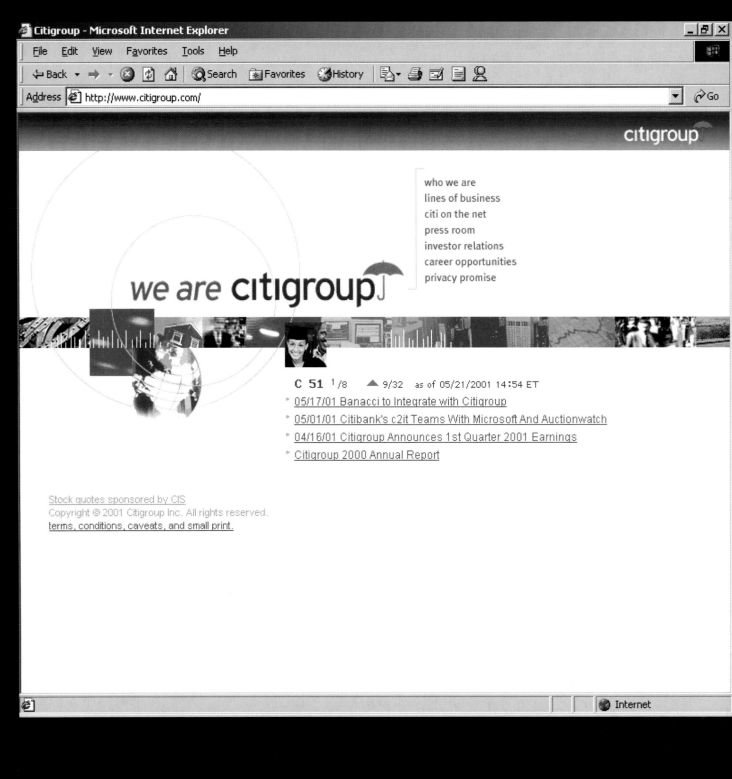

Citigroup.com is the site for the Citigroup conglomerate company, which contains, among other companies, Citibank, Traveler's property and life insurance, and Salomon Smith Barney.

Citigroup's homepage is remarkably sparse, especially when you consider that it represents a complex conglomerate. While simplicity is a good goal to strive for, it must be balanced by an appropriate level of content. Citigroup's homepage, while fairly simple, doesn't tell users what Citigroup is or does, which is one of the most fundamental duties of a homepage. Users must drill down to even find out which major companies are part of Citigroup. Where would a user find Citibank from this homepage? Citigroup suffers from vapid homepage chic, including vacuous whitespace, gratuitous stock art graphics, and trendy all-lowercase titles. It would be better off trying to look less hip and being more informative at the homepage level. Citigroup's façade of simplicity increases the complexity of the user experience. Not only do users have to understand a complex company, they must dig in multiple places to find the information.

Window Title
  While this simple window title is suitable for bookmarking, it would be better if it also included a brief description of what the site is.

Tag Line
  We Are Citigroup tells users absolutely nothing they don't know already. Any user surprised or informed by this information clearly got to this homepage accidentally.

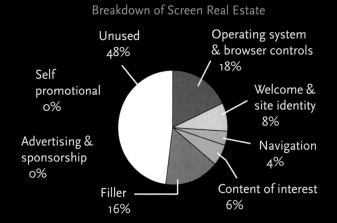

Breakdown of Screen Real Estate

- Unused 48%
- Operating system & browser controls 18%
- Self promotional 0%
- Welcome & site identity 8%
- Advertising & sponsorship 0%
- Navigation 4%
- Filler 16%
- Content of interest 6%

www.citigroup.com

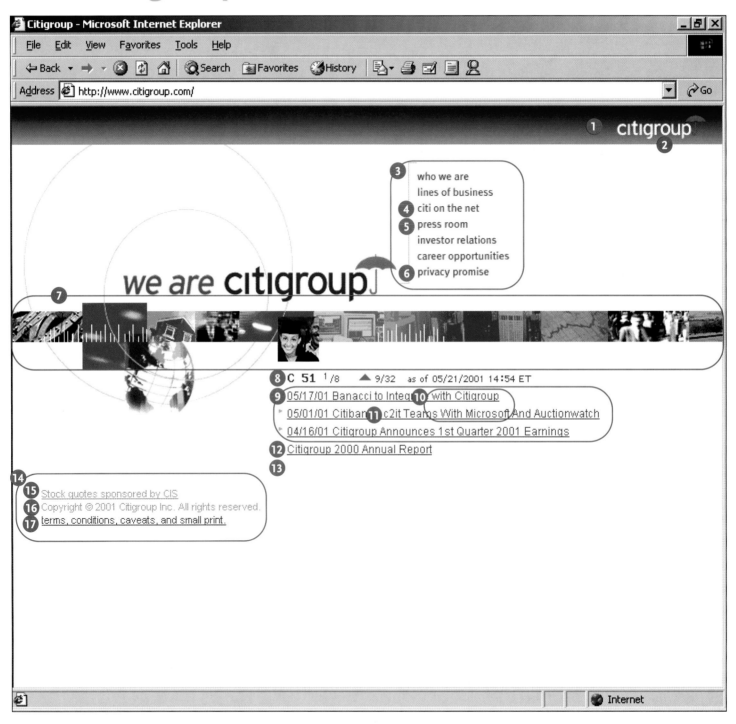

1 Every homepage should include access to the site's search feature, including a text box. This is especially important for an organization as large as Citigroup, for which it's better for users to have tools for accessing content directly instead of drilling down through the site's information architecture.

2 No need to repeat the logo on the homepage, which actually decreases the branding impact because it splits focus. It would be much better to use some of this space on a tag line that describes what the company is all about—the mysterious umbrella doesn't help to do so.

3 These areas overlap too much. One would expect **Who We Are** to describe the lines of business, which makes the separate **Lines of Business** link confusing and seemingly redundant.

4 **Citi on the Net** is a mysterious and ill-defined area (even once you go to it). Wouldn't this homepage qualify as "citi on the net?" In fact, **Citi on the Net** launches an obnoxious Flash demo without warning, which eventually offers links to information users can find in **Who We Are** and **Lines of Business**.

5 Good to include a prominent **Press Room** link to the PR area.

6 This is odd and rather cutesy wording for the company's privacy policy.

7 This gratuitous and chaotic strip of graphics does nothing to inform users about Citigroup or enhance the site. On the contrary, it is quite distracting, especially since one of the squares (the photo of the graduate) is animated and flashes a different stock art face approximately every second. On a homepage with so few elements, every element needs to add value. It would be more informative to show the logos of the different major companies that Citigroup comprises.

8 Yes, it was a 200-year old tradition, but now that the NYSE and the Nasdaq use decimals instead of fractions for stocks, so should this site. Otherwise, the site's quote won't match the official quote. Also, only Citigroup stockholders will likely recognize the obscure stock abbreviation "C" for Citigroup— better to label the area as a stock quote for Citigroup, which should be clickable so users can link to a full quote.

9 It's odd that there are only three news items for a month-long timeframe. This begs the question: Were these the only news items, or just the most important? It's also not clear whether these releases are exclusively for Citigroup, or for the other business lines, such as Citibank, since there are releases for both.

Too, it's better to give the headline first, then the date. Users will scan the first word in links for differentiating content. It looks like these are verbatim press release headlines repurposed for the Web, which should have been edited first for optimum scannability.

10 Inconsistent capitalization styles detract from a professional appearance and can make users trust the site less because they perceive it as careless or sloppy. This homepage mixes all lowercase links with initial caps links and even uses different capitalization rules within a single area ("with" is lowercase in the first news headline and uppercase in the second). It looks like Citigroup tried unsuccessfully to use the lowercase it uses in its logo throughout its homepage. This style inevitably leads to problems as soon as you need to include a proper name.

11 The bizarre **c2it** acronym detracts from the readability of the whole headline.

12 No need to include "Citigroup" here. This link would be more scannable and differentiable if it were simply "Annual Report 2000."

13 There should be a link to an archive of recent press listings here, so users can access stories they might have seen on a previous visit to the site. Although users can get to this information through the **Press Room**, they'll likely look for items where they've seen them before.

14 The two links in this area break the browser's Back button, making it impossible for users to use the most common method for going back a step. Sites should preserve browser conventions—especially this site, because users have to actually click many links to figure out what they contain.

15 This hyperlink seems rather irrelevant and purely informational. What is **CIS** anyway, and why would the user care who is *sponsoring* a stock quote? Does this mean that CIS paid for it, or generated it? In fact, this leads to important information for users, well hidden under this poorly named link. When users click here, they learn that CIS (Citibank Investment Services) will no longer be available after a certain date and that Citibank is offering another investment resources site in its place. This message should have been featured on the homepage in a more informative way—one that tells users of CIS's demise and announces the purpose and existence of the new site.

16 Too, while it's fine to list the copyright at the bottom of the homepage, doing so on a page with so few elements draws more attention to it than is deserved. Better to include it in the **terms and conditions**, **caveats**, and **small print** category.

17 This playfully self-deprecating description of the legal information on the site instills hope that a more humanized version of the usual legalese resides here. Unfortunately, this link takes users to a typical, unreadable, and intimidating disclosure statement, made worse by uppercase letters.

www.cnet.com

CNET | Price comparisons | Product reviews | Business solutions | News | Downloads | Site map   Free e-mail

cnet CNET.com
The source for computing and technology.™

CNET - Domain Name Search
Is you.com taken?
Find out now!   [name.com] **GO!**

▼ advertisement
Memory - Outpost.com   **Search** [   ] [All CNET ▼] [Go!] Site map   **Premier desktop sponsor:**Dell

Today on CNET

Thursday, April 19

8 mobile projectors
Take your show on the road in style with a road-ready projector. Use our roundup to find the perfect one to make your presentations pop.

- We review Microsoft Outlook 2002
- The first Java-enabled phone has arrived

Top 10 must-haves
From handhelds to MP3 players to digital cameras, our editors have created a comprehensive list of the coolest gadgets available now.

- Dealing with the blue screen of death
- A guide to freelance Web building

CNET services

Hardware Reviews
Desktops, Notebooks, Memory, Networking...

Electronics Reviews
Music, Wireless, Digital Photo, Home Theater...

Enterprise Business
E-commerce, IS, Security, Linux, App Dev...

Tech News
Enterprise Computing, E-business...

Tech Auctions
Desktops, Monitors, Storage, Electronics...

Latest Prices
Desktops, Networking, Software, Notebooks...

Software Reviews
Operating Systems, Utilities, Business & Productivity...

Web Services
Access, Web Hosting, Web Developers...

Finance & Investing
Real-Time Stock Quotes, My Portfolio, IPOs...

Downloads
Games, Business, Handhelds, Linux, Mac...

Today's Editors' Top 5:
Digital camcorders

- Sony DCR-TRV20
- Sony DCR-PC110
- JVC GR-DVL9800U
- Canon GL1
- Canon Elura 2 MC

All Editors' Top 5's

News.com top stories

IBM announces chip for Internet devices

ARM shares rise on profit growth

Future bright, Juniper chief says

Judge lifts ad restraints on Juno

More news

News.com video

FEEDBACK

CNET.com positions itself as "the global source of information and commerce services for the technology industry" in the site's official **About CNET** area. CNET offers services such as reviews and price comparisons to help users make purchase decisions. The site also provides technical news stories and links to many other web services.

Overall, CNET does a good job of revealing a great deal of the site's content on the homepage. However, it could show even more featured stories or CNET services by removing some unnecessary navigation links and ads at the top of the page. The headline quality is also uneven on the site. The headlines are fairly succinct in the news area, and the categories in **CNET services** are clear, but the headlines in the **Today on CNET** area, which are most critical because of their prominence, need some editorial attention.

Window Title

Although CNET is likely just trying to be friendly with its "Welcome to" salutation, it makes this page useless for bookmarking because it will appear under "W" instead of "C." Also, no need for the exclamation mark or the two instances of "CNET." Better to simply start the title with "CNET" and follow it with the tag line.

Tag Line

This tag line is simple and straightforward, but would be more descriptive if "source" were changed to "resource." After all, CNET doesn't supply you with computers; it's a place to get information about the beasts.

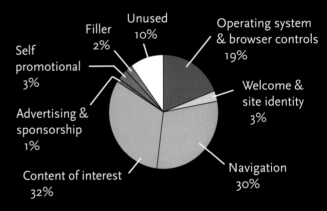

Breakdown of Screen Real Estate

- Unused 10%
- Filler 2%
- Self promotional 3%
- Advertising & sponsorship 1%
- Content of interest 32%
- Operating system & browser controls 19%
- Welcome & site identity 3%
- Navigation 30%

1 CNET should remove this top navigation area, which takes up space and adds more confusion than value. Not only are most of the links redundant to those featured in the categories in the main body of the page, they have different names, so it's not clear they're the same. For example, **Product reviews** in the top line goes to the same place as **Hardware Reviews**, not a general reviews page. Better to offer one clear navigation choice. We favor the main page categories, since they more effectively show users what's in them.

2 It's confusing to have an active link to the homepage on the homepage. It's even more confusing in this case, because the active **CNET** link can make it seem like this might not even be the "real" CNET site.

3 This is really just an ad disguised as a CNET feature, and it should be moved to the **CNET services** area under **Web Services.**

4 CNET's logo links to a subsite called CNET Insider, but gives no indication of that from the homepage. Instead, the site logo should link to the main homepage from all other pages on the site and not be clickable on the homepage. Insider information should be accessed through a link called "About CNET."

5 If CNET typically uses this space for internal ads, it would be better to display it as a featured service in a special area of the main body of the page, which gives real information and doesn't look so much like an ad. This would free up space to show CNET content and would ensure that more users would see it.

6 CNET deserves some credit both for finding a way to make this featured ad less intrusive than many web ads and for convincing the advertiser that this low-key approach was worth the cost. Chances are, users are more likely to read the link than a busy graphical banner ad (like CNET's own on this page), which users tend to block out.

7 Great that **Search** has an input box on the homepage—it should be wider, though, so that users can edit and review their entries more easily.

8 This is a waste of scoped search. The only other choice available is to search the entire Web—something users use their own preferred search engines for.

9 No need for the exclamation mark on the **Go** button.

10 Highlighting a sponsor like this could cause users to wonder how neutral CNET's hardware reviews are. On the other hand, at least CNET is forthcoming about this information so that users can decide for themselves.

11 It's not clear what the difference is between **Today on CNET** and **News.com**. Also, the different fonts for these headings, as well as the **CNET services** heading, make the site look busy and adds no value.

12 The date stamp is not necessary on this site, especially because this section is called **Today on CNET.**

13 This headline's wording is awkward—it would be simpler to say "Today's Top 5" or "Editors' Top 5."

14 None of the headlines in this section makes the best use of few words. Many of them begin with unnecessary words, such as "We," "The," "A," and even "8," in the **8 mobile projectors** headline. Eliminating these words would make the headlines more succinct and allow users to scan for the keywords more easily. Another example, **Top 10 must-haves** would be shorter and give more information if it said "Top 10 gadgets" (unless "top 10" is a misnomer—the text below the headline promises a **comprehensive list**).

15 It's doesn't help users to offer separate links to all these different camcorders, without any comparison of them. Users can get the individual specs on each device but no comparison information among the top picks or editor's commentary on why these five were chosen.

16 While many users might already know that the "blue screen of death" refers to Windows crashing, it would be better to use a more straightforward and informative headline, so that all users know immediately whether this story is of real interest to them when they are scanning the page. Clever titles make people pause, even if they're eventually understood. It would also be better to start the headline with a more precise verb phrase than "dealing with," which could mean so many things—does the article teach you how to fix the problem, or does it help you work through your feelings about the whole traumatic affair?

17 This wording is awkward and confusing. Does **All Editors' Top 5** refer to all the editors at CNET, or does this mean all the top five lists? Also, **5's** shouldn't have an apostrophe, but CNET could avoid this problem by calling these "Top 5 Lists."

18 It's unclear from this headline whether this is a news update or a review of the new product.

19 Should provide a link to archived stories from this feature area, so that users can access these stories once they're moved off the homepage.

20 These headlines are more clear and concise than the headlines in **Today on CNET**. This news area works well to showcase several top stories and allows users to access more news.

21 This Yahoo-style navigation model works well for CNET because it allows the site to show many categories at once and to feature top picks within each category. These category names are simple and understandable. However, the ordering of the categories seems a bit random. It would be better to group all reviews, followed by other categories that relate to acquiring or purchasing products, such as **Latest Prices**, **Tech Auctions**, and **Downloads**. This would then group service categories in the opposite column.

22 It would be better to unify the information architecture for product information. **Latest Prices** should be integrated with the reviews instead of treated as a separate category. With the current structure, users have to learn two navigation schemes for finding all the information they need for a purchase.

23 CNET popularized the left navigation area in this shade of yellow, although it now mainly uses category-style navigation, popularized by Yahoo. This small yellow strip is a nice, unobtrusive nod to CNET's web design history.

cnnfn.cnn.com

CNNfn.com is the online home to the cable business and financial network of the same name. Users can track stock and bonds worldwide, get business news from a variety of sources, and visit special areas for small businesses and personal finance. Program information about the cable network is available, but except for a few featured ads, it's the least emphasized.

CNNfn is packed with good financial content, but much of the page feels packed. It's good that the center of this page features stock and bond updates, and top news stories with concise, well-written headlines and decks. However, venturing outside of this area to find something is like the dizzying experience of finding your stock flying by on the ticker during Moneyline. Why the disparity?

Although the page's center uses tried-and-true inverted pyramid journalism techniques to hook users with the big picture and progressively disclose details, the surrounding navigation areas give all the details up front, making it hard to get the big picture. Too many navigation and search options, and too many items in too many lists. With such a complex wrapper to desired content, most users will navigate from the center, ignoring the scary list on the left.

Window Title

Good window title. Not only will it bookmark under the company name, but it includes a concise tag line that describes the site.

URL

The official URL is http://cnnfn.cnn.com. Because this site is part of CNN.com, it must contend with a three-element domain name. It's good, then, to make the default name cnnfn.cnn.com instead of complicating it with the "www" prefix. Although it's good that the site supports the alias www.cnnfn.com and redirects users to the official URL, the official URL doesn't support the "www"—that's bad. In other words, typing www.cnnfn.cnn.com, causes a "server not found" message. Users frequently type "www.companyname.com," so it's important to support the prefix and "companyname.com."

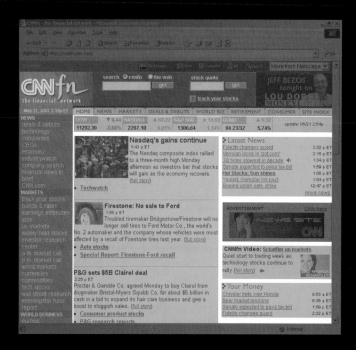

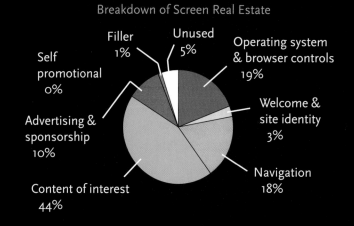

Breakdown of Screen Real Estate

Filler 1%
Unused 5%
Operating system & browser controls 19%
Self promotional 0%
Welcome & site identity 3%
Advertising & sponsorship 10%
Navigation 18%
Content of interest 44%

Tag Line

Good, simple, concise tag line that sums up the site. Nicely placed under the logo so there's no confusion about what it is.

cnnfn.cnn.com

1 Unless users have registered for one of the Netscape services at the top of the page, they'll see this generic **Welcome!** message. Unfortunately, it looks like an ill-designed afterthought, and is right next to the important logo area for the site.

2 Because of the AOL/Time Warner merge, Time Warner content websites, like CNNfn, now feature this Netscape toolbar at the top of every page. It's reminiscent of Lotus Development Corp's attempts to reestablish market awareness over Microsoft by putting SmartCenter on the desktop. Whatever Netscape's reasons are for doing so, it results in potential usability problems. It's confusing to have two search boxes on the page, it takes a big stripe of space away from the real homepage, and potentially confuses users with features like IM and Calendar that they wouldn't expect on this site. It would be better for Netscape to focus on making each service as great as possible and then providing targeted cross-reference links when appropriate on content sites.

3 Good that neither the logo or **Home** tab just below and to the right of it are clickable.

4 This search area is unnecessarily complex. No need to search the Web—users will do that from their favorite search engine. Instead, default to searching the entire site. Also, it would be clearer and more standard to have a simple "Search" button after the input box instead of the **get** button.

5 This input box looks too much like the search box to the left of it and will likely confuse users. It's also not clear whether you can enter a company name or whether you must enter the stock symbol. One way to improve this would be to replace the **get** button with a link that specifically tells what is going to happen, such as "Get Stock Quote."

6 It's not necessary to include a widget to tell users they can click a link. In fact, this link is one of the few on the page that is underlined and looks like a link—no extra help required.

7 These tabs duplicate navigation elements on the left side. Worse, they do so in a different order and change the hierarchy. For example, **deals & debuts** is part of **News** on the left. On the tabs, **Deals & Debuts** is a separate main heading and comes after both **News** and **Markets**. It would be better to provide one clear navigation choice for users.

8 What would compel someone to click a tab called **Consumer**? Being one? Needing them to run a business? Category names such as **Consumer** usually make more sense to the company that made them up than to the people it's trying to serve. In the navigation area on the left (scrolled off the screen in our shot), the parent category of **Consumer** is **Personal Finance**, which at least makes some sense.

9 Great to feature high-priority news—stocks and bonds, in this case—so prominently. Good to include the color coding for up or down, but not to rely on it solely—the arrows help colorblind users to quickly get the gist of the trend. To be consistent, though, the bond market gain or **5.764%** should be colored green, not black. It's also good to show the percentage change in addition to the points gained or lost.

10 It's critical to have a date and time last updated stamp on a page that shows financial information. It's a bit confusing the way this page shows two dates and times in different formats. The date and time stamp below the logo doesn't say if it's the time last updated or just the current time. It's good for international users, though, that the month is spelled out. In the stocks and bonds area, the time is the update time, but the month and day are numerically abbreviated, which is bound to cause confusion at least 12 days out of each month. Better to write out the month. Finally, throughout the page, p.m. is incorrectly abbreviated as just "p."

11 These are great examples of well-written headlines and decks. Good to have the headline and the **full story** link to the complete story. The headlines are succinct and informative, and the decks give more information, without just repeating the headline.

12 This photo is too detailed for the small size and doesn't convey more than any generic market floor shot. Better if the photo could zoom in on one positive reaction to the upward Nasdaq trend featured in the story.

13 These little graphics don't serve any purpose, but they do give users the impression that they're clickable. Alas, they're not. Don't distract users with unnecessary graphical elements.

14 As long as there is an updated time on the page, it's not necessary to include the times with the headline for each article. It's important to include the time with the main story, however.

15 These are well-written headlines, but what is the difference between **Latest News** and the three stories featured on the left?

16 It's extremely difficult to scan this navigation list, especially when items wrap to the next line, as they do in **financial news in brief**. The list is too long and intimidating, even when unexpanded, and it's hard to find the logic in the way the items are ordered in each category. It lacks the perceived affordances to show that it's expandable and the feedback to show current position, making it difficult to keep track of your place. Many, but not all, of the items expand when clicked, but the list doesn't scroll the user's current position onto the screen. This list needs an information architecture overhaul, and some items should move off the homepage. Better to limit the list to higher-level categories and show more of the breadth in the main body of the page.

continues

cnnfn.cnn.com

17 Good to provide a specific link to **more news**. It would be good to make the **Latest News** heading clickable as well.

18 This photo has an appropriate level of detail for its size and works well with the headline to make it clear that the topic is tires.

19 Although it's good that this advertisement is labeled as such, it wouldn't be necessary to do so if it provided more information. This ad currently deserves the label **Advertisement**, because it tells nothing about what's on **News Site**; instead, it just tries to lure users off of CNNfn. Much better to positively position this as integrated content across CNN web pages by offering users the kind of content contained in the CNNfn video feature below this ad.

20 Great to have cross references to other relevant articles at the end of each of these stories, especially on a site that has so much content. Good to harness the captive audience and cater to their known interests.

21 What's the difference between **world markets** and **World Business**?

CNNfn's left navigation is too dense and hard to scan, and it doesn't adequately show the currently selected topic. Worse, the look changes completely when you select a topic, as shown here. And because there's no indicator of the current selection (**Tech Stocks**, in this case), it's difficult to find your place again. The tabs on the top, which repeat categories from the left, are overkill.

www.coles.com.au

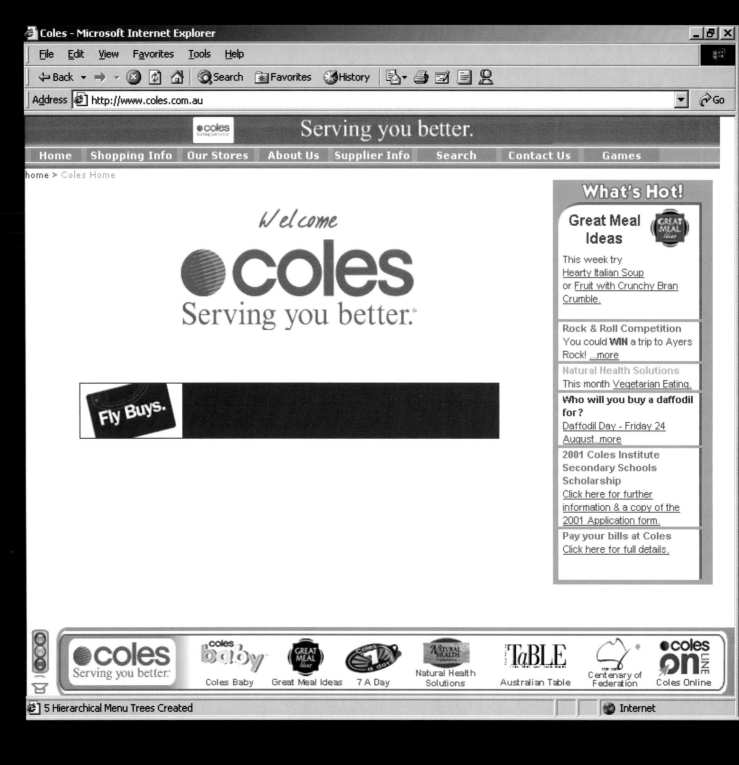

Coles.com.au is the online home to an Australian-based supermarket chain that operates more than 430 stores throughout Australia and employs more than 57,000 people. This homepage has corporate information about Coles, as well as product information and program information for shoppers and suppliers.

The first, and probably most-lasting impression of Cole's homepage is the "elevator music," or "Muzak," that greets users when they open the site. Isn't it enough that we're all tortured by Muzak during our trips to the grocery store? Isn't avoiding Muzak a major impetus to shop online? Apparently, Coles doesn't think so and has faithfully copied the art form online. What you (thankfully) don't get in most brick-and-mortar stores is lots of flashing signs. Unfortunately, you do get lots of them here. And although Cole's homepage is visually and audibly busy, it actually doesn't offer users much content. It doesn't connect the parts of the site in a uniform way, so it's hard to tell what value the site has and to whom it's catering. Can you actually shop on this site? Can you learn about the company? Can you apply for a job? Coles' homepage offers several links to other sites, yet even many of these sub-sites offer more splash screen than content.

Window Title
  Although this window title will bookmark appropriately, it would be better if it included a brief and meaningful tag line for the site.

Tag Line
  Serving you better is about as bland and uninformative a tag line as you can get.

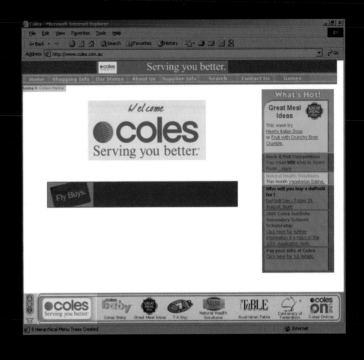

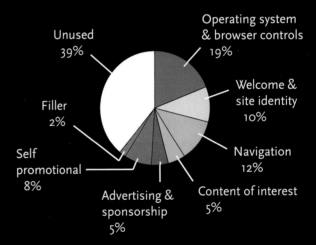

Breakdown of Screen Real Estate

Unused 39%
Operating system & browser controls 19%
Welcome & site identity 10%
Navigation 12%
Content of interest 5%
Advertising & sponsorship 5%
Self promotional 8%
Filler 2%

www.coles.com.au

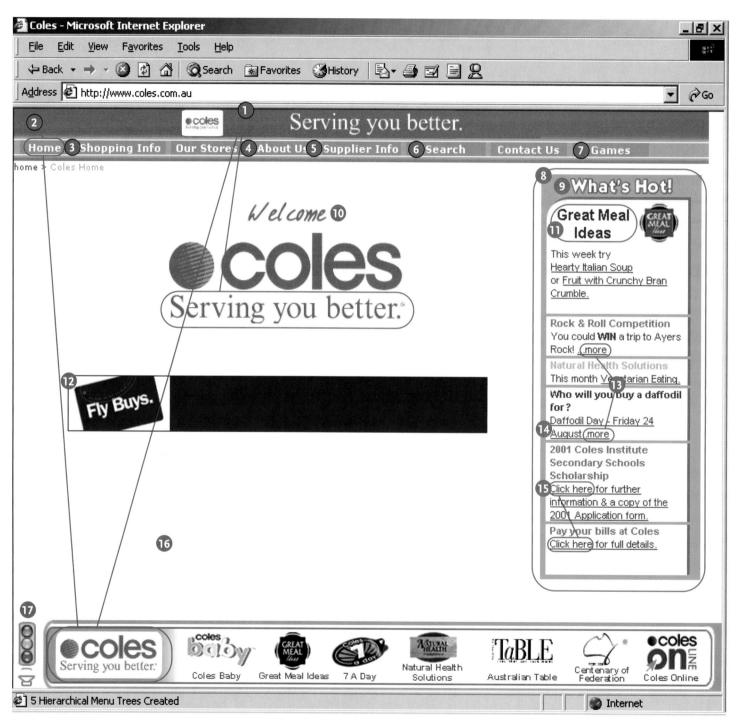

1. Big waste of space to repeat the tag line four (!) times, especially when the tag line doesn't give users useful information. Even worse, the Coles logo and tag line at the top of the page are animated—they zoom in and out and on and off the page in an annoying and distracting way. What would serve users better is some real content.

2. It's never good to have active links to the homepage on the homepage, as Coles does here with this **Home** button and linking logo. The effect is even worse on this homepage, because the user must turn off the Muzak again after the page reloads.

3. **Shopping Info** is a misleading label for this pull-down menu. First, the menu has several items about Coles philanthropic efforts, which would be better in a "Philanthropy" link. Next, you can't shop at all from any of the choices. You can learn about different offerings available at Cole's stores, but you still have to go to the store to get them.

4. This **About Us** link leads to a pull-down menu. Some of the choices on this menu go to items that should be directly on the homepage, such as investor information and philanthropic activities.

5. If Coles really wants suppliers to use this site, it should promote and feature supplier information on the homepage, instead of burying it beneath this link.

6. **Search** should have an input box on the homepage. Users often overlook search when it is buried beneath a link, as it is here.

7. Odd choice to have **Games** on a grocery store site, especially one that doesn't feature much content on its homepage. Why choose to use precious homepage real estate on something that is very unlikely to be a top user task. In fact, this link doesn't go to "games"; it brings up just one: a very simplistic coloring program.

8. Most of the font colors used in this section, such as red, pink, and green, are difficult to read. Also, the one familiar color here, blue, isn't used in the standard way—to show a link. The net effect of all these colors is a busy interface in which everything has so much emphasis that nothing seems important.

9. This title doesn't help to clarify the contents of this boxed area, especially since each item has a heading that defines it. The box is sufficient to give focus to these items—only use a title if it adds value.

10. No need to welcome users to your website. In this case, it looks like the site is welcoming itself ("Welcome, Coles").

11. No need to repeat **Great Meal Ideas** in the title and the logo. Better to eliminate the logo (especially since it's also at the bottom of the page) and instead show a photo of the featured recipe.

12. Bad enough to put a big, animated ad right in the middle of your homepage—even worse when it just flashes the marketing name of one of the site's rewards programs without giving any real information. Cole's could have used this central homepage space in many more valuable ways, such as promoting current specials at the store or listing and explaining the vague links currently at the bottom of the page, such as **Coles Baby** or **7 A Day**.

13. Avoid generic hyperlinks like **more**, as used here. Better to rewrite these sections to make the hyperlinks stand out and tell users exactly what they'll get by clicking them. For example, the contest could use "Entry Details" for its link.

14. This text assumes that everyone understands the significance of Daffodil Day. Although it's good that the date for the event is given, it would be better to give more specific information about the purpose, such as "Buy a daffodil and help fund cancer research."

15. No need to use **Click here** in hyperlinks—it wastes space and isn't as scannable as beginning the link with a more meaningful word. Better to use a specific and brief hyperlink that tells users what comes next. For example, the scholarship blurb could easily use the title as the hyperlink and then give some real details in the blurb below it, for example, "Win up to $1000 toward your college education."

16. A missed opportunity for Coles: We couldn't find any employment information on the homepage for job hunters.

17. Couched behind this unintuitive, upside-down traffic signal lies the key to turning off the Muzak that greets users on the homepage. Figuring out that this is *where* to do that is tricky enough—actually *doing* it is even trickier. The user must carefully click the tiny target of the red light. There's no readily perceptible difference between the yellow and green lights—both will start the torture all over again. (Although we think the yellow light makes it play a bit more softly, it could just be our ears ringing.)

continues

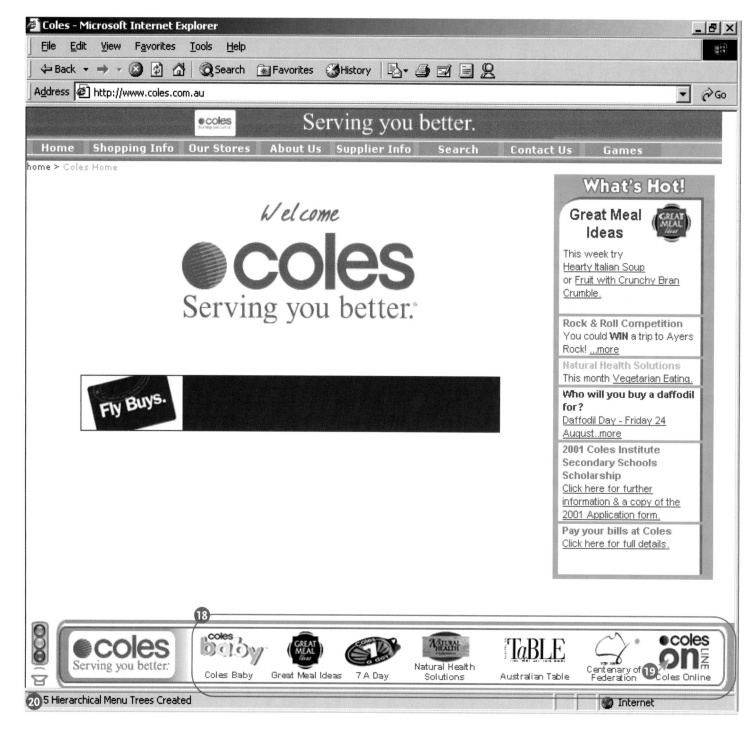

18 This navigation area could be much more usable. First, it's redundant to show both a branded icon and the text name for each item, unless you're doing so to make the icons accessible to visually impaired users. That isn't the case here, because the text name is part of the graphic. Second, why relegate important navigation to the bottom of the page when the rest of the page is so empty? Our recommendation: use simple text links in lieu of the graphics, move the navigation up, and feature some content from each area so users don't have to dig down just to figure out the rather obscure names of some of these categories. For example, **Coles Baby** offers shoppers with children many advantages, such as store savings and VIP treatment in checkout lines. Entice users with some of the details.

19 **Coles Online** is a startling name; aren't users already online at Coles? In fact, this is the entryway to actually buying groceries online from Coles—albeit a few links down from here. Much better if the homepage featured some of the products users can buy on the site and let them start shopping from the homepage.

20 Hmmm... not likely any end user cares about **Hierarchical Menu Trees** at all, let alone how many are created when the page first loads.

The Coles homepage links to this Coles Online page. This page is closer to what one would expect from a grocery store website and provides more straightforward information than the site's main homepage. Although better than the homepage, this page still acts more as a gateway than presenting real content—users must enter a password or postcode to proceed.

www.directv.com

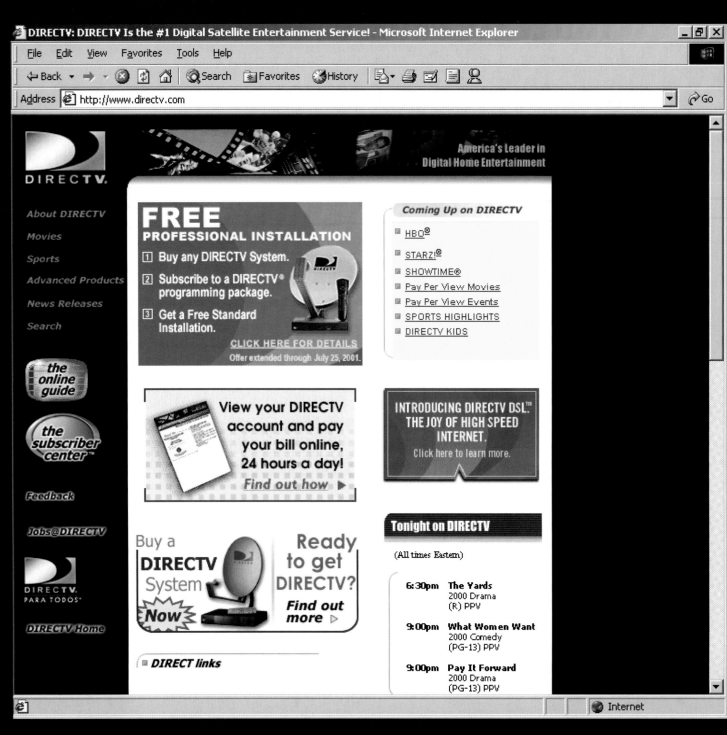

Directv.com is the corporate homepage for the digital satellite television programming service. Besides company information, users can learn where to buy and how to setup satellite dishes, and they can also get information about different service packages, view program guides, and manage their DIRECTV account online.

Pushy, pushy, pushy. DIRECTV is a cool service, but only if you know what it is. Chances are, many users come to this site to figure out what DIRECTV is and how it works. This homepage needs to address the needs of these potential customers in a less superficial way. The focus is more on hard sell than education. Existing customers, too, must dig down a few levels before getting any real information. Overall, the focus is too much on *looking* cool and not enough on explaining what actually *is* cool about the product. Many viewers flock to cable television in an effort to get advertising-free content—ironic that this site bombards these same viewers with ads and buries the content.

Window Title
Good that this window title starts with the site name, so it will bookmark well. It's also good to include a description of the service, although no need to include "DIRECTV Is"—it reads like an awkward sentence instead of a tag line. It would be best to update the tag line, as suggested below, and include it in the window title.

Tag Line
America's Leader in Digital Home Entertainment is okay as a tag line, but doesn't quite nail it because "Digital" and "Home" don't adequately convey the core concepts of "Television" and "Satellite." Also, the tag line's visual treatment and placement on the page put it at risk. The small, blurry orange font and the busy background graphic make it hard to see, and convey "ad" more than "information." This, coupled with the classic ad placement in the upper-right corner, almost ensures that users will ignore it.

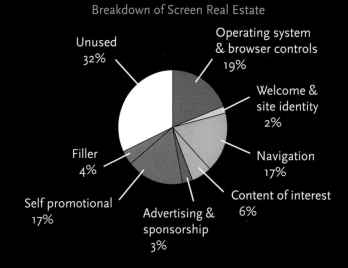

Breakdown of Screen Real Estate

- Unused 32%
- Operating system & browser controls 19%
- Welcome & site identity 2%
- Navigation 17%
- Content of interest 6%
- Advertising & sponsorship 3%
- Self promotional 17%
- Filler 4%

www.directv.com

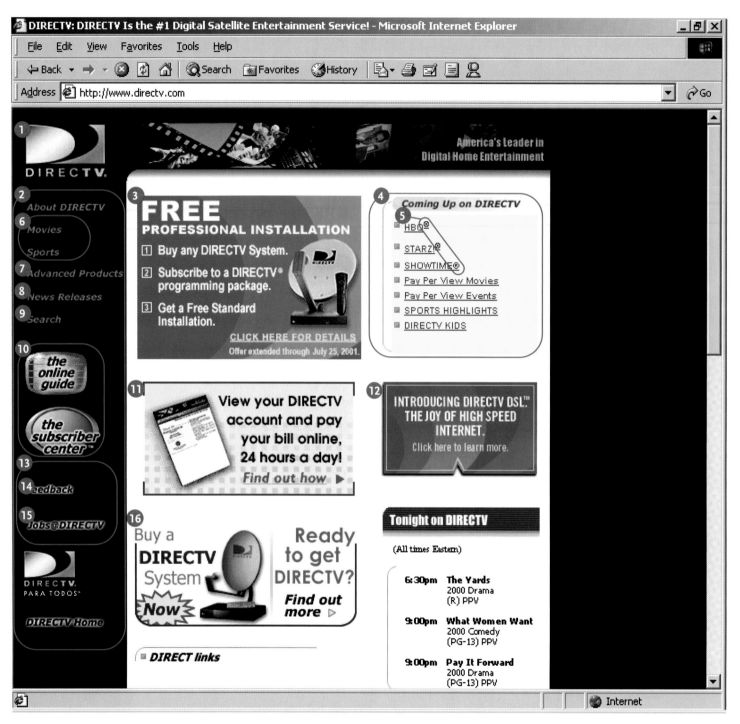

1. This logo, which links to the homepage, shouldn't be clickable from the homepage.

2. Although it's actually one of the simpler navigation bars we looked at, it's organized and formatted in a way that makes it look unnecessarily complex. All the links should have the same visual treatment—we recommend using simple text links in a more traditional left-side navigation bar. Also, group the items according to corporate information (about, jobs, and news) and subscriber information (account management and programming).

3. This featured special is better than the other ads shown. At least it gives some information about the offer and includes an expiration date. Still, it could be done more succinctly, such as "Free installation with purchase of any DIRECTV system and subscription to a programming package." No need to include **Click Here For** in the link to details.

4. This is a good section that shows some of the many programming offerings, but the heading is misleading. **Coming Up** sounds like these channels aren't currently available but will be in the future. Better to use a simpler heading like "Premium Services," which is how they're usually classified by cable service providers.

5. The trademark symbols on these three items are pretty much impossible to see—they look like screen artifacts.

6. These links for **Movies** and **Sports** go to information pages that tell how you can get more of both of these by subscribing to DIRECTV, which isn't clear from the names. If anything, these links might make users think they can access programming information from them. Because DIRECTV touts wide selections in both of these categories, it would be better to incorporate this message into the main body of the page and link to more details for both.

7. **Advanced Products** is a blandly evasive title for some of DIRECTV's more interesting add-on and partner services, such as TiVo and Microsoft's Ultimate TV. The whole purpose of these products is to make television recording easier to do—calling them "Advanced" might deter users' interest.

8. This link to **News Releases** isn't compelling and buries information about the company. Better to feature a couple of recent headlines in the main body of the page and link to more news stories.

9. Users often overlook **Search** on the homepage when it's accessed through a simple link, but they'll certainly miss it buried in the middle of the navigation bar. Always give users a search input box on the homepage and feature it prominently at the top of the page.

10. Too much emphasis usually isn't a good thing. Why separate these two links so much from the rest of the navigation? By trying to call attention to them, DIRECTV makes them look too much like ads—they have the trademark graphic treatment that takes up a lot of space but conveys no information.

Don't include "the" in link names—it makes them less scannable. Also, it's better to list a couple of the services in **the subscriber center**, such as online bill paying, than to make users guess at what it offers.

11. Allowing customers to manage their accounts online is a great service, but don't undermine it by overselling it. This graphical treatment is too ad-like, and the good information gets lost. We recommended deleting this ad and instead offering one section of the subscriber center page that includes links to the main tasks you can do there. It's fine to include a graphic next to this new area, but use a better close-up of the bill (unskewed, please).

12. Another potentially interesting offering buried in an ad and marketese—better to give some real information about the DSL service, including a description that conveys the value proposition. Is this a cheaper way to get DSL than all the other providers? More convenient? Include the price in such a description and give users a meaningful link to more information—**Click here** is a waste of space.

13. While someone likely thought this font looked cool, it's difficult to read and looks too different from the other navigation links. Better to avoid fancy halo techniques, stick to simple fonts, and use colors that provide ample contrast with the background.

14. **Feedback** is too vague of a term to use here. Often, sites use feedback links for feedback on the site. In this case, the link takes users to a form where they can send questions to DIRECTV on everything from billing to service; it should be called "Contact Us."

15. Better to spell out "Jobs at DIRECTV" so that users don't mistakenly overlook this standard corporate link as a URL.

16. This would be a pushy ad on any other website, but it's over the top here. First, there's already an ad for new subscribers (two ads up on this ad-heavy page). This ad tells users nothing about *why* they should buy the dish and sign up for the service. Instead of telling users to **Find out more**, just tell them more up front. The cartoonish **Now** in the corner is especially tasteless. It would be better to abandon all such ads and instead design a tasteful section of the homepage that explains the service and any current promotions.

continues

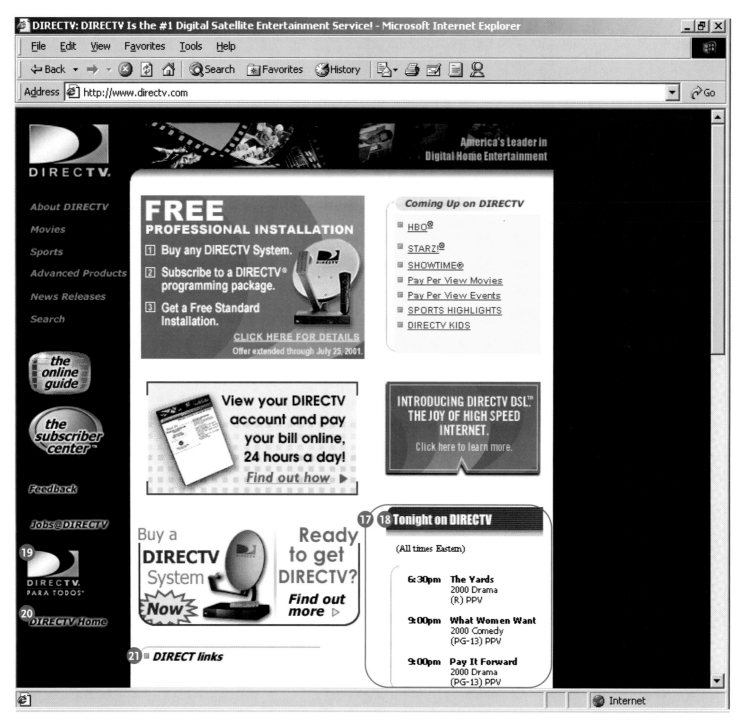

17 Here's a spot crying out for pictures, and there aren't any. This programming list flashes and changes every few seconds, making it distracting and hard to follow. Also, the all-text descriptions give too much boring information, like the category of the show and the year produced, without first giving any interesting information, like a description or picture of the stars. Better to feature a few top programs for the evening (without rotating the content) and link to the program guide.

18 This area should include the date, so that users can feel assured that "tonight" truly is applicable for that day. This probably wouldn't be necessary on a site that had plenty of obviously current content, but because this is the only time-bound content on this page, it's important to do so.

19 No, it's not just careless redundancy. Although it looks like this is yet another logo, it actually leads to a Spanish version of the site—something the tiny **Para Todos** doesn't adequately convey. It's great to provide native language content for your user base, but don't bury the feature. Better to prominently feature a simple link in the language, such as "en Español."

20 This is an odd place for a link to the homepage—most sites include them in the upper-left corner, if they include them at all on the homepage. Also, there's no need to use the company name; a simple "Home" link is more readily recognizable. Last, this shouldn't be an active link on the homepage.

21 This heading covers some links that spotlight areas of the site, like FAQs, subscriber news, and new channels included in the service. There's no need to label an area like this, especially in such a generic way as **links** that, if anything, might make users think these are links off the site. It's also better to avoid branding your headings with the company name or portion thereof, as is done here with **DIRECT**. This practice buries keywords and makes headings and links less scannable—and it often results in a nonsense phrase, as it does here.

www.disney.com

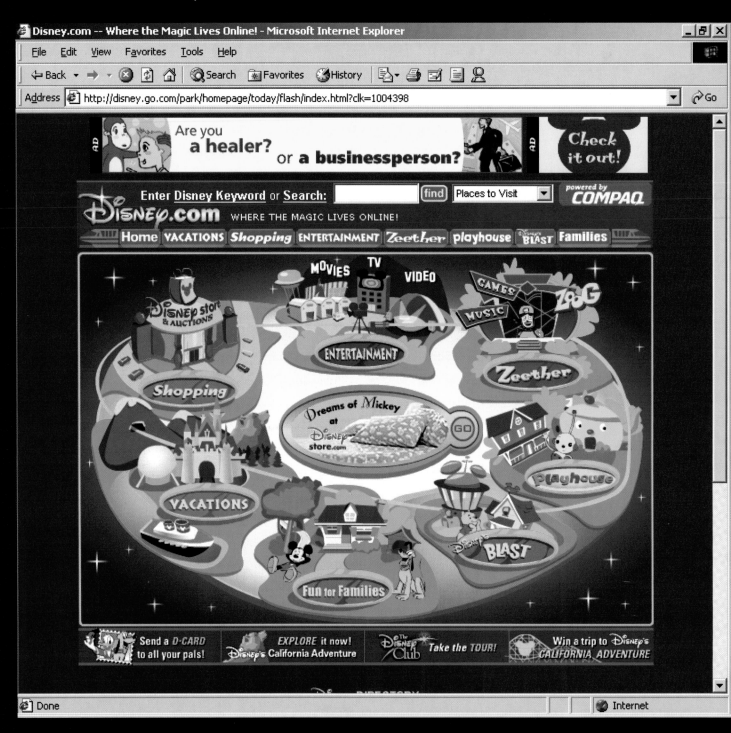

Disney.com integrates games and information about the Walt Disney Company's characters, theme parks, and other entertainment ventures. According to the site's official About Disney.com page, the goal is to offer an "engaging experience for everyone in the family, every hour of every day." Scary as it might be to be fed all Disney every single hour of the day, this might be feasible, given the breadth of content produced by the company. Luckily for parents who want their kids to think for themselves, the site comes nowhere near fulfilling this mission.

Disney's homepage suggests a totally useless site, even though there are several valuable features inside, such as areas for buying tickets for the theme parks and Disney merchandise.

Disney tries so hard to make the page *look* interesting that it neglects to show content that actually *is* interesting. Additionally, this homepage doesn't serve the needs of any of its multiple user populations well. Adults will likely be annoyed at the overabundance of sounds and animation, as well as the dearth of real information on the homepage level. This forces users to go into multiple categories to figure out what they even contain. Children might be initially charmed by the cacophony and colors, but young children will surely struggle with the text menus that lurk behind every bright picture. It would be much better to combine realistic photos and meaningful text links to show and describe the actual charm of the Disney empire, rather than create an unhappy new world on the Web. This would better serve all Disney customers, young and old.

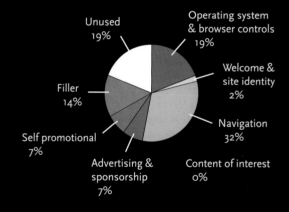

Breakdown of Screen Real Estate

- Unused 19%
- Operating system & browser controls 19%
- Welcome & site identity 2%
- Navigation 32%
- Content of interest 0%
- Advertising & sponsorship 7%
- Self promotional 7%
- Filler 14%

Window Title
Although it's good for bookmarking and recognition that "Disney" appears first, the goofy tag line is unnecessary because it doesn't say anything about the site.

Tag Line
This tag line tells nothing about what the site contains.

URL
Disney's URL is far too long and complex. Also, users cannot confirm that they are on the official Disney site because the domain is go.com (the name of Disney's ill-fated venture into Internet portals).

www.disney.com

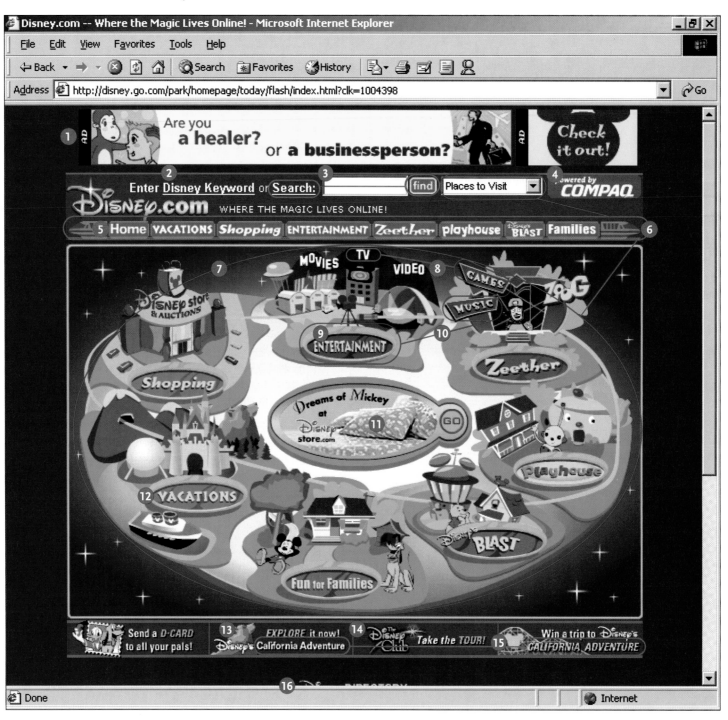

1 It seems like all the ads on the site are internal ads for Disney. If so, it would be better to eliminate them and use the space for real content, possibly promoting the same features. Users tend to ignore anything that looks like a banner ad, so this is a poor way of promoting site elements.

2 It's too much to invent a special navigation convention just for this site in the form of **Disney Keyword**s. Better to simply have the search accept these special terms and serve up the most relevant page as the top hit.

3 It's not clear whether you have to click **Search** or **find** to activate a search.

4 Don't waste space telling users what hardware runs the server. Before agreeing to promote your service or hardware providers in such ads, carefully consider whether any benefit you receive is worth lessening the effectiveness of your website.

5 This **Home** button is clickable and links to the same page. A wasted click is even worse on this homepage than on others, because here you have to wait for the monorail train to pull out of the station and drive back onto the screen each time you load a new page.

6 Considering that all you can do on this page is navigate to a page inside the site, it's overkill to have three different ways of doing so: a pull-down menu, the "monorail" navigation bar, and the pseudo-geographical map.

7 It would have been better to feature real content instead of a virtual theme park that has been made up for this site. Disney specializes in so many characters and real environments that are exciting for kids—why not show this? Users would certainly be more interested in real pictures of Disney theme park attractions and news and updates on recent movies.

All the center page choices have sounds that play when the mouse pointer passes over them. These rollover effects are fun the first time but quickly become jarring—especially when you are simply moving the mouse across the screen.

The category names in this virtual theme park (and also in the monorail navigation bar), such as **Zeether** and **Blast**, are mostly meaningless. According to the PR area of the site, **Zeether** is intended for older kids, whereas **Playhouse** is intended for kids ages 3–6. Why don't these areas say so? The large graphic for each category is equally unenlightening. It would have been better to avoid the cutesy marketing names and meaningless graphics, and give users some real clues about the site's organization.

8 On a page without much content and many nonsense words, users will naturally be drawn to any understandable words, such as **TV** and **Games**. Unfortunately, neither of these words are clickable; instead, when the pointer approaches them, the site pops up the full menu for an entire category, like **Zeether**. It's never good to take users from a specific choice, such as "Games" back to a broader category.

9 **Entertainment** is a nondescript category for this site, which is *all* about entertainment.

10 Although this homepage offers few choices, it has a great deal of redundancy. For example, **Music** is shown as one of the labels on the **Zeether** area, yet **Music** is also one of the choices on the menu that pops up when you point to **Entertainment**.

11 The center area doesn't pop up anything when you point to it. Normally this would be fine, but not in this context, where everything else does something when you point to it. The center feature feels inactive in comparison, even though it is the space for current promotions.

12 The site's primary navigation interface is highly visual and auditory, so it might be intended to appeal to kids. Yet, the result of pointing to any of the areas, such as **Vacations**, is to pop up a completely textual menu—suited for the very young.

13 This page format doesn't lend itself to presenting new content or informative content. For example, the new theme park California Adventure is buried at the bottom.

14 This button for **Disney Club** is a waste of space that could have been used to explain the club better. It's not very motivational to take a tour of something if you don't know what it is.

15 The two buttons for **California Adventure** are confusing and unnecessary.

16 At the bottom of the page (not visible in the screenshot) is a feature to switch to the **Disney Lite** version of the homepage. This is great, especially for users with a slow connection or people who cannot stand the sound effects. It is also good that the site remembers the user's preference and shows the user's chosen version of the homepage on subsequent visits. Paradoxically, the "lite" page actually has more information on it than this standard page.

Disney Lite

www.drugstore.com

Drugstore.com sells prescription and nonprescription drugs, vitamins, and beauty, health, and personal care products. Drugstore.com also offers advice on nutrition and health issues.

Drugstore.com has taken the drugstore metaphor too literally and has slavishly copied all the departments of a drugstore. One of the key values of this site is its low prices on prescription drugs delivered to your home. However, the large and banal promotional item overshadows this value. Drugstore.com features its core functional areas, such as checkout and the shopping cart, fairly well. Unlike some store sites that link to vaguely named departments, Drugstore.com gives some good examples of what products are in the various departments. It would be better, though, if the site showed a few more small product pictures to enable users to quickly scan the departments. This homepage also wastes some space on chatty salutations and marketing-speak that could delay users on the way to the products. Finally, the site uses purple for unvisited links, which is confusing because purple is the standard for showing visited links.

Window Title

This is a good descriptive title, highly suitable for bookmarking. It would actually be a better tag line for the site than the tag line currently used.

Tag Line

Although this tag line is better than the one on the very similar PlanetRx site, "healthy way to shop" doesn't mean much. Mentioning both of the main components of the site— shopping and advice—is good, but how does information differ from advice? It's unnecessary to include "Drugstore.com" in the tag line.

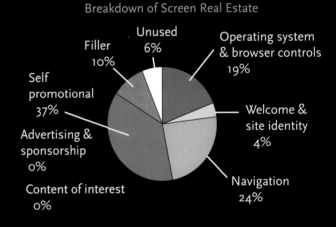

Breakdown of Screen Real Estate

- Unused 6%
- Filler 10%
- Operating system & browser controls 19%
- Self promotional 37%
- Welcome & site identity 4%
- Advertising & sponsorship 0%
- Navigation 24%
- Content of interest 0%

www.drugstore.com

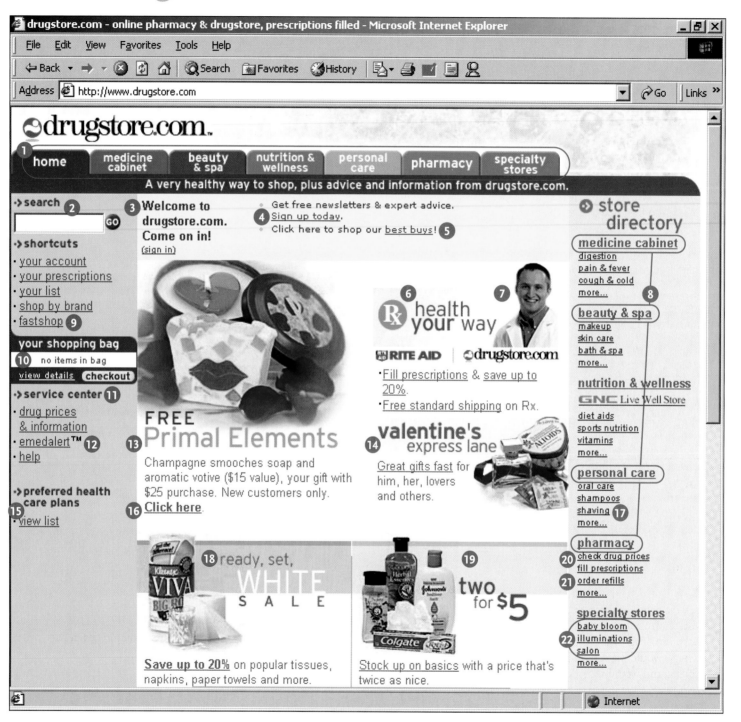

1. The tabs supply no additional value to the links in the **store directory**. A better approach would avoid redundant navigation options on the homepage.

2. This search box is rather small, and **Go** is not as easily recognizable to users as "Search."

3. This meaningless and hokey welcome message totally overshadows the more important sign-in feature.

4. **Sign up today** is not a motivating user action, especially because there's no information about what's in the free newsletters. A better design could reveal some sample content and use "Find Out More..." as the link text.

5. **Best buys** are lost in this area. A better plan would show product pictures and prices of some best buys and integrate them into the center of the page.

6. The phrase **health your way** is totally meaningless. This space would be better used to explain the interesting partnership between Rite Aid and Drugstore.com.

7. At least this picture of a real person is relevant to the site's content. Because this is an actual Drugstore.com pharmacist, it would be even better to list his name and title.

8. The **medicine cabinet** and **pharmacy** and categories should be next to each other. The **personal care** category should be next to the **beauty & spa** category.

   There is confusing overlap between these sections as well. Bath products implies things like shaving products, but those items are found under **Personal Care**.

9. How does **fastshop** differ from **your list**?

10. The term **shopping bag** is not as standard or recognizable as the term "shopping cart."

    It's good to integrate the **checkout** and the **shopping bag** in this way, to tie them together.

    This message clearly shows that the shopping bag is empty; the bag fills with items as the user adds them.

11. What exactly is the **service center**? What is the difference between the drug prices that you get here and the ones that you get from the **pharmacy** in the **store directory** on the right? Why are drug prices part of a service center at all? A better design would have a simple link to Help in the upper-right corner and would include the other items in the **pharmacy** so that users have one place to look for drug information.

12. The word **emedalert** is odd and hard to scan quickly. It's better not to make up cutesy new words. Also, the trademark symbol doesn't belong in the navigation bar—it should be included only on the page to which this links.

13. It's doubtful that the phrase **Primal Elements** will mean much to most people. A better solution would highlight the promotional aspect and include the text "Free Gift." The description of this item is so silly that it's unreadable.

14. More emphasis should be given to this Valentine's Day section than the one freebie gift to the left. Rather than using the vague link to **Great gifts fast**, a better design would include explicit delivery information right on the homepage.

15. What does **preferred** mean in this case? To whose preference is the site referring? **View list** is unhelpful, vague, and unnecessary. A better solution would just describe briefly what "preferred provider" means and have that description link to the list, or feature a few big providers and a link to other providers.

16. **Click here** should not be the link because it doesn't give any information. A better design would underline "Gift with $25 Purchase."

17. Categorizing with words alone involves a lot of reading and doesn't facilitate quick scanning. A better option would be to show some small pictures of the items in each category so that the user can visually make a sweep of the store.

18. Although it's good to promote unexpected product lines on the site and show pictures, this headline is needlessly clever marketese. Also, how do these items fit in the site's information architecture? Besides the homepage, what department would you choose for buying paper towels?

19. This sale is easy to understand because of the simple headline and the photo of the featured items.

20. Rather than checking prices, the site should emphasize its low drug prices. This **pharmacy** area should also specify whether it offers generic drugs.

21. Placing the **order refills** feature on the homepage is good because it reveals one of the major values of this site over a physical store.

22. Funky, fancy names such as **baby bloom** make the user think too hard to figure out what they contain. **Illuminations** sheds no light on what that category contains. What is the difference between **salon** and the **beauty & spa** department?

www.ebay.com

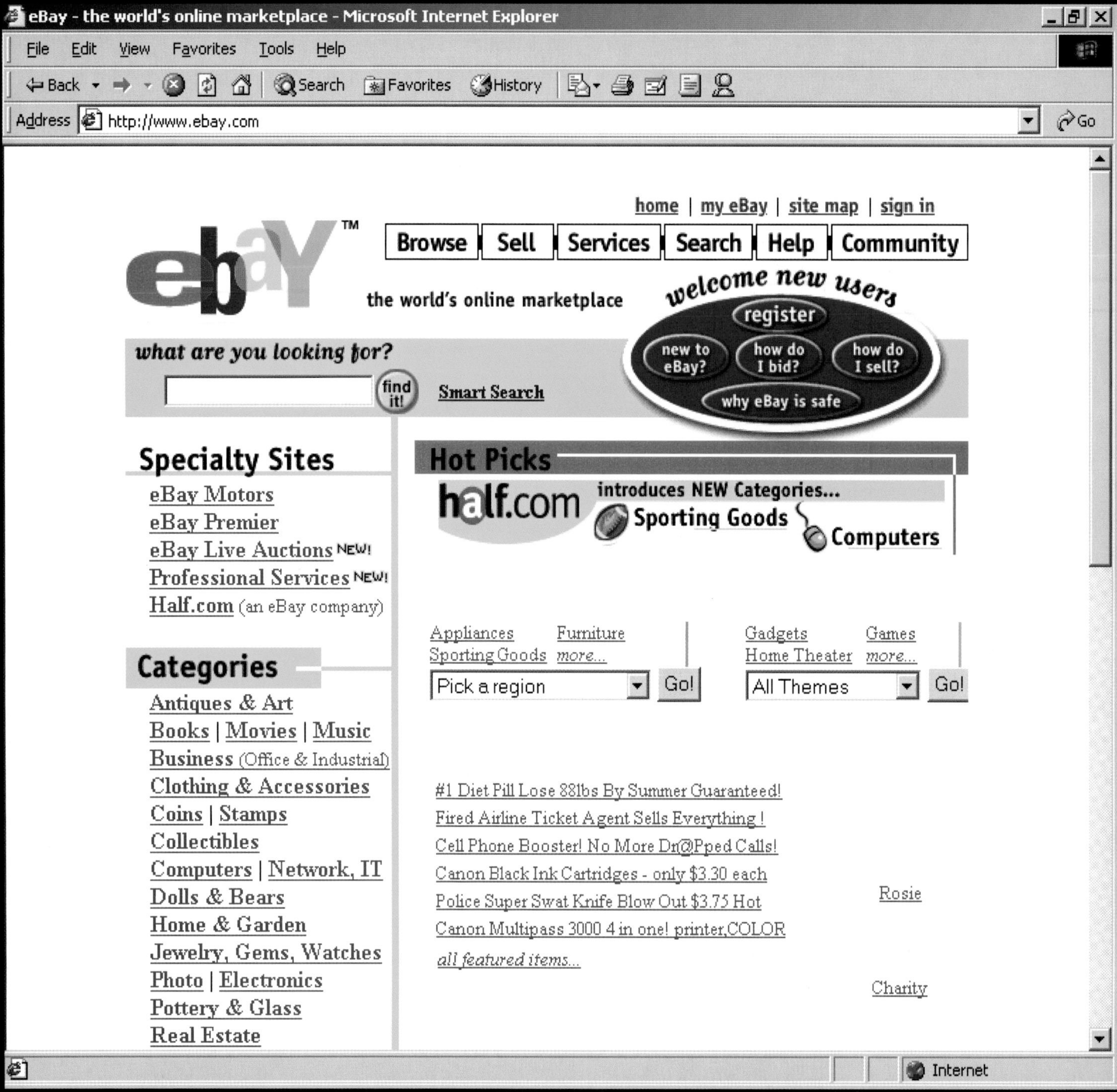

eBay - the world's online marketplace - Microsoft Internet Explorer

File   Edit   View   Favorites   Tools   Help

⬅ Back ▼ → ▼ ⊗ ⟳ ⌂ | ⊘ Search ⛉ Favorites ⟲ History | ⬃▼ ⊜ ⊠ ⊟ ⊠

Address 🖻 http://www.ebay.com   ▼   ⟲ Go

home | my eBay | site map | sign in

eba̲Y ™

Browse | Sell | Services | Search | Help | Community

the world's online marketplace

welcome new users

register

new to eBay? | how do I bid? | how do I sell?

why eBay is safe

what are you looking for?

[   ] find it!   Smart Search

Specialty Sites

eBay Motors
eBay Premier
eBay Live Auctions NEW!
Professional Services NEW!
Half.com (an eBay company)

Categories

Antiques & Art
Books | Movies | Music
Business (Office & Industrial)
Clothing & Accessories
Coins | Stamps
Collectibles
Computers | Network, IT
Dolls & Bears
Home & Garden
Jewelry, Gems, Watches
Photo | Electronics
Pottery & Glass
Real Estate

Hot Picks

half.com introduces NEW Categories...

🏈 Sporting Goods   🖱 Computers

| Appliances | Furniture |
| Sporting Goods | more... |

[Pick a region ▼] Go!

| Gadgets | Games |
| Home Theater | more... |

[All Themes ▼] Go!

#1 Diet Pill Lose 88lbs By Summer Guaranteed!
Fired Airline Ticket Agent Sells Everything !
Cell Phone Booster! No More Dr@Pped Calls!
Canon Black Ink Cartridges - only $3.30 each
Police Super Swat Knife Blow Out $3.75 Hot
Canon Multipass 3000 4 in one! printer,COLOR

all featured items...

Rosie

Charity

🖻   🌐 Internet

eBay is the world's leading online marketplace for goods and services. eBay's mission is to help anyone trade practically anything on earth. Indeed, the breadth of products and services available is remarkable. Where else can you find one-stop shopping for airplane parts, alligator heads, Shirley Temple dolls, and people to write your next marketing plan? In 2000, the value of goods traded on eBay exceeded five billion dollars.

eBay's homepage is visually overwhelming. The sheer number of items available feels formidable enough—no need to add to the confusion. This homepage has too many areas warring for emphasis, which could be greatly simplified by reducing the number of buttons and tabs, and by using fewer typefaces. This homepage is on the right track in its attempts to reveal the site's contents; the current implementation, however, needs a redesign. Redundant category listings weigh down the page, while some links appear without headings or explanation. eBay would be better off toning down the graphics in its design elements and including more pictures of the actual products users can buy.

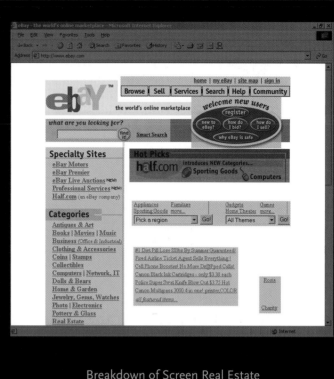

Window Title

This window title is good. Not only will it bookmark in the appropriate alphabetical order, it also explains what the site is all about.

Tag Line

This is one of the few simple tag lines that adequately explains the purpose of the site without venturing into marketese.

Breakdown of Screen Real Estate

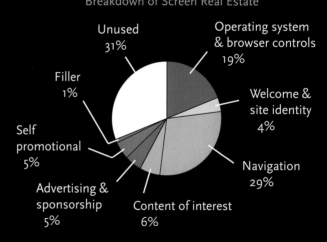

- Unused 31%
- Operating system & browser controls 19%
- Filler 1%
- Welcome & site identity 4%
- Self promotional 5%
- Navigation 29%
- Advertising & sponsorship 5%
- Content of interest 6%

www.ebay.com

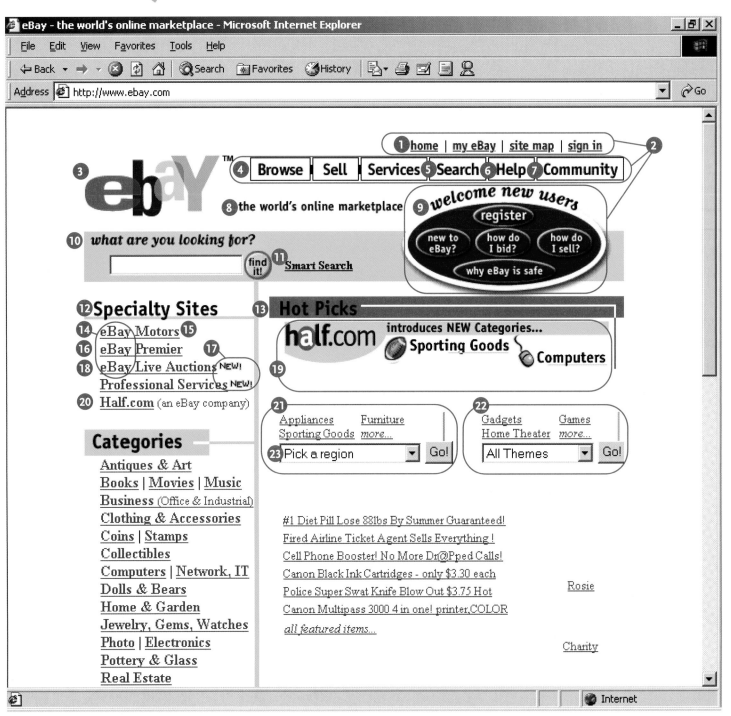

1 Don't provide an active link to the current page. In this case, users might wonder what page *this* is, if not home.

2 It's confusing and visually overwhelming to have these three navigation areas on top of each other.

3 Throughout the site, the company name is written **eBay**—it's confusing that the logo is all lowercase (**ebay**).

4 These navigation buttons don't look as clickable as simple links do.

5 It's confusing to have a link to **Search** when there's a large search area on the page below.

6 **Help** should be grouped with the other options that help users to use the site, such as **my eBay** and **site map.**

7 A generic link to **Community** doesn't tell users anything about eBay support communities on the site. Better to feature some specific chat topics or forum threads on the homepage.

8 This tag line should be integrated with eBay's logo, to tie the image with the message. It looks like the designer placed the tag line next to the whole block for the logo, and the trademark sign pushed the tag line too far out to the right.

9 Although it's good to provide a visible starting place, this area overdoes it. It wouldn't be so bad if this area disappeared once an existing user had signed in, but it remains regardless, using valuable homepage real estate, detracting from the products, and cluttering the page.

10 This search area tries too hard to grab the user's attention. This approach often backfires, since users tend to screen out blocks of text in banner shapes because they look like ads. The search area would draw the eye more if there were less around it. Better to just have a wide input box and a "Go" or "Search" button, and get rid of the **what are you looking for?** heading in the fussy italic font.

11 **Smart Search** implies that the basic search *isn't* smart. Typically this is called "Advanced Search." Because many users are overwhelmed by advanced search features, better to call it what it is and not lure unwary users in over their heads.

12 Calling these pages **Specialty Sites** unnecessarily separates them from the eBay identity. Even if they are separate sites, users will likely think of them as collections, or part of the regular eBay site.

13 It's unclear whether **Hot Picks** refers to just the **Half.com** ad below it, or to all the items below this part of the page. In any case, it's not very helpful for explaining this part of the page.

14 There's no need to use the site's name when referring to its own services. The list would be more scannable if the three links were simply called "Motors," "Premier," and "Live Auctions" (even better if the names were fixed as well).

15 **Motors** is not as precise as "Automotive."

16 Hard to know what **eBay Premier** is from the name.

17 Good to have a **New** icon so users can quickly find recent additions to the homepage. A typeface this small, however, calls for a simpler font—the yellow background adds adequate emphasis on its own.

18 Because the main eBay service is to run auctions in real-time over the Internet, it's hard to imagine what type of service this link leads to.

19 This ad for **Half.com** uses a lot of space and takes a lot of visual focus, yet tells the user very little. In the same space, the ad could tell what **Half.com** *is* and also give a couple of examples from the new categories. Or, this area could be simplified and made smaller, so it's not as intrusive.

20 It's not clear what type of products **Half.com** offers, so why not delete **an eBay company** (who cares?) and use the space to describe the site.

21 It's unclear why these category links are grouped with this **Pick a region** dropdown.

Why are these categories here at all, rather than in the **Categories** area on the left of the page? If eBay is trying to promote certain categories, it should show some of the featured items from those categories to pique users' interests.

22 The entire implementation of the **Themes** area is clunky and obscure. First, it's difficult to figure out what eBay means by "theme"—the links above the dropdown seem like regular categories. Themes should be clearly differentiated from categories—better to just list some and include a link to "More Themes." Second, why mix UI devices by having links *and* a dropdown? Dropdowns are difficult for users to navigate, especially if the list is long.

23 The meaning behind this **Pick a Region** dropdown is a real mystery. Dropdowns that instruct users to perform a specific action often make them think they *must* perform that action. This is more likely to happen here because this dropdown is located in the center of the page—one of the first places users look. In fact, users don't need to pick a region here. This dropdown takes users to listings of items in their local area and focuses on items that are difficult to ship.

continues

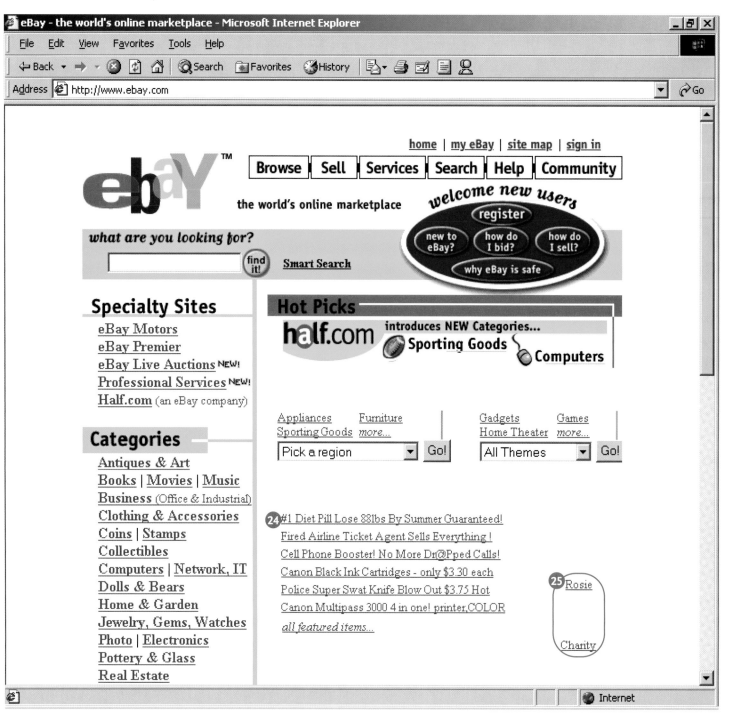

www.ebay.com

24 It's good to feature some items on the homepage, so users can see a variety of products up front. However, this area needs some type of title, like "Featured Items," to let users know what they're looking at. It would also be helpful to see pictures of some of these items.

25 These obscure links floating out in space are odd and confusing. At first glance, one might guess they're seller's names for the items featured in the list to their left. Because they actually go to pages for charitable fundraising (the **Rosie** one is run by Rosie O'Donnell), why not tout the good deeds and save users confusion by providing more information in the links?

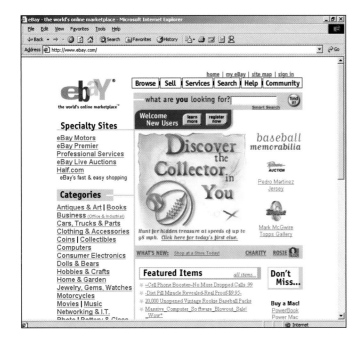

After we wrote this review, eBay launched the redesign shown here. The new design is somewhat cleaner and better-looking, but retains too many of the usability problems we've pointed out. The new design fixes 55% of the weaknesses addressed in the old design, leaving 45% in place.

www.emagazineshop.com

eMagazineshop, formerly known as magazineshop.co.uk, is the UK's leading online magazine subscription service.

This website does a good job of featuring some of its products on the homepage. Unfortunately, however, the graphical magazine covers don't have the visual impact or get the brand recognition they should, because they must compete with the overdone visual design on the rest of the page. When you have so much graphical content, it's important to make the core site elements very simple, so they provide a subtle backdrop to the content.

Window Title

Bravo to a window title that will bookmark appropriately and that includes a simple and straightforward tag line to tell users what the site's all about.

URL

This URL is more complex than it should be. Best to keep the URL in simple, real language whenever possible. It's odd that a UK-based website is not accessible with the .co.uk extension, especially since **www.magazineshop.co.uk** was the original URL.

Tag Line

This is a great tag line. It tells users exactly what the purpose of the site is, and it is well situated right below the site's logo.

Breakdown of Screen Real Estate

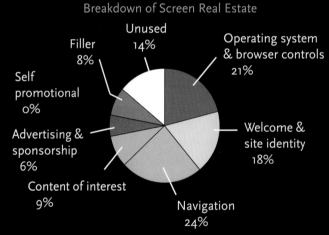

- Unused 14%
- Filler 8%
- Self promotional 0%
- Advertising & sponsorship 6%
- Content of interest 9%
- Navigation 24%
- Welcome & site identity 18%
- Operating system & browser controls 21%

1. Two flaws in this otherwise clear, prominently placed logo and tag line area: The logo links to the homepage from the homepage, and the **e** in the site name isn't clearly visible. If users remember the site name as "magazineshop.com," they'll go to a different magazine site, located on a different continent.

2. This graphic is animated—the square (a magazine, perhaps?) in front goes in and out of the house. Bad enough that the graphic is meaningless, worse that it adds confusion and detracts attention from the real products on the page.

3. Both of these areas flash internal promotions for the site. The movement is distracting. Much better to eliminate the animation and use the main body of the page to feature titles.

4. No need to give the date on a noncontent site, let alone dedicate this large amount of real estate to it.

5. Too many instances of **Home** here. It's silly to devote such a large amount of space to the house icon and static text, and it's worse to include an icon that links to itself.

6. No need to use icons with these standard site links. In fact, the words are clearer than the graphics and don't add the same clutter to the page.

7. It's good to have a direct link to the shopping cart. It would be better to include the term "shopping" in the name though—users have more success finding the shopping cart when "shopping" is the first word of the link.[*]

8. **Info** is not as standard as "About Us," or "About [site name]" for linking to information about the site, which is where this link goes.

9. This **Find** heading doesn't add any value—neither of the items below it need an additional heading. **Find** also looks clickable, but it isn't.

10. There's no reason to make all these links into graphics. The shaded backgrounds only clutter the screen, and don't effectively show the hierarchy of headings and subheadings Simple links would be much more effective and would provide a more subtle backdrop for the graphical content in the main body of the page. Also, all uppercase letters are not as easy to read as mixed case.

[*]For more information, see our report at
http://www.nngroup.com/reports/ecommerce/checkout.

11. It's great to feature magazine categories in this prime real estate spot. However, the area is so busy that it lacks focus, looks very ad-like, and is in danger of being overlooked. There are a number of ways to simplify this area. Remove the **Click Here** links and the word **Magazines** from the boxes. Give each box a straightforward category name, and include other text only if there is a special for that category. Simplify the font formatting on all the text, so that the magazine logos don't have to compete with other fancy fonts and thus get the most emphasis.

12. It's not good to mix this **Gift Selector** in with search and navigation. Worse though, is that this isn't a gift selector at all. The name implies that it guides users to the right gift using certain criteria, but the link goes to static text telling them to give magazine subscriptions as gifts. A link from this text takes users to a gift certificate purchase area. The **Gift Selector** link should go directly to the gift certificates page and be called "Gift Certificates," because selling gift certificates is its ultimate goal.

13. Several things are wrong with this search implementation. First, better to locate search at the top of the page. Next, the input box is too small—users need to be able to edit and review their entries. In fact, this 13-character box can't display many common magazine titles, such as *Good Housekeeping*. Last, the heading for this area is not only unnecessary, it doesn't even look connected to search because of its separate boxed area—it just wastes space.

14. It would be better to show a couple of magazine covers for these categories, rather than generic clipart. Also, the boats and yachting photo is too detailed for this small size.

15. This editor's letter tries too hard to force a magazine metaphor onto something that's not even a virtual magazine—it's a magazine shop. If anything, this should be "Shopkeeper's Picks" or the like. Also, this text looks like it was written for print. It's too verbose and dense to be scannable online.

16. These headings are disproportionately large compared to the text that follows them. This not only takes focus away from the content in the text that follows them, it makes the area look less like serious content and more like ads.

continues

17 It's not good to mix this customer service policy (**Risk Free Titles**) with this magazine categories area. Better to include it in an area that describes overall benefits of the site, such as lower prices, ordering convenience, and the ability to cancel if unsatisfied.

18 **Play**, **Friends & Family**, and **Enthusiast** are all vague category names. In fact, the magazines in these three categories have so much overlap that they are practically identical. It would be better to eliminate these broad categories and instead promote some of the categories that are currently one click down from the homepage.

19 Great that this area features certain magazines and both shows the cover and describes the content. It would be better to include the actual price as well as the percentage savings and to put this information right at the top, near the title, so users don't miss it.

20 **Renewals** is not a category; it's a customer service that should be included under the user's account information. Worse, this link takes users to their account page, not straight to renewals. Either remove this link, or if it's a common enough task for users, place a link that goes straight to renewals next to the shopping cart and account links in the upper right of the screen.

eMagazineshop.com's homepage uses graphics for almost everything, but it doesn't use ALT text to identify the areas. This can make the site inaccessible to visually impaired users and forces all users to wait for the images to download before they can take action on the site. This picture shows what the page looks like without the graphics.

www.espn.com

ESPN.com is the online home to the cable sports news channel. From this site, users can get news and scores on all major sports of interest in America. Users can also get programming information for the ESPN television and radio channels. The site offers interactive games in the Fantasy area, where players can set up their personal dream teams of sports players.

Kudos to ESPN for delivering a content-rich site. The biggest strengths are the many clear links to articles and good photos. In fact, the site gets weak mainly when it abandons content richness and ventures into web coolness.

Window Title
This window title will bookmark appropriately by site name. However, it would be better to skip the ".com" part of the title and simply call the page ESPN—possibly followed by a brief explanation.

URL
It would be much better for this well-known company to have its own domain at **www.espn.com** than to appear as a subdomain under **go.com**, but at least users can enter **www.espn.com** and be automatically redirected to **espn.go.com**.

Tag Line
This site doesn't have a tag line, but it should have a brief one to tell what it's all about.

Breakdown of Screen Real Estate

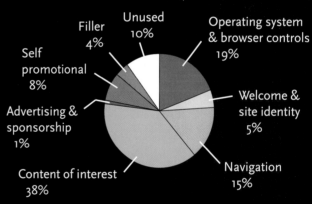

- Filler 4%
- Unused 10%
- Operating system & browser controls 19%
- Self promotional 8%
- Welcome & site identity 5%
- Advertising & sponsorship 1%
- Navigation 15%
- Content of interest 38%

1 This top navigation area poses usability problems. First, many users will likely never notice it, because they often have banner blindness for anything within or above the main banner area at the top of the page. Also, some of the items here, such as **NBA.com**, link to outside sites, while others, such as **RPM**, go to ESPN.com pages. Most of the ESPN links are already offered elsewhere on the page. Better to eliminate this area and incorporate the items into the main left side navigation area, if they're not there already. The links to external sites could be labeled "Sports Resources" at the bottom of the navigation list.

2 This area flashes different upcoming programs on the ESPN television station and the site's chat. This is implemented better than some ticker-like content—it's slower, for one thing, so there is time to read the listing—but it's still a distracting screen element and an inefficient way to view programming data. Much better to have a prominent link to what's on chat and the television station.

3 This busy ad area doesn't tell users anything useful and distracts them from all the adjacent real content. ESPN uses this space for internal promotions, but often lists an external sponsor. It would be better to separate this area from the main body of the page. And because the site does a good job already of promoting content on the main body of the page, it would be even better to abandon the idea of sponsored content, if it's going to be so content-free. Sponsorships will be much more successful if they sponsor something that users are actually interested in and that has a meaningful connection between the sponsor and the content. For example, a company selling baseball memorabilia could sponsor a section about the sport's history.

4 This link to **Photos** isn't noticeable enough—it looks like part of the ESPN banner. The photos on this site are excellent and deserve a prominent link. It would also be good to provide a cross-reference to "More Photos" from the featured photo in the main body of the page.

5 Who cares who's powering the site? Likely not sports fans. One useful aspect to this thinly veiled ad for Compaq: If you click the little button, a very businesslike ad for Compaq's Inspiration Technology appears. Nice panic button if you're checking sports scores at work and your boss walks in.

6 Good headline that's well matched to the photo and fun to read, without being overly clever. Punctuation correction needed, though—the apostrophe on **'OL** should come after, not before, the word.

7 Good that the homepage has a search input box, but it should be wider, so users can see and review their entries. Currently you can't search for "Bret Saberhagen" without the query scrolling out of sight. Also, the input box and the **Find** button aren't properly aligned.

8 Exciting, clear, well-cropped photo. Makes it clear right away that this is a sports site. Also good that there's an informative and concise caption below it. Because the photo changes with the story, it does double duty as content and as a simple way to direct users' attention to the lead story. Admittedly, ESPN is privileged because sports generate a daily stream of great photos.

9 When these links are visited, they turn a light gray color, which doesn't provide enough contrast with the gray background.

10 This perplexing UI allows users to load a sports scores ticker in a window or frame on their computer. Although some users might like this feature, there's nothing likable about the way to get it. The icons don't make sense without the ToolTips, and the ToolTips use nerdy computer implementation language. For example, the down arrow means you want the "Frame" option (the scores will display in a frame at the bottom of the screen). Since the buttons are close together, it takes precise mousing to get them to appear. Also, if you choose the frames version, you can close it only from this close box—likely not the remote control users will find intuitive. Last, whenever you pass your mouse over one of the little buttons, the text on the right, currently **Live Scores** updates with a short description of the button. Because these are right in the main navigation path, chances are good that this text will flash different words often, in a distracting manner.

11 Odd to have the **Hall voting** headline boldfaced and not bulleted. If it's considered the main story, it should be at the top of the list. If it's simply a sidebar to the **Hall inductions** story, it would be more appropriate to present it with less prominent typography.

12 It's not clear that **Scores** are separate links and go to a different page from the sports name that appears in the same box. One contributing factor is that the perceived affordance for these being separate, clickable items is inconsistent with the other items in the navigation list. When you hover the mouse over a sports name, such as **MLB** the cursor changes to the hand and the word highlights. When you hover the mouse over **Scores** you get the hand cursor, but the word doesn't highlight. Because of this, it looks like **Scores** might just be a status indicator to tell users that scores are now available in this category. It would be better to eliminate these **Scores** links and offer one scores area on the site, which links to each sport that has current scores available. Each individual sports page should also have a clear link to current scores.

13 This navigation area is too small to offer these separate links to NFL topics, especially so close together. If anything, the second choice should be right justified so they are clearly different.

continues

www.espn.com

14 The headline would be more scannable if it started with the salient terms (Yashin, Isles) instead of the word **Report**, which has close to zero meaning (after all, everything that's reported on the site is a report of some sort). If the editors want to distance themselves from the possibly unsubstantiated rumor, a better headline might have read "Yashin, Isles reportedly close to record deal."

15 Not good to list this as a web address—**www.rpm.espn.com** doesn't exist. The actual URL that appears when you click here is **http://rpm.espn.go.com/rpm/index**, but most users will try "www" first. Better to not distance it from the website anyway by listing it as a separate site—just list it as "RPM."

16 Good to have a link to more headlines. It would be better to right justify or indent this link more, however, to differentiate it from the ones above it.

17 Not necessary to have the icon for **Insider**, since the link includes the name already.

18 These two areas use tabs to fit more content in limited space. Although we've advised against navigation tabs in some sites in this book, such as AsiaCuisine, because they bury content, in this case they are implemented pretty well. The tabs use dynamic HTML, meaning that they update instantly so users can check out the various choices easily and quickly. Each tab has good descriptions of feature stories, so even if you're unfamiliar with a category like **Page 2**, you can get a fairly good idea of the type of material it contains. The site also rotates which tab in a set is the default, thus exposing users to the different categories.

19 The **Insider** is a great example of how to make it worthwhile for users to give up personal profiling information. Users must register to access Insider content, but they get clear benefits from doing so. Before they register, they can see a list of articles available on the Insider site at that time. The Insider focuses on expert editorials and analyses, as well as offering a comprehensive daily link service to other sports content on the Web.

20 No need to emphasize that Jayson Stark works for ESPN.com, in contrast to Peter Gammons who works for ESPN. After all, ESPN.com *is* ESPN on the Internet, so the two entities shouldn't be differentiated.

21 Poor link choice here—if you scan it, it merely insults the Angels without telling the story. Better to link the phrase **Anaheim Angels are making a wild card push**.

22 Good content prioritization to optimize what's visible above the fold at 800×600. For users with higher resolution settings, the brighter visual treatment of the top area gives it priority over the lower items.

23 Good to have a link to live content, in this case games in progress.

24 It's good to feature specific programming from the ESPN television network on the website, but the design has a few usability problems. The time should indicate whether it is a.m. or p.m., and a space is needed between the time and the time zone (ET). Also, while it's great to actually list the topics for this show, it would be better to use a simpler font and to left justify the text. It's appropriate to use the font formatting for show's name, but not good to do so for actual content because users often screen out highly formatted text.

ESPN uses well-cropped photos with succinct headlines and descriptive captions to enrich the site's content. One reason for their effectiveness is that they relate directly to the content, rather than bloat the page with gratuitous eye candy.

www.exxon.mobil.com

ExxonMobil - Microsoft Internet Explorer

File Edit View Favorites Tools Help

Back • → • ⊗ ⟳ ⌂ | Search Favorites History | ☒ • ☐ ☑ ☐ ☒

Address http://www.exxon.mobil.com/index_flash.html ▼ Go

ExxonMobil

About ExxonMobil | Newsroom | Jobs & Careers | Shareholder Information | Brands & Products

ExxonMobil,
the world's premier petroleum
and petrochemical company

► **Financial & Operating Review**

► **Summary Annual Report 2000**

News Headlines

ExxonMobil Selected as Leader in Saudi Gas Venture

May 18, 2001 - Exxon Mobil Corporation announced today that the
Kingdom of Saudi Arabia has selected ExxonMobil as the leader in a
significant project, Core Venture 2 in the Saudi Arabian Natural Gas
Initiative, and that ExxonMobil has also been selected to participate in
the implementation of another major project, Core Venture 1. Full
story

Texas Wild!

May 17, 2001 — Opinion Editorial. The Fort Worth Zoo's new exhibit
called Texas Wild! demonstrates how with careful stewardship nature
can flourish in co-existence with human activities. Full story

ExxonMobil Announces Kashagan West-1 Well Test Completion

May 4, 2001 — Exxon Mobil Corporation announced today the
completion of testing at the Kashagan West-1 well by the North
Caspian Sea consortium.   Full story

2:35 PM EST on May 21

$ 89.05 ↓ -1.15

© Exxon Mobil Corporation.
All Rights Reserved.

Financial Info

119th Annual Meeting of
Shareholders of Exxon
Mobil Corporation
Wednesday, May 30,
2001
9:30 A.M., Central Time

You are invited to join
Lee R. Raymond, CEO
and Chairman, for a live
audio Broadcast and
slideshow during
ExxonMobil's 119th
Annual Shareholder's
Meeting via the Web.

(Click here to register)

Sitemap | Privacy | Contact Us   Search for [   ] go

Done   Internet

ExxonMobil Corporation formed from a merger of Exxon and Mobil in 1999 to form one of the world's largest petroleum and petrochemical fuel companies. From the corporate website, users can get standard information about the conglomerate and its family of companies, such as product information, press releases, financial data, job opportunities, and philanthropic activities. Users can also join webcasts of shareholder meetings.

The positives for this homepage are that the information is fairly well organized and the content is refreshingly straightforward and focused on educating users about the company and its products, instead of putting a public relations spin on what a good global citizen it is. A downside is that the site's fairly simple content looks more dense than it should because it's not written for online viewing. The site also breaks too many web design and accessibility conventions with missing ALT text, blue non-linking text posing as links, and text strings that should be links but aren't.

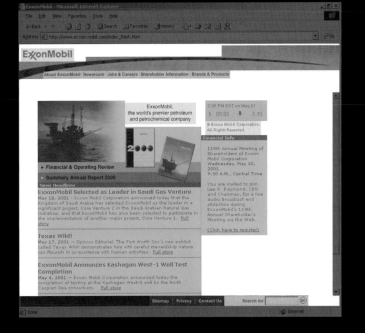

Window Title
This window title will bookmark appropriately by company name.

URL
This URL is too complex for a homepage, and the flash part of it is confusing, since nothing on the page seems to move. Better to hide the implementation details from users, so they can focus on their task. On the other hand, it's helpful that ExxonMobil owns both **www.exxonmobil.com** and **www.exxon.mobil.com**, since users sometimes have difficulty entering concatenated domain names,. It would be best to choose one as the official default name and redirect users to it if they entered the alternative.

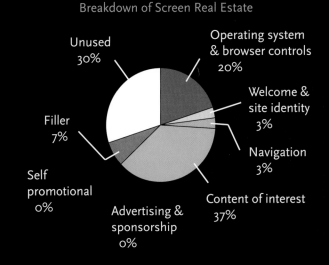

Breakdown of Screen Real Estate

- Unused 30%
- Operating system & browser controls 20%
- Welcome & site identity 3%
- Navigation 3%
- Content of interest 37%
- Advertising & sponsorship 0%
- Self promotional 0%
- Filler 7%

Tag Line
The tag line **ExxonMobil, the world's premier petroleum and petrochemical company** is fairly straightforward, although the word "premier" is a bit vague and subjective. Is this their opinion, or is it based on an outside measure? At least this tag line tells what the company does. It would be more identifiable as a tag line, however, if it were located next to the logo in the upper-left corner.

www.exxon.mobil.com

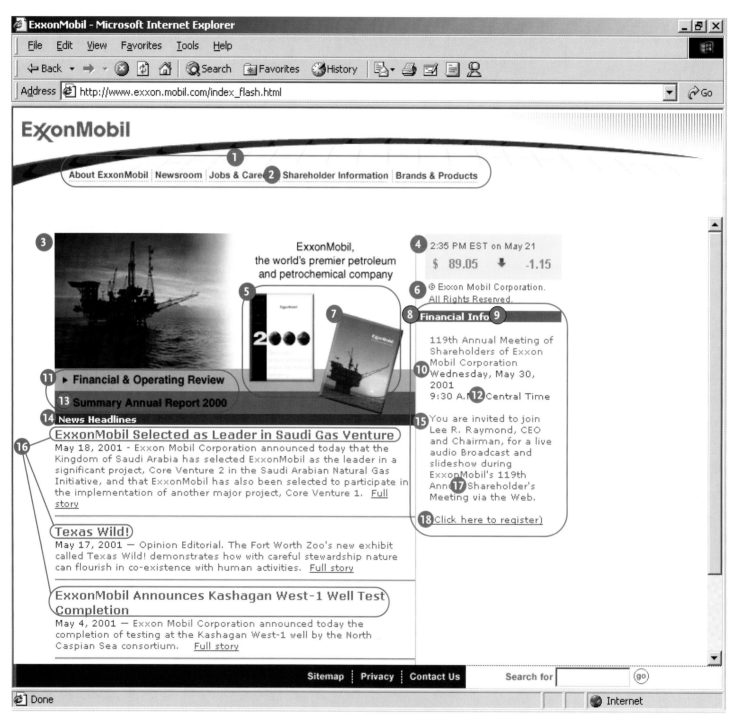

(1) Good to have all the corporate information in one place. However, when you pass your mouse over these links, you get another row of navigation links for each choice. These links are standard enough that they don't need subcategories on the homepage. Better to take users straight to a main page for each link.

(2) **Shareholder Information** implies that this area is only for people who already own stock. Because the information is pertinent to potential stockholders as well, better to call it the more standard "Investor Relations" or "Investor Information."

(3) Although it's good that this photo's content is relevant to the company's product, this particular shot might not be the best choice from a PR perspective. The dark sky framing a shadowed offshore oil rig looks brooding and ominous. In general, oil companies would best avoid photos that show large dark shadows in the water next to their rigs.

(4) This area gives us clues that we're looking at a stock quote, and one would *assume* it's for ExxonMobil, but we can't be sure. First, the quote needs to list the stock name and symbol: ExxonMobil (XOM). Second, stock quotes should link to a full quote. Third, the time is listed as EST (Eastern Standard Time), but it should be EDT (Eastern Daylight Time), because the date is May 21, more than a month into daylight savings time. The time also needs to specify that it's the *time last updated*, not just the current time. And it shouldn't be blue—it looks like a link, but it's not. It's good, however, that the month is spelled out to avoid confusion for international users.

(5) These thumbnails of publications are too detailed and recognizable only if you already know what the publication covers look like. It's not clear which of these is the Operating Review and which is the Annual Report. Worse, even though these are links, they don't have any ALT text.

(6) This is a rather high-visibility placement for the site's copyright information. Better to put this at the bottom of the page.

(7) It's strange to see the homepage graphic repeated in this thumbnail.

(8) Because this **Financial Info** area is used often for webcasts of company meetings, why not call it "Webcasts?" The current heading seems too broad for this one entry, and it's covered under **Shareholder Information**.

(9) These headings look too small in comparison with the body text.

(10) Too many different font colors here. This looks busy, and the link color gets lost.

(11) Although it's fine to give these links to high-profile items special visual treatment, it's not okay to make them graphics without giving them ALT text.

(12) Many international users (and some U.S. users) won't know what Central Time is—give the time differential from GMT as well, such as "GMT −5" (or 6, if the time given represents daylight savings time). Also, reserve blue for links—this looks like one, but it's not.

(13) Why is **Summary** included in the title for the annual report? As far as we can tell, this goes to the full annual report, not a summary. This extra word makes the link less scannable.

(14) The **News Headlines** heading should link to an archive of news stories. There should also be a link to archives at the bottom of the featured headlines, so that users have a way to access past content.

(15) This paragraph is too wordy for online reading and repeats all the information from the heading above. Better to delete it.

(16) These headlines should link to the full story. Some users will want the full story from the headline alone, so you can't assume they'll read down and find the **Full Story** link at the end of the summary.

(17) Presumably, the company has more than one shareholder, so the correct spelling is "Shareholders' Meeting" (with the apostrophe *after* the s). Although almost all users will miss this minor typo, it highlights the need for careful editing, especially for anything that's allocated prime real estate on a major company's homepage.

(18) No need for the link to say **Click here**. Link names should tell users what they will get when they click. A simple rewrite to integrate after the title and time of the meeting: "Join CEO Lee R. Raymond for a live web audio broadcast and slideshow. Register for webcast."

The very word "register" will prevent many users from taking advantage of this potentially useful feature. Users hate to register, both because doing so is usually an arduous task and because it requires them to abandon the safe anonymity of traditional web browsing, making them fear that their privacy will be violated. It should certainly be possible to listen to the webcast without registering. Users might be offered the option of having the site email them a reminder shortly before the start of this live event, but such a feature should be given a different name (perhaps "reminder") and not referred to as a registration.

continues

www.exxon.mobil.com

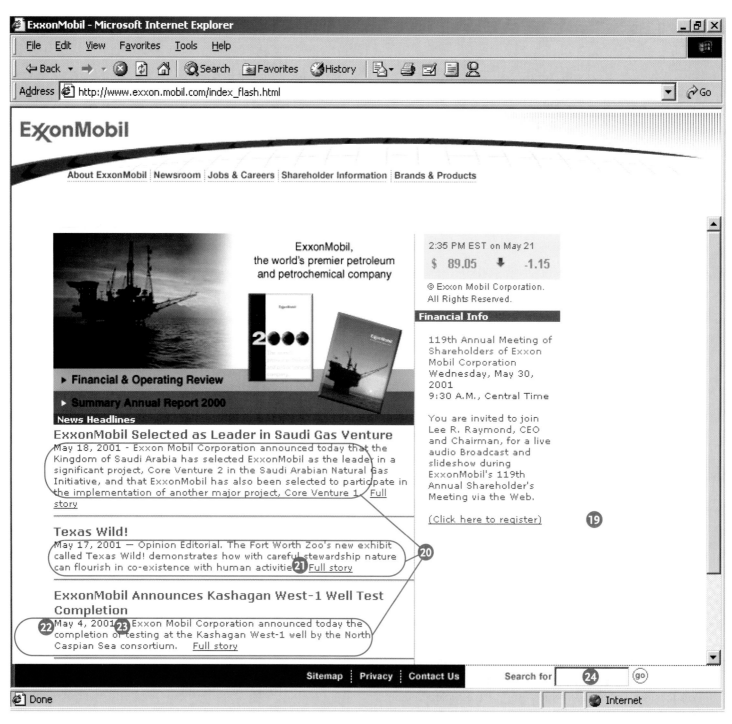

19 A typical example of frozen page layout that wastes a large amount of space in this area because the text does not reflow to fill up the available space. A liquid layout would probably allow users to see all the news items above the fold.

20 These decks take up several lines, but don't tell users much more than what they get from the headline. That they begin **Exxon Mobil Corporation announced**... is a tip-off that they're verbatim press releases pasted into the website and not optimized for online viewing. Although an automated pull of press releases onto your homepage might seem like a good idea, it's not worth the price of reduced readability. Better to invest in an editor to craft news content for your homepage. Give brief, meaningful blurbs on news stories; don't repeat headline content, and definitely don't waste words attributing the content to the company. It's implicit, since this is the corporate site.

21 These **Full story** links open a new browser window. No need to do this—it's fine to open the story in the current window. Users often get confused by multiple browser windows.

22 It would be better to reveal the outcome of the test in the deck than to keep the user in suspense as to whether oil was found at Kashagan West. In general, the homepage summary of an article should be straightforward and cover its main points. Teasers don't work in the long run because users get tired of clicking articles that turn out to disappoint them.

23 Because these stories span a few weeks' time, it's good to include the date. Even better, though, to update the news more frequently on the homepage, so that it's all more current.

24 Although it's good that **Search** has an input box, this low-visibility location almost guarantees that many users will overlook it. To make matters worse, the horizontal line above it separates it even more from the main body of the page. Best to put **Search** in the most common spot: the upper-right corner of the page. Also, the input box should be wider so users can edit and review their entries.

About ExxonMobil | Newsroom | Jobs & Careers | Shareholder Information | Brands & Products
Careers Home | Why ExxonMobil? | Benefits | Campus Graduates | Experienced Opportunities | FAQ
Apply Yourself | InternationalOpportunities

When you hover the mouse pointer over the links in the top navigation area, a second row of navigation links appears, as shown here for **Jobs & Careers**. No need to show this much detail for these standard links. Better to take users straight to a Jobs & Careers page, which explains the choices there in more detail. Also, JavaScript menus are error prone and can require delicate "mousemanship." If the user moves the mouse from the main **Jobs & Careers** field to select the **FAQ** link, the cursor will likely pass over the **Shareholder Information** field, causing a completely different set of links to appear.

www.fedex.com/us

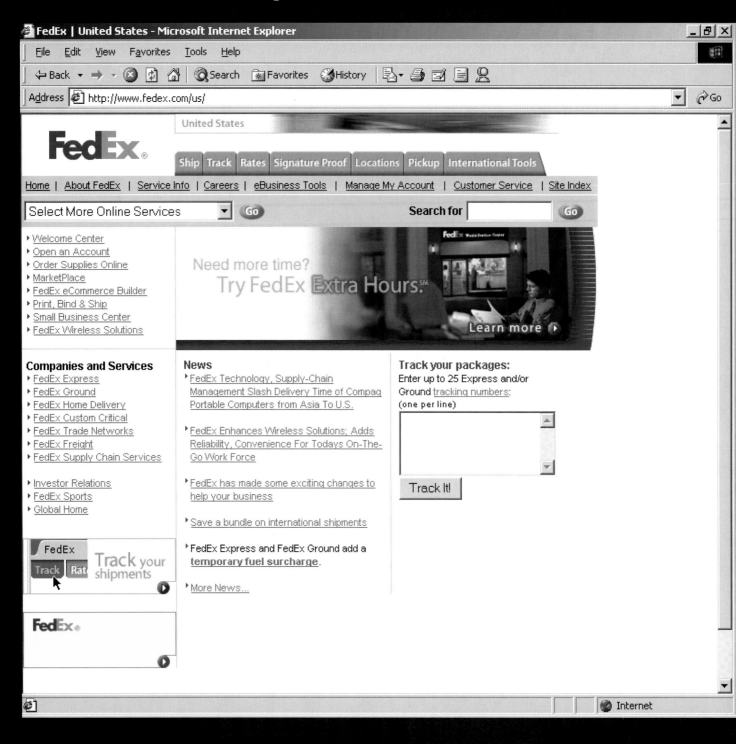

Fedex.com/us is the United States corporate homepage for FedEx, described in the official About FedEx information as a "$20-billion market leader in transportation, information, and logistics solutions." FedEx Corporation comprises five major companies: FedEx Express (of Federal Express fame), FedEx Ground, FedEx Freight, FedEx Custom Critical, and FedEx Trade Networks. The FedEx homepage directs users to homepages for these companies, provides corporate information and news, and supports online account management and tasks, such as scheduling and tracking deliveries.

The site offers users an easy way to perform many common tasks related to shipping and receiving packages. Unfortunately, it makes the tasks look harder than they are. The main problem is that the page needs an information architecture overhaul. There are far too many navigation areas, and the items within them seem randomly grouped. FedEx faces the challenge of all conglomerate companies—adequately representing all the companies involved and providing overall corporate information. FedEx also supports many applications to let users do business tasks on the Web. It's better to put all navigation in one place and chunk it according to corporate information, subsidiary information, user account management, and primary user tasks.

Breakdown of Screen Real Estate

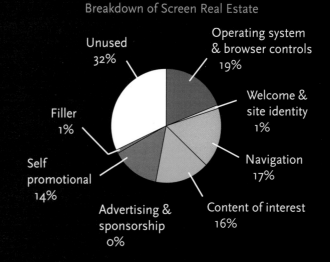

Unused 32%

Operating system & browser controls 19%

Welcome & site identity 1%

Filler 1%

Navigation 17%

Self promotional 14%

Content of interest 16%

Advertising & sponsorship 0%

Window Title
This window title will bookmark appropriately by company name. It's good to include **United States,** because that will help users find the correct site when using search engines.

Tag Line
Although FedEx is a name recognized around the world, this homepage should have a brief tag line to explain what the site's all about.

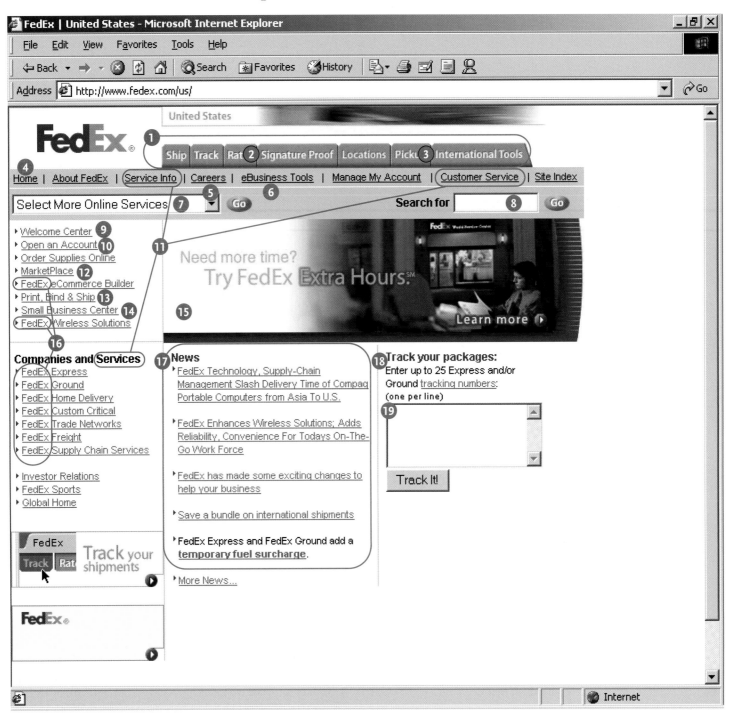

www.fedex.com/us

1 Looks like FedEx is trying to give special emphasis to these high-priority tasks by putting them in this tab navigation bar; however, this attempt could actually have the opposite effect. Users often have "banner blindness" and overlook big graphical rectangles at the top of pages. Although it might be possible to make these tabs look more identifiable by altering the visual design, the real problem is that this page has too many different navigation areas, all vying for focus. This section crams too many options in a small space. Better to eliminate these tabs and instead include the content in a package shipping and tracking area on the main part of the homepage.

2 **Signature Proof** is a great feature that offers users a printable copy of the signed delivery slip for packages they've sent. This should be next to, or incorporated into, the **Track** feature, however. It seems a bit odd as a stand-alone feature.

3 It would be better to call this "International Shipping," because all the items on the page that follows pertain to shipping packages outside of your own country.

4 Sites shouldn't include an active link to the homepage on the homepage.

5 **Careers** gets lost in the middle of these unrelated items. FedEx needs a clear section for corporate information, including a press room, **Investor Relations**, **About FedEx**, and this link to employment information.

6 **eBusiness Tools** should be next to other FedEx web-based services, such as **eCommerce Builder**.

7 Beware of prominently placed dropdowns like this. Users often flock to them as a recognizable item, especially on busy pages like this one. Once users get there, though, they struggle with unclear menu choices and an unwieldy UI. It's unclear whether this menu has low-priority choices that didn't make the cut for homepage links, as implied by the word "more," or whether it contains high-priority items. Best to provide fewer navigation devices and better information architecture.

8 Although it's good to have a search input box on the homepage, it would be better if the box were wider so users could enter and review longer queries. The **Search for** label probably isn't necessary—it would be even less so if the **Go** button were a "Search" button instead.

9 **Welcome Center** is a rather hokey link title. Much of the information here could go in **About FedEx**.

10 **Open an Account** and **Manage My Account** should be in the same area, along with any relevant customer service options, such as ordering supplies.

11 Too many choices on this page contain the word "service," and it's hard to differentiate among them without following their links. **Service Info** is an especially vague name.

12 What does **MarketPlace** mean in the world of FedEx? Answer: nothing. This link goes to one of those annoying shopping portal pages that encourages users to link off the site and spend their money elsewhere on unrelated items. The remote, common thread: all ship via FedEx. Unfortunate to mix this link in with several useful account management links.

13 This link refers to a partnership service between FedEx and a document reproduction company. The link unexpectedly brings up a second browser window with the other company's website. If you have such partnership arrangements, write clear links so that users aren't startled by the affiliation. For example, the link here could have been something like "Print at Kinko's, Ship FedEx."

14 It's not clear what **Small Business Center** is. Should small businesses go here first to perform their FedEx tasks? In fact, this goes to a general resource center for small businesses and would be better named "Small Business Resource."

15 On a page that suffers from so much crammed-in text, it's a pity to see such a large percentage of the space used for an internal ad that doesn't give users any information about the feature advertised. FedEx would be better off using homepage real estate to explain the site's major areas more fully, with a small, relevant graphic for each area, instead of this irrelevant stock photo used here.

16 Although "FedEx" is part of these official company names, including it on all these links makes them difficult to scan and differentiate from each other. Better to include all these links in one place and add "FedEx" to the heading above the list.

17 All these news headlines are too long to scan. Eliminating "FedEx" from most cases and cutting to the chase, such as "Wireless Solutions Add Reliability and Mobile Convenience" would save a lot of space.

18 This heading should link to the package-tracking page, which lets users track packages using a variety of criteria.

19 It's great to enable a common user task from the homepage, as FedEx has done here. However, this tool will likely confuse some first-time users. It doesn't tell users what a tracking number is or where to find one, even in the link by that name. The tool also doesn't tell users how to enter their tracking numbers (with or without spaces); luckily, it's pretty forgiving and works even if users don't enter the exact number of spaces or delete them entirely.

continues

www.fedex.com/us

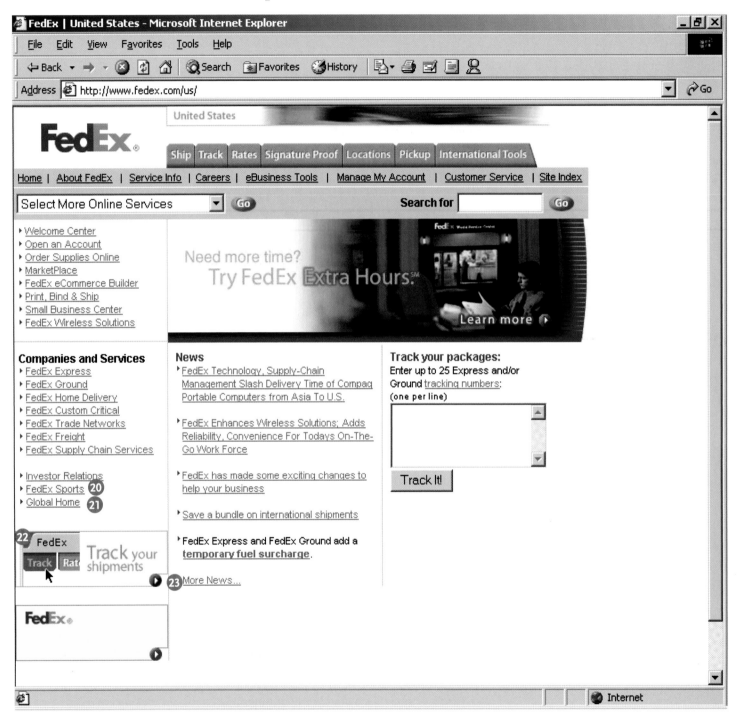

20 **FedEx Sports** is a puzzling link name, especially if you're not a sports fan or haven't noticed the big FedEx banners at certain sporting events. No, FedEx hasn't reinvented the gladiator games—this link goes to information on FedEx Sports sponsorships and should be named accordingly.

21 **Global Home** is a bit of an overstatement for what's basically a country routing page with a couple of links on it. Users who select a country on this page and have their browser set to accept cookies will likely not see it again anyway. "Global" is also a tricky word—if users think of it as meaning "comprehensive," they'll likely think first of the FedEx homepage for their country. It would be better to phrase this link in terms of what users do there (select their country).

22 Why clutter the homepage with ads that merely reproduce links and tools already on the page? Users can track shipments using the tab at the top of the page or the **Track your packages** tool on the right.

23 Good to provide a link to more news stories so users can look for past items as well.

FedEx uses a routing splash screen, shown here, to get users to choose their location. The information is stored in a cookie, so users go directly to their country's homepage on subsequent visits. This is a common way to handle multiple geographical sites. It's odd, though, that the page also includes links to corporate information. If users click **About FedEx** or **Investor Relations**, they are routed to that information on the United States version of the site, and it's not easy to figure out how to switch to another location from the U.S. site. This is the major drawback of using a first-time-only UI—inevitably, some users will need to return to that page, and they won't be able to access it.

www.fhwa.dot.gov

Federal Highway Administration Home Page - Microsoft Internet Explorer

File Edit View Favorites Tools Help

← Back ▼ → ▼ ⊗ ⊞ ⚹ | ⊕ Search ⊡ Favorites ⊛ History | ⊟▼ ⊜ ☑ 🗐 ⊠

Address 🗐 http://www.fhwa.dot.gov/   ▼ ⇨ Go

U.S. Department of Transportation
Federal Highway Administration

What's New

FHWA Programs

Legislation and Regulations

Electronic Reading Room/FOIA

Press Room

FHWA Web Sites

About FHWA

Employee Phone Directories

Doing Business with FHWA

Search

FIRSTGOV

News:
Tuesday, July 3, 2001
U.S. Transportation Secretary Mineta Announces Initiative to Develop First-Ever National Tunnel Management System
FHWA, FTA to Produce Inventory, Guidance for Inspection, Maintenance
U.S. Transportation Secretary Norman Y. Mineta today announced a U.S. Department of Transportation initiative to develop a tunnel management system for the nation's highway and transit tunnels. "Safety is President Bush's highest transportation priority. A systematic framework and analytical tools to manage America's highway and transit tunnels better will help to afford safety and mobility for motorists," U.S. Transportation Secretary Norman Y. Mineta said. "By working together within the department to develop the system, we will maximize service and efficiency for those who stand to benefit from the information."
[Read the full release]

Monday, June 25, 2001
FHWA Names Public Affairs Officer In Agency's San Francisco Office
The Federal Highway Administration (FHWA) has appointed Steve Moler, a 15-year journalism veteran, as public affairs officer in its Western Resource Center office in San Francisco. [Read the full media advisory]

FHWA Press Releases

Employment Opportunities
Jobs in the Federal Highway Administration

Planning A Trip? Your first stop should be the National Traffic and Road Closure Information web site.

Stop Red Light Running
Each year, more than 1.8 million intersection crashes occur. In 1998, red light running crashes accounted for 89,000 crashes, 80,000 injuries and nearly 1,000 deaths. Public costs exceed $7 billion. The goal of the Stop Red Light Running (SRLR) Program is to reestablish respect for traffic signals to enhance the safety of drivers and pedestrians in communities nationwide, while reducing the number of trauma center admissions caused by this traffic problem.

STOP RED LIGHT RUNNING

The **Millennium MUTCD** was published as a final rule in the Federal Register on December 18, 2000. The Millennium MUTCD text can be found at: **http://mutcd.fhwa.dot.gov**. The Internet version of the MUTCD is the primary outreach and education medium for the FHWA. Hard copies of the MUTCD will be available in Spring 2001 through national

🗐 Done   🌐 Internet

The Federal Highway Administration is the division of the Department of Transportation responsible for United States highways.

The major areas of this homepage are well defined and easily recognizable. The site offers easy access to past news items (below the fold in our screen-shot). On the other hand, the **News** area of this page is very crowded. It gives too much detail on certain programs, but doesn't comprehensively cover many of the programs that the administration sponsors. The site is also weighed down by too many logos and acronyms—a sign of "program creep," which is common on government sites. There are also several redundant navigation options that, if eliminated, would simplify the design.

Window Title
This window title will bookmark alphabetically, but it's not necessary to include the words "Home Page" in it.

Tag Line
Unlike most company names, which need further explanation, the nature of the Federal Highway Administration's business is clear from the name, so no tag line is necessary.

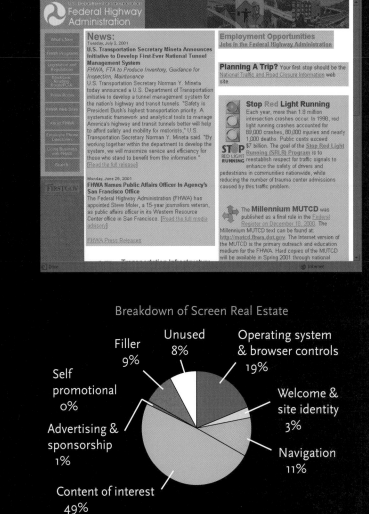

Breakdown of Screen Real Estate

- Filler 9%
- Unused 8%
- Operating system & browser controls 19%
- Self promotional 0%
- Welcome & site identity 3%
- Advertising & sponsorship 1%
- Navigation 11%
- Content of interest 49%

www.fhwa.dot.gov

Federal Highway Administration Home Page – Microsoft Internet Explorer

File   Edit   View   Favorites   Tools   Help

Back • → • ⊗ ⊉ ⌂ | ⊗Search ⊛Favorites ⊛History | ⊞• ⊜ ⊞ ⊟ ⊇

Address ⊜ http://www.fhwa.dot.gov/   ▼ ⊘Go

U.S. Department of Transportation
Federal Highway
Administration

What's New

FHWA Programs

Legislation and Regulations

Electronic Reading Room/FOIA

Press Room

HWA Web Sites

About FHWA

Employee Phone Directories

Doing Business with FHWA

Search

FirstGov

News:
Tuesday, July 3, 2001

U.S. Transportation Secretary Mineta Announces Initiative to Develop First-Ever National Tunnel Management System

FHWA, FTA to Produce Inventory, Guidance for Inspection, Maintenance

U.S. Transportation Secretary Norman Y. Mineta today announced a U.S. Department of Transportation initiative to develop a tunnel management system for the nation's highway and transit tunnels. "Safety is President Bush's highest transportation priority. A systematic framework and analytical tools to manage America's highway and transit tunnels better will help to afford safety and mobility for motorists," U.S. Transportation Secretary Norman Y. Mineta said. "By working together within the department to develop the system, we will maximize service and efficiency for those who stand to benefit from the information."

[Read the full release]

Monday, June 25, 2001

FHWA Names Public Affairs Officer In Agency's San Francisco Office

The Federal Highway Administration (FHWA) has appointed Steve Moler, a 15-year journalism veteran, as public affairs officer in its Western Resource Center office in San Francisco. [Read the full media advisory]

FHWA Press Releases

Employment Opportunities
Jobs in the Federal Highway Administration

Planning A Trip? Your first stop should be the National Traffic and Road Closure Information web site.

Stop Red Light Running

Each year, more than 1.8 million intersection crashes occur. In 1998, red light running crashes accounted for 89,000 crashes, 80,000 injuries and nearly 1,000 deaths. Public costs exceed $7 billion. The goal of the **Stop Red Light Running (SRLR) Program** is to reestablish respect for traffic signals to enhance the safety of drivers and pedestrians in communities nationwide, while reducing the number of trauma center admissions caused by this traffic problem.

STOP RED LIGHT RUNNING

The **Millennium MUTCD** was published as a final rule in the Federal Register on December 18, 2000. The Millennium MUTCD text can be found at: **http://mutcd.fhwa.dot.gov**. The Internet version of the MUTCD is the primary outreach and education medium for the FHWA. Hard copies of the MUTCD will be available Spring 2001 through national

Done   Internet

① Good to clearly show the relationship with the Department of Transportation, while still giving proper prominence to the name of this site. Would be better if users could click **U.S. Department of Transportation** to go to that site.

② No, they're not just pretty pictures; these are actually navigation devices, which is not obvious at all. It's difficult to tell what the different pictures represent—what unique message does each road convey? Why is Oscar working construction? Also, there is too much detail for photos of this size—it's hard to tell where one photo ends and the next begins.

③ Good to have dates on these articles, because the site doesn't update frequently. The day of the week, however, is unnecessary.

④ Either of these two lines would be sufficient to lead to job listings. This would be better as an element of the general navigation area on the left. It should be in the center of the page only if specific jobs are featured.

⑤ Need to explain what **FTA** means at some point (Federal Transit Administration).

⑥ Tell users *why* they should go to this website, not just that they *should* go there. Also, **Planning a Trip?** limits the use of this link. Better to rename this section "Road Closures" and use the description to tell users how often it is updated, as well as give the link to the site.

⑦ This area of the site should just be called "Publications." Emphasizing **Electronic Reading** is silly when users are already reading online.

⑧ Good to have a direct, visible link to press releases under **Press Room**. The **What's New** link has too much overlap, however, and should be combined with **Press Room** so users aren't confused by multiple links to news areas.

⑨ **Web Sites** is not an appropriate term for what are probably departments of the FHWA. Use of the term more likely indicates that the FHWA developed these pages in isolation, with different budgets. To the user, these are all parts of one website—the FHWA website. In any event, almost all these pages are repeated in the **Programs** link as well, which would suffice.

⑩ The generic banality of this quote adds nothing to this deck except an extra inch.

⑪ No need to color the word **Red** in red—the red traffic light next to it is sufficient. This actually makes the headline harder to read, because it draws undue focus to the one word.

⑫ Good that this story conveys a large amount of data in a small amount of space. The statistics about the number and cost of crashes caused by red light running are especially informative.

⑬ **About** information is typically the last or first item in lists like this.

⑭ No need to use a plural for directory here. Also, it seems odd to call this an **Employee** directory, since users can search by department name or contact person.

⑮ Don't repeat the headline. The simple headline is better so the area doesn't get overloaded with graphics, but if you must use the program logo, eliminate the headline.

⑯ If there's ever a stereotype of bureaucracy in government, this overuse of meaningless abbreviations is it. **SRLR** doesn't help users remember the government program name in any way, so there's no reason to include it.

⑰ **Search** should be an input box on the homepage, not buried down here.

⑱ Why have three terms for press releases? Even if there are some differences among these, the distinctions are likely only meaningful to the FHWA, not to the user.

⑲ Presumptuous to think that all users will recognize the name **FirstGov** as the portal to all government sites. As long as this concept is still new, it should have some kind of explanation next to it.

⑳ This headline would be more informative and shorter if written "Steve Moler Named San Francisco Public Affairs Officer."

㉑ This deck repeats 80% of the headline. Without the redundancy, the deck could have been one line shorter or offered one more line of unique content.

㉒ Need to explain up front what **MUTCD** stands for—the term is used everywhere, but never explained.

㉓ It's good that this link to the **Federal Register** goes straight to the register for that day instead of a general page. It would be better if the link took users straight to the rule, which is rather difficult to locate on the page due to the many other government agencies listed there.

㉔ When we reviewed this site in July 2001, the page still referred to this publication availability date of Spring 2001. Either the publication had been delayed or the content needed to be updated. In either case, the information was outdated.

Florida Department of Revenue - Homepage - Microsoft Internet Explorer

File   Edit   View   Favorites   Tools   Help

Back | Search   Favorites   History

Address   http://sun6.dms.state.fl.us/dor/   Go

MyFlorida.com

my

GO   **help | 411 | feedback | directory**

Gov. Bush's E-Newsletter

Florida Department of Revenue

Child Support   Taxes   Forms   Property   Law   Businesses   Governments   Home

Search this Site

Find it!

Contact Us

Taxpayer Services

Refunds

850-488-8937

Child Support
1-800-622-KIDS (5437)

FLORIDA
DEPARTMENT
OF REVENUE
e
SERVICES

DOR JOBS

Florida
Tax Law
Library
Online

Florida
NEW HIRE
REPORTING

DOR Expands Electronic Services

FLORIDA
DEPARTMENT
OF REVENUE
e
SERVICES

Registration for Sales & Use Tax plus other taxes is now available online. Click on the new "Revenue e-Services" icon for information on registration, paying by credit card, telefiling and more...

Florida Tax Relief Act of 2001

During the week of July 28 through August 5, 2001, Florida residents will receive a sales tax exemption for clothing, footwear and certain accessories having a sales price of $50 or less per item, and certain school supplies having a sales price of $10 or less per item.

- Download the Tax Information Publication (TIP), which includes a list of taxable and exempt items.
- View the emergency rule notifying the general public and retailers of the Florida Residents Tax Relief Act of 2001.
- Download a poster for your place of business.
- View the frequently asked questions.

Forms

Download tax forms, Order forms direct from Distribution Center, EDI/EFT, more...

Business

Beginning your relationship, Registering, Workshops, Industry info, more...

Child Support

How-to information, Guidelines, Payments, New Hire, more...

Property

Appraisers, Tax Collectors, Definitions, Exemptions, more...

Director's Message

It's part of my job to make our information and services easily accessible to you. I hope you find what you need and will give us your suggestions for improvement.

Our annual report.

Our Mission

- Increase voluntary payments.
- Reduce the burden on those we serve.
- Continually improve the way we do business.

Taxpayer Bill of Rights

Our Taxpayer Rights Advocate helps taxpayers resolve problems.

Department News

Combined Communications Services Tax To Affect

Done   Internet

From Florida's Department of Revenue (DOR) homepage, users can download tax forms, get tax law information, and perform a variety of business and personal tax-related tasks.

This homepage is at once too simple and too complex. It's too simple because the page doesn't adequately represent the breadth of content on the site. It mentions only a few specific tax laws and describes a couple of programs. The page is, however, filled with icons for these programs, which make it look complex but convey no real information. The writing doesn't really attempt to humanize the complexity of the laws, but instead reports them verbatim, complete with verbose and confusing names. Concern for completeness is often death to fundamental web design principles, such as concise headline writing. This isn't to suggest that sites should bend the truth or be inaccurate, but in order to succeed online, you must give relative priority to elements on the page. It's not enough to just list "official" names of laws and programs—you must craft new content that communicates just the salient information.

Window Title

Good that this window title begins with the site name, so that it will bookmark appropriately. No need to include the word "Homepage" though.

URL

This URL is so complex that it would be difficult for most users to reach the site by typing the name. Unfortunately, because the site is part of the general Florida state Internet infrastructure, it's stuck with Florida's unmemorable domain name: http://sun6.dms.state.fl.us.

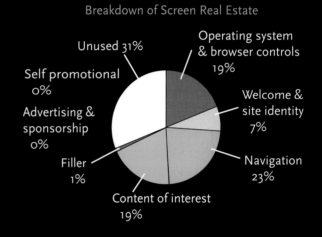

Breakdown of Screen Real Estate

Unused 31%

Operating system & browser controls 19%

Self promotional 0%

Advertising & sponsorship 0%

Welcome & site identity 7%

Filler 1%

Navigation 23%

Content of interest 19%

http://sun6.dms.state.fl.us/dor

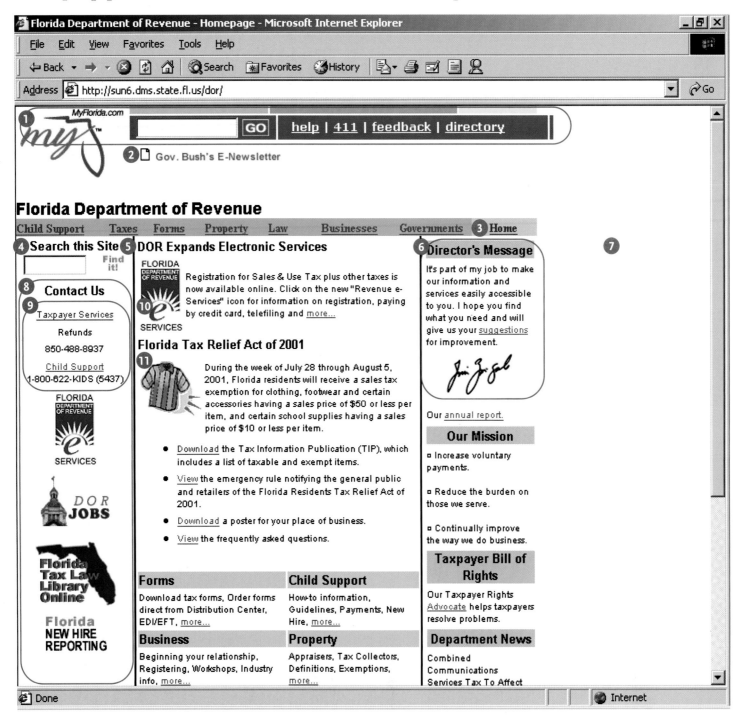

① This navigation area for the MyFlorida.com site, of which the DOR site is a part, is likely to cause more usability problems than it's worth for the benefit it provides. Users will almost certainly encounter problems from the two different search boxes. Users who notice both will wonder which is the correct one, whereas users who go to this search will likely get too many untargeted search results.

The features in this top navigation area, such as search, **411**, and **directory**, help users access other departments within MyFlorida.com—something they can do from the MyFlorida.com homepage. As long as there is a clear link to MyFlorida.com from this page, there is no need to repeat the links here.

The issue is whether to consider the entire State of Florida government as the unit of interest (of which case the DOR would be a subsite) or whether to consider each department as a site and view the statewide level as a summary that is treated the same way as the homepage for a conglomerate or holding company. Because we expect that most users will find the departments to be the most pertinent level of the hierarchy to form coherent websites, it's better to just provide a link to the state site and move the navigation bar up to this top level, instead of viewing all state content as a unified whole.

② Just because Governor Bush wrote it isn't reason enough to compel users to go to yet another online newsletter. Better to give some hint at the content—is this really a message from Governor Bush, or some other sort of newsletter that he sponsors? More frustrating though, the little icon and wording of the link imply that users will go directly to the newsletter—instead, they go to yet another newsletter sign-up that doesn't tell them what they'll get in return for giving away their personal data.

③ This link to the homepage shouldn't be clickable from the homepage. Also, homepage links are most commonly on the left side of the page for sites in languages that read from left to right.

④ No need to label a regular search area **Search this Site**. In this case, they've likely done so as a Band-Aid® for the greater usability issues that come from having two search boxes on the homepage. In any case, it would be better to use a search button than the overly perky **Find it!**, which doesn't look particularly clickable. Also, while it's good to provide an input box, this one is far too small for users to be able to view and edit their entries. Only half of a typical query, such as "sales and use tax" fit in the current box.

⑤ Although there's nothing wrong with the way this headline is written, the content isn't interesting from a user's perspective. Users are probably not interested in the DOR's overall effort to move its services online. Users likely come to the site to do one thing and need to know *how* they can do it here (online, download, by mail, by phone).

⑥ A message from the director is more common in a print publication than on a web page. In this case, the message really doesn't tell users anything of value and takes up more space than a simple feedback link would. Although the director's message is probably a well-intentioned attempt to meet the third point of the department's mission statement (**Continually improve the way we do business**), the request for suggestions is not nearly as open-ended as it sounds. Below it lurks a 12-question survey (all of which are required fields), which goes against item two of the mission (**Reduce the burden on those we serve**).

Too, never use a scanned signature without also providing the person's name in regular type. If you don't know that the DOR's director is Jim Zingale, you likely won't figure it out by his handwriting. Ironically, despite the prominence given to the director's message, it is impossible to discover information about the department's management structure or the biographies of top executives—something that's often requested by the press. *

⑦ This frozen page layout wastes a large amount of space in this area because the text doesn't reflow to fill up the available space. A liquid layout would have allowed most or all the content to be above the fold at 800×600.

⑧ Centered text is less scannable and more visually busy than left-justified text.

⑨ Although it's good to list contact numbers directly on the homepage, this implementation is confusing. **Contact Us** is typically a link that goes to a page with all contact information, but here it isn't clickable, and it isn't visually connected to the items that follow it in an obvious way. Additionally, the spacing is inconsistent between the contact names and numbers, so it's not easy to see what name goes with what number.

⑩ Use links, please. Don't send users to an icon to navigate when you can link directly from a meaningful phrase within the text.

⑪ This graphic doesn't effectively communicate that clothing and school supplies will be tax-free. As it would be difficult for any graphic to do so, it's probably better to spend the resources on designing the content to be scannable and effective.

* **http://www.nngroup.com/reports/pr**

continues

http://sun6.dms.state.fl.us/dor

Florida Department of Revenue - Homepage - Microsoft Internet Explorer

File   Edit   View   Favorites   Tools   Help

⇐ Back → · ⊗ ⊠ ⌂ | ⊗ Search ⊞ Favorites ⊛ History | ⧏· ⊜ ⊟ ⊟ ☒

Address 🗐 http://sun6.dms.state.fl.us/dor/

MyFlorida.com

my

[GO]   **help | 411 | feedback | directory**

🗋 Gov. Bush's E-Newsletter

Florida Department of Revenue

Child Support   Taxes   Forms   Property   Law   Businesses   Governments   **Home**

Search this Site

Find it!

Contact Us

Taxpayer Services

Refunds

850-488-8937

Child Support
1-800-622-KIDS (5437)

(13) FLORIDA
(14) DEPARTMENT OF REVENUE
e
SERVICES

DOR **JOBS**

Florida Tax Law Library Online

Florida
NEW HIRE REPORTING

DOR Expands Electronic Services

FLORIDA
DEPARTMENT OF REVENUE
e
SERVICES

Registration for Sales & Use Tax plus other taxes is now available online. Click on the new "Revenue e-Services" icon for information on registration, paying by credit card, telefiling and more...

Florida Tax Relief Act of 2001

(12) During the week of July 28 through August 5, 2001, Florida residents will receive a sales tax exemption for clothing, footwear and certain accessories having a sales price of $50 or less per item, and certain school supplies having a sales price of $10 or less per item.

(17) • Download the Tax Information Publication (TIP), which includes a list of taxable and exempt items.

(18) • View the emergency rule notifying the general public and retailers of the Florida Residents Tax Relief Act of 2001.

(19) • Download a poster for your place of business.

(20) • View the frequently asked questions.

(21)

(22) **Forms**

Download tax forms, Order forms direct from Distribution Center, EDI/EFT, more...

Child Support

(23) How-to information, Guidelines, Payments, New Hire, more...

(24) **Business** **(25)**

Beginning your relationship, Registering, Workshops, Industry info, more...

Property

Appraisers, Tax Collectors, Definitions, Exemptions, more...

Director's Message

It's part of my job to make our information and services easily accessible to you. I hope you find what you need and will give us your suggestions for improvement.

Jim Zingale

(15) annual report.

(16) **Our Mission**

▫ Increase voluntary payments.

▫ Reduce the burden on those we serve.

▫ Continually improve the way we do business.

Taxpayer Bill of Rights

Our Taxpayer Rights Advocate helps taxpayers resolve problems.

(26) **Department News**

Combined Communications **(27)** Services Tax To Affect

🗐 Done   🌐 Internet

12 This paragraph isn't scannable. Better to use fewer words; for example, replace **During the week of** with "From," and bold or bullet key phrases, such as "Clothing Less Than $50" and "School Supplies Less Than $10".

13 Too many icons here—probably a symptom of government program mania. Even if you develop icons for internal program initiatives, such as getting the law library online, resist the urge to share them with users unless they are widely known and recognized. The icons end up separating these items too much from the rest of the site and making the important standard links, such as job listings, look like they go to external sites. Worst of all, these icons have no ALT text.

14 This icon is particularly inscrutable. The glowing **e** may lead to enlightenment, but it is impossible to tell what kinds of services it represents (without reading the temporary news item in the middle of the page). The icon contains three lines of embedded text at the top, but they simply repeat the name of the department and thus serve no purpose.

15 The link to the annual report should include the year and should be in a location separate from the **Director's Message**. The site needs a true "About Us" section to unify the pieces of information about the department that are currently scattered all over the page.

16 Better to include "official" mission statements in an "About Us" section and instead write a tag line for online use that briefly states the website's purpose. This mission statement area takes up a good deal of space without telling users much about what the DOR does. Eliminate the third bullet completely—an unspecific "do better" item doesn't belong in a mission statement, online or in print.

17 Good to spell out this publication name before using the acronym. This helps all users, but it's especially useful for users who use a screen reader because many acronyms read aloud are meaningless or unintelligible. However, this description should be written based on the benefit to the user, and the link should be on the information-carrying phrase; for example, "Tax Information Publication (TIP) tells you what items are taxable and which are tax exempt."

18 No need to have a separate bullet for reading the rule. Instead, link to the rule from the main paragraph above.

19 Need a description of the poster—this bullet is too general. Better to say something like "Download a Tax Exemption Poster for your business."

20 Another bad link name. To be scannable, this bullet should be "Frequently Asked Questions about the Tax Relief Act."

21 Oh no! What's clickable here? Actually, only the little **more...** phrases are clickable—none of the categories or subcategories are links. Why bother to give users this detail and then prohibit them from accessing it directly?

22 This category should be called "Tax Forms" because that's all you get here. This would eliminate the need to use the word "tax" in the subcategories below this heading. The second subcategory is poorly worded. Who cares where you're getting the tax forms *from*? The key information to provide here is what differentiates this option from the preceding one to download tax forms, so this link should be "Get Forms by Mail." It would be best to refer to the EDI/EFT (electronic data interchange and electronic funds transfer) forms as "Electronic Filing." This makes sense to users who understand what EDI/EFT means and to those who don't have a clue what it means.

23 **How-to information** doesn't give users any meaningful information about what they'll find in the child support section. Avoid using such non-specific links. Instead, list specific topics, such as "Locating Parents," "Establishing Paternity," and "Enforcing and Modifying Support Orders."

"New Hire Reporting" would be a clearer link name than **New Hire** in this context. Florida requires employers to register all new employees so the state can withhold child support payments if the person is delinquent in paying them. It's also important to include this link in the section for employers, because they'll likely think of the task as a reporting requirement, not as the final product of their labors (child support).

24 "Business Tax Filers" would be a more precise heading. **Business** has too many different meanings to use as a heading by itself.

25 **Beginning your relationship** is an ironically humorous way to describe a business's first tax payment. "Getting Started" would be more appropriate.

26 The word **Department** in this heading makes it seem as if it covers office news from departments within the DOR, rather than news from the DOR as a whole. Avoid repeating your company name (or parts of it) in homepage links.

27 This five-line headline (shown in part in our screenshot) appears to have been written for a print medium. If it had been rewritten for online scannability, it would have been more understandable and would have fit on just two lines—for example, "Communications Tax Affects Thousands."

www.ford.com

Ford Motor Company Home Page - Microsoft Internet Explorer

File   Edit   View   Favorites   Tools   Help

Back   →   Search   Favorites   History

Address   http://www.ford.com/servlet/ecmcs/ford/index.jsp   Go

Ford Motor Company

Visit our websites around the world.   GO

SEARCH
Advanced Search

Visit our vehicle brands.   VOLVO   mazda   LINCOLN   Ford   Mercury   JAGUAR   ASTON MARTIN   LAND ROVER

Visit our service brands.   Ford Credit   QualityCare   Kwik-Fit   Hertz

Welcome to Ford Motor Company
Striving to Make the World a Better Place

OUR VEHICLES

Use our shopping guide to find the vehicle that fits your lifestyle and budget, or explore our showroom with one of our many browsing options.

- **See All Vehicle Options**
- Cars
- Trucks
- Minivans & Vans
- SUVs
- Environmental Vehicles

VEHICLE SELECTOR ○○○○○○

Know exactly what you want?
(US Only)

Choose a Brand ▼

Choose a Model ▼

GO

OUR DEALERS ○○○○○○

Breaking News

Read the 2000 Corporate Citizenship Report. Review our environmental, social and economic performance, and learn more about how we're changing the way we do business.

OUR SERVICES

- **Access All Services**
- Safety & Maintenance Tips
- Financial Services
- Smart Buying Guide
- Extended Warranties
- Special Buying Programs
- Rentals from Dealers

OUR COMPANY

- **Learn About Us**
- Investor Information
- Newsroom
- Careers
- Environmental Initiatives
- Corporate Citizenship
- Heritage

There's a dealership near you!
(US Only)

Choose a Brand ▼

GO

RACING ▶▶▶▶

Feel the speed. Hear the thunder. Experience our century-long tradition of winning.

Site Map | Privacy | FAQs | Contact Us   Note: ▣▶ leads to an external site

©Copyright 2001 Ford Motor Company. All rights reserved.

Internet

Ford.com is the corporate website for the Ford Motor Company. Here, users can find general information about Ford, such as PR information, financial data, employment listings, and philanthropic news, as well as information about all vehicle brands owned by Ford Motor Company. Users can also find Ford dealerships.

Kudos to Ford for coming up with well-organized categories, which for the most part have straightforward link names and not cutesy marketese. Ford does a good job of balancing a fair amount of content while still maintaining an uncluttered appearance in the main content area; however, it wastes about one third of its space in welcomes and logos, which could be condensed to a much smaller area. And while the Ford homepage contains most of the content basics, it doesn't convey a good sense of what's fun and attractive about its product. If any homepage is calling out for a picture of a sexy model, this is the one—car model, that is. Why not showcase at least one car model on the homepage? The one car shown is in such a screened back and patterned graphic that it's virtually unrecognizable.

Window Title

This window title is straightforward and suitable for bookmarking and searching. No need to include the words "Home Page" though.

URL

This URL is overly complicated and might make users think they've gone to something other than the main homepage for Ford.

Tag Line

Striving to Make the World a Better Place is more suitable for a philanthropic organization than a multi-billion dollar corporation and takes Ford's desire to position itself as a good world citizen to a silly degree. Users in search of a better world don't likely think of going to www.ford.com to make it so. That aside, this tag line says nothing about what Ford is famous for—automobiles—and thus serves no useful purpose.

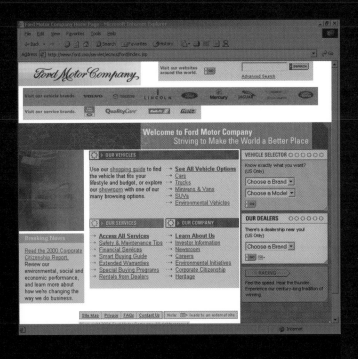

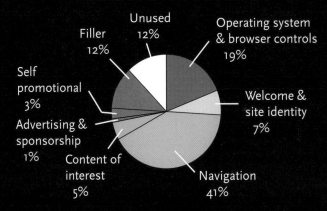

Breakdown of Screen Real Estate

- Unused 12%
- Filler 12%
- Operating system & browser controls 19%
- Self promotional 3%
- Welcome & site identity 7%
- Advertising & sponsorship 1%
- Content of interest 5%
- Navigation 41%

www.ford.com

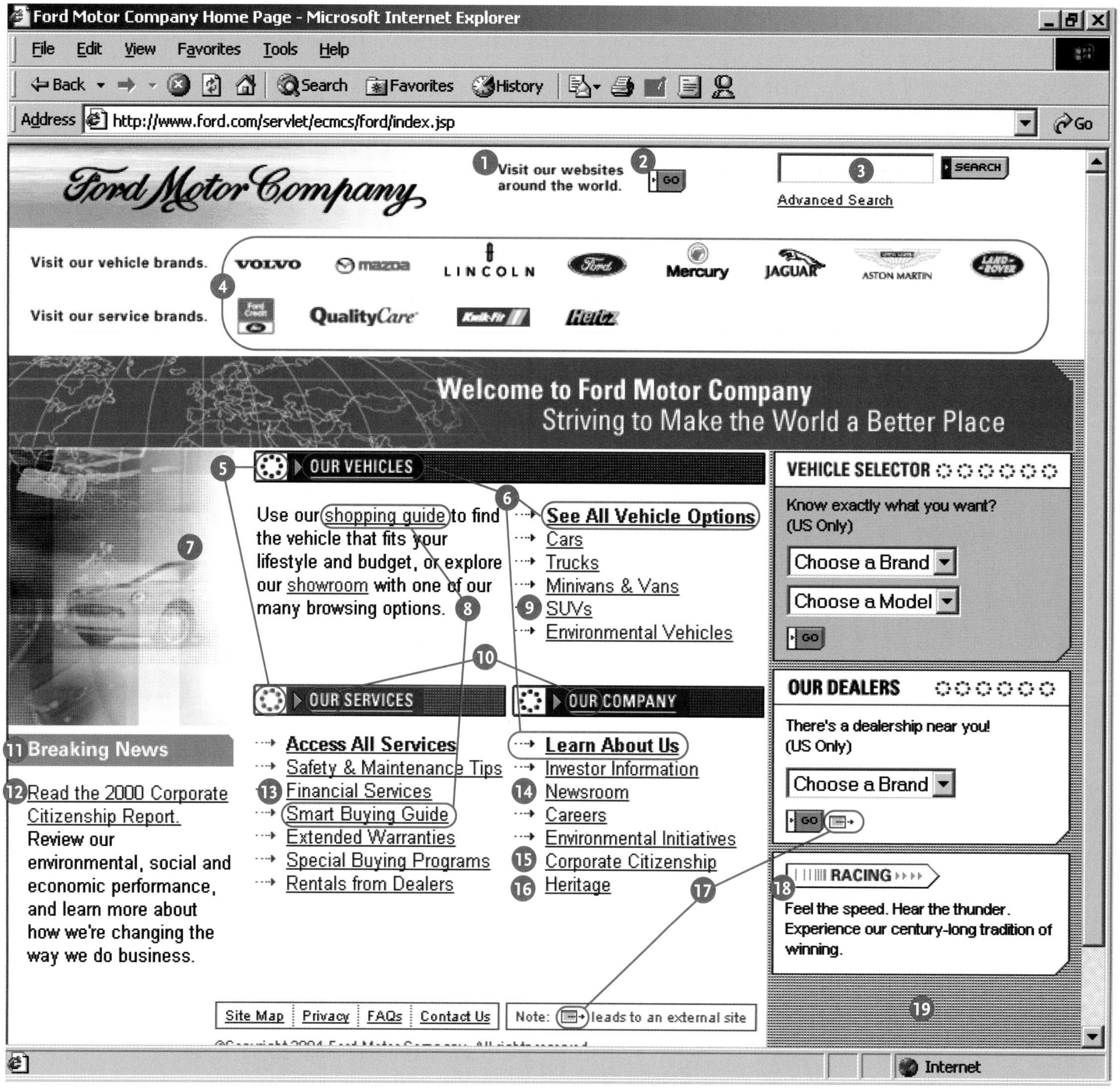

Ford Motor Company Home Page - Microsoft Internet Explorer

File   Edit   View   Favorites   Tools   Help

⇐ Back ▾ ⇒ ▾ ⊗ ⊡ ⚙ | ⊙Search ⊞Favorites ⊙History | ⊟▾ ⊜ ⊡ ⊟ ⊠

Address ⬚ http://www.ford.com/servlet/ecmcs/ford/index.jsp   ▾ ⟳Go

Ford Motor Company

1 Visit our websites around the world.   **2** | GO

3 | SEARCH
Advanced Search

Visit our vehicle brands.   **VOLVO**   ⊙ **mazda**   **LINCOLN**   *Ford*   **Mercury**   **JAGUAR**   **ASTON MARTIN**   **LAND ROVER**

4

Visit our service brands.   **Ford Credit**   **Quality**Care   **Kwik-Fit**   **Hertz**

Welcome to Ford Motor Company
Striving to Make the World a Better Place

5 ▶ OUR VEHICLES

Use our shopping guide to find the vehicle that fits your lifestyle and budget, or explore our showroom with one of our many browsing options.   **7**   **8**

6 → **See All Vehicle Options**
→ Cars
→ Trucks
→ Minivans & Vans
9 → SUVs
→ Environmental Vehicles

10

VEHICLE SELECTOR ○○○○○○
Know exactly what you want?
(US Only)

Choose a Brand ▾

Choose a Model ▾

| GO

5 ▶ OUR SERVICES

11 Breaking News

12 Read the 2000 Corporate Citizenship Report. Review our environmental, social and economic performance, and learn more about how we're changing the way we do business.

→ **Access All Services**
→ Safety & Maintenance Tips
13 Financial Services
→ Smart Buying Guide
→ Extended Warranties
→ Special Buying Programs
→ Rentals from Dealers

▶ OUR COMPANY

→ **Learn About Us**
→ Investor Information
14 → Newsroom
→ Careers
→ Environmental Initiatives
15 → Corporate Citizenship
16 → Heritage

17

OUR DEALERS ○○○○○○
There's a dealership near you!
(US Only)

Choose a Brand ▾

| GO | ⊞→

18 ▐▌▌▌ RACING ▶▶▶▶
Feel the speed. Hear the thunder. Experience our century-long tradition of winning.

19

Site Map | Privacy | FAQs | Contact Us   Note: ⊞→ leads to an external site

©Copyright 2001 Ford Motor Company. All rights reserved.

Internet

1. Although it's great that Ford has a vast number of international websites, this description and **Go** button are not clearly linked, and **around the world** doesn't make clear that the button leads to global sites. Because most users likely will choose the appropriate website once, and because Ford has a large number of international sites, it might be worth it to give users a one-time splash screen to select location and then to include a link to go to the website for another country in a less prominent place.

2. These buttons are too graphically detailed for their small size. More important, though, is that these buttons don't have ALT text, making all of these features, even **Search**, potentially inaccessible to visually impaired users.

3. Good to have a simple **Search** feature with a link to **Advanced Search** right at the top of the homepage. Better if the search box were wider, to allow users to easily review their entries. There is one potential drawback to this location: because it appears above two graphical banners, users might screen out this entire area and overlook **Search**. Better to place the banners above the search area.

4. It's a good idea to give these vehicle brands top billing on the homepage, to give users a snapshot view of Ford's diverse vehicle brands and an easy way to access its corresponding websites. The value of the service brands at this top level is questionable. Aside from Hertz, these brands aren't as instantly recognizable, and the logos are hard to decipher— it's nearly impossible to read **Ford Credit** and **Kwik Fit**. This means users will have to click them to find out what they are and will be taken off the Ford site. To make matters worse, the **Kwik Fit** logo breaks the Back button, so users can't easily return to the Ford site. It would be better to abandon the logos and use a link that describes these services.

5. All of these little circles spin at seemingly random times as you move around the page. They don't add anything to the page, and look rather silly. They look more like bullet chambers than wheels (if that's what they're supposed to be). This detracts from the mostly clean appearance and makes it hard to concentrate on the content.

6. Each of these three sections has a main, bold link, such as **See All Vehicle Options**, which merely repeats the section heading link, such as **Our Vehicles**. It's best to avoid redundant navigation because it adds clutter and confuses users—it's especially unnecessary when the options are so close together.

7. This busy and faded out graphic is difficult to decipher. It would be better to showcase one vehicle and update the content regularly. This would immediately establish what the website is all about and provide a good opportunity to promote different product lines. People who like cars like to look at them.

8. The difference between the **shopping guide** and the **Smart Buying Guide** isn't clear from a user's perspective. Ford likely separates them because they represent totally different branches of the company. The **Smart Buying Guide** extends beyond choosing car models into purchasing options like leasing, pre-owned vehicles, and financing. From the user's perspective, though, these decisions are all part of buying a car, so it's better to group them with the product.

9. **SUVs** should be next in the list after **Trucks**, so users can differentiate between them.

10. **Our** is not necessary in these headings, and it makes them less scannable, because users look for action words at the beginning of headings.

11. **Breaking News** should offer a link to past news stories, so that users can access items they've seen featured during recent visits.

12. Because this headline has body text, format it as a headline—remove **Read the** at the beginning and the period at the end.

13. Good site features often get lost under non-specific names like **Financial Services**, especially when the company isn't famous for providing these types of services. Better to specifically list a few high-profile tasks, such as making a car payment online or calculating a car payment, and link to more options.

14. Good to have a prominent link to news and press releases.

15. **Corporate Citizenship** is a vague name for Ford's philanthropic efforts. Better to call this category "Philanthropy."

16. It's great to include a homepage link to a company's history, especially for a company with as much historical impact as Ford. **Heritage** is rather odd wording—it would be more accurate to call this link "History of Ford."

17. This well-intentioned symbol, meant to show users when links lead to external websites, is odd and will likely confuse more users than it informs. First, you shouldn't rely on users finding the explanation at the bottom of the page. Second, the little icon looks clickable (it isn't), so users might try clicking it instead of the **Go** button.

18. Neither the **Racing** title nor the text in this section clearly explains that it links to some interesting content for car racing enthusiasts. This section is a good candidate for a photo of one of Ford's racecar models, accompanied by some more meaningful text.

19. Many areas of this homepage show undesirable and distracting dithering; it is especially pronounced in this background area.

www.gateway.com

Gateway.com serves as the corporate homepage for Gateway Inc., as well as the entry point for its e-commerce business. Gateway.com allows customers to research and purchase personal computers, as well as a broad range of, as Gateway describes them, "complete technology solutions" for business, home, government, and education customers.

One of the strengths of this homepage is that, because of its incredible simplicity, it makes a powerful first impression. It's initially very calming to see such a spare homepage. However, simplicity doesn't necessarily equal usability. Often, simple pages are deceptively complex, because users must go deep into the site to find what they need, as is the case with Gateway.com. Gateway's homepage doesn't give users any content—it's strictly a navigational gateway to the rest of the site. It also doesn't clearly convey what the company is all about—if you don't already know what Gateway sells, you're in trouble. Gateway works hard to imbue its homepage with its company culture and branding. From its friendly greetings, to the Holstein box, to the folksy category names, Gateway attempts to communicate that customers will still get the kind of personal attention that Gateway has delivered since it was a two-person startup in a barn. Often though, the net effect of all of this folksiness doesn't live up to Gateway's motto, "Keep it personal, make it simple." Users have to work too hard to figure out the meaning behind the links and can't access basic e-commerce necessities like search and shopping cart.

Window Title
This simple title tells exactly what this page is. For use in bookmarking and to make search results scannable, however, it would be more informative to use the title "Gateway Computers" instead of "Gateway Homepage."

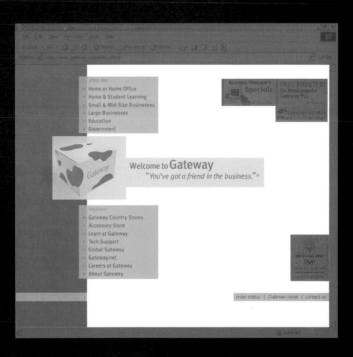

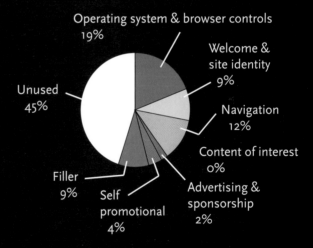

Breakdown of Screen Real Estate

- Operating system & browser controls 19%
- Welcome & site identity 9%
- Navigation 12%
- Content of interest 0%
- Advertising & sponsorship 2%
- Self promotional 4%
- Filler 9%
- Unused 45%

URL
This URL isn't terrible, but it would be better if it were simply www.gateway.com.

Tag Line
This vaguely chummy tag line doesn't say anything about what *type* of business Gateway is. Tag lines need to explain what the company is all about and, ideally, communicate what differentiates the company from its competitors. Interestingly, if Gateway's major differentiator is exceptional friendliness, it's good to communicate that; however, in the absence of defining business information, the promise rings shallow.

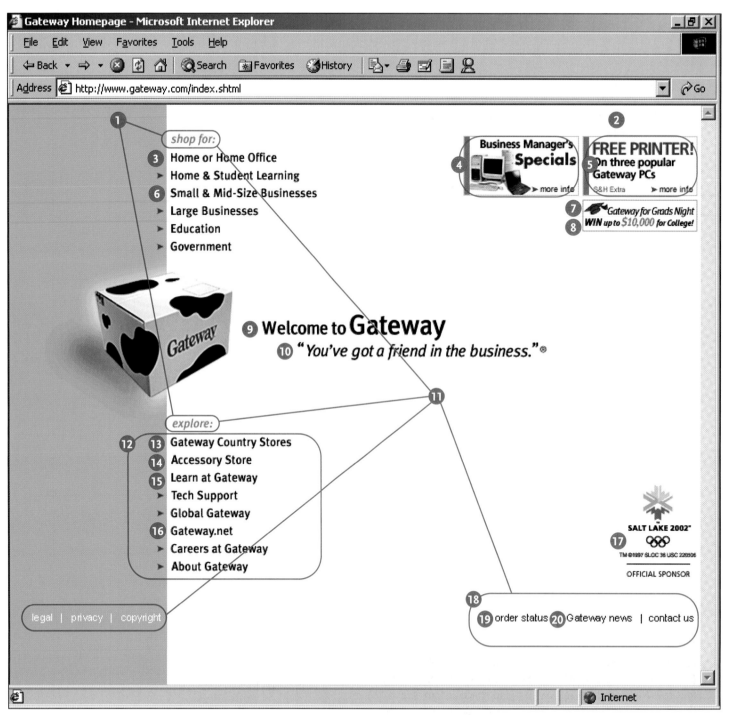

1. **Shop for** and **explore** are oddly phrased category names and are not easily distinguishable from each other. In fact, the first two items under **explore** (**Gateway Country Stores** and **Accessory Store**) seem like shopping items. To Gateway, the difference likely is clear—transaction versus content. But users think of tasks in a much less fragmented way, where exploring is often a part of the shopping process.

2. Where is "Search"? Every homepage needs a search input box right at the top of the page. Some users use search as their primary tool to find things; other users rely on it as a fallback if they have trouble with the categories. In either case, users need and expect it.

3. It's confusing to have two choices both called **Home.** Better to begin links with differentiating words.

4. Why give users all these words and tell them nothing? This ad makes users read two sentences, but they still need to click through to get any idea of what the **Business Manager's Specials** are. It's much more enticing to show the specials and offer links to more sale items than it is to offer a generic **more info** link.

5. This small ad has a lot of text for users to take in at once, but it conveys very little information. The wording is odd—what does it mean that you get a printer "on" popular Gateway PCs? It would be better to tell more about the featured items by showing a small picture of one of the printers, or by listing the model numbers or prices. While it's great to be forthright about additional shipping costs, this **S&H Extra** note is so small that it looks like the site is trying to hide it.

6. Market segmentation like this often makes more sense to the seller than the buyer. Users don't generally think of themselves as belonging to a market segment—and often they don't neatly fit one category, but rather several. If you work exclusively out of your home, are you **Home Office** or **Small Business**? And when does a **Mid-Size Business** become a **Large Business**? Classifying your users on who they *are* is less meaningful than classifying them by what they *need to do* using your products.

7. While the cap icon is fine for the U.S., it doesn't internationalize well, because many countries don't give mortarboard caps to graduates.

8. At least this contest promotion tells users what it offers (money for college). However, the gimmicky name, **Gateway for Grads Night**, clutters up the small ad space and makes the user work to figure out what it means. Better to ditch the program name and just use the straightforward **Win up to $10,000 for College** in a bigger font.

9. The **Welcome to Gateway** text is unnecessary—the entire concept of saying "Welcome to our homepage" is a nostalgic leftover from the early days of the Web.

10. Dedicating prime center homepage real estate to the company tag line is a bold choice by Gateway. This tag line doesn't explain what Gateway does, however, so it's not particularly helpful. Also, no need for quotes around a tag line.

11. Why are these headings and links in lowercase while other choices are in uppercase? Mixed case is easier for users to read, and inconsistent formatting can confuse users, or make them think the site is less professional or sloppy.

12. It's unnecessary to include the word "Gateway" in these navigation choices. In fact, omitting "Gateway" and adding in more descriptive words would clarify their meanings and differentiate them. For example, the alliterative but ambiguous phrase **Global Gateway** could be "International Sales."

13. **Gateway Country Stores** is a confusing name. Do users go to this area to shop, or to learn about Gateway stores?

14. While it can be good to offer users direct access to accessories shopping, it can also be a sign that the site too rigorously segments core offerings from accessories. Users appreciate advice and recommendations on accessories in context with the core product information, so it's important to integrate accessories into the regular product pages.

15. **Learn at Gateway** is not as clear as "Online Training," which is what users can get from this link.

16. It's not clear what **Gateway.net** is (even after you go there).

17. Because the page is so sparse, this Olympics logo really stands out. It seems odd to showcase Olympic sponsorship so much when Gateway plays down its own products.

18. These items should be in a more visible position on the page. It's especially important to elevate the prominence of the **order status** item. If a user doesn't see the link down here, where would he go? Back to the shopping area, where he would have to choose his market segment?

19. Gateway doesn't offer a link to the shopping cart from its homepage. Most e-commerce sites do offer a link because it gives users a quick way to access their items without having to navigate through the shopping area.

20. **Gateway news** doesn't indicate that journalists can find PR contacts and company information here. We recommend using "Press Room."

Designing websites to maximize press relations: Guidelines from Usability Studies with Journalist. See **http://www.NNgroup.com/reports/pr.**

www.ge.com

GE.com is the corporate website for GE, self-described as a "diversified services, technology, and manufacturing company." GE's business units produce a vast range of products and services, from home appliances, to industrial parts, to loan services, to television programming. GE ranks fifth in the Fortune 500 index.

Designing a corporate homepage for a company as diverse as GE is a daunting task. When there is such a great need to convey a lot of information in a limited space, it's important to trim out all redundancies. Many redundant areas weigh down GE's homepage, which allows less space for unique material and risks confusing users by providing multiple paths to the same information. For example, this homepage offers a good area at the top of the page for accessing corporate information, but then repeats this option in many other places. The page also wastes space with fancy formatting—many of the buttons, graphical ads, tabs, and finder tools could be pared down to simple links, which would allow users to see more actual information about GE's business units.

Window Title
   While it's good that the window title begins with the company name, this one is about as bare bones as you get. If the site had a meaningful tag line, it would be good to include it here.

Tag Line
   It's good that this homepage includes GE's well-known corporate tag line **We bring good things to life**. GE also includes a site tag line of sorts, under the **Welcome** area. This is a great idea—unfortunately the implementation here is rather weak. The vague slogan **A Community of Ideas and Solutions that Work for You** sheds absolutely no light on what this site is all about. The same slogan could have applied to almost any other site in this book, and if it's good for all, it's good for nobody.

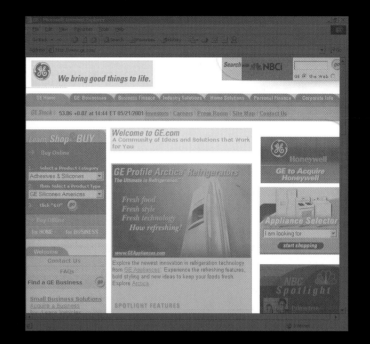

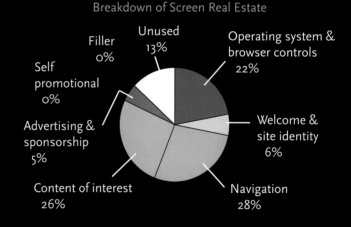

Breakdown of Screen Real Estate

Filler 0%
Unused 13%
Operating system & browser controls 22%
Self promotional 0%
Advertising & sponsorship 5%
Welcome & site identity 6%
Content of interest 26%
Navigation 28%

www.ge.com

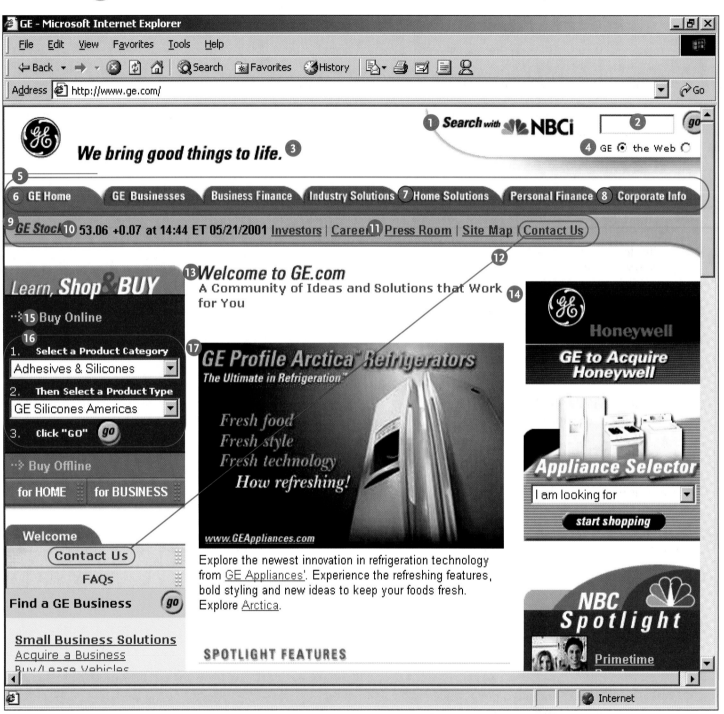

1 It's critical to have a prominent and usable search function on the homepage, especially for a site as large as GE.com. GE's choice to promote NBCi here makes this area look too much like an ad and demotes the prominence of **Search**, especially since **Search** ends up effectively unlabeled because it's overshadowed by the NBCi logo. This problem is made worse by several drop-down menus found on the homepage, which users often mistake for **Search**. Even the curved border around the area effectively separates **Search** from the rest of the page and makes it easy for users to ignore it as a banner ad. If you must include such logos, better to keep them as far away from the feature as possible—in this case, better to put the logo off to the right of search.

2 While it's good that there is a text box for **Search**, it should be wider, so that users can review and edit their queries.

3 No period necessary at the end of a tag line.

4 The ability to search the entire Web is an irrelevant feature. Users who want to do so will go directly to their preferred search engine and not to GE.

5 These tabs repeat many of the product categories from the **Learn, Shop & Buy** area. Better if the site has one clear way to access product areas.

6 This **GE Home** tab shouldn't be clickable—pages shouldn't link to themselves.

7 Users often get confused by the trendy use of **Solutions** to describe products. Better to just call them "Products."

8 The **Corporate Info** tab links to a page almost identical to the homepage—the only difference appears to be some featured tech stories, which should be featured in the **Press Room**. Because the homepage offers links to specific corporate information in the section below this, eliminate this tab.

9 Good to group this general corporate information in one area.

10 Nice to have the stock information with date and time at the top of the page. Good to have the stock name link to a full quote.

No need, however, to include the year in a time stamp for a stock ticker. Simplifying the date would allow room for spelling out the name of the month, which makes the date format more international.

11 Great that this homepage includes a prominent **Press Room** link to the PR area, so that journalists can easily find information about the company.

12 Why have two **Contact Us** links? The upper-right location is more standard than the one found in the site's **Welcome** section.

13 It's unnecessary to welcome users to your site. This welcome takes up a good deal of space—one of the **Spotlight Features** would have been visible if it had not been here.

14 This area announcing GE's pending acquisition of Honeywell looks more like an ad than a news area. Users tend to ignore all things that look like ads—it would be a more effective use of space to include a story about the acquisition with a link to more information.

15 **Buy Online** misrepresents what users can do from this area, to a large extent. Users can't buy many of the products this area links to, such as aircraft and appliances, online.

16 These three steps are overly complex and not necessarily the best way to get users to GE's vast product line. Users have a hard time manipulating long drop-down menus, especially when they are interdependent, as these are. Also, many of the choices, such as **Clubs** and **Money Management**, seem out of place for GE and are impossible to understand without actually going to the new page. The instructions for the drop-downs should be the default in the drop-down menus—no need to take up two extra lines by listing them above each dropdown. This solution would also hide the current defaults (**Adhesives and Silicones** and **GE Silicones Americas**), which, while alphabetically first in the list, are not the first things most users think of when they think GE.

The menu choices on the dropdown for step 2 are **GE Silicones Americas**, **GE Silicones Europe**, and **GE Adhesives**. The first two are not product types, but geographical business units.

There's no need to give instructions and a **go** button (shown with step 3). Better to give a simple "Search" button instead.

17 This huge ad for a new line of refrigerators offers no information about the product line and repeats information that the paragraph below it gives, such as the URL for appliances. The only moderately useful item in the ad is the photo, but even that is too distorted to be a great selling tool. Better to show a clear product photo, without marketing text in it, and write a helpful and informative paragraph that entices users to click through based on the actual merits of the product.

continues

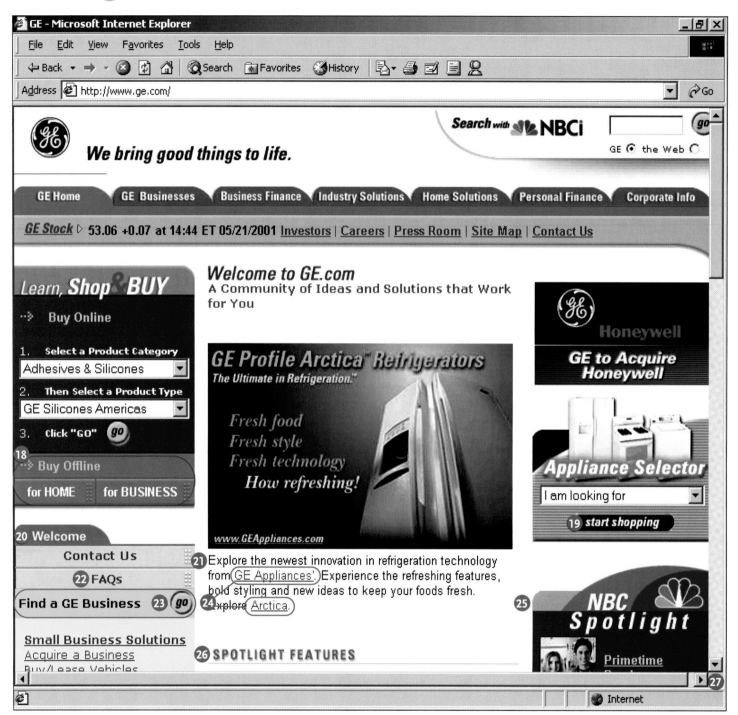

18 Both the label and the UI for this area are unintuitive. While it's good in theory to balance the **Buy Online** area by naming this area in a similar way, **Buy Offline** forces a computer metaphor onto an experience (shopping in the real world) that users need no metaphor to understand; instead, it sounds stilted. The perceived affordances are misleading: users will definitely try to click the very clickable-looking arrow next to **Buy Offline**, but unfortunately this whole area is unclickable. The Braille-like bumps on the **For Home** and **For Business** buttons look more like they should be dragged than pressed, and these buttons look separate from, rather than connected to, the **Buy Offline** header.

19 **Start shopping** is a misleading button name. First, because it's a standalone action, unlike "Go" or "Search," it's not clear that you must select an item from the drop-down menu before you can start shopping. If you do click the button without choosing an appliance category, the page merely reloads and gives no feedback to the user. Since the rest of the page uses **Go** buttons with drop-down menus, this area should as well. Second, it's unclear how this area relates to the large **Learn, Shop & Buy** area on the left.

20 This **Welcome** tab is odd—as is the collection of items lumped together in this area. Not only does it repeat the welcome at the top of the page , which is itself unnecessary, but it does so for an area that doesn't need a heading to begin with. This is also an odd place for a welcome, since it's so far down the page. And why use a tab in this instance? Single tabs don't make sense.

21 This paragraph is loaded with marketese, but light on information. Why make users work to figure out that an "innovation in refrigeration technology" is a refrigerator? Also, better to tell users a few of the new features to pique their interest—it's too vague to refer to "refreshing features" and "new ideas."

22 It's unclear what these **FAQs** pertain to. Are these about the company or about the website? Most websites provide links to site help in the upper right or in the footer.

23 **Find a GE Business** should be a simple link—the **go** button is unnecessary when the user hasn't chosen anything yet. Since this area sits on top of a long list of GE businesses, it's better to give users a text box here, so if they know the business name, they can enter it directly.

24 These links don't help users scan to get the most important information. **GE Appliances'** is too general of a link (and shouldn't have the apostrophe at the end). **Arctica** should be "Arctica Refrigerator" at least, so users can understand what it is.

25 This ad for an NBC program seems rather out of place on GE's corporate website, especially if users don't know that GE owns NBC. Users don't likely come to this website to get information about television shows.

26 Weak headline. Since you cannot see what's below the headline in this screenshot, try guessing what it covers. Based on multiple visits to the site, we believe that the items listed below the fold are abbreviated versions of promotions that had been more prominently featured at the top of the page in earlier weeks. Such an archive of recent lead stories is great for usability: Users often remember seeing something that was the most visible element on a homepage, but they cannot find it once it moves off that spot.

27 The layout ought to be visible without any horizontal scrolling in an 800-pixel wide window.

www.gm.com

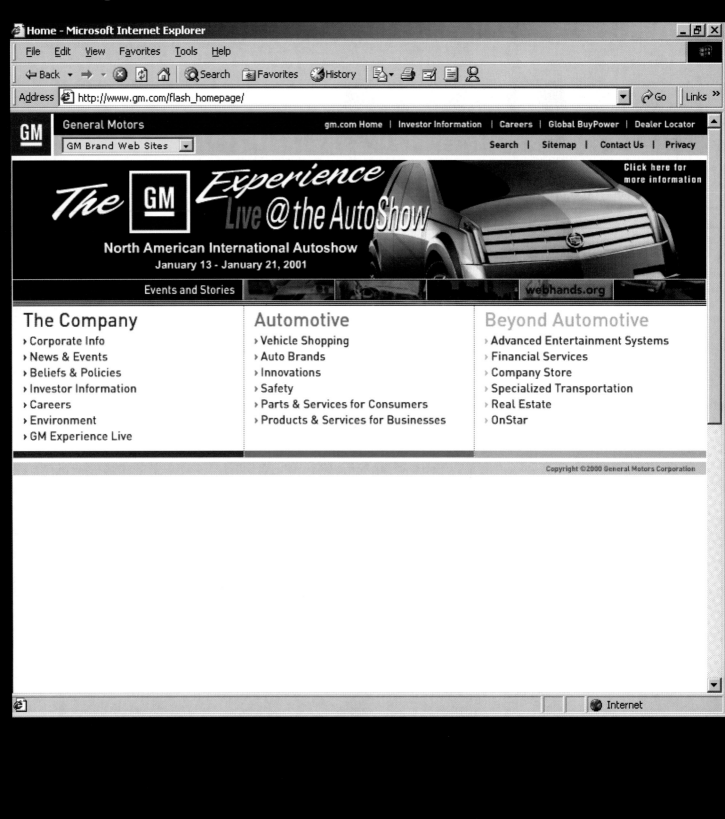

GM.com is a multipurpose corporate website that gives information about the company, GM cars, car-related services (such as insurance), and non–car-related services (such as home loans and relocation services). The site links to e-commerce sites that support these services.

GM.com is at war with its own purpose. This homepage doesn't make clear whom it is trying to serve or what users can do here. It's not clear whether you can buy a car on this site or just look at online brochures. Although GM has a lot of content to offer, it buries that content off the homepage. In an effort to keep the homepage simple, GM gives only category names. Without drilling down through these categories, which users hate to do, it's nearly impossible to ascertain the broad variety of products and services that GM describes on this website besides cars. GM dedicates about half of its homepage's precious real estate to a useless Flash demo and whitespace, showing a deeper commitment to superficial marketing than to information delivery.

Window Title
This title doesn't give any information about GM and will be useless if the user bookmarks the site.

URL
Needlessly complex: users shouldn't have to care what technology is used to implement the page.

Tag Line
GM is famous enough that the company itself doesn't need a tag line. We know they make cars. Still, the website would benefit from a tag line that summarized the intended customer benefits.

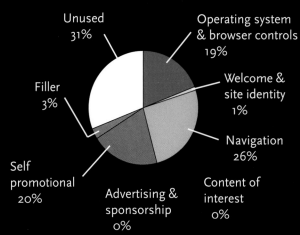

Breakdown of Screen Real Estate

Unused 31%
Operating system & browser controls 19%
Welcome & site identity 1%
Navigation 26%
Content of interest 0%
Advertising & sponsorship 0%
Self promotional 20%
Filler 3%

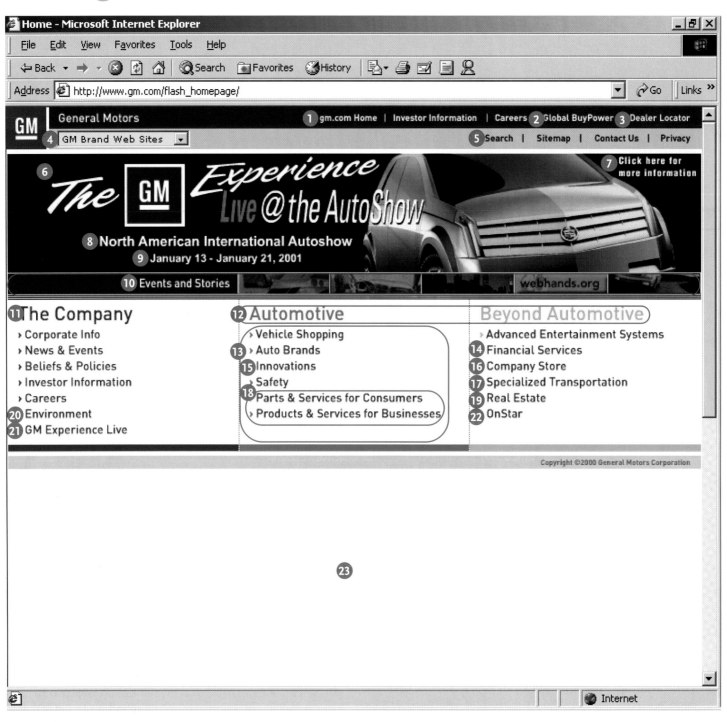

(1) There shouldn't be a homepage button on the home page—you're already there.

(2) **Global BuyPower** is too obscure a term to serve as a major navigation link without explanation. In general, it's better to name navigation categories after their purpose as far as users are concerned, using natural language terminology. Specialized, company vocabular may be used in subtitles or inside the site, but not as standalone links.

(3) Although it's good to have a dealer locator, it's odd to separate it from the **Automotive** section. In fact, this option *is* located in **Automotive**, but it's buried. Better to feature this prominently in one place on the homepage rather than bury it twice. At least the name is good: somebody who wants to find a dealer will know to click on **Dealer Locator.**

(4) **GM Brand Web Sites** means nothing from a customer's perspective. The choices in this dropdown menu go to sites for all the different products that comprise the GM brand. A dropdown menu is an awkward way to access this information—users won't be able to see all choices simultaneously, and often have trouble making the correct selection on long lists. Better to include a clear link to GM products and services, as well as feature some of this information, such as the car brands that GM produces, on the homepage.

(5) The **Search** feature needs an input box on the homepage.

(6) This area flashes various promotions for GM products and events. It would be better to use this ad space to show a few relevant news stories and some of the product line.

(7) What information do you get here? This link is too separated from what it refers to (the auto show) and implies that you get more information about the car pictured next to it.

(8) The auto show ad should include a more specific location than just North America.

(9) This date format is one of the more internationally recognized. One might argue that the North American Autoshow doesn't need an international date format, but it surely doesn't hurt North Americans to write dates in a way that is easily understood in other countries. It's possible to save a little space and thus make the homepage faster to scan by writing the dates as "January 13–21, 2001" instead of **January 13 - January 21, 2001.**

(10) This seemingly decorative strip of graphics actually contains buttons that link to some of the site's categories. If the user hovers the mouse pointer over one of the buttons, a category name, such as **Events and Stories,** appears to the left. For some categories, a URL also appears to the right (**webhands.org** in our example), conceivably to show where this link goes. This is an incredibly unintuitive and cumbersome way to navigate. First, because of its proximity to the large, animated ad, most users will never think to explore this area, and thus will never discover that some navigation lies beneath the mysterious graphics. Second, users should never have to work to discover navigation in the first place. This is akin to boarding up all of the doorways to your store and making your potential customers remove the boards, if they can find where you hid the hammer.

(11) Good to have company information separate from product information (Automotive). A better design would use the more standard phrase "About GM" as a title.

(12) While it makes sense to have a specific **Automotive** category for a company that is primarily known for producing cars, it doesn't make sense to fit a car metaphor on the company's other services with **Beyond Automotive.** Better to be less clever and give users a more straightforward category name.

(13) Although it's good that these menus are fairly simple and contain a manageable number of items, it's difficult to tell what these titles contain because they're overly brief. They should be better explained, as in "Shop for a Car" and "Innovative Car Features."

(14) The **Financial Services** category is too all-encompassing and not informative enough. It artificially separates car loans from the **Automotive** section of the website, probably reflecting the organizational structure of GM more than the user's perspective.

(15) Does **Innovations** refer to new GM cars or features on cars?

(16) Why is **Company Store** not in the **Company** category?

(17) **Specialized Transportation** is an obscure category that covers locomotives (called "Electro-Motive" in an attempt to further obscure matters), military transport, and engines. Compounding the problem, most of the military products, such as ambulances and troop carriers, look suspiciously like automotive products.

(18) This unnatural segmentation probably reflects GM's internal organization, not customers' perspectives. People don't think of themselves as "consumers," especially in this context. Likely, a person dealing with GM thinks of himself as a car owner.

(19) **Real Estate** is an unexpected category on a site that seems focused on cars. A bit more explanation would save users a lot of guesswork.

(20) The **Environment** category needs more explanation to be understandable. Is this GM's environmental awareness policies or its company culture?

(21) What is **GM Experience Live?**

(22) Use of the company name **OnStar** incorrectly assumes that everyone will recognize the function of this feature. Also, because the system is intended for in-car use, it would have been more appropriately categorized under **Automotive.** Most likely, **OnStar** is placed in the non-car category because it's managed as such inside GM's orgchart, but a website's information architecture should be driven by the way *users* think about the concepts.

(23) This layout leaves too much whitespace at the bottom of the screen. Although it's good to prioritize homepage content so that the most important items appear above the fold, it would be better for a company as complex as GM to more fully utilize its homepage space, so that users could get a feel for what the company has to offer without having to click a lot of links.

www.globalsources.com

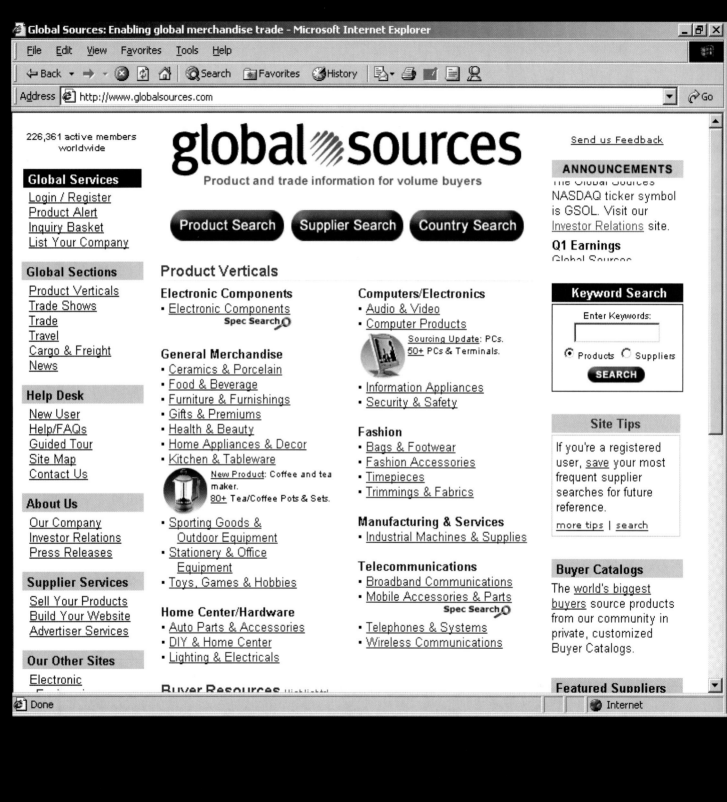

Global Sources describes itself as "a leading enabler of global merchandise trade." Its aim is to "develop and operate independent net marketplaces, and offer software solutions that facilitate cross-border transactions in public and private environments." Global Sources Online is the world's 8th largest net marketplace and comprises 27 vertical and 14 geographic portals. Global Sources began 30 years ago as a global trade magazine publisher and has developed and sold trade management software for the last ten years. From this site, buyers can get information on many products available for high volume purchase. The site also offers buyer and supplier resources on worldwide trading.

This homepage is busy, intimidating, and crowded. Communicating a richness of services is good, but users may wonder what the site is really about and what benefits it offers over other ways of trading. More is not always better—this homepage suffers from redundant links and features and feature-explanation overkill. The homepage needs an overhaul to eliminate redundancies and clear areas for corporate information, site services, buyer resources, supplier resources, and a single way to search. The best implementation currently is when the main body of the page lists various centers with links to sample content within them. Right now each "center" is treated like a different website, and most centers launch a new browser window, giving the site a fragmented feel. It would be better to present a unified experience as a whole site. Many sites catering to vertical markets get too broad and offer too many services, attempting to become users' starting page—almost always a doomed effort that only dilutes the focus of the site.

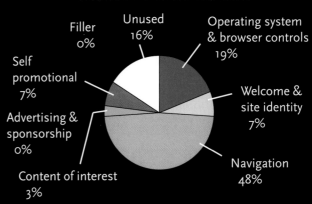

Breakdown of Screen Real Estate

Filler 0%
Unused 16%
Operating system & browser controls 19%
Self promotional 7%
Welcome & site identity 7%
Advertising & sponsorship 0%
Content of interest 3%
Navigation 48%

Window Title

Although it's good that the window title begins with the company name and will bookmark appropriately, it would be better to use the straightforward tag line from the homepage (with our suggested modification) instead of this more general marketing-oriented phrase.

Tag Line

This tag line is close to being good, but makes it seem like the site offers more general product and trade information than actual product specs. Better to modify slightly to "Product Descriptions and Trade Information for Volume Buyers."

www.globalsources.com

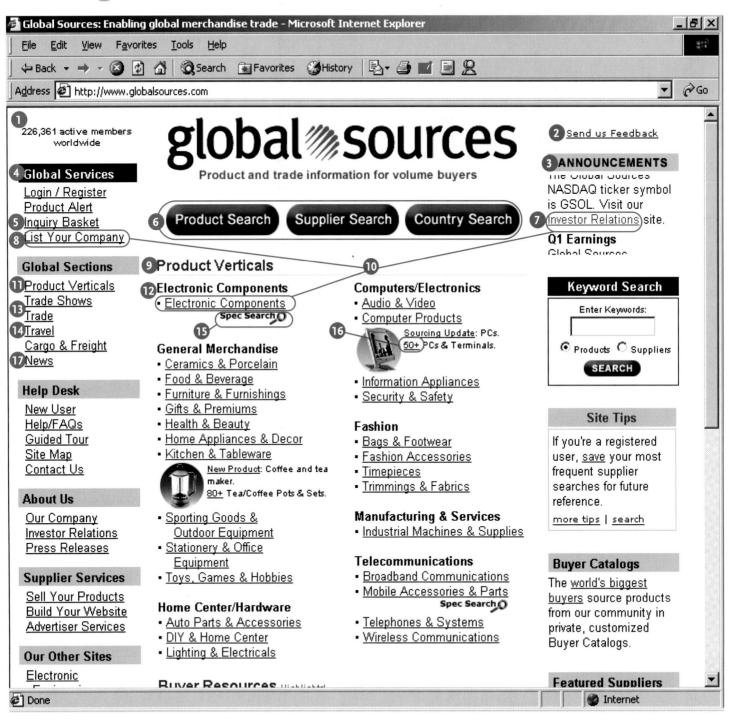

Global Sources: Enabling global merchandise trade - Microsoft Internet Explorer

File   Edit   View   Favorites   Tools   Help

Back   →   Search   Favorites   History

Address http://www.globalsources.com

1 226,361 active members worldwide

global sources
Product and trade information for volume buyers

2 Send us Feedback

3 ANNOUNCEMENTS

The Global Sources NASDAQ ticker symbol is GSOL. Visit our **7** Investor Relations site.

4 Global Services
- Login / Register
- Product Alert
- **5** Inquiry Basket
- **8** List Your Company

6 Product Search   Supplier Search   Country Search

Q1 Earnings
Global Sources

Global Sections
- **11** Product Verticals
- **13** Trade Shows
- Trade
- **14** Travel
- Cargo & Freight
- **17** News

9 Product Verticals   **10**

12 Electronic Components
- Electronic Components
  15 Spec Search

General Merchandise
- Ceramics & Porcelain
- Food & Beverage
- Furniture & Furnishings
- Gifts & Premiums
- Health & Beauty
- Home Appliances & Decor
- Kitchen & Tableware

New Product: Coffee and tea maker.
80+ Tea/Coffee Pots & Sets.

- Sporting Goods & Outdoor Equipment
- Stationery & Office Equipment
- Toys, Games & Hobbies

Home Center/Hardware
- Auto Parts & Accessories
- DIY & Home Center
- Lighting & Electricals

Computers/Electronics
- Audio & Video
- Computer Products

16 Sourcing Update: PCs.
50+ PCs & Terminals.

- Information Appliances
- Security & Safety

Fashion
- Bags & Footwear
- Fashion Accessories
- Timepieces
- Trimmings & Fabrics

Manufacturing & Services
- Industrial Machines & Supplies

Telecommunications
- Broadband Communications
- Mobile Accessories & Parts
  Spec Search
- Telephones & Systems
- Wireless Communications

Keyword Search

Enter Keywords:

○ Products   ○ Suppliers

SEARCH

Site Tips

If you're a registered user, save your most frequent supplier searches for future reference.

more tips | search

Buyer Catalogs

The world's biggest buyers source products from our community in private, customized Buyer Catalogs.

Help Desk
- New User
- Help/FAQs
- Guided Tour
- Site Map
- Contact Us

About Us
- Our Company
- Investor Relations
- Press Releases

Supplier Services
- Sell Your Products
- Build Your Website
- Advertiser Services

Our Other Sites
- Electronic

Buyer Resources

Featured Suppliers

Done   Internet

① This number would be more meaningful if it were divided into registered suppliers and registered buyers, or if it listed a sales outcome, such as total sales generated on this site.

② A link to send feedback should go in the **Contact Us** section or be listed next to the other site services.

③ This **Announcements** area scrolls content in a little window. Animated text is distracting and takes focus away from other items on the page, and it's not a pleasant or effective way to read. The content only stays still for moments at a time, and users must read quickly before it moves out of view. Ironically, users will tend to ignore this area despite the intended visual emphasis provided by the animation. Since animation usually indicates something useless and since it is extra work to deal with, users often avoid looking at animated text.

④ **Global** is a nerdy computer development way to refer to things that appear throughout the entire site and is not a meaningful top level of information architecture. It's not necessary to tell users that any item on your site is "Global"—just make it so. Users expect that things they need will be there when they need them and where they expect them. "Global" is an especially problematic term on this site, since it's in the site name and the nature of the business is global trade. The items in these areas need to be recategorized into areas, such as site services, corporate information, and trade resources.

⑤ Because this site uses a shopping cart metaphor for a place where sellers can collect products about which they want more information, it would be good to use a shopping cart icon as well.

⑥ It's confusing to have so many redundant search options on this page. Although the intention behind these buttons—to give prominence to a high-priority task—is good, these search options aren't as noticeable as they would be if users could enter their search query directly on the homepage. The current **Keyword Search** is dwarfed in comparison to these buttons and seems like a different search feature. This page needs a single, wide input box at the top with scoping for products and suppliers and a link to more advanced options, such as searching within particular countries. This is the kind of big and heterogeneous site on which advanced search is worth the added complexity. Users should also be able to search the entire site for customer service and site features, such as an explanation of the **Inquiry Basket** (shown in the **Global Services** area).

⑦ There are three problems with this link. First, it's hard to catch a moving target in the scrolling window. Second, although the company might have developed **Investor Relations** as a separate site, to the user it's all one site for one company—sections of it shouldn't be referred to as places users visit. Instead, link to sections by describing what users will get there, such as "Detailed Stock and Investment Information." Last, this link opens a new browser window, which is confusing for users. No need to do so; just take users to the **Investor Relations** area in the same window. All pages on the site should have a clear link back to the homepage.

⑧ **List Your Company** should be part of **Supplier Services**, not general site services.

⑨ Although "vertical" is a common term for narrowly focused markets, using the term as a noun rather than an adjective is too jargonistic. Better to call these something like "Vertical Product Centers" or simply "Product Categories."

⑩ These link colors are misleading and confusing. None of the link colors change once they are visited. Visited link colors help users keep track of where they've been on the site, especially when they are searching for something. Also, the unvisited colors should be the same throughout the site—instead, this page uses three different link colors, making it seem as if some are visited and some aren't. The gray on the left makes the choices look like they aren't available, and it's confusing to have two different colors of blue links that mean the same thing. It would be clearest if all unvisited links used the standard blue.

⑪ No need to have a link to **Product Verticals** on the homepage, since the majority of the main body lists the different vertical markets in the same way as the page that follows this link. If anything, some of the details about each vertical market could link from this category or be incorporated into the main body of the page.

⑫ Avoid redundant category/link names and single-item bulleted lists. **Electronic Components** should either link directly from the category name or be part of **Computers/Electronics**.

⑬ It's confusing to have two **Trade** links right next to each other. **Trade Shows** makes sense, but **Trade** on its own is too general for a site that is all about trade.

⑭ **Travel** should be called "Travel Resources" to clarify the site area that follows this link. Users likely will have their own preferred methods for booking travel already, so the idea of a travel category should be eliminated—a site as complex as this one does not need extra features that are unrelated to its core mission.

⑮ **Spec Search** is a useful tool that lets users search for electronic components or telecommunications products by specific technical criteria. Because this is likely an important task for this site's users, it's good to elevate this tool to the homepage so users can access it directly, without having to navigate through the category page. Although we advocate integrating the site's major search functions into one area, **Spec Search** has too many levels of detail and is too narrowly targeted to justify complicating all of search by integrating it.

⑯ **50+** isn't an adequate link name—it seems like the site is trying to prove that it offers adequate selection. If the site indeed has the breadth of product offerings it claims, it shouldn't be necessary to list the number of products—and it's better not to do so when the number is low relative to how huge the selection is.

⑰ A plain link to **News** isn't compelling. Much better to feature a few headlines in a news area with links to more. News could be integrated with announcements because users are unlikely to distinguish between these two concepts.

www.globalsources.com

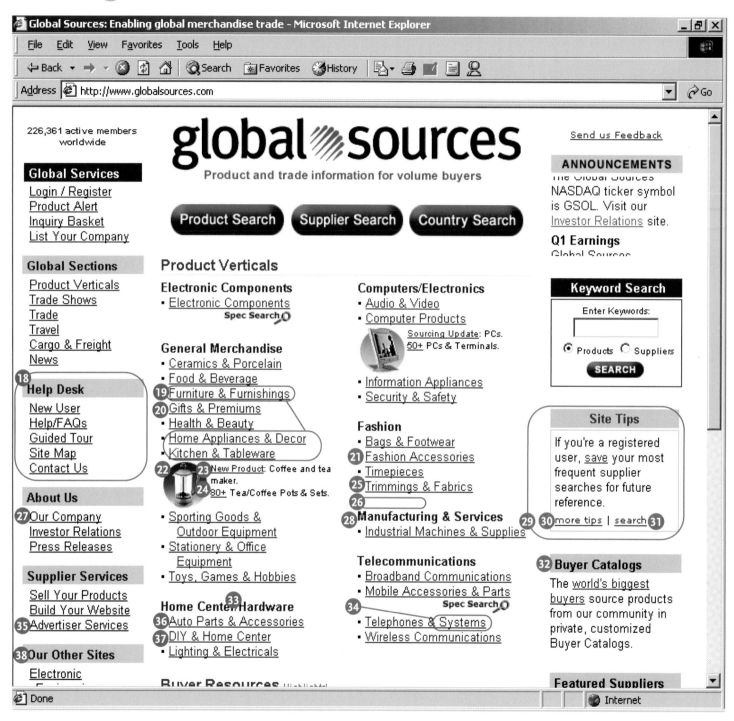

Global Sources: Enabling global merchandise trade – Microsoft Internet Explorer

File   Edit   View   Favorites   Tools   Help

Back   →   Search   Favorites   History

Address   http://www.globalsources.com

226,361 active members worldwide

global sources
Product and trade information for volume buyers

Send us Feedback

ANNOUNCEMENTS
The Global Sources NASDAQ ticker symbol is GSOL. Visit our Investor Relations site.

Q1 Earnings
Global Sources

Global Services
Login / Register
Product Alert
Inquiry Basket
List Your Company

Product Search   Supplier Search   Country Search

Global Sections
Product Verticals
Trade Shows
Trade
Travel
Cargo & Freight
News

Product Verticals

Electronic Components
- Electronic Components
  Spec Search

Computers/Electronics
- Audio & Video
- Computer Products
  Sourcing Update: PCs. 50+ PCs & Terminals.
- Information Appliances
- Security & Safety

Keyword Search
Enter Keywords:

○ Products ○ Suppliers

SEARCH

(18) Help Desk
New User
Help/FAQs
Guided Tour
Site Map
Contact Us

General Merchandise
- Ceramics & Porcelain
- Food & Beverage
- (19) Furniture & Furnishings
- (20) Gifts & Premiums
- Health & Beauty
- Home Appliances & Decor
- Kitchen & Tableware
(22) (23) New Product: Coffee and tea maker.
(24) 80+ Tea/Coffee Pots & Sets.

Fashion
- Bags & Footwear
- (21) Fashion Accessories
- Timepieces
- (25) Trimmings & Fabrics
(26)

Site Tips
If you're a registered user, save your most frequent supplier searches for future reference.

About Us
(27) Our Company
Investor Relations
Press Releases

- Sporting Goods & Outdoor Equipment
- Stationery & Office Equipment
- Toys, Games & Hobbies

(28) **Manufacturing & Services**
- Industrial Machines & Supplies

Telecommunications
- Broadband Communications
- Mobile Accessories & Parts
  Spec Search
(34)
- Telephones & Systems
- Wireless Communications

(29) (30) more tips | search (31)

Supplier Services
Sell Your Products
Build Your Website
(35) Advertiser Services

Home Center Hardware (33)
(36) Auto Parts & Accessories
(37) DIY & Home Center
- Lighting & Electricals

(32) **Buyer Catalogs**
The world's biggest buyers source products from our community in private, customized Buyer Catalogs.

(38) **Our Other Sites**
Electronic

Buyer Resources

Featured Suppliers

Done   Internet

18 The amount of screen real estate devoted to **Help Desk** makes it look like the site requires a lot of help to use. This organization is reminiscent of long help menus in big software packages, which probably explains why Global Sources, a software manufacturer as well as an Internet marketplace, chose to organize this way. Most of these items are standard links to site and corporate information that shouldn't be labeled "Help," since users resist using anything labeled as such. Better to eliminate this category and integrate the items into site services (**Global Services**) and corporate information (**About Us**).

19 All these items should be in the **Home Center** category.

20 **Gifts & Premiums** is too general a category to be useful, especially as a subcategory of the broad **General Merchandise** category. Although some products seem like traditional gift fare, such as key chains and pens, some don't seem like good gift or premium items. For example, the featured new product when we checked was a latex Frankenstein mask—just the thing for your best salesperson.

21 This link should just be "Accessories," since **Fashion** is already the category name.

22 This photo is pretty clear for being such a small size. It's also good that the photo has clear ALT text with the product name and a link to the specific product page with a much larger photo.

23 Although it's good to show a new product, it would be better to use the specific product name, "Coffee and Tea Plunger," as the link and use a "New" icon next to the picture or link.

24 **80+** is not a meaningful link name. Because this item goes with the featured item above it, better for the link to be "More Coffee/Tea Pots and Sets." Also, it would be simpler and more credible to state the actual number instead of **80+**.

25 Suggest reversing the word order here to "Fabrics & Trimmings," which is more common in the garment industry because trimmings adorn fabrics. The revised order also facilitates scanning by placing the more salient word first and by making it clear what kind of trimmings you are talking about—not the ones that are served with a Thanksgiving turkey.

26 There should be categories for men's, women's, and children's clothing under **Fashion**, because these items are featured on the site. Currently, many clothing items, such as cashmere sweaters and men's overcoats, are miscategorized under **Fashion Accessories**.

27 **Our Company** is not as standard as "About Global Sources."

28 Another single-bullet category—better to just list the heading and make it linkable or list a couple of specific links in this broad category.

29 Like the extensive **Help Desk** area, this **Site Tips** area makes the site seem more complicated than it needs to and is reminiscent of a complex software package. Better to integrate any tip information in context in the UI.

30 **More tips** seems like it would take you to an archive of all site tips offered. Instead, this link goes to product search tips, which should be offered only as a "Tips" or "Advanced Search" link from the main search area, not here.

31 Because this **search** link appears within the tips box, it implies that it searches all the tips available, which isn't the case. Instead, this is a redundant link to **Product Search** and should be eliminated.

32 This description is confusing. Part of the problem is the name of these catalogs. These are special catalogs *for* buyers, which list *suppliers*, not catalogs for suppliers, which list buyers, as the name suggests.

33 **Hardware** is a potentially confusing term on a site that also features computer hardware.

34 **Systems** is too general—better to call this link "Telephones and Fixed Network Systems."

35 **Advertiser Services** is a vague link name and just goes to a section called "Sell Your Products." No need to list it separately. Sell Your Products adequately describes the task from a user perspective, and this feature should be a main offering on that page.

36 Auto parts don't fit in the **Home Center** category.

37 **DIY** (do it yourself) is a colloquial phrase, even when spelled out. It shouldn't be used in acronym form as a category name, especially on a site that encourages international members. Also, **Home Center** is redundant because it's the name of the larger category.

38 **Our Other Sites** seems to be a mix of translated versions of this site and other Global Sources specialty sites, such as Electronics. These groupings should be separate. Links to translated sites should appear in a prominent place, and the link should be in the language that the translation is in. Links to related sites should be labeled as such.

www.ibm.com

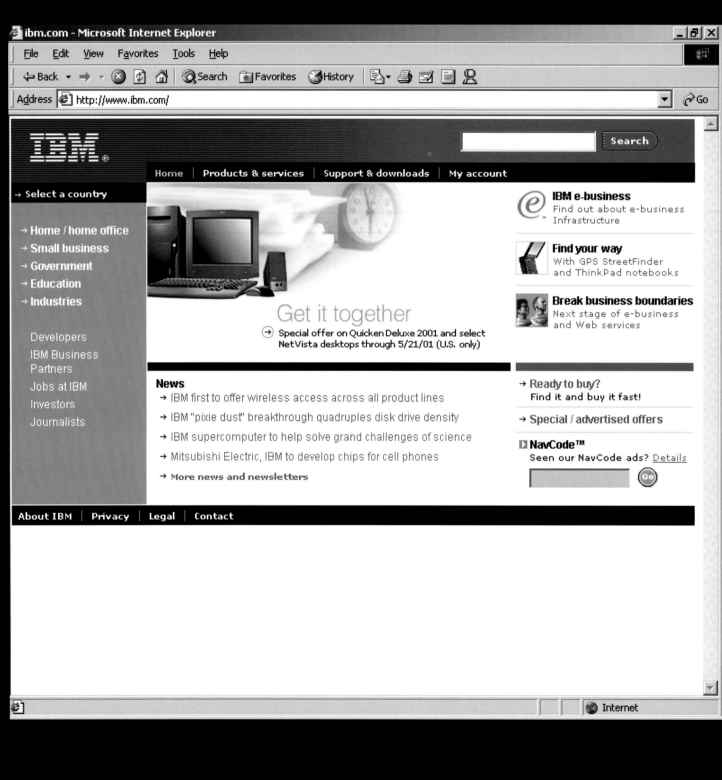

IBM.com serves as the corporate homepage for IBM, as well as the entry point for IBM's e-commerce site. IBM is one of the world's largest developers and manufacturers of information technologies, including computer systems, software, networking systems, storage devices, and microelectronics.

IBM's homepage has a clean, calm, professional, and organized look overall. For such a simple look, however, the page actually has a lot of starting point complexity, especially for new users. This homepage forces users to define themselves before going on to the rest of the site. Users must figure out which key factors differentiate them—should they define themselves by the products they want to buy, by business size, by industry, or by individual work title? Another twist in IBM's quest for utter simplicity: The consistently minimalist phrasing borders on vague and makes users work too hard to discern the meaning. Often one more word in the links would bring more clarity.

Window Title

This window title will bookmark appropriately. A small note: Because it looks a little funny to see ibm in all lowercase letters, it might be better to use the uppercase "IBM" the world is used to seeing.

Tag Line

IBM doesn't have a tag line on its homepage, but it should. A good tag line for IBM would briefly describe both the breadth of the site (corporate and e-commerce) and the breadth of its product line.

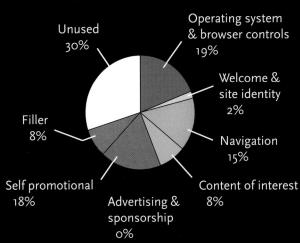

Breakdown of Screen Real Estate

Unused 30%

Operating system & browser controls 19%

Welcome & site identity 2%

Navigation 15%

Content of interest 8%

Advertising & sponsorship 0%

Self promotional 18%

Filler 8%

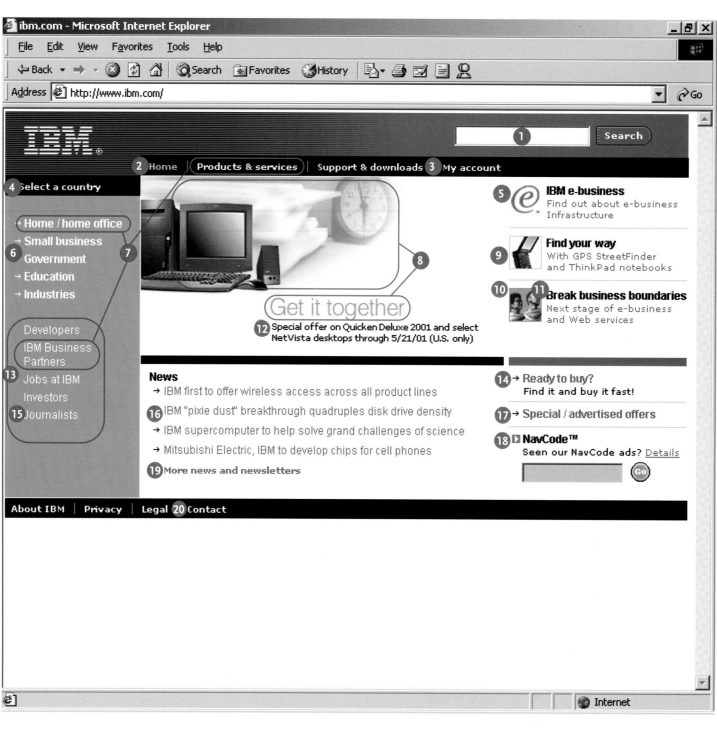

www.ibm.com

1. Good to have **Search** prominently featured in an uncluttered area at the top of the page. Also good that the input box is wide enough for users to review and edit their entries. The bullet-like button is a bit odd, however. The perceived affordance of the little bumps reads more "drag me" than "press me." It would be better to use a more standard button shape.

2. There shouldn't be an active link (or any link, for that matter) to the homepage from the homepage.

3. IBM should offer a link to the shopping cart from the home-page like most e-commerce sites do, because it gives users quick access to their items without having to navigate through the shopping area.

4. The placement and formatting of the **Select a country** link makes it look like a header for the navigation that follows it giving a humorous amount of undue emphasis to market segmentation. Are you a citizen of **Small business** or **Industries**? On the positive side, for a site with as many country sites as IBM, it's good that they made this a simple link, instead of a long, cumbersome dropdown menu. Unfortunately, when users click the link, a dropdown menu is exactly what they get.

5. This bland and uninformative text doesn't explain IBM's e-business marketese or appropriately focus on the featured infrastructure discussion that follows. A better phrase, **INFRASTRUCTURE: Buzzword or E-Business Necessity?**, lies one link down and would be a more intriguing choice here.

6. Market segmentation often makes more sense to sellers than buyers. Users don't generally think of themselves as belonging to a market segment—and often they don't neatly fit one category. If they work exclusively out of the home, are they **home office** or **small business**? If they're part of a 500-person electronics manufacturer, should they go through **Industries** or **Small business**? Finally, how do users know whether to start here, by market segment, or go straight to **Products & services**?

7. These links follow inconsistent capitalization rules. Some use sentence capitalization, such as **Products & services**, while others use initial caps, such as **IBM Business Partners**. These inconsistencies might seem minor, but they make the page look more cluttered and users perceive the site as less professional.

8. This graphic and headline don't adequately convey the special offer. **Get it together** would work well if the photos depicted a good product photo of Quicken and a NetVista desktop. The NetVista photo is fine, but the connection of the generic clipart paperwork mound and analog ticking clock to Quicken is a mystery and seems like a negative product connotation.

9. In the era of PDAs, running GPS from a laptop is a tough sell. It would be better to focus on any value that the laptop has (such as using the laptop in a car or giving bigger views of maps) over a more portable device. Also, the photo is too small to show much, but it would be nice if it could communicate GPS in some way, rather than only show the laptop.

10. This photo is far too detailed for its size, and it's tough to tell how the men in little blue suits relate to e-business and web services.

11. This nonspecific headline and deck don't give users any real information about what services IBM offers that can break business boundaries. It would be better to highlight one specific web service or e-business feature, with links to more. Users are more often put off than intrigued by fact-free marketing generalizations.

12. Why not summarize the offer right here? Users love to see prices and offer terms right on the homepage. Good, though, to list the expiration date and specify that it's U.S. only.

13. It's not clear without looking whether these links, such as **Developers** and **IBM Business Partners**, are *for* these people or *about* these people. This is further muddled because the link to **Jobs at IBM** doesn't fit this writing style (it would have to be "Job Seekers," for parallel construction, which would be silly).

14. It's unclear how this **Ready to buy** area relates to the **Products & services** link at the top of the page. Because users can't enter a product name or number directly on the homepage, how does this save them any time? If anything, this feature implies that the products section is a slow way to go.

15. Although it's good to have a homepage link to information for the press, "Press Room" would be a clearer and more standard name for the link than **Journalists**—and it's actually the name of the page this link goes to.

16. These headlines would be more scannable and differentiable if **IBM** was removed and they started with the key phrases, such as **"pixie dust" breakthrough**.

17. Good to have a link to all specials and advertised offers. Better, though, to place it right next to the special offer featured in the center of the page and call it "More Specials/Advertised Offers."

18. As if the made-up name **NavCode** isn't confusing enough, this inquiry about whether users have or haven't seen a particular ad is entirely unhelpful. Should users enter "Yes" or "No" in the input box below it? In fact, users who know what NavCodes are can enter them in the box—but there should be instructions to this effect.

19. Great to have a link to **More news**, so that users can access the archives, but it's a bit odd to pair this specific feature with the less clear **newsletters** feature. To interest users in newsletters, you need to sell the value of what they'll get, rather than offer them another way to clog their inbox.

20. **Contact** is vague. Who is contacting whom? Better to use the more standard "Contact Us," "Contact Information," or just "Contact IBM," which is what the page it links to is called.

www.jamesdevaneyfuel.com

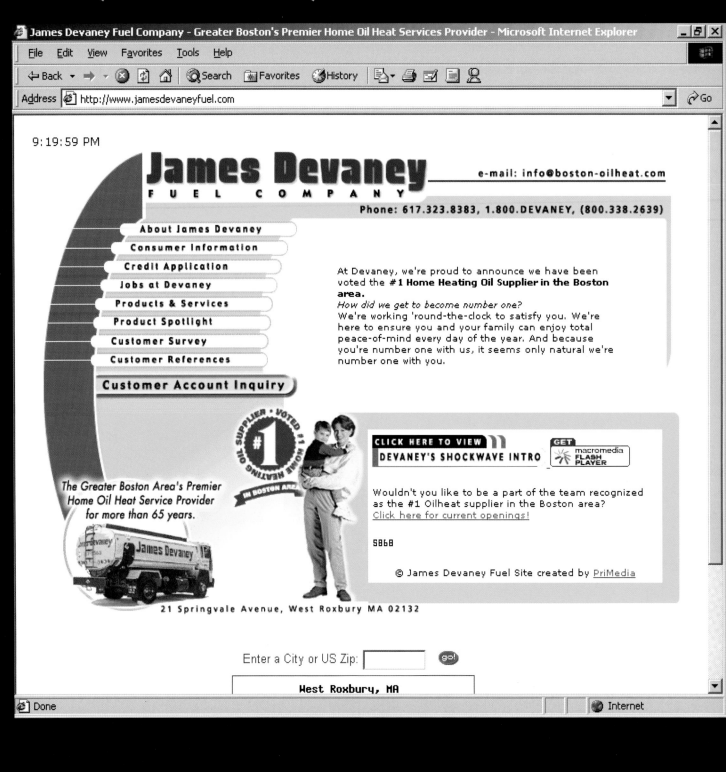

James Devaney Fuel Company primarily offers oil heat and air conditioning services to residential and commercial customers in the Boston area. From the site, customers can learn more about the company and its services, or manage their existing accounts through online bill payment and credit services.

This homepage is fairly simple and clean, except for a few areas that we recommend eliminating or redoing. It competes admirably well with some much larger companies. Because this company offers a specific and narrowly focused product line, it could afford to focus the homepage more specifically, as well, and reveal more offerings up front. It's striking that although the company offers many more services and products than home fuel delivery, none of them are mentioned on the homepage or in the tag line. Although the company services business customers, it only emphasizes residential customers on the homepage. The good news is that this page has plenty of room left (especially if our design suggestions are implemented) to showcase some of these other products and give airtime to business customers. It would also be good to give a bit more information about the oil delivery service, including prices, up front.

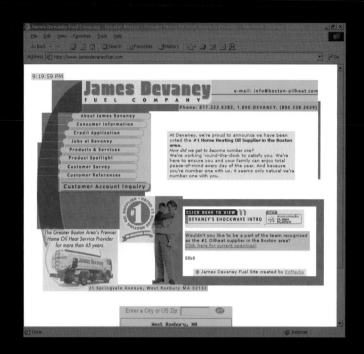

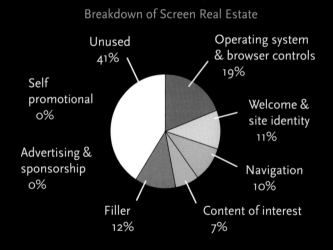

Breakdown of Screen Real Estate

- Unused 41%
- Operating system & browser controls 19%
- Self promotional 0%
- Welcome & site identity 11%
- Advertising & sponsorship 0%
- Navigation 10%
- Filler 12%
- Content of interest 7%

Window Title

This window title will bookmark appropriately by company name. It's good that it also includes a description of the company.

Tag Line

The statement above the truck graphic would work fairly well as a tag line, but is a bit too wordy, compared to the more succinct description in the window title, which is a better choice. A potential downside (depending on Devaney's business goals) to this tag line is that it narrowly focuses on one aspect of the business (home customers). In any case, the final tag line should be located next to the logo, to give it more prominence.

www.jamesdevaneyfuel.com

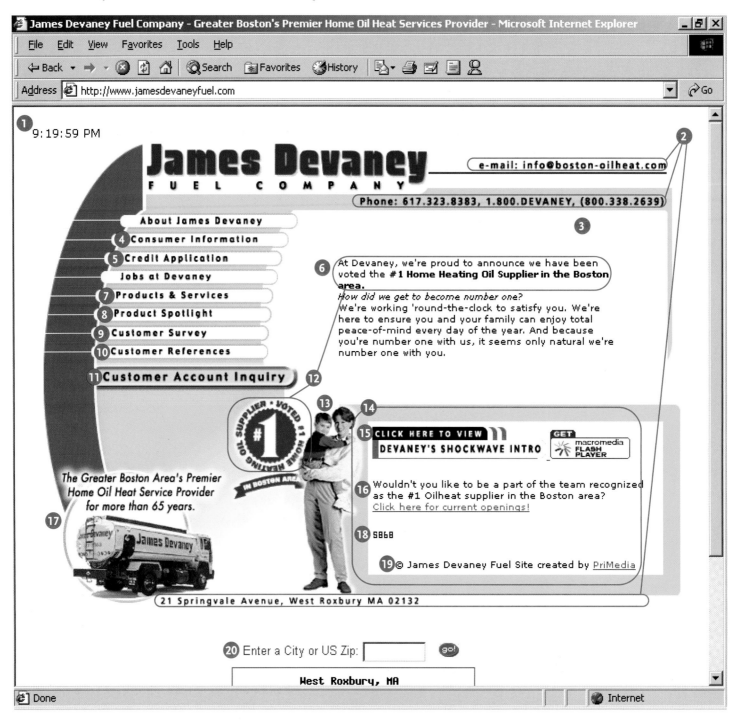

1 9:19:59 PM

James **Devaney**
F U E L C O M P A N Y

e-mail: info@boston-oilheat.com **2**

Phone: 617.323.8383, 1.800.DEVANEY, (800.338.2639)

3

About James Devaney
4 Consumer Information
5 Credit Application
Jobs at Devaney
7 Products & Services
8 Product Spotlight
9 Customer Survey
10 Customer References
11 Customer Account Inquiry **12**

6 At Devaney, we're proud to announce we have been voted the **#1 Home Heating Oil Supplier in the Boston area.**
How did we get to become number one?
We're working 'round-the-clock to satisfy you. We're here to ensure you and your family can enjoy total peace-of-mind every day of the year. And because you're number one with us, it seems only natural we're number one with you.

SUPPLIER • VOTED #1 HOME HEATING OIL **#1** IN BOSTON AREA

13 **14**

15 CLICK HERE TO VIEW
DEVANEY'S SHOCKWAVE INTRO
GET macromedia FLASH PLAYER

16 Wouldn't you like to be a part of the team recognized as the #1 Oilheat supplier in the Boston area?
Click here for current openings!

18 5868

19 © James Devaney Fuel Site created by PriMedia

The Greater Boston Area's Premier Home Oil Heat Service Provider for more than 65 years.

17 James Devaney

21 Springvale Avenue, West Roxbury MA 02132

20 Enter a City or US Zip: [ ] go!

West Roxbury, MA

Done   Internet

1 This time stamp faithfully updates every second of the current time—an unnerving characteristic that could make users feel like they're being timed. Showing users the current time isn't helpful—most operating systems give users a nice little clock in one of the corners of the screen. While it's appropriate on content websites to show users the time the content was last updated, there's no reason to include the time in any form on this site.

2 Great to include contact information on the homepage, especially for a service provider. All the information should be in one place, however, so users don't mistakenly think one element is missing. Also, the email address needs some explanation of when to use it. It would be best to give users a standard "Contact Us" link that goes to a page with the preferred method of contact for all situations (billing questions, service calls, etc.).

3 It's fine that a relatively simple site like this one (less than 100 pages) doesn't have a search feature.

4 **Consumer Information** is an uninformative link name that doesn't reflect the content from a user's perspective. This link should be called "Energy Saving Tips," because the content explains how investing in upgrades and regular service to your heating system can decrease your energy bill.

5 **Credit Application** should be listed next to other account tasks.

6 It's good to devote central homepage space to describe what makes your company a good one to do business with. This text could use some improvements to make it more scannable and specific, however. To improve scannability, cut down the word count and use bullet points to outline the key advantages over competitors. Give specific examples of these benefits from a customer's perspective. For example, saying you're working "'round the clock to satisfy" isn't as specific and useful as saying a customer can reach a service representative 24 hours a day and always schedule a visit within 12 hours.

7 This category name is too general for a company with a small product line. Better to use separate links for the two major product and service categories: "Air Conditioning" and "Oil Heating."

8 **Product Spotlight** leads to a page that features one product from each of the different lines of products the company offers, such as water heaters, air conditioners, and water treatment systems. It would be better to feature these directly on the homepage, with links to more information. This would help show the breadth of products the company offers and take an ambiguous item off the navigation area.

9 Getting customer feedback from a self-selected sample of users on your site will likely lead to skewed and misleading data. If you must include something like this, include it in the "Contact Us" section and phrase the link from the customer's perspective, such as "Give Feedback on Our Service."

10 Most websites refer to customer recommendations as "Testimonials" or by describing the content more clearly, such as "Read What Our Customers Say about Us." Because this homepage emphasizes that the company is number one in its service category, it would be good to use a couple of quotes from customers to back up this assertion.

11 This wording is confusing—it sounds like you can inquire into another customer's account here. Better to call this the standard "Your Account" or list the tasks, such as "Pay Bills Online."

12 The big graphic should appear closer to the text that describes it.

13 We couldn't figure out the connection between the person with the baby and James Devaney Fuel. Happy customers? A very young Mr. Devaney? In any case, this photo competes with the more appropriate fuel truck photo. Better to show some gratuitous happy *warm* people, if any.

14 This boxed area draws a lot of focus, but it doesn't give users any value and should thus be removed. This is prime homepage real estate—use it judiciously.

15 While it's good that this page lets users choose whether or not to see a Shockwave intro, it's bad that the option gets so much focus on the homepage. Like most Shockwave intros, this one is eminently skippable; unlike most, it conveys a few facts, such as the year the company was established, and the basic concept that the company delivers oil to homes.

16 There's no need for this verbose sentence—the **Jobs at Devaney** link in the left side navigation does the job just fine.

17 This photo of a company fuel truck is good for establishing brand identity. Many users will recognize the company name because they've seen the trucks around town. This photo could even be a bit bigger to get more focus.

18 It took closing and reopening the site to confirm our fears. This was a visitor counter—something no homepage should publish, especially not without explanation.

19 Try to work out a deal for site design that doesn't include giving the design firm a credit on your page. This information doesn't help the user and detracts from the site's real content. If you must give credit, best to do it in the source code, so those who are truly interested in finding out how things were done can do so, without cluttering the regular UI.

20 Danger! If you follow these directions, you'll leave the site and go to your city's Weather Channel site. Although the boxed area below this line (just barely showing in our screenshot) shows a weather forecast, it's not at all clear that it's connected to this line. In any case, users come here to buy fuel, not check the weather. They already know it's cold. Resist the urge to pack superfluous content onto your website, especially one that serves a narrow set of tasks. Reserve directive text ("Enter a City or U.S. Zip") for mandatory tasks or qualify the statement appropriately ("To See Your Local Weather").

www.jobmagic.net

Jobmagic.net is a UK-based employment service website. Companies with employment vacancies post their listings on the site, and people seeking jobs enter criteria about the types of jobs they're looking for and view listings. Job seekers can also enter their *curriculum vitae* (CV) online, so that it's available to prospective employers.

JobMagic faces the difficult task of designing one homepage for two distinctly different markets: job seekers and employers. Several usability problems we note stem from this burden. Most problems center around the navigation area, where the approach was to create two versions of some standard homepage links—one for job seekers and one for employers. This dichotomy spawns other side effects as well. Because both groups share homepage real estate, neither gets an adequate share of homepage content. While there's room for actual job listings and success stories from satisfied employers and job seekers, much space is wasted on ads and animated messages. Another problem is that the segmentation works okay if you fit neatly in one of intended user groups, but the segmentation also makes it difficult to find general corporate information, such as investor information. JobMagic would be better off putting this and other company information in a category of its own that could appeal to all users, regardless of their market segment.

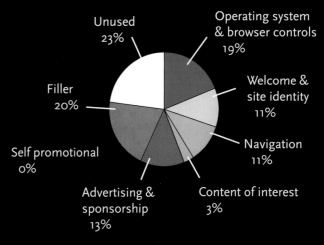

Breakdown of Screen Real Estate

- Unused 23%
- Operating system & browser controls 19%
- Welcome & site identity 11%
- Navigation 11%
- Content of interest 3%
- Advertising & sponsorship 13%
- Self promotional 0%
- Filler 20%

Window Title

While it's good that this window title gives some information about the website's purpose, it's far too wordy. Also, because the title starts with **UK** instead of the company name, the site won't bookmark alphabetically under "J," which would work for "jobs" or "JobMagic."

Tag Line

This site has an okay—albeit fleeting—tag line. The company name and the tag line **online recruitment services** flash briefly across the middle of the screen every few seconds (shown in our picture as the large, blank, brick-colored rectangle, since we caught it at an off moment). The tag line paints on letter by letter, and no sooner do all the letters appear than they all disappear, just the way they came. If users bother to look at what seems like just another of this site's numerous ads, they'll have to be quick to see and retain the tag line.

www.jobmagic.net

1 It's not clear whether the jobs on this site are from the UK only or include continental Europe. In any case, this should be a clear part of the tagline for the site, as well as in the **About** section.

2 A date is useful on this site so users can know whether content has changed since their last visit. This date, however, doesn't tell whether it's the date of the last update (the only useful information) or just an automatically generated display of the current date.

3 Good to tell how many vacancies there are on the site. It would lend more credence and be more informative to also give the number of vacancies filled through postings on this site.

4 JobMagic's relationship to **RexOnline** is unclear, and this **Powered by** credit doesn't help to clarify. It seems as though Rexonline is JobMagic's parent company, but if you don't recognize them, you can't get more information here—the logo doesn't link to RexOnline's site. If it's important to credit a parent company, integrate the information with the site logo ("a division of <company name>").

5 This **Home** button shouldn't be clickable; don't include an active link to the current page.

6 Big waste of space here. This area hosts a senseless animation, which ends with the company name and a brief description of the site. It would be much better to make the tag line a permanent fixture next to the logo and move up the content on the main body of the page into this area. By doing so, there would be room to list some actual job postings on the main body of the page.

7 It's not clear what the **Featured Companies** are. Are these companies that have paid JobMagic for more prominent placement, or has JobMagic culled the available listings and is featuring some of the most interesting companies on the homepage?

8 **About** is vague here, since it comes under both **Jobseekers** and **Clients**. It's confusing enough that there are two identical links—but *who* is **About** about? Is this where you get information about the site's job seekers or clients? In fact, this is a typical "About Us" section, except that one is tailored for each customer type. Better for credibility and comprehension to give all users the same story in one place, and go to it from an "About JobMagic" link.

9 It seems odd to single out **Login** as an isolated task on the homepage, especially in two different areas. Users are unlikely to think of login as a task to perform in isolation from other tasks unless they gain some immediate benefit, such as the homepage becoming a customized view that shows appropriate job vacancies, from doing so. Because no such benefit is offered here, better to prompt users to register or log in when they choose parts of the homepage that are "members only." Better yet for the site to remember its registered users with a cookie, so they don't have to sign in at all.

10 Both **Jobsearch** and **Search Vacancies** go to the same place—an expanded version of the search tool that appears on the homepage. Redundant navigation links confuse users—this instance is worse because the outcome is identical, but the names are different. Worse yet, **Search Vacancies** is inconsistent with all other headings on the page—it's the only one that is also a link.

11 These two options for registration are a bit confusing. **Register CV** makes more sense than the plain **Register** link under **Clients**. In fact, employers need to complete this registration before they can post job vacancies or search through CVs. It would be better if the site had one central area for all users to register or sign in.

12 **Clients** doesn't adequately differentiate employers, or job posters, from job seekers. Aren't job seekers clients of the site as well?

13 No need to welcome users to your site. This would instead be an excellent place for a brief tagline to tell users what JobMagic is all about.

14 Although we credit JobMagic for honesty, it's likely not be the best policy to use the word "possibly" when positioning your company. Better to say "one of the largest and most up to date." Better yet, tell how frequently it's updated and how many jobs are posted on average within a given timeframe.

15 **HR Central** leads to an odd collection of disparate links—everything from information about the company, to product descriptions, to contact information. Many of these links already appear elsewhere on the homepage—it's difficult to determine their value here, especially when listed under such a vague category name.

continues

www.jobmagic.net

UK Jobs and Recruitment at JobMagic - find uk job vacancies, direct from employers and companie - Microsoft Internet Explor...

File   Edit   View   Favorites   Tools   Help

Back   Search   Favorites   History

Address http://www.jobmagic.net

JOBMAGIC.net

Tuesday 3rd July 2001 - Currently 24,534 Vacancies Online

Powered by Rexonline Plc

Home
Contact
JOBSEEKERS
About
Login
Jobsearch
Jobs by Email
Register CV
Career Ahead
CLIENTS
About
Login
HR Central
Products
Register

Welcome to JobMagic

JobMagic is possibly the largest, most up to date vacancy web site.

(17) Simply search our database of jobs offered by leading Employers throughout UK and Europe and apply instantly online.

Your next job could be minutes away.

SEARCH VACANCIES

Select Discipline/Role...

(16) [Enter Skills & Keywords]

[Enter Locations]

e.g. *nt* and *programmer*
hampshire, hants, south

(18) GO

(19) FEATURED VACANCIES

Rex Online — Rexonline Plc Sales Executives Required.

FEATURED COMPANIES

Ine
neteffect EUROPE LTD
Microsoft
Anite
STRATUMSOFT
CherSoft

(20) SEE MORE

Pi Computer Systems
Electronic Document Management Magicians   JOB VACANCIES AVAILABLE - CLICK HERE

© 2001, JobMagic is a division of Rexonline Plc, view privacy statement

Done   Internet

206

It's great to facilitate a top user task on the homepage, as JobMagic does with this tool that searches for job vacancies based on user-input criteria. This tool needs some usability improvements, however. It's not clear which, if any, of the three fields are required before doing a search. Users must navigate an unwieldy pull-down menu and try to fit their profession into one of the listed categories. It's not clear in what format users should enter their skills, keywords, or desired locations. It's also unclear whether users can enter single or multiple words. It would be better at least to provide examples next to each field and a link to tips.

17 This watermark of JobMagic's logo adds nothing except clutter and detracts from the company description above it. The logo in the upper-left corner is sufficient for branding.

18 This over-designed **Go** button is a bit confusing. Users will be drawn to click the most clickable-looking part—the arrow icon, but it's not clickable. Either make the whole thing clickable or, better yet, keep it simple.

19 What do you think is clickable in this section? Not the job description, so if you're interested in this particular listing, you need to find it again on the sponsoring company's job postings site. In fact, only the company logo is clickable. This is misleading, since this area is supposed to feature actual job vacancies, not just companies with job vacancies.

20 **See More** what? It's not clear that this is a navigation link—at first glance it looks like just another ad, since this area is devoted to them. Better if this were a simple link that specified what the user will get, such as "More Featured Companies."

Although popups are always annoying at some level, JobMagic's popup, shown here, deserves some credit for trying to serve a useful purpose. It introduces job seekers to two of the site's major features and offers the opportunity to go directly to them. A big downside to this approach is that users are unlikely to trust this site if they haven't seen it yet. Another downside is that it caters only to job seekers and misses the opportunity to offer employers a shortcut to a frequent task. Better to avoid popups entirely and focus design efforts on the homepage, so that it guides users to high-priority tasks.

www.learn2.com

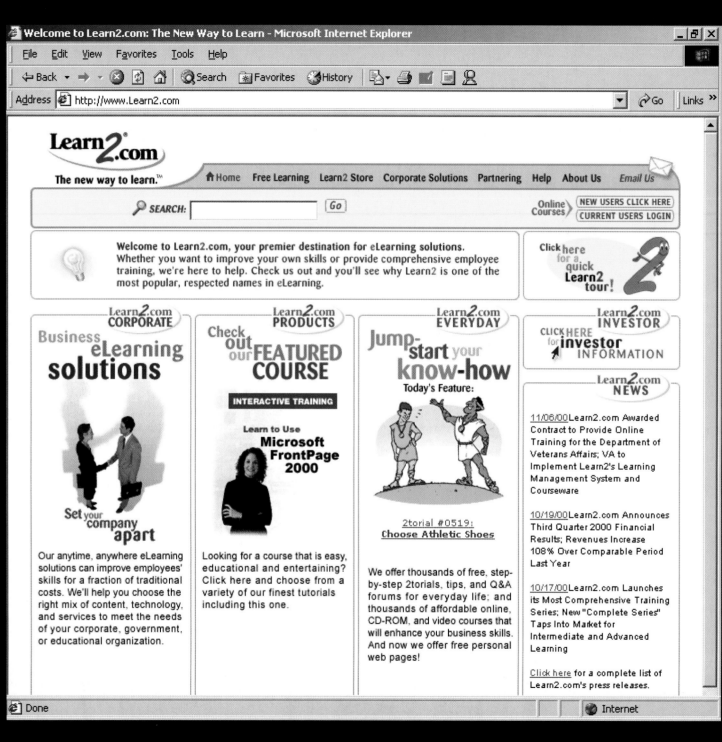

Learn2.com offers web-based, CD-ROM, and video tutorials for both businesses and consumers. Tutorial topics range from software applications, operating systems, and programming courses, to guidelines on more rudimentary topics, such as how to avoid and cure hangovers or how to tie a necktie.

Learn2.com tries to appeal to both corporate and consumer markets from its homepage, with mixed results. This increasingly common split of user focus makes it difficult to clearly convey the site's purpose. This is compounded by the marketese that dominates the homepage. Although the site has a lot of text, it doesn't offer much in the way of solid content. If the site has interesting courses to offer, why not give users more samples of them?

Window Title
This page title will be virtually useless if the user bookmarks this page because the site will be listed under "W" for "Welcome" in Favorites.

Tag Line
This tag line is okay, although it would be better if it conveyed a bit more information, such as the concept of online learning.

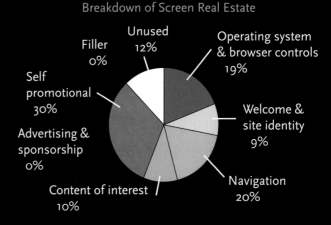

Breakdown of Screen Real Estate

- Unused 12%
- Filler 0%
- Self promotional 30%
- Advertising & sponsorship 0%
- Content of interest 10%
- Navigation 20%
- Welcome & site identity 9%
- Operating system & browser controls 19%

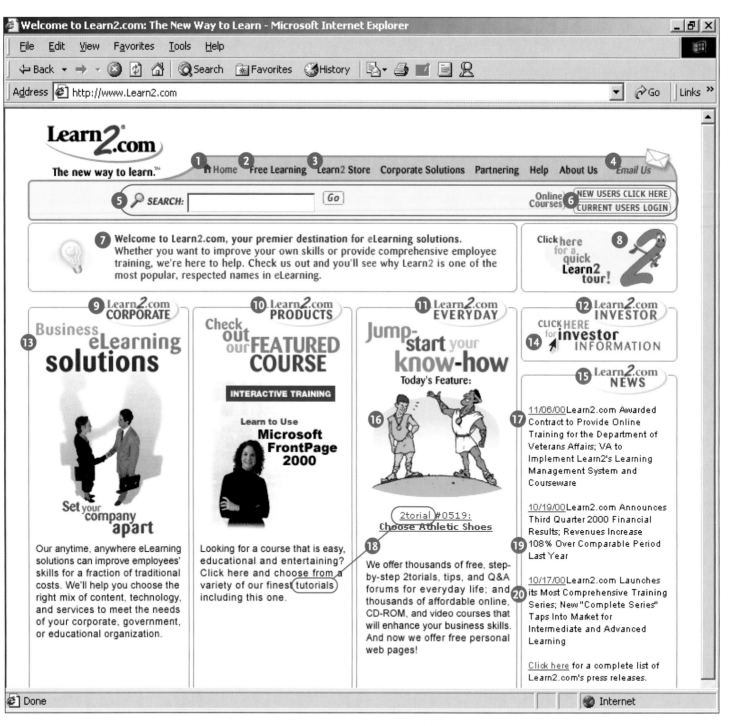

1. A homepage icon on the homepage is not only unnecessary, but it's also potentially confusing. The red color accentuates the problem.

2. **Free Learning** is not as straightforward of a label as "Free Courses."

3. **Learn2 Store** begs the question, "What do they sell there?" Users frequently guess that stores sell company clothing and promotional items. Better to just call this what it is: a course catalog.

4. **Email Us** is not as standard and not as representative of the actual content as "Contact Us." The different font formatting is unnecessary and adds visual noise to the page.

5. It would be better to switch the order of the search box and the login area. This would put search in the more standard upper-right corner and would give login a more central focus.

6. This login area is hard to see. The combination of all uppercase letters and a small font makes the text difficult to read, and it's not as noticeable as the segmented content areas below it.

7. Although it's good to have a dedicated area to explain the site's purpose, this description is vague and makes many promises. It would be better to offer information about the site instead.

8. This cartoonish **2** character has a distinct consumer feel and doesn't target the corporate market well.

9. Although the **Corporate** category seems sufficiently differentiated from the other categories, the difference between **Products** and **Everyday** is much less clear and won't serve first-time or return users well. First-time users won't be able to easily tell what these categories are, and return users will have to remember which category includes the course they are currently taking or would like to take.

10. Are **Products** courses intended for fun or business purposes? The description uses words such as "easy" and "entertaining," yet the example suggests that this may be related strictly to software training.

11. Are **Everyday** offerings intended to provide personal tips, like choosing running shoes, or to "enhance your business skills," as the description claims?

12. Although it's good to have one easily viewable logo in the upper left-hand corner of the homepage, these smaller logos add clutter without adding benefit.

13. The fancy font formatting in these headings detracts from scannability and takes up a great deal of screen real estate, without adding content. Users tend to block out large, graphical text because it looks like a picture or an ad. This information could have been handled in a simpler yet more descriptive link or links to real investor content.

14. This link to **Investor Information** looks more like an ad than a link. It would be much better to use simple underlined text.

15. This **News** area uses a great deal of homepage real estate but probably will interest only a limited subset of the site's visitors. A link to current news from the Investors' section probably would suffice and would leave more room to include course content on the site.

16. There's no clear purpose to the mix of real (but relatively meaningless) photos and cartoon graphics.

17. If these news stories had meaningful descriptions, it would be better to make them the links, rather than the dates.

18. What is the difference between **tutorials** and a **2torial**?

19. These news links don't offer enough information for users to know what they're selecting without clicking through all of them. The initial capital letters in all the words reveal that these are merely repurposed press release titles rather than a much more useful description of the news story. Note the unnecessary inclusion of **Learn2.com** in each title. This redundancy reduces scannability.

20. News titles like this are too vague to be useful. What was the topic of the "most comprehensive training series" ever offered?

www.microsoft.com

Microsoft is the ruler of the known universe. The company is the main supplier of software for personal computing and also has ventures in other areas of technology, such as games and telephony.

Microsoft's homepage has a very attractive, clean layout with simple and fast-downloading images. However, the homepage's content lacks a single, clear voice and tone. Much of the text is technical and serious and seems aimed at the IT professional, but in some places marketese rears its cheery face with phrases, such as "test drive anywhere, anytime communication" and "cool deals." It's difficult to find information about future trends and technology roadmaps, and there is no link to the company's big research department. Gamers must feel like a second-rate customer group, despite Microsoft's sizeable bet on Xbox.

Window Title

Not only is this **Welcome** unnecessary, it will make a bookmark to this page begin with "W" instead of "M."

Tag Line

Where do you want to go today? might have been a goofy tag line, and we would recommend something better, but the site does need a tag line that summarizes what you can do here.

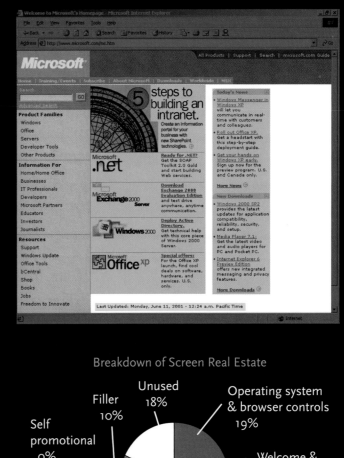

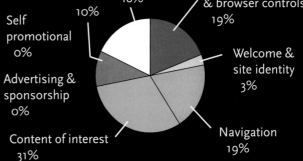

Breakdown of Screen Real Estate

- Unused 18%
- Filler 10%
- Self promotional 0%
- Advertising & sponsorship 0%
- Content of interest 31%
- Operating system & browser controls 19%
- Welcome & site identity 3%
- Navigation 19%

www.microsoft.com

Welcome to Microsoft's Homepage - Microsoft Internet Explorer

File   Edit   View   Favorites   Tools   Help

⇐ Back ▾   ⇒ ▾   ⊗   🔄   🏠 | ⬡ Search   📓 Favorites   🕒 History | 📑 ▾   🖨   📝   📄   👤

Address   🔤 http://www.microsoft.com/ms.htm   ▾   ↪ Go

Microsoft®

1   2 All Products | Support   3 Search | microsoft.com Guide

4
Home | Training/Events | Subscribe   5 About Microsoft | Downloads   6 Worldwide   7 MSN

Search

8 GO

Advanced Search

10

Product Families

Windows
Office
Servers
Developer Tools
Other Products

Information For 13

Home/Home Office
Businesses
IT Professionals
Developers
Microsoft Partners
Educators
Investors
Journalists

Resources

Support
Windows Update
Office Tools   16
bCentral   17
Shop   18
Books
Jobs
Freedom to Innovate   19

5 steps to building an intranet.

Create an information portal for your business with new SharePoint technologies. ⊕

11

Microsoft **.net**

14

Microsoft **Exchange** 2000 **Server**

Windows 2000

Microsoft **Office** XP

Ready for .NET?
Get the SOAP Toolkit 2.0 Gold and start building Web services.

Download Exchange 2000 Evaluation Edition and test drive anywhere, anytime communication.

Deploy Active Directory.
Get technical help with this core piece of Windows 2000 Server.

Special offers:
For the Office XP launch, find cool deals on software, hardware, and services. U.S. only.

12

Today's News   9

• Windows Messenger in Windows XP will let you communicate in real-time with customers and colleagues.

• Roll out Office XP. Get a headstart with this step-by-step deployment guide.

• Get your hands on Windows XP early. Sign up now for the preview program. U.S. and Canada only.

15 **More News** ⊕

New Downloads

• Windows 2000 SP2 provides the latest updates for application compatibility, reliability, security, and setup.

• Media Player 7.1: Get the latest video and audio players for PC and Pocket PC.

• Internet Explorer 6 Preview Edition offers new integrated messaging and privacy features.

More Downloads ⊕

20 Last Updated: Monday, June 11, 2001 - 12:24 a.m. Pacific Time

🔤 | 🌐 Internet

(1) The global menu looks like a banner, not navigation. Users will often overlook it because it merges with the browser borders. Compounding this problem, the tab-like graphic surrounding the main Microsoft graphic makes the menu look like background.

(2) **All Products** is a weird name for a menu. Why not just call it "Products?"

(3) Although it's good to have a search box on the page, the need for this one is probably a symptom of the difficulty users have in spotting the **Search** command in the menu bar. For those users who *do* see both searches, it will be confusing that there are two. Are they different?

(4) These screen objects do not look like menus. Their perceived affordance is purely "click me" and not "pull-down menu." It is quite startling to mouse over some of these words and have a menu appear.

(5) Conventionally, "About Us" is the last option in a navigation bar, not the middle.

(6) **Worldwide** is a vague name for a menu. It is particularly unhelpful as the name of the finder for U.S. sites and office locations.

(7) The full menu for all the different areas of **MSN** should not be here. Better to link to that site and allow users to find their way from a more fully explained homepage.

(8) **GO** should not be in all uppercase. Mixed-case "Go" is easier for users to read.

(9) These little triangles are just widgets that show off the technological prowess of developers. But what do they accomplish? Users can hide or show the lists of news and downloads, but doing so is purely a futile exercise that doesn't help users be more efficient or use the site in different ways. Now, if there were a way to customize the information shown in these areas, maybe adding widgets to manipulate it would have some use.

(10) This is one of the best-structured left-hand navigation bars on the Web. The three categories are clear and well-separated, both visually and conceptually.

(11) Very attractive abstract graphic, but it doesn't communicate anything about intranets.

(12) Inconsistent punctuation: Some headlines end with a period, some end with a colon, and some have no punctuation. Headlines don't need final punctuation. These headlines and decks should all follow a consistent style as well: Note that the deck below **Download Exchange 2000 Evaluation Edition** is a continuation of the headline, while the other two headlines are self-contained.

(13) Audience segmentation works well here because most of the categories are concrete.

(14) Since Microsoft product logos are widely known by their target audience, they serve two useful purposes: they help users to find these products quickly and they give users an immediate idea of what products the site offers when they first open the page.

(15) Good link to archived news and downloads, but there's no need for the little arrows to indicate that a link takes you someplace else.

(16) Although it's good to promote frequently used tools, such as **Windows Update** and **Office Tools** from the homepage, they should be grouped as sub-choices under the main links for **Windows** and **Office**. Users will think about them as part of those products, rather than as a generic resource.

(17) **bCentral** needs to be explained. Best to avoid made-up names. If you have them, always explain them and don't use them as navigation choices, which forces users to click them just to find out what they are.

(18) Don't have a special **Shop** link when there is a product section. The natural thing for users is to find the product first and then decide to buy it.

(19) **Freedom to Innovate** really means "Don't bother us with any pesky anti-trust regulations." This is an understandable attitude on the part of this company, but the link is misplaced, because it's not a resource but a campaign. Also, because it's placed under **Resources**, the language reflects a misleading perspective: one would expect this to be a resource to help the *user* innovate. Resources should be named after what they do for the user.

(20) Good to have the complete date and time for the latest update on this site, because Microsoft often needs to react to critical security scares. In such situations it's important for users to know whether they are getting the latest official information. Also good to use internationalized date and time formats without abbreviations.

www.mothernature.com

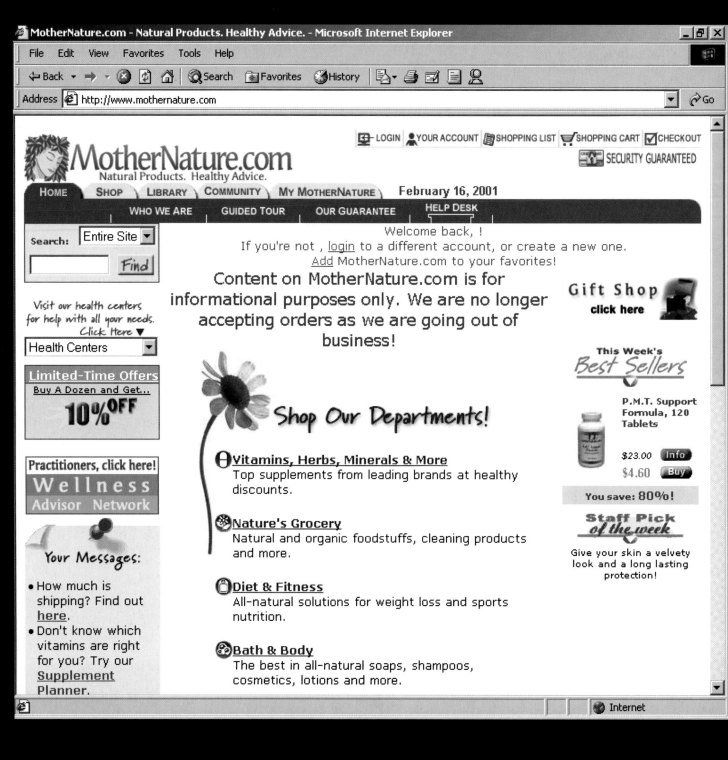

MotherNature.com sells natural products such as vitamins and health supplements, natural foods, and bath items. The site also has health and natural product content.

MotherNature.com goes overboard in trying to create a brand identity and ends up hiding that identity in unidentifiable clutter—at odds with the simple, natural products sold here. The site uses far too many fonts; it looks like the designer tried to find and use every font in nature. MotherNature.com adds to that clutter by including unnecessary trendy website features, such as a customized homepage option and a message area that, in fact, are not customized. When we reviewed it, MotherNature.com was in the process of closing down and was no longer accepting orders. Aside from one unhelpful message, the company had made no effort to remove sales and ordering information, which creates a confusing and misleading user experience.

Window Title
This title is good for bookmarking.

Tag Line
This tag line is better than most tag lines on the web; however, it could be a bit more specific because "products" could mean any number of things.

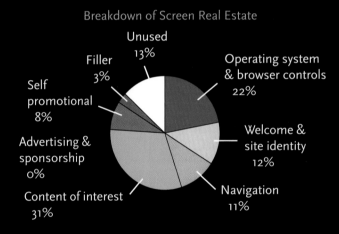

Breakdown of Screen Real Estate

Unused 13%
Filler 3%
Self promotional 8%
Advertising & sponsorship 0%
Content of interest 31%
Operating system & browser controls 22%
Welcome & site identity 12%
Navigation 11%

www.mothernature.com

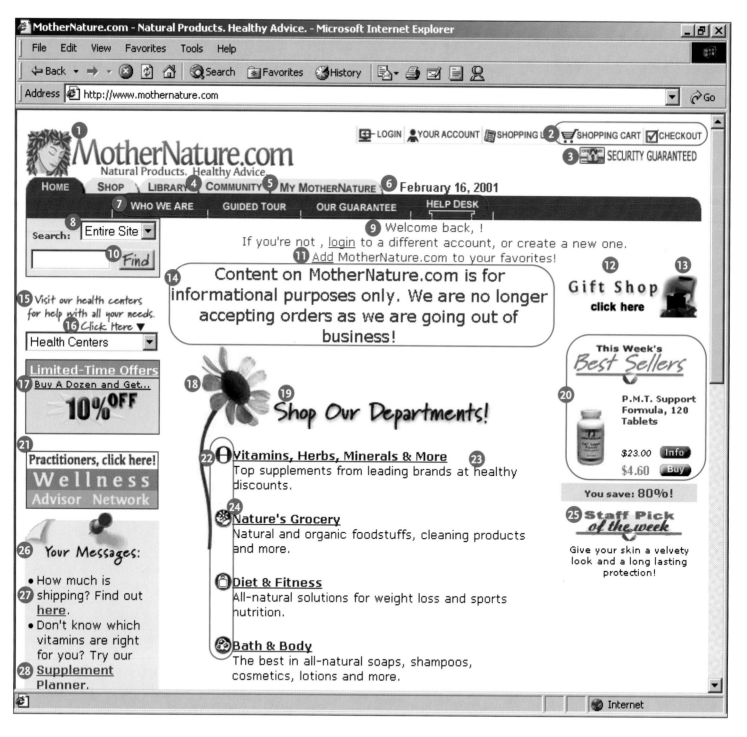

1. The logo has a clearly identifiable font and overall look. Unfortunately, because the rest of the site is cluttered with fonts, the visual impact of the logo is lost.

2. Although it's good that the shopping cart uses the standard icon and is in the expected location, it would be even better if the shopping cart showed the items inside and was integrated into every page of the site. It's good also that you can go to **Checkout** without having to go to the shopping cart.

3. The security logo is so small that it's not really useful.

4. The **Library** label is too generic to be helpful—better to tell users what type of information is here, such as "Health Information." Too, **Community** is vague Internet lingo that doesn't tell users the value of what they can do there.

5. Using separate areas for personalized content is not as good as just personalizing the homepage. Why make the user work to get this content?

6. There's no reason to show the date here.

7. **Guided Tour** and **Help Desk** should be next to each other. Does "Help Desk" mean help or customer support? Also, the desk icon doesn't help and makes the button less readable. Finally, it's hard to know what you'd get from **Our Guarantee**. If there is critical information here, it's better to elevate it to the homepage and include anything else in **Who We Are**. Finally, **Who We Are** is not as standard as "About."

8. Placement of the search box on the homepage is good, but the box is too small, which makes it hard to enter and review queries.

9. Don't say "welcome back" if you don't have the user's name. This makes a poor first impression.

10. This nonstandard **Find** button is difficult to quickly identify. The color and the font are not readable.

11. Replicating browser features has questionable value and quickly clutters a site. Also, the link **Add** is not as helpful as "Add Mothernature.com" would be.

12. Making the **Gift Shop** a separate place on the site is not as helpful as directly assigning gift-finding functionality to a tool on the homepage.

13. Whatever is pictured in the gift area is totally unrecognizable. With a picture this small, it's better to show a simple line drawing than a realistic photograph.

14. This going-out-of-business message doesn't help existing customers at all and could only confuse new visitors because the rest of the site implies that you can still make purchases. It would be better to take down the rest of the website and provide links that explain what happens with outstanding orders for existing customers only.

15. Labeling health centers and then including **Health Centers** in a pull-down menu is unnecessarily redundant. Also, the font used here is hard to read.

16. No need to explain how to use standard widgets. In any case, "click" is not a good description of what you do to a pull-down menu.

17. **Limited-Time Offers** is a worthless ad because it doesn't give enough information to entice customers to click. It's not clear what you need to buy a dozen of—this could be a link to a flower site.

18. The daisy and its cheerful direction to go shopping waste a lot of space that could be used to show products.

19. Messages encouraging users to shop at a site that is closing are confusing. It would have been much better to make some effort to clear all purchase functionality off the homepage.

20. Why is **Best Sellers** plural if only one product is featured? Too, **PMT Support Formula** should have a better explanation of what it is. Finally, it's good that the **Buy** and **Info** buttons are right next to the item rather than making the user go to the product page.

21. What type of **Practitioners** does this refer to? What is the **Wellness Advisor Network**? Does this help you network with wellness advisors or teach you how to be one?

22. Category icons are hard to see. It would be much better to show some of the products so that users could quickly scan the departments rather than have to read descriptions and interpret icons.

23. Clever word play, such as **healthy discounts**, detracts from quick readability.

24. **Nature's Grocery** is too cutesy. Other headlines are good because they precisely describe what you will find in each category.

25. Odd to use the use of **Staff Pick of the week** as a selling device if you don't explain why your staff recommends something. It would be simpler to use "Featured Products." The **Pick of the week** also doesn't give any explanation of what the product is or how much it costs. This item could be anything: a vitamin, a cream, or content.

26. **Your Messages** implies personalization that this message board doesn't offer. Too, why does the site alternate between "your" and "my" options, such as **Your Account**, **MyMotherNature**, and **Your Messages**? (See also the shopping cart and navigation bar areas.)

27. Shipping should be integrated into all prices. Users want to see prices in context; it doesn't make sense to see this from the homepage before shopping. To facilitate scanning, **shipping** should be underlined, not "here."

28. The **Supplement Planner** could be a useful tool, but it is buried in this location and is incorrectly categorized as a message.

www.mtv.com

MTV.com - Microsoft Internet Explorer

File   Edit   View   Favorites   Tools   Help

Back | Search   Favorites   History

Address   http://www.mtv.com/   Go

NEWS | MUSIC | BANDS | SHOWS | CHAT | XTRA | SHOP | E-MAIL

mtv.com

search

mtv news
updated 05.21.2001
2:13 PM EDT

Mariah Carey Gets 'Glitter'
In Her Eyes

Music Industry Giant
Vivendi Universal Buys
MP3.com

Bono's New Son Respects
Daddy's Tour Schedule

Weezer Drought Turns
Into A Flood

all headlines >>

mtv news gallery >>

Last Week to Vote
for MTV's Movie
Awards: What's
Your Pick for Best
Movie?

Join the BBMak Screening Preview
Streaming video from their latest DVD, only on MTV.com

Destiny's Child: Three The Hard Way
Ain't no stoppin' them now

Sign Up for Free MTV Mail
We'll give you a hip new e-mail address--you@mtv.com

PHOTO: EVERETT COLLECTION

Vote On *TRL* for Your Favorite Video

Catch Highlights from Laugh Out Loud Weekend

Check Out Daria's Take on Love

New Releases
From Hot Artists

Weezer
"H*** Pipe"
(Geffen)

R.E.M.
"Imitation of Life"
(Warner Bros)

Depeche Mode

mtv360

MTV

See How It
Ended on *Real
World/Road Rules
Challenge*
Tonight

MTV2

You've got the
power: Pick the
videos you
watch on Control
Freak

EP

Check out
Train's Live
Version of
"Drops of
Jupiter"

join mtv.com
> Free E-mail Account
> Free Newsletter
> Chat

radio mtv.com
MTV Radio
TRL
MTV2 Radio

Internet

Mtv.com is the online home for the popular music and entertainment cable television station.

The content on mtv.com is alienating to non-MTV fans, and understanding the site relies on insider knowledge. For most other websites, this would be considered in very poor taste. For a site that appeals to teenagers, however, this is probably part of the appeal. Users who understand the lingo are "in," and any dork who doesn't can just leave.

One thing the young don't often possess is a great deal of patience, which they'll need while waiting for the slow download of this homepage. On the positive side, the three primary organizational schemes—news, artists, and television shows—work well. This page also delivers a good deal of information without feeling overwhelming, largely because of the effective use of white space.

Window Title
   This title will bookmark appropriately in alphabetical order.

Tag Line
   Although MTV is a widely recognized name, it would still be good to have a tag line to let users know what the site is all about, in particular to define what added value the site has over the television channel.

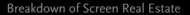

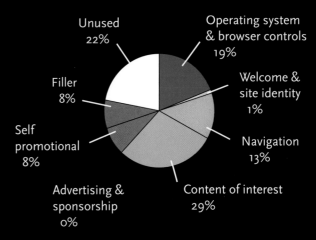

Breakdown of Screen Real Estate

Unused 22%

Operating system & browser controls 19%

Welcome & site identity 1%

Filler 8%

Self promotional 8%

Navigation 13%

Advertising & sponsorship 0%

Content of interest 29%

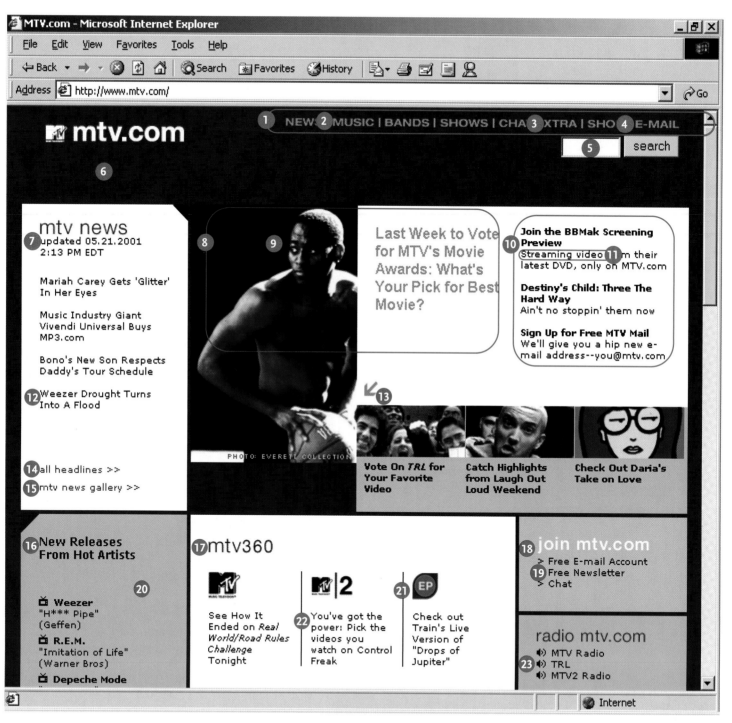

1. This navigation area fades to obscurity. Both the dark gray text and all capital letters are very hard to read.

2. Because this entire site is about music, it's confusing to have a link to music here. Better to be more specific about what aspects of music this area covers.

3. XTRA is a nondescript label. It's hard to know what you get, even once you're there. Seems like a general holding tank for leftover links.

4. E-mail is not an appropriate service for a content website to offer. Doing it well requires deep thinking on collaborative features, remote access, and other specialties that MTV likely doesn't possess. Providing free email was a big craze a few years ago, when many sites felt compelled to offer web services, even when that wasn't their specialty.

5. Although it's good to have the search box available right at the top of the page, this one is so small that it's bound to cause usability problems. Users like to be able to review and edit their queries. Also, the search button isn't aligned properly with the input box. Finally, clicking the search button pops up a new window, which is annoying and often disorients users.

6. Although this homepage uses white space fairly effectively throughout, this large black area is excessive.

7. Should use an international date format and spell out "May."

8. This related photo and headline are a bit too visually separated by white gutter space, so it's not clear that they go together.

9. This photo should have a caption because the associated headline is about the general awards, not about this particular movie.

10. If the content is not alienating enough, most users over 40 will struggle to read the tiny font size. More serious, however, is that the font size is fixed, so a visually impaired user can't adjust it to a comfortable reading size. Why discriminate against teenagers with poor vision?

11. Streaming video of a new hit from a popular artist is a great use of the multimedia aspects of the Web—you can't get that in *Rolling Stone* magazine.

12. This overly clever headline doesn't give enough information about the story. In this case, since Weezer fans have waited five years to get a new album (hence the "drought"), and now are expected to get two albums in rapid succession (the "flood") it would be better to come right out and say so.

13. This mysterious arrow points to nothing and links to even less. It looks clickable, but it's not.

14. Good to include a link to all headlines, so that users know where to go for more.

15. mtv news gallery doesn't adequately communicate the great feature that lies beneath. Although one would think this goes to photos, it actually goes to news sorted by artist. No need to include mtv in the link name, however, when you're already on MTV's site.

16. What decides who is a Hot Artist? It's not clear on this site why some artists are promoted over others. It would be good for MTV to explicitly say if they maintain editorial independence from the industry, or if placement is sponsored.

17. No need to have a title at all in this area, especially not one as obscure as mtv360. The logos for the channels suffice.

18. This whole join mtv.com area is wasted space, since users can access these items elsewhere on the page. Much better to use this space to foster real community for visitors by listing featured chat sessions and topics as they are available.

19. Links to free newsletters are not sufficiently attractive for users to junk up their mailboxes with unknown information, arriving with unknown frequency. Tell users what they'll get from the newsletter and how often it will arrive ("Get Top Music Headlines by Email Every Day").

20. This is a lot of empty space in what is potentially one of the most interesting areas for users. Also, who cares about the distributor? Better to just list more artists and titles.

21. EP is an interesting transmedia feature. When viewers see the EP logo on a music video, it means the website has extended versions of the song or more information about the artist. Why not explain this up front so users who don't know about it can discover it?

22. Although it's good to reveal content on the homepage, this description implies that the link goes straight to the Control Freak area, when in fact it goes to a general MTV2 page. Better to go to the general area from the logo and to the specific area from the link.

23. It's clear that users can click one of these to get a radio station, but how do they know what the difference is among the different stations? It would be better if users could see what the station was currently playing.

NewScientist.com is the online home of the British print magazine that chronicles science and technology news. From this website, users can read news stories online, as well as access current and archived content from the magazine's print edition. The website also features a listing of jobs in the science industry.

This is a nicely organized page that doesn't look cluttered, even though it shows a good deal of content. Strengths include revealing content by example through clear, well-cropped photos and concise headline and copy writing. A weakness is that the site is too self-conscious about its web presence, as evidenced by how it labels web material as "Online" and "Links." Users will think about the company as a whole entity and don't benefit from this separation. Although the content has been designed for online viewing, the page still needs some tweaks on link colors to make sure users can keep track of where they've been on the site. The site is in desperate need of a search feature as well as an archive of past exclusive stories so that users will have a chance to access the rich content beyond what's currently featured.

Window Title

This window title will bookmark appropriately by company name. No need to include the ".com," though, especially since the site (appropriately) added a space between **New** and **Scientist** to make the magazine name more human-readable (but different than the domain name).

Tag Line

This site doesn't have a true tag line, but the description of the print edition almost does double duty as a tag line: **Global science & technology weekly**, thus telling users what the site is all about.

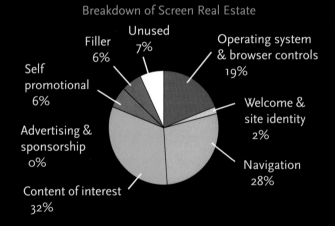

Breakdown of Screen Real Estate

- Unused 7%
- Filler 6%
- Self promotional 6%
- Operating system & browser controls 19%
- Advertising & sponsorship 0%
- Welcome & site identity 2%
- Content of interest 32%
- Navigation 28%

www.newscientist.com

1. Unfortunate choice to waste the entire top of the page with banner ads for the print magazine. Better to include the promotion in context, within the print edition section. This catches users when they are most interested and frees up more space on the main page for real content. Users ignore advertising banners, so anything that looks like a banner is a poor use of space (unless you can con some other company into wasting its advertising budget). A website's promotion also deserves better than to be hidden in a banner. The repeated **New Scientist** name detracts from the logo.

2. Two bad things about this newsletter signup. First, it looks just like a search feature. We frequently see users mistakenly enter search queries into boxes like this. Next, it tells users nothing about the content or frequency of the newsletter, but requires them to give away their private email address up front.

3. Where's search? You won't find it on the homepage or anywhere on the site. All sites of this size should offer access to site-wide search on the homepage. Some users prefer search as their primary tool for finding information, while others rely on it as a backup method when browsing and categories fail them.

4. Although it's good to differentiate the website from the print publication, no need to call this content **Latest online news**— that's a given on the Web. Better to reserve the word "online" for offline references to your website.

5. The time and date should indicate when the site was last updated, not the current time. Also, better for international readers to write out "2001," so users don't mistake this date for August first.

6. It's odd to use a city to refer to a time zone, especially for a science site. It would be better for international readers to give the time in GMT or relative to GMT (such as "GMT+1," while London observes daylight savings time).

7. No need for two links to **all the news**; the one at the bottom of the news area is enough. Also, "More News" is a more precise link name.

8. It would be good to also include a link to the cover story, rather than just offer a generic contents link.

9. Great to show the current cover for the print magazine, rather than recycle an out-of-date issue for the job.

10. Overall, these headlines and decks are well written and concise.

11. As long as all stories on the page are within the week, no need to list the date and time on the deck of each story, unless it is truly a breaking news item. The time and date at the top of the page are enough to show users that content is current. It is good, however, to list the date in the full article. Timestamps should only be used for content that is truly time-critical or can change during the day (say, stock quotes or announcements of new Nobel Prize winners).

12. This deck could convey the same message in fewer words: "Officials to decide if damaged fuel injector will delay launch."

13. Richard L. Garwin's name gets lost in this deck. Better to bold it so that it's scannable. Other than that, the deck offers an intriguing description of Dr. Garwin in a small amount of text.

14. **About us** typically describes the company relative to its website. It's best to have just one **About us** that describes the whole of the company, including the print magazine and website, but this homepage has a second one, **About newscientist.com**, at the bottom of the page (not visible in our screenshot).

15. Great to feature quirky, interesting, reader-generated content like this on the homepage. The description aptly describes **The Last Word**, while the two questions reveal content in the best way, by example.

16. Listing jobs in the science field is a great feature of the site. It would be better to use a more descriptive heading for this area though, since users could easily mistake it for a listing of jobs at New Scientist.

17. Unnecessary to say **Online** here—it's all online. It's also better for scanning to start the link with the information carrying word, "Conference."

18. Great photos illustrate some of the hot topics. However, if a topic is showcased above, it shouldn't appear in the list below, especially not in a different order. By avoiding duplication, it would have been possible to reduce the number of bulleted topics from 15 to 10 and have a more easily scanned list.

19. This photo (hamburger?) is too detailed for this size.

20. These little icons are too detailed for the available space and don't add much to clarify these opinion sections. More captivating to use the space to feature one of the interesting topics, such as one of **Feedback's** "strange but true" tales.

21. Calling a category of items "links" on the Web is not as informative as describing the content and letting the delivery method speak for itself. A more appropriate heading would be "Science Resources."

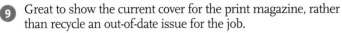

Managers face reprogramming after defeat
Robot footballers play better without a manager screaming at them from the touchline
14:23 20 August 01

Seasonal trend in abortions linked to depression
Annual peaks in voluntary abortion mirror peaks in depression and suicide, say Italian researchers
10:32 20 August 01

Which story has already been read? It's tough to tell, since the visited (top) and unvisited (bottom) link colors are so similar. Better to reserve standard blue for unvisited links and use an obviously different color for visited links, preferably a less saturated color (but not gray, which is hard to read).

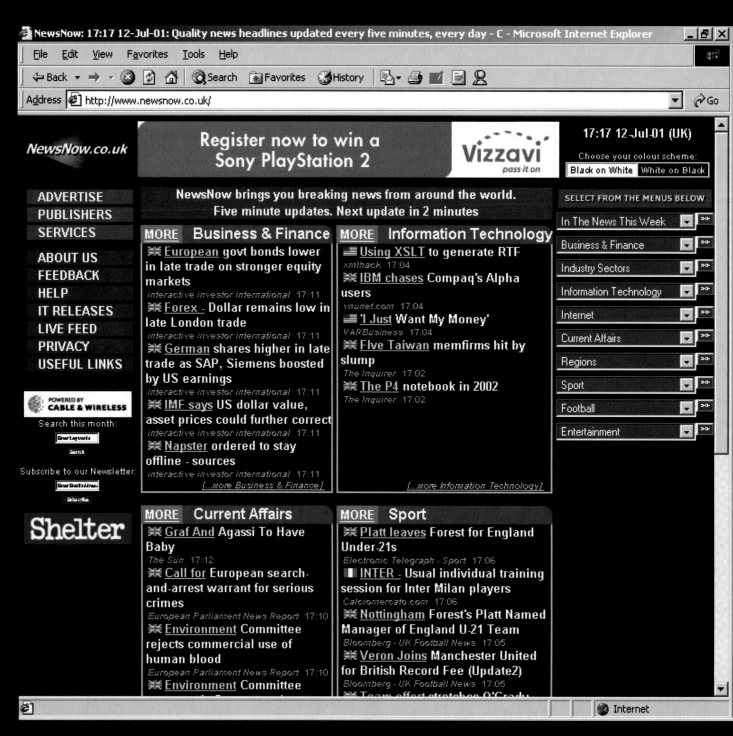

NewsNow.co.uk was the United Kingdom's first "news aggregation" company, meaning it compiles and categorizes news from sources around the world. The company claims to offer users "the widest range of quality online news sources from a single, convenient location." On this site users can see the latest headlines from 3,000 leading news sources without visiting each site separately and then read their choice of stories in full on the publishers' websites.

Although the site offers good content aggregation, the homepage is visually overwhelming. The current crowded design mirrors some of the chaos of the Web that the site is supposed to help users avoid and is actually at odds with the site's purpose. The major benefit of a site like this is that it consolidates information. But because all headline links open new browser windows, the site's most common action is to throw users back out into the big World Wide Web. The site's much touted five-minute updates similarly introduce chaos, as the site takes control of the browser and leaves users with a whole new world every five minutes. It's ironic that a site intended to let users control the Web often takes control away from users. The site suffers from many bad headlines that violate our guidelines for web writing. Ideally, the site should employ an online-savvy editor to rewrite all headlines to conform to the guidelines instead of simply repurposing headlines from sources that often employ a print writing style.

Breakdown of Screen Real Estate

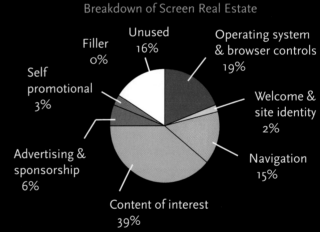

- Unused 16%
- Filler 0%
- Operating system & browser controls 19%
- Self promotional 3%
- Welcome & site identity 2%
- Advertising & sponsorship 6%
- Navigation 15%
- Content of interest 39%

Window Title

Good that the window title starts with the company name so it will bookmark appropriately. No need to put the date and time in, however—all the numbers in the middle of the text make the whole thing hard to read. Users who bookmark this site will see the date **12-Jul-01** in the Favorites/Bookmarks menu forever, making them likely believe that the page contains old news.

Tag Line

The sentences at the top of the page serve as a tag line. It would be better to edit them to one sentence. The next update time isn't really necessary, especially since the site updates so frequently. Also, **Breaking News from Around the World** isn't really a strong differentiator, considering the many other good news sites on the Internet. Aggregation and topic classification are the true strengths of this site, and the associated user benefits should be promoted in the tag line.

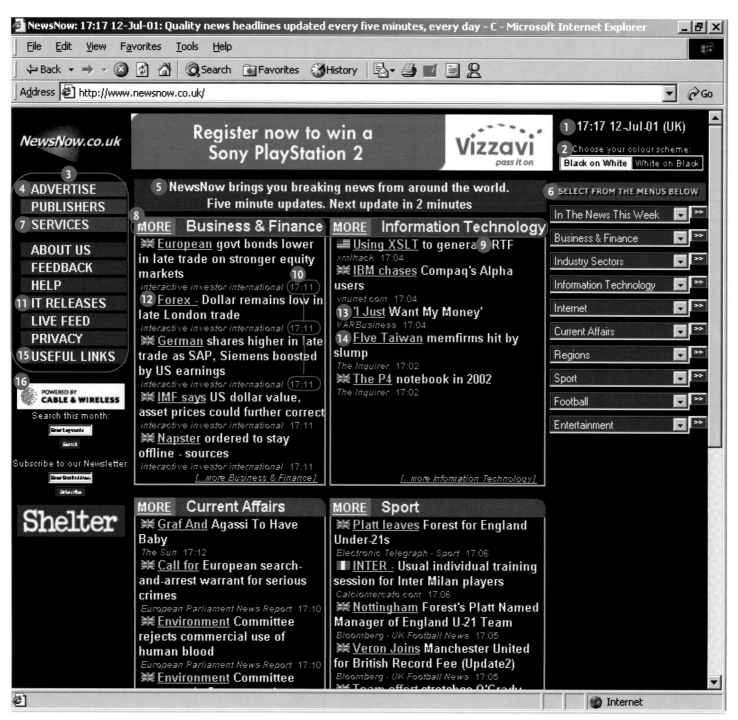

www.newsnow.co.uk

1 Need to list and label this as the time last updated here—it's not clear if this is the current or updated time. Also, better for international users to write out the year "2001" and give the time in relation to GMT (GMT +1, in this case).

2 Although it's well intentioned to offer users color choices like this, most users would rather get straight to business on websites without having to fiddle with customizing the site's design. It's likely that NewsNow offers customization for its enterprise offerings, so companies can make the site fit with their corporate look, and decided to offer it here as well. Better to offer one design that is as readable as possible for the majority of users and let users who need to modify colors further do so through their browser controls. Additional usability issues: the **Black on White** box resembles, and is in the standard location for, a search box; it also looks like it's the currently selected option because it stands out from the (black) background.

3 Because this page layout has so many big blocked groupings, it would be a nice visual relief to use simple links here instead of these big, blockish buttons. Also, mixed case is easier to read (and quieter) than all caps.

4 Making **Advertise** the topmost link on the site sends a rather disconcerting message to news seekers. It's more standard to have such links for "doing business with us" placed near the **About Us** link at the end of the navigation options.

5 Telling users when the site will update next is misleading, because this number only updates when the page updates, meaning it can promise an update in four minutes even if the update is only seconds away. Worse, the page refreshes automatically, which means that once the page is through refreshing, users must search to find what they were looking for—many headlines get replaced with new content during each update.

6 This feature lets users choose to see news stories for one content area within these major categories. That's good. The problem is, they must do so by manipulating a rather tricky UI. The dropdowns are long, and they don't allow users to see all available choices at once for a category. Also, users can choose only one content area at a time—rather inconvenient if you're interested in multiple areas. The little arrows next to the dropdown add clutter and are pretty much obsolete because they only work to go to the main categories, which are available elsewhere on the page—the items in the dropdowns link immediately when selected.

Better to integrate this feature into the main body of the page by offering it as a standard link in each category. The link could go to a page that listed all content areas, so that users could see all available choices at once.

7 Since NewsNow offers three enterprise and customized news services in addition to this website, why not list them directly on the homepage? These other services are likely where the biggest for the company lie, and promoting them to the homepage would show users up-front all that the company has to offer.

8 No need to include the link to **More** in these heading sections. First, it's redundant, because each section has a link at the bottom. Second, it makes the section heading less scannable because all sections begin with **More**, rather than with the differentiable phrase. Each section heading should be a hyperlink that leads to more articles in that category.

9 Abbreviations are okay to use in this instance, as long as they are defined in the first usage in the article. The headline would be quite unwieldy with the long versions ("eXtensible Stylesheet Language for Transformations" and "Rich Text Format").

10 Although it's good to show the time in the main body of the story, it's not helpful to display the time at the headline level, especially since the site updates so frequently and the times are so similar. Eliminating the times here would simplify the interface and give more prominence to the differentiating words in each headline.

11 Odd to have a dedicated button for **IT Releases**, which simply seems to be a topic area under information technology and thus would fit more logically in the dropdown on the right side of the page. It's also jarring to find a button that displays a filtered subset of the headlines in the middle of a set of buttons that relate to the general nature of the site (**Help**, **Feedback**, and so on).

12 **Forex** (for foreign exchange) isn't as informative or scannable as beginning the headline by telling *which* dollar is weak (presumably U.S. based on other headlines in this category).

13 This headline doesn't give enough information about the story.

14 A better headline would be "Taiwan Memory Manufacturers Hit by Slump." This would eliminate the tech jargon (**memfirms**) and begin the headline with an information-carrying phrase.

15 **Useful Links** has a collection of non-news websites that NewsNow recommends, such as Google for searching the Web. This link literally takes users off the site, as it opens a new browser window. Better to limit the tasks to what the site is really about and avoid the impulse to offer users everything on the Web.

16 Who cares who powers the site?

continues

www.newsnow.co.uk

NewsNow: 17:17 12-Jul-01: Quality news headlines updated every five minutes, every day - C - Microsoft Internet Explorer

File   Edit   View   Favorites   Tools   Help

⟵ Back ▾ ⟶ ▾ ⊗ ⟳ ⌂   Search   Favorites   History   ▾ ⊟ ✉ 📄 👤

Address   http://www.newsnow.co.uk/

Register now to win a Sony PlayStation 2

Vizzavi *pass it on*

17:17 12-Jul-01 (UK)

Choose your colour scheme:
Black on White   White on Black

NewsNow.co.uk

**NewsNow brings you breaking news from around the world.
Five minute updates. Next update in 2 minutes**

ADVERTISE
PUBLISHERS
SERVICES

ABOUT US
FEEDBACK
HELP
IT RELEASES
LIVE FEED
PRIVACY
USEFUL LINKS

POWERED BY
CABLE & WIRELESS

Search this month:
18
Search

Subscribe to our Newsletter:
22
Subscribe

Shelter

SELECT FROM THE MENUS BELOW

In The News This Week ▾ »
Business & Finance ▾ »
Industry Sectors ▾ »
Information Technology ▾ »
Internet ▾ »
Current Affairs ▾ »
Regions ▾ »
Sport ▾ »
Football ▾ »
Entertainment ▾ »

MORE Business & Finance

European govt bonds lower in late trade on stronger equity markets
interactive investor international 17:11

Forex - Dollar remains low in late London trade
interactive investor international 17:11

German shares higher in late trade as SAP, Siemens boosted by US earnings
interactive investor international 17:11

IMF says US dollar value, asset prices could further correct
interactive investor international 17:11

19 Napster ordered to st 20 offline - sources
interactive investor international 17:11

[...more Business & Finance]

MORE Information Technology

Using XSLT to generate RTF
xmlhack 17:04

IBM chases Compaq's Alpha users
vnunet.com 17:04

'I Just Want My Money'
VARBusiness 17:04

Five Taiwan memfirms hit by slump
The Inquirer 17:02

17 The P4 notebook in 2002
The Inquirer 17:02

21

23 [...more Information Technology]

MORE Current Affairs

Graf And Agassi To Have Baby
The Sun 17:12

Call for European search-and-arrest warrant for serious crimes
European Parliament News Report 17:10

Environment Committee rejects commercial use of human blood
European Parliament News Report 17:10

Environment Committee

24

MORE Sport

Platt leaves Forest for England Under-21s
Electronic Telegraph - Sport 17:06

INTER - Usual individual training session for Inter Milan players
Calciomercato.com 17:06

Nottingham Forest's Platt Named Manager of England U-21 Team
Bloomberg - UK Football News 17:05

Veron Joins Manchester United for British Record Fee (Update2)
Bloomberg - UK Football News 17:05

Team effort stretches O'Grady

Internet

17 Don't begin headlines with articles, such as "the" here. Begin instead with the key phrase, such as "P4 Notebook."

18 This search box seriously needs a redesign. First, it's too far down on the page and overshadowed by the big, white, rectangular ad above it. Better to put search at the top of the page. Second, the instruction text in the input box is unnecessary clutter—users know to type in input boxes. Better to give a link to search tips, if you have them. Third, this stacked layout isn't as clear as just showing the input box with the action button to the right of it. Fourth, the font size is much too small for readers to see what they are typing. Last, the text above the box implies that you can only search for items during the last month. It would be much better if users could specify the time parameter to search in an advanced search feature.

19 This headline is good, except for the - **sources**.

20 Good to provide the publication name for each headline, since news-loving users on this site will likely have strong preferences for certain ones. It would be nice if users could sort articles by publisher.

21 Systematically hyperlinking the first word or two of each headline doesn't help users a bit and clutters the entire site by emphasizing the wrong phrases in many cases, such as **European**, or **I Just**. It's also tricky to have only a portion of the headline link to the article. Well-written headlines should begin with an information-carrying word or phrase and contain no unnecessary verbiage. For this reason, no extra emphasis should be necessary on a headline site and the entire headline should be hyperlinked.

22 Don't ask users to blindly give away their email address for an item of unknown content or frequency. Instead, explain the value to the user and ask for the necessary information once they're interested.

23 This link to more articles is too small and too far from the list of articles. Better to keep the overall UI simpler and use the same font as the headlines, but indent it slightly to differentiate it from the headlines above it. It's good that the **more** link specifies what you get more of.

24 These flags are a clever idea, but they are likely to cause more usability problems than add value. The flags signify the country that *reported* the story, although the natural first interpretation is that they mean that the story *takes place* in that country. This gets especially confusing when the headline has a country name and the flag depicts a different country, for example, the UK flag next to the story about German shares and U.S. earnings. Since the links all show the publication name, it's not necessary to credit the country as well. The reporting country would be good to show in the full article, however.

www.pbs.org

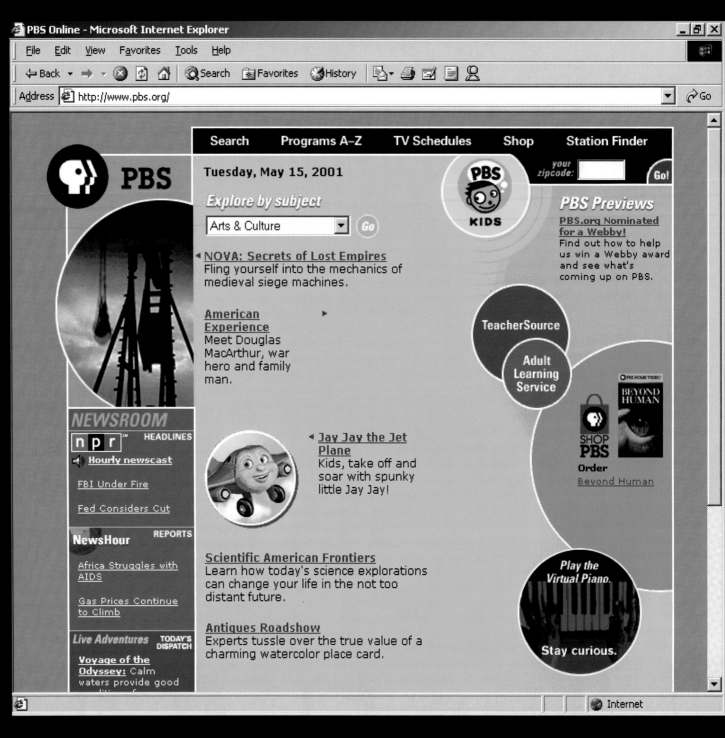

PBS.org is the online companion site to more than 450 PBS television stations. The site offers PBS programming information, educational content, and games, and it enables users to customize the site for their local PBS station. The site also sells PBS merchandise, such as videotapes of television programs.

This homepage battles form and fashion. It looks like the primary focus of the design was to get the site to match the look of PBS's television identity. Indeed, the colors and the circles are signature PBS. However, trying to retrofit user interaction design into a predefined visual design is an all too common recipe for usability problems and a shallow interpretation of branding. A company's image is about so much more than how it looks; it's about the experience that the user has with the company and what the company offers its customers. All of the overlapping circles on this site take up valuable space that could be used to communicate the programming breadth and rich community resources that PBS offers. Instead, this page is rather sparse, and makes it seem like PBS doesn't have much going on. PBS would be better off revealing more of its cool content than filling the page with cool shapes.

Window Title

This window title will bookmark appropriately. No need for the "online" though—users know they're online. Better to give a brief description of the site.

Tag Line

Although the site demonstrates a fair amount of its content by example, a tag line could be a good place to convey the *public* nature of public television.

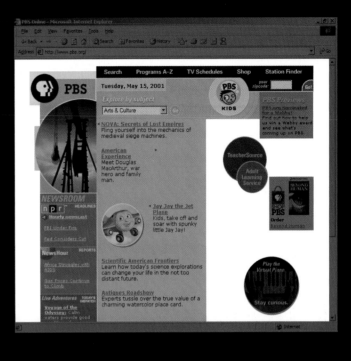

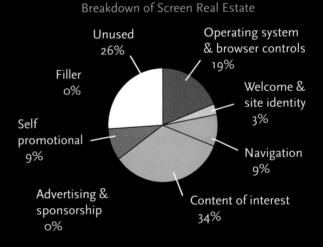

Breakdown of Screen Real Estate

- Unused 26%
- Operating system & browser controls 19%
- Filler 0%
- Welcome & site identity 3%
- Self promotional 9%
- Navigation 9%
- Advertising & sponsorship 0%
- Content of interest 34%

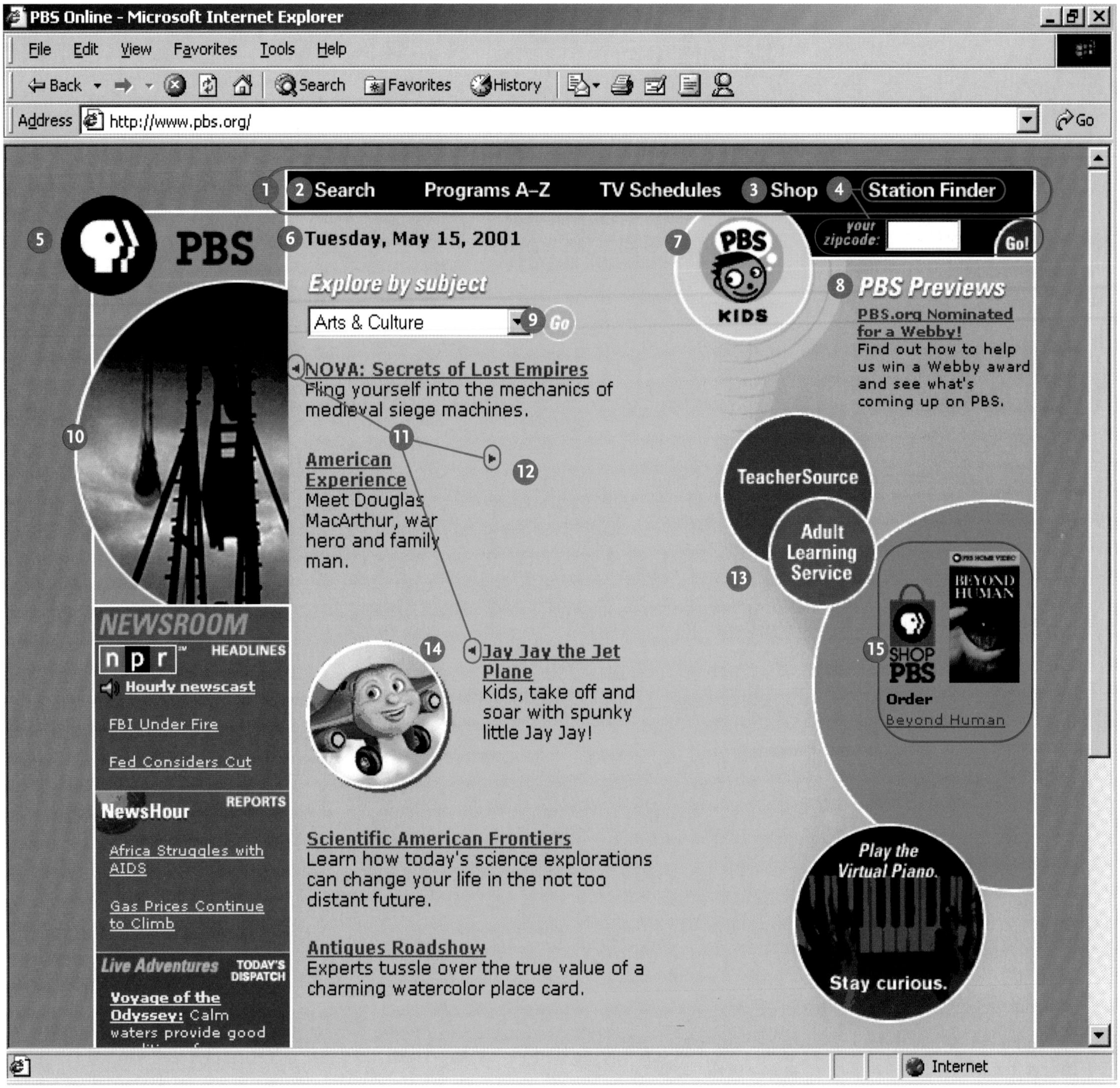

1 This navigation area has some design problems that, while not showstoppers, will likely lessen the usability of it. First, the links don't look particularly clickable. It would help if they were underlined or had some type of vertical separator, so they looked like separate, clickable elements. Second, the **PBS Kids** bubble and the **zipcode** text box keep this area from having a standard rectangular navigation bar shape. What will probably save this weak design are the very straightforward navigation choices, which clearly relate to expected top tasks on the site, such as **Programs A-Z** and **TV Schedules**. Also, because the rest of the page is relatively sparse, users will probably take more notice of this area with its identifiable words.

2 To be easily visible; **Search** should have a text box on the home page. **Search** is especially invisible on this homepage, where there are two elements that look like search boxes on the page (**Explore by Subject** and **Station Finder**).

3 **Shop** is not as clear as "Shop PBS" or "PBS Store" would be. This would let users know that the shop sells PBS merchandise and isn't just the increasingly common generic link to partner special offers.

4 The **Station Finder** is a nice feature that helps users customize the site to contain information for their local PBS station. The UI for the **Station Finder** needs some improvement. The three elements (title, search box, and **Go** button) aren't visually connected. It would be better if all three elements had a different color treatment or a border to group them. The nonstandard **Go** button is oddly shaped, probably to match the circle design on the rest of the site, and too far from the input box. A simple go or search button would be clearer.

5 Good to use the same, classic PBS logo that viewers are used to seeing on television. This instantly identifies the site as PBS.

6 Because this site has time-sensitive content, it's good to show the date; however, it should clearly indicate that this is the date (and time) that the site was last updated. This helps users know how current the news is.

7 While most kids who watch PBS programming will recognize the **PBS Kids** logo, it's not immediately clear that it's clickable. It would be better to crop the logo a bit, and have some links to PBS Kids content.

8 **PBS Previews** is a misleading title for this area of the screen. In fact, the area on the left side of the screen has all the programming previews. The only story here is a plea to get users to support PBS for an award, with a quick mention that you can also see "what's coming up" on PBS. This title also doesn't look clickable. It's formatted in the same style as **Explore by subject** on the left, which isn't clickable.

9 This **Go** button's color isn't noticeable enough—there should be much more contrast with the background color.

10 This graphic, although large, is blurry and doesn't do much to illustrate the Nova story. If this graphic were not here, the **Newsroom** area could feature a few more stories, with short descriptions.

11 These little arrows are more confusing than helpful. It appears they point to graphics associated with the text, but they're so small they're difficult to see. The one next to **American Experience** is so far away from it that it wouldn't effectively connect anything with the headline. Better to eliminate the arrows and use good labels and descriptions, and place graphics close enough to the relevant text to make their interdependence clear.

12 Looks like a graphic for **American Experience** was missing here.

13 Although these large circles match the visual design PBS uses on TV, they aren't an effective navigation design for the Web. They look more decorative than functional (they don't look clickable), and the wasted space is more than a visual detail. Because the circles can fit only a few words, PBS misses the chance to educate users about the breadth of its services. While a teacher might experiment and click **TeacherSource**, those non-teachers who might not won't learn about this valuable community service. It's better to use simple links and give more description. **TeacherSource** and **Adult Learning Service** are programs that PBS proudly offers and explains elsewhere on the site, but this design makes them look like ads or afterthoughts.

14 This area for **Jay Jay the Jet Plane** makes better use of text and graphics to show content than other parts of this homepage. It's the one example where the homepage uses the circle-shaped graphic well—it offers the user a peek at the program with a picture that is clearly intended for children. It's also good that the link identifies the program name. Because it looks like Jay Jay is suited for young children, the description could probably skip the **Kids** introduction (kids will click on the picture) and could instead give parents a quick description of what educational angle the show supports.

15 Although it's good to show the video box and title that you can order from PBS, it would be nice to have a brief description of the video as well. It's important when featuring a specific item like this to also offer a link to the broader category of items; however, the **Shop PBS** logo doesn't serve this purpose well. It adds too much visual clutter and it's not clear whether **Shop PBS** is separate from the specific video—if you click it, will it take you to that video or a general store? (It does the latter). Better to use a simple link, such as "More Videos."

continues

www.pbs.org

PBS Online - Microsoft Internet Explorer

File   Edit   View   Favorites   Tools   Help

Back   •   →   •   ⊗   ⟳   ⌂ | ⊗ Search   ⊞ Favorites   ⟳ History | ⧉ •   ⊕   ⊠   ⊟   ⊗

Address http://www.pbs.org/   ⬇   ⤳ Go

Search   Programs A–Z   TV Schedules   Shop   Station Finder

PBS

Tuesday, May 15, 2001

PBS KIDS

your zipcode: [   ] Go!

Explore by subject

[Arts & Culture ▼] Go

PBS Previews

PBS.org Nominated for a Webby!
Find out how to help us win a Webby award and see what's coming up on PBS.

◀ **NOVA: Secrets of Lost Empires**
Fling yourself into the mechanics of medieval siege machines.

American Experience
Meet Douglas MacArthur, war hero and family man.   ▶

TeacherSource

Adult Learning Service

PBS HOME VIDEO

BEYOND HUMAN

SHOP PBS

NEWSROOM   **(16)**

n p r   **HEADLINES**

(17) 🔊 **Hourly newscast**

FBI Under Fire

Fed Considers Cut

(18)

NewsHour   REPORTS

Africa Struggles with AIDS

Gas Prices Continue to Climb

◀ **Jay Jay the Jet Plane**
Kids, take off and soar with spunky little Jay Jay!

Order
Beyond Human

(19)
Scientific American Frontiers **(20)**
Learn how today's science (explorations) can change your life in the not too distant future.

(21) *Play the Virtual Piano.*

Stay curious.

Live Adventures   TODAY'S DISPATCH

Voyage of the Odyssey: Calm waters provide good

Antiques Roadshow
Experts tussle over the true value of a charming watercolor place card.

Internet

16 It's not clear that you need to click **Headlines** and **Reports** to see more of them than the two listed in each section. Both of these words look like part of the section heading, not links. The page then breaks this convention with **Today's Dispatch**, which is not clickable. Better to either underline headings like this so that users know they can click them, or include links to "More Headlines," "More Reports," and so forth.

17 Good to include this icon to show that this link goes to an audio file. It's important to indicate if a link is going to go to anything other than another web page, so users don't get startled by a new medium.

18 It's unclear what the difference in types of stories is between the **npr Headlines** and **NewsHour** reports. If a user is looking for a particular news story, how does he know whether to look in **npr** or **NewsHour** first? This is also a surprisingly small number of headlines for a network that offers a fair amount of news coverage.

19 Either or both of these stories are good candidates for a small illustration, such as a photo of the antique described in the **Antiques Roadshow.**

20 It would be better to give an example of one type of exploration and one of the effects it would have, instead of teasing users with this general description.

21 Neither the picture nor the text helps users know what to expect from this section. Does this refer to a PBS program? Can you actually play a virtual piano here? Or is it just helpful advice?

www.petsmart.com

Petsmart.com is an online pet supply and product site. The site offers advice and information about pet issues, such as selecting, feeding, behavior, and health. The site also provides information about the physical Petsmart chain of pet stores.

Petsmart.com's biggest strength is that it shows examples of the products and content offered on the site. Market segmentation is more appropriate and more easily defined on this homepage than it is on many other sites that try to segment customer groups. Whereas many people don't know whether they are a "home office" or a "small business" user, people can easily tell whether their pet is a dog or a cat. The **Search**, however, does some additional scoping that likely will confuse users. Although the site is fairly clean-looking overall, some formatting and style inconsistencies detract from its professional look.

Window Title

It's good that this window title begins with the site name. The text that follows doesn't really tell users much. How is this "smarter" shopping?

Tag Line

Although this site doesn't have a tag line, the large featured special, as well as the other content shown on the homepage, makes it pretty clear that this is a place for pet supplies. Even so, a tagline that describes what you can do here and why this site is better than the competition would be helpful.

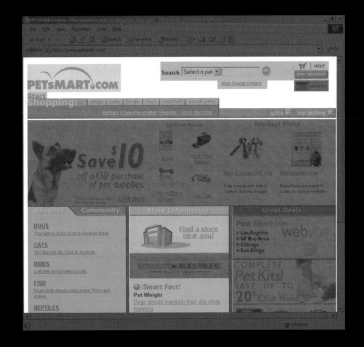

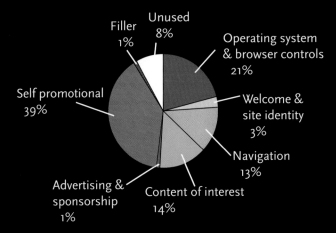

Breakdown of Screen Real Estate

www.petsmart.com

1 Although it's good that the site has **Search** on the homepage, this implementation is a bit confusing. First, it's not clear which actions are required. The dropdown default instruction makes it seem that you must select a pet—in fact you don't need to. On the other hand, you must enter a search term to get any results, although there is no indication of this. Second, it seems you can successfully enter anything in **Search**, since there are no instructions or limits explained. Actually you can only enter product search information. You must go to **More Search Options** to search for articles or advice. Last, there is no way to search the entire site. It is very misleading to scope **Search** without telling users how you are limiting their results.

2 This entire area is one graphic and only has ALT text for **your account,** leaving the shopping cart and help unlabeled. The shopping cart icon alone without text is not as recognizable as a link, though it does help that the site uses the "standard" Amazon.com two-wheeled cart.

3 Who cares if **Visa** is welcomed? Does this mean that other credit cards are not? Ads like this can confuse users and aren't beneficial to them. This ad should at least link to information about why users should use Visa and a general credit card policy.

4 These navigation options aren't well integrated—this area looks cluttered because its three sections (tabs, links under tabs, and the graphical buttons on the right) look very different from one another and aren't easily differentiated. If the tabs are for shopping, why aren't **gifts** and **top sellers** there as well? Why are reorders in a different place?

5 Petsmart likely used this drop-shadow font to call attention to this area. Unfortunately, the font reduces visibility because the white shadow makes it look blurry, and there isn't enough contrast between the font color and the background color.

6 This small white font on a red background is difficult to read.

7 **Banfield** is an obscure link name that assumes too much Petsmart knowledge on the part of the customer. Although some users will know that this is Petsmart's pet hospital and health insurance provider, many will not. Better to be more straightforward and call it "Pet Hospital and Health Insurance."

8 **Register** and **Quick Re-Order** should be grouped next to **your account** and the shopping cart.

9 These icons look out of place and inconsistent with the other navigation links on this page. An image of an item from **gifts** and **top sellers**, with a link to more items, would make these links more intriguing.

10 Why clutter the interface with different font sizes for these similar section headings?

11 It's good to show a pet photo to help users feel instantly oriented. However, since the site serves several categories of pets, it would be good to show a few types of animals. Otherwise users might think this site is only for dogs.

12 While it's good that these featured products have photos and descriptions, it would be better to list prices as well. Users *always* want to know the price—it's nice not to make them dig for it.

13 Featuring this rather unusual but interesting product is great, but it would be better to use a more specific link name. It's not clear what type of emergency the kit helps. Also, because the kit is for saving unweaned kittens, providing the delivery time is critical. If you really need the kit, it's probably best to buy it at the brick-and-mortar store.

14 **Click here** isn't necessary—just link from the offer itself.

15 These don't look like standard tabs, so users might not know to click on them. To make matters worse, the **Store Information** and **Great Deals** section headings to the right of these headings are not clickable. Also, these tabs look completely different from the tabs at the top of the page. Sites shouldn't have two different implementations of the same UI device.

16 **Answers** is a rather vague name for this collection of articles, especially since none of the links are written in a question/answer format.

17 One would expect that these links to pet categories would bring up answers for that type of pet. Instead, they take you to the generic category page for that pet type. It's not good to suddenly take users from specific to more general information.

18 Why are these two generic articles about **Be Kind to Animals Week** featured specifically in the **Dogs** and **Cats** sections?

19 Exclamation marks add unnecessary urgency to these headings and hit the user like a too-loud voice.

20 This promotion for Webvan doesn't communicate either of two major user benefits: getting Petsmart orders delivered along with grocery orders, and $25 off of a Webvan order if the order includes pet food. Instead, it implies that users can get fast delivery of their Petsmart orders in only four cities—leaving users to wonder if delivery is even available in other cities.

21 This is a strange title, unless it goes into a chat area, which it doesn't.

continues

www.petsmart.com

22 It's not clear why these items are listed under **Store Information**. In fact, this entire section could be a simple link to the store finder.

23 This promotion for **Pet Kits** doesn't explain what they are. Better to take out the gratuitous picture of the lady and the cat and show a product photo of the items that come in a pet kit, along with the price and retail value.

24 This homepage uses inconsistent capitalization, which detracts from a professional appearance and adds clutter. For example, the links under **Dogs** and **Cats** use initial caps, but the links under **Birds** and **Fish** use sentence-style capitalization.

25 The word **Read** is extraneous here; the title would be more scannable without it.

26 It's great to feature a pet facts section and to list the tip on the homepage. However, this particular tip doesn't lead to any specific information on the topic. Instead the link goes to an article on general travel tips for cats and dogs. It's important to ensure that links adequately reflect the content they lead to, or users can become disoriented. Also, the subtitle **Pet Weight** is unnecessary.

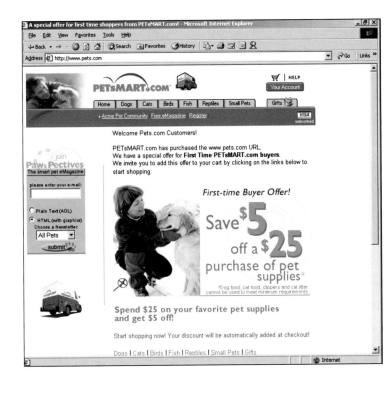

This homepage shows how Petsmart nicely handled the acquisition of another pet supply company's URL, Pets.com. Rather than just redirecting users to Petsmart.com, Petsmart explained the acquisition and gave first-time buyers a discount at Petsmart.com. This not only gave users an incentive to give their business to the new company, it eased them into the transition.

Note: The special offer shown here is a lesser value than the special offer featured on the Petsmart site. However, these screenshots were taken at different times. The Pets.com URL later offered the same incentive (save $10 off a $30 purchase).

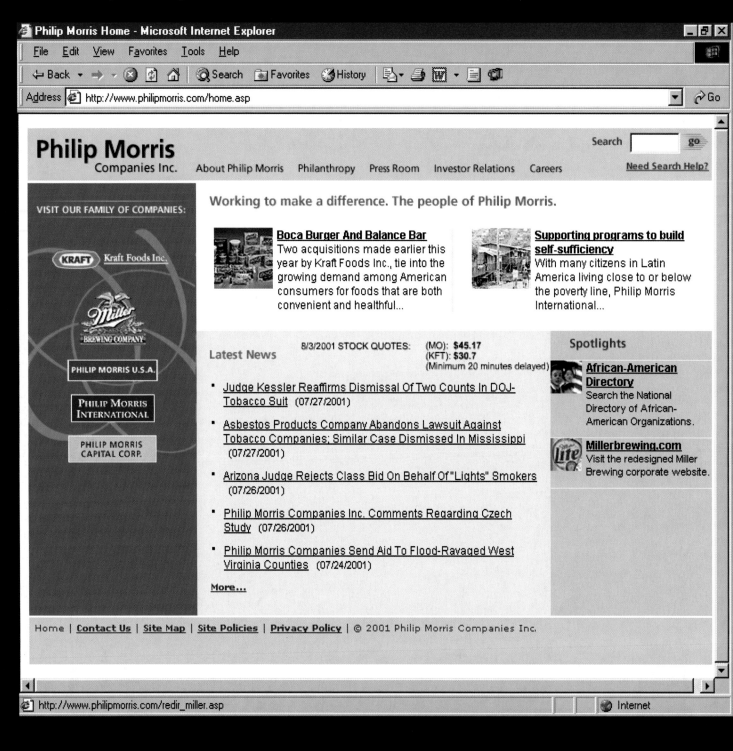

www.philipmorris.com

The Philip Morris family of companies is the largest and most profitable producer and marketer of consumer packaged goods in the world. The company's total 2000 operating revenues exceeded $80 billion. Some of the Phillip Morris companies include Kraft Foods, Miller Brewing Company, Philip Morris USA, and Philip Morris International. The Philip Morris Companies, Inc. website points users to the websites of the individual companies and provides corporate news and information.

This is a well-organized and clean homepage—in fact, it's almost too clean. Like many homepages, the interesting story is in what's *not* on the page. This page includes a fair amount of content, yet much more of it's devoted to detailing good deeds and intentions than to detailing what the company actually produces. Granted, this is a tough task for all conglomerates, because their product lines span many different categories. It's interesting to note how greatly Philip Morris' public relation efforts outweigh its desire to inform about its products—there is only one news item that deals with an actual product line, but there are multiple (and just about an equal number of) items devoted to ongoing litigation and philanthropic activities.

Window Title

Good that the window title starts with the company name so that it will bookmark alphabetically, but no need to include the word **Home**.

Tag Line

This site has an animated tag line area that flashes between **Working to make a difference. The people of Philip Morris** (as shown) and **Makers of the world's finest products**. These platitudes tell more about Philip Morris' desired positioning than they inform users about what the company does.

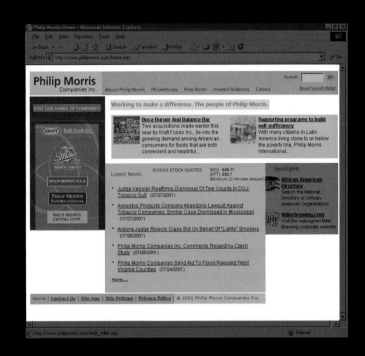

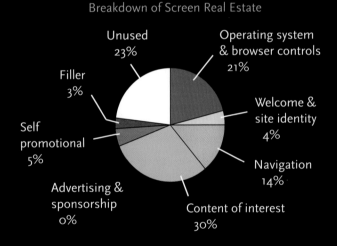

Breakdown of Screen Real Estate

- Unused 23%
- Operating system & browser controls 21%
- Filler 3%
- Welcome & site identity 4%
- Self promotional 5%
- Navigation 14%
- Advertising & sponsorship 0%
- Content of interest 30%

www.philipmorris.com

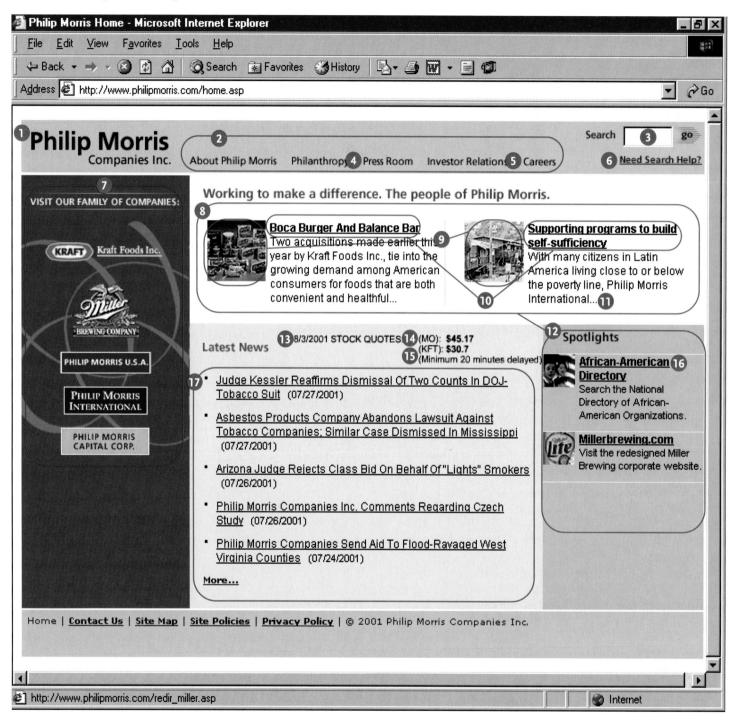

1 This logo links to the homepage, which is fine for other pages, but shouldn't happen here. Don't provide active links to the current page.

2 Good to have all corporate information in one place on the page.

3 It's good to have a search input box on the homepage, but this one is far too small for users to be able to review and edit their search entries. Many average queries wouldn't fit here—the box can just fit the word "tobacco," but nothing more.

4 Good to have a clearly visible and separate link for the press from the homepage.

5 **Careers** is not as direct or standard as "Employment" or "Jobs at Phillip Morris."

6 Good to keep **Search** simple and have an option to go to help or advanced search. "Search Tips" would be a better link name. Users are more attracted to "Tips" than the dreaded "H" word (help), and this name would better represent the advanced search features that users can access from this point.

7 Although it's good to show recognizable logos of the companies that make up the Philip Morris conglomeration, this area takes up a large amount of space relative to the amount of information available. If you're not familiar with what these companies do, it seems like you have to go to their sites to find out. In fact, if you hover your mouse pointer over the logo, you get a description of the company in a popup, but nothing indicates that this is so. Better to simplify the visual design of this area by removing the background graphic and adding a brief description of each company next to its logo.

8 Philip Morris has skillfully used this area to showcase its activities in two areas: product innovation (left) and philanthropic contributions (right). Featuring content to support a message is good, but without a link to other specific content, it's easy to give users too narrow a view of your product line. It seems suspicious that a company known for cigarettes, beer, and macaroni and cheese touts only health food and help for the homeless. In addition, this area updates randomly each time the homepage reloads and displays different stories. While it can be a good idea to rotate content, it's disorienting to do so this frequently and without providing links to the other content. If users comes back to the site to check on a particular story, there's no way to access it and no explanation of where it went.

9 These photos are too detailed for the display size. Better to use simpler, close-up images.

10 The **Boca Burger** and **Supporting programs** headings use inconsistent capitalization styles—capitalization should be consistent throughout the homepage.

11 The trailing ellipsis makes this deck into too much of a teaser. Philip Morris does *what* to help poor Latin Americans? Even though there are only 4–5 short lines available, it should be possible to write a better deck that summarizes the article and helps users decide whether they want to read it. In contrast, the **Boca Burger And Balance Bar** deck is fairly good at telling the highlights of the story in the available space.

12 It's not clear what the difference is between the featured stories on the top and those featured in **Spotlights**. After a good deal of digging on the site, we found a repository of the stories from the top area. The Boca Burger/Balance Bar story was in a **Business News** category; the Latin American self-sufficiency story was in a category called **Initiatives**. If the homepage listed these categories, it would help to differentiate them from **Spotlights**, as well as help explain their relevance to Philip Morris.

13 It's better to spell out the month, so that dates make sense for international users—this is especially true for a company with as much worldwide influence as Philip Morris.

14 These stock quotes don't give enough relevant information and should link to a full quote. It's best to spell out the stock name if it's not completely obvious from the abbreviation, as is the case with **MO**. Also, the selling price isn't very meaningful unless it's combined with the percentage change in the price.

15 Although it's good to acknowledge a delay in the quote price, giving users a minimum delay time isn't very helpful, let alone reassuring. Such time-sensitive material needs a time last updated stamp instead.

16 This unexplained link to the African-American Directory seems like a site non sequitur or, from a cynical perspective, like a shameless ploy to position the company as a good citizen. The page that follows this link explains that Philip Morris offers this online directory as a service and to show its commitment to equal opportunity efforts. Better to explain this up front. Regardless, it defies any stretch of the imagination to think that a user looking for an African-American organization would do so by going to the Philip Morris homepage, so the link is completely useless and a waste of prime real estate on a major corporate homepage. If the company wants to highlight its commitment to equal opportunity efforts, a better way of doing so would be to run a feature story about some of its own employees, or to run a story on how the company supported the development of the directory and what was learned in the process.

17 Because all these are press releases, rather than outside news stories, it would be more accurate to call them that.

continues

www.philipmorris.com

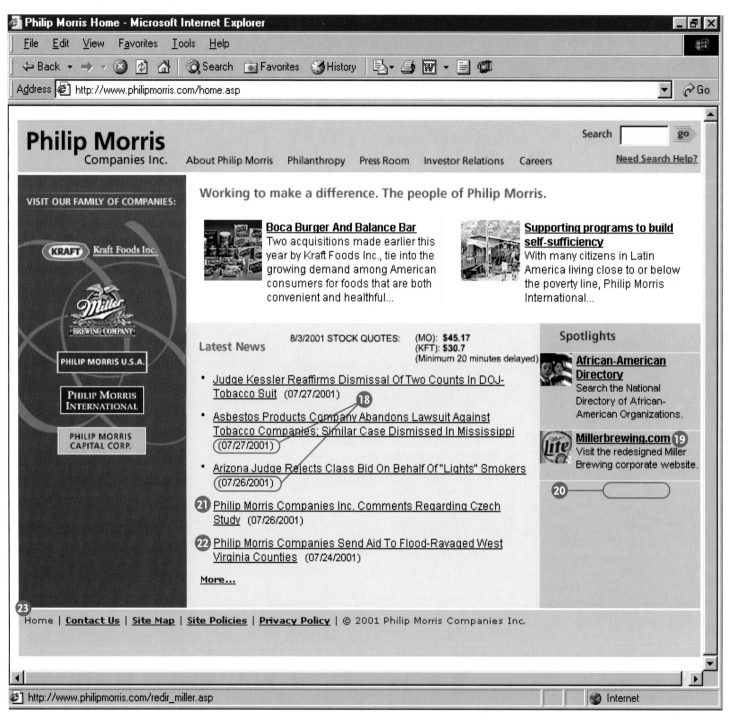

18 The dates in this news area often add a full line to these stories without adding much value, since all of the items occur within one week of each other. Dates would be more helpful on a site with infrequent news pieces. Although it's good to give the dates in the full story and the archive area, recent corporate news like this can probably go without the dates, as long as the content is updated regularly.

19 While the site redesign might be big news within the walls of Miller Brewing Company, it's not interesting on its own from a user's perspective. Rather than give users a general update on your site release, offer them specific examples of benefits they'll get from the new design, such as new content areas.

20 Need to provide a link to past spotlights so users have a way to find stories they've seen on previous visits.

21 This headline doesn't tell anything about the release that follows. Including the company name is a waste of space (all of these stories come from Philip Morris) and doesn't tell anything about what the "Czech Study" is. This is probably by design, because the study was a PR nightmare for Philip Morris and this press release was necessary cleanup. It would be truly good PR for Philip Morris to build credibility by honestly acknowledging and taking responsibility for this incident—they do so in the full story, but better to do so here.

22 Good to have a link to additional news stories. It would be better to give this link a more specific name, such as "News Archives."

23 Good that this **Home** link isn't active on the homepage. However, this is a rather unexpected and out of the way place for the link—typically Home links are in the upper-left corner.

www.planetrx.com

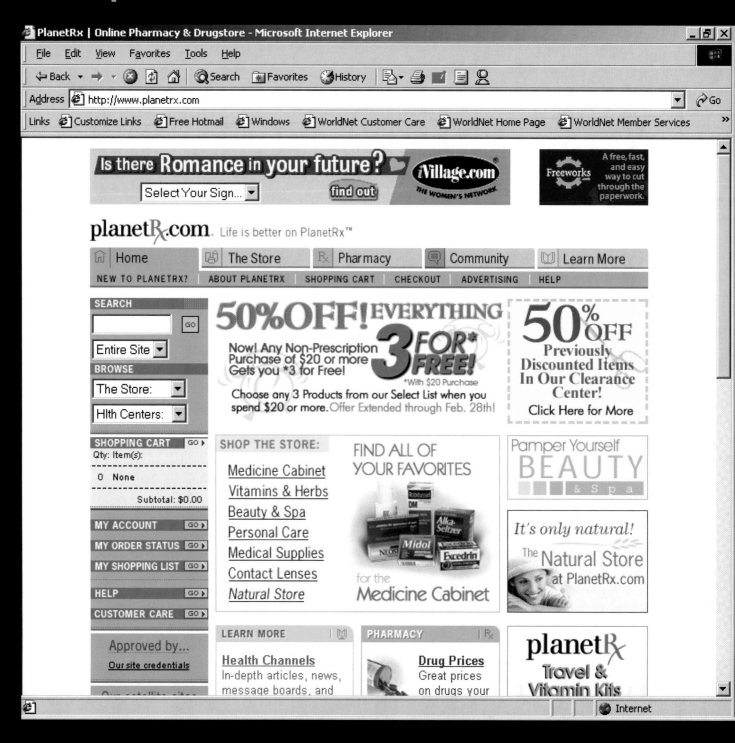

PlanetRx.com is an online pharmacy that offers prescription and nonprescription drugs, beauty and healthcare items, and medical supplies. PlanetRx also offers information, advice, and community forums on medical and healthcare issues.

The PlanetRx homepage is busy and difficult to scan. Much of the page is wasted on large graphics that don't provide enough information to clearly convey what the site has to offer. PlanetRx crowds its home-page with ads for in-store specials, but it doesn't show very many of its products. Although drugstores are imminently scannable, PlanetRx keeps its inventory a secret from the customers, leaving them guessing at the meaning and value behind vaguely defined departments, such as **Natural Store**. It seems as though PlanetRx tried to directly copy the rather unhelpful department names from a brick-and-mortar drugstore, but it neglects to give users a peek down the aisles so that they can find the right place.

Window Title
This title is good for bookmarking purposes because it begins with the company name and includes a description. This clear description of PlanetRx would make a great tag line for the site.

Tag Line
This cheerfully banal tag line doesn't explain anything about PlanetRx.

Breakdown of Screen Real Estate

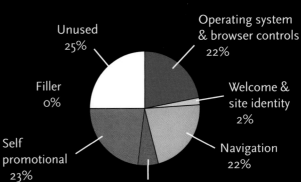

Unused
25%

Operating system
& browser controls
22%

Filler
0%

Welcome &
site identity
2%

Self
promotional
23%

Navigation
22%

Advertising &
sponsorship
6%

Content of interest
0%

www.planetrx.com

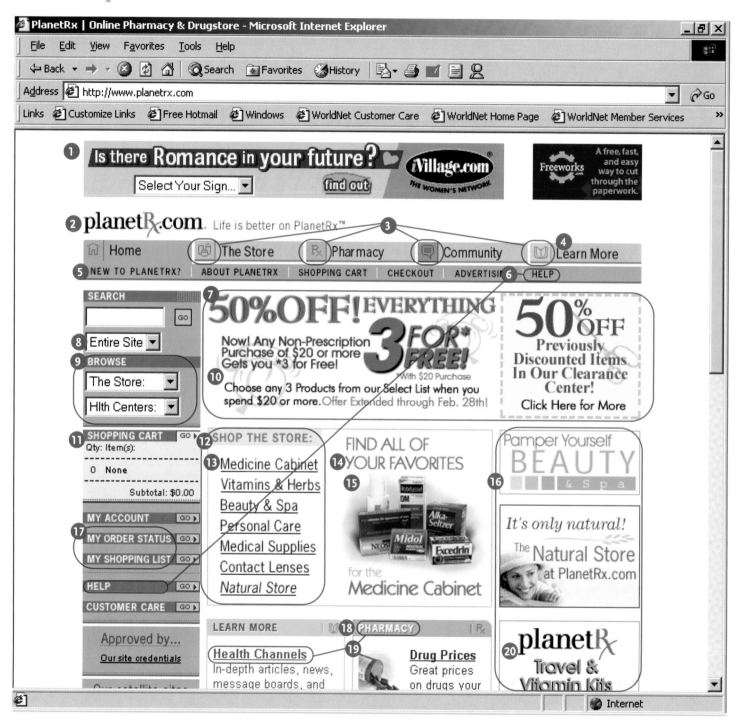

1 Not only does this banner area monopolize the homepage, but this particular ad seems like the tag line for PlanetRx, a romance site.

2 This logo is too small relative to the large ad banner above it. If you must include an ad banner, make sure that it doesn't supersede your site's identity and message, as happens here.

3 These color-coded site areas aren't obvious enough because the site uses so much color everywhere else.

4 The option **Learn More** is vague and seems redundant with **About PlanetRx** and **New to PlanetRx?**. A better title would be "Health Topics."

5 This **New to PlanetRx?** link goes to a hodgepodge of information, much of which is appropriate for all users, not just new users, and should be in **About PlanetRx**. Any information that new users must have to use the site should be featured in the middle of the page, not hidden behind an unnoticeable link.

6 Why are there two **Help** options? The link in the upper-right corner is in the more standard location and thus is preferable over the **Help** option in the lower-left corner.

7 This entire promotional area is confusing. Is the sale 50% off, three for free, or both? What is the difference between these two 50% off discounts? What does the * refer to? Presumably, this asterisk refers to the note below it about products available from a **Select List**, but this is unclear. It would be much better to show some of the items featured in the special.

8 It's good that the scoped search defaults to search the entire site. Users often get confused when they unknowingly end up searching limited areas of sites.

9 These browsing options are unnecessary on the homepage. Homepages should show—not hide—content, as these drop-down menus do. These long dropdown menus repeat the department names already featured on the page and are unwieldy for users to manipulate.

10 This alarm clock watermark adds no value, and it further clutters an already cluttered area.

11 This **Shopping Cart** shows an appropriate and helpful level of detail. It's good that it updates when users add items to the cart. However, the oddly worded default values of **0** and **None** detract from the otherwise clear presentation. It would be better to simply say "Nothing in cart."

12 It's difficult to differentiate among these store departments. What is the difference between **Beauty & Spa** and **Personal Care**? Where would you go to buy shampoo? What about facial soap? Why is **Natural Store** in italics?

13 This use of **Medicine Cabinet** is too metaphorical, and it is not sufficiently different from **Medical Supplies**. Where exactly do you buy a bandage on this site? "Medications" would be a better word choice. This category should be listed next to **Medical Supplies**.

14 **Find All of Your Favorites** puts undue emphasis on the task of "finding" on the site, making it sound like users will have to work to find what they want here.

15 This graphic could be very helpful because it shows actual products, but it's wasted because it doesn't clearly convey what **Medicine Cabinet** contains. In fact, it adds to the confusion between **Medicine Cabinet** and **Medical Supplies** because it shows Neosporin, used for first aid, which falls in the Medical Supplies category. Better to feature fewer products in the photo, and make sure they clearly represent the category.

16 These promotions for PlanetRx departments serve no user purpose, but merely show redundant information in an unhelpful way and add to the general clutter and advertising noise on this homepage. PlanetRx would be better off allocating this space to show more detail of what's in the departments. This woman pictured doesn't show users what's in the **Natural Store**; it would be much better to see pictures of some of the items.

17 It's good to have all of these shopping-related items next to the **Shopping Cart**, but what is the meaning of **My Account**, compared to **My Order Status**? My Account contains profile information about the user that is probably more meaningful to PlanetRx's marketing department than to the end user.

18 Although it makes sense to give **Pharmacy** its own area, it doesn't make sense to give it such a low-priority position on the page, since it's one of the major components of the business.

19 The **Health Channels** and **Pharmacy** promise some actual content; it's unfortunate that these are below the fold on 800×600.

20 Why does the site logo appear here, and why is it larger than the logo in the upper-left corner?

www.redherring.com

RedHerring.com offers news, analysis, and commentary about the technology business. Users can read RedHerring's columns online or register to have them sent to their email account. RedHerring also offers pre-IPO and IPO tracking, investment advice and strategies, and a report series on the business of technology.

RedHerring's official **About RedHerring.com** section describes the site as having "unmatched depth of analysis and insider perspective" and says, "RedHerring.com explains how technology business news and events affect you." This might very well be true, but the homepage doesn't effectively convey these messages. The homepage instead tries to show how cutting edge it is by being "edgy." This shallow interpretation of trendsetting only calls into question the validity of the real content that lies behind all the cleverness.

First, the site gets caught up in gimmicks that tie in the company name with other fishy titles. It focuses too much on incorporating the fish theme and not enough on straightforward, meaningful titles that help users find the content. Second, the homepage doesn't communicate the "insider perspective" the site offers. Because many of the columnists are in fact industry insiders, it would be more effective to market these areas as perspectives and explicitly state which perspective you get in which column (Wall Street broker, venture capitalist, or CEO, for example). Last, this homepage is overloaded with internal promotions—better to have confidence in the useful content and let it sell itself.

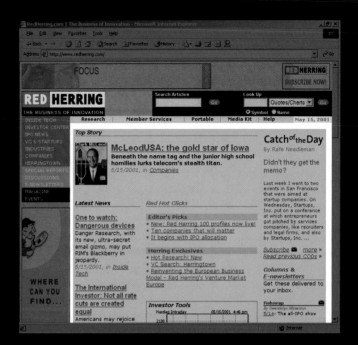

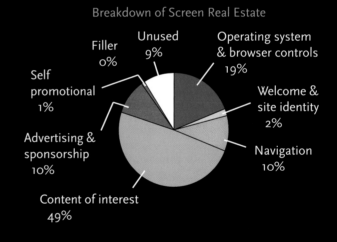

Breakdown of Screen Real Estate

- Filler 0%
- Unused 9%
- Operating system & browser controls 19%
- Self promotional 1%
- Welcome & site identity 2%
- Advertising & sponsorship 10%
- Navigation 10%
- Content of interest 49%

Window Title

This title will bookmark well, both because it alphabetizes appropriately and because it repeats the tag line, which reminds users about the site's purpose.

Tag Line

This simple tag line works fairly well for this site, although **The Business of Innovation** is less precise than "The Business of Technology," which is how the company describes itself in the **About RedHerring.com** section of the site.

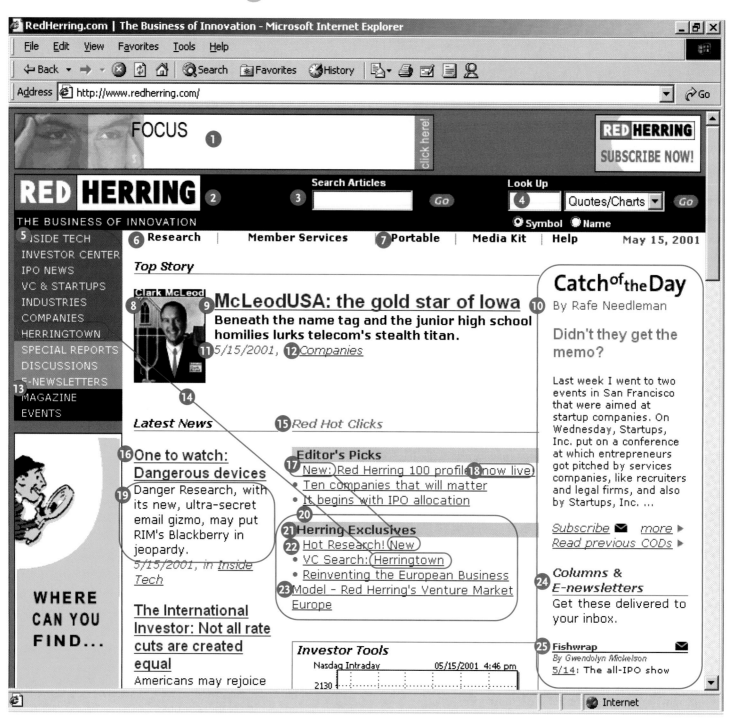

1 This homepage is swamped with ads, most of which are internal ads for Red Herring. Many of the ads are animated, which creates a chaotic and distracting experience and undermines the business nature of the site. Because users come to the site for content, give them as much of it as possible—don't waste their time telling them how great a site is that they've already chosen to visit.

2 This logo shouldn't be clickable—pages shouldn't link to themselves.

3 Good that **Search** has an input box on the homepage and that it labels what is being searched (**Articles**). However, a limited search like this likely means users can't search for features of the site, such as customer support services. In fact, the site has a separate **Search** in the customer support area, but many users struggle when the search function is scoped on the homepage.

4 "Stock Lookup" would be a clearer label for the first input box. Also, the input box's width is fine for stock symbols, but would be too small if the user were entering a company name.

5 These content categories are not easily differentiated from one another and have some overlap. For example, what are the differences between **Investor Center**, **IPO News**, and **VC & Startups**? Are **Companies** all non-startup companies? Where do you look if you're thinking of investing in a pre-IPO startup? **Inside Tech**, **Investor Center**, or **VC & Startups**?

6 **Research** is a confusing label. Users might think they can research companies from this area. In fact, this is where users can buy Red Herring reports. Better to just call it "Reports."

7 It's great that the site offers a special version of the site for mobile devices—so good, in fact, that it's probably worth giving this a more descriptive title, such as "Portable Edition."

8 It's good that this photograph includes the person's name. It would be easier to read, however, if it were a small caption below the photo, rather than integrated into the graphic. Also, changing the caption from a graphic to real text would make it possible for visually impaired users to enlarge the characters as much as needed.

9 No need to use a bold font in the deck. The larger headline and the photo give this story sufficient emphasis without it.

10 It's a great idea to produce a column that begins on the homepage. However, it's important to craft this initial part of the article carefully so that it conveys enough information to lure people into clicking for more. The headline, for example, likely relates well to the entire story, but doesn't convey much information about or relate to the visible part of the story.

11 As long as these stories are current and the homepage has a date, why repeat the dates for these top stories?

12 This link to the broader category (**Companies**) could potentially confuse users by taking them from a specific story to a more general area of the site. Better if users can just click on the story and see it displayed in the context of, or with cross-references to, the appropriate site section. It would be good, however, to provide a link to past top stories in this area.

13 It's not clear why these different areas of the navigation bar have different background colors. In fact, the light gray looks like it is a highlighted selection, which is not the case.

14 **Herringtown** doesn't give users a clue about what this part of the site contains, and there's no need for redundant navigation to it. In fact, **Herringtown** has a database that matches investors and companies—likely very interesting to its users, but hidden under this gimmicky name.

15 Not only is **Red Hot Clicks** a rather silly heading, but it's not necessary to have a heading here at all. The headings that follow are more precise and are fine on their own.

16 **One to Watch** should be smaller because it is not part of the headline itself. Users should start scanning this story with **Dangerous Devices**.

17 If you're going to mark content as "new," use a consistent means to do so. It's doubtful there's any value in doing so here. Because the content updates daily anyway, one would assume everything here is new. Generally, it is best to facilitate scanning by starting with an information-carrying term.

18 It's enough to say that this area is new—**now live!** is overkill. The combination of the exclamation point and the unnecessary words takes away from the professional credibility of the information.

19 Excellent deck that summarizes an interesting article with a minimal word count.

20 Inconsistent capitalization in these headlines—other headlines on this page use sentence-style capitalization—this section uses initial uppercase letters.

21 It would be better to use the full name of the company, rather than just **Herring**. The company name is quirky enough—it's better to use it consistently and keep users oriented than to start throwing nicknames at them as well.

22 This link is uninformative and rather bizarre. What **Hot Research** does it refer to? Providing one insightful research result with a link to more would be much more compelling than vague enthusiasm. Hyperlinks should give users enough information to know where they're going when they click them.

23 This headline is too long and doesn't wrap well enough to be easily scannable.

24 This text doesn't successfully connect the **Columns and E-Newsletters** heading with the links below it (starting with **Fishwrap**). In fact, because the heading is a link, it looks at first like the heading and this sentence are all there is to this section. Better to cut this sentence and just include a "Subscribe" option for each of the columns.

25 **Fishwrap** truly takes the herring theme too far. This column name doesn't differentiate this column from the others the site offers in any meaningful way.

www.slussers.com

This corporate homepage for Slusser's Green Thumb, Inc. explains the company's commercial and highway landscaping services, such as seeding, sodding, erosion control, and landscape design. Users can submit requests for bidding and pricing from the site. Users can also see prices, photos, and descriptions of Slusser's used landscaping equipment that is for sale.

Slusser's homepage needs some infrastructure and landscaping help. This page uses too many separate navigation areas for a relatively simple body of content. It would be best to settle on one main navigation area, with a clear grouping of corporate information in one place. The current design underutilizes the main body of the page, loads it with too many styles of over-formatted text, and too many words without enough information. It would be much better to simply describe Slusser's services and then show some before-and-after pictures to convey the company's value by example, instead of by hype. For aesthetics, weed out most of the font styles and consistently apply a small set of style and formatting standards.

Window Title

It's good that this window title begins with the company name and includes a straightforward description of what they do. One minor suggestion for clarity: Move the word "landscaping" to the end, because it applies to both commercial and heavy highway.

Tag Line

Transforming landscapes and heavy-highway into beauty is better than many tag lines, but still not as straightforward as the window title. Probably better for Slusser's to reserve the word "landscape" for verb usage, so it's clear what they add to the land.

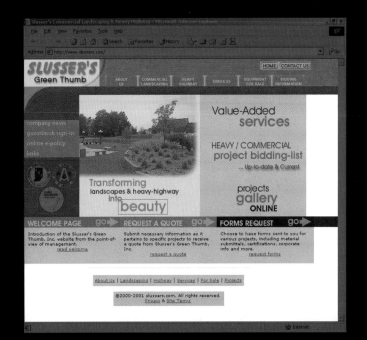

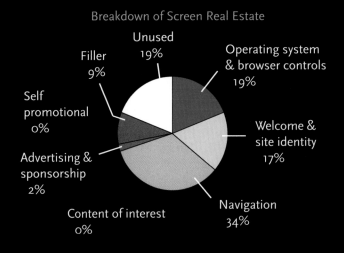

Breakdown of Screen Real Estate

- Unused 19%
- Operating system & browser controls 19%
- Welcome & site identity 17%
- Navigation 34%
- Content of interest 0%
- Advertising & sponsorship 2%
- Self promotional 0%
- Filler 9%

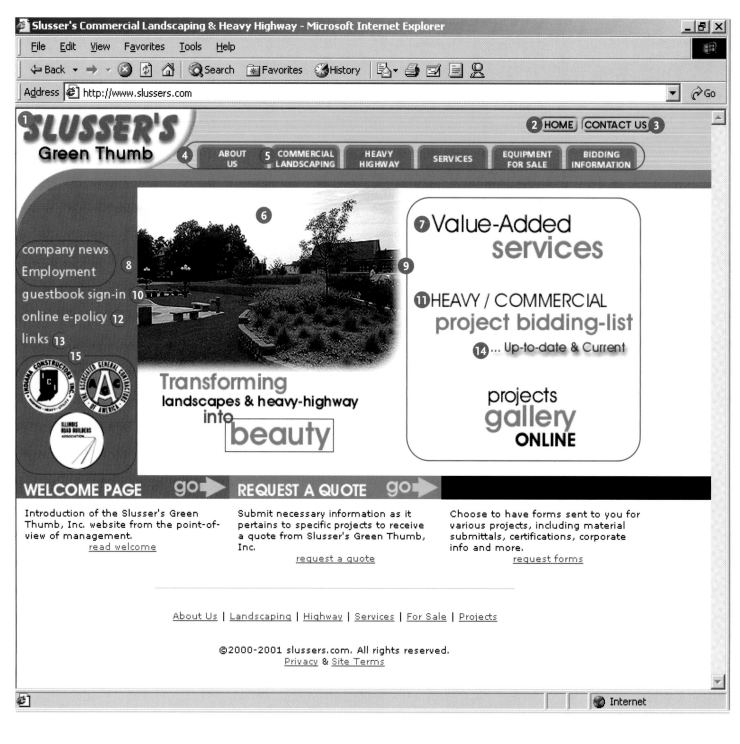

www.slussers.com

1 It's not clear at first that **Green Thumb** is part of the company name—it looks like a tag line. It would be better to use the same font for both parts of the name to visually unify them.

2 There's no reason to separate the link to **Home** from other main navigation—it's better to keep similar information, such as navigation options, together so users know where to look for it. Also, this **Home** button shouldn't be active on the homepage.

3 **Contact Us** should be grouped with and formatted in the same way as the other standard company information (**About Us**, **Employment**, and **company news**).

4 Tabs add complexity to this fairly simple site and repeat navigation items that are already available in the main body of the page. On the positive side, these tabs have clear, straightforward labels. Better to remove the tabs and consolidate the navigation to one area of the page, but retain the good, simple labels.

5 The ALT text for this tab is "Comm. Landscaping." Imagine this text read aloud by a screen reader, and you will realize why abbreviations are rarely a good idea in ALT text.

6 It's good to feature a relevant photo like this photo of some of Slusser's work. It would be better to label it with a caption, or ALT text at a minimum, to explain that this is an actual project and not just stock photography.

7 Although landscaping *is* a value-added service, calling it that just adds complexity and makes this seem more like a marketing pitch than a link to a description of services. Because the company's services fall into a few simple categories (seeding, sodding, landscaping, and erosion), it might be possible to list them on the homepage so that users could get a good idea of what the company does. If that list is too long, one simple link to "Products and Services" would suffice.

8 Need to use consistent capitalization rules throughout the site. Right now it's a hodgepodge of different styles, from all lowercase, to sentence capitalization, to mixed uppercase and lowercase within the same phrase. Not only does such inconsistency add visual clutter to the page, but also users often perceive it as careless and unprofessional.

9 These three links are a great example of how fancy font formatting can make links look less clickable and reduce their importance relative to other items on the page. These items don't look any different from the marketing slogan to the left of them—and they don't look particularly clickable. They also don't tell users anything, but do take up a lot of space to deliver a navigation phrase. It would be much more powerful to use simple links and then use the recaptured real estate to show some before-and-after examples of Slusser's services.

10 This **guestbook sign-in** is really a way for Slusser's to gather potential customer information and offers no value to the user. Guestbooks are usually seen on amateurish personal sites and don't belong on a business website. Better to be honest about asking for customer data and explain the outcome. For example, "Sign Up to Receive More Information about Slusser's."

11 Odd punctuation and capitalization and awkward, wordy phrasing make this link difficult to read. As far as we can tell (because this goes to a password protected part of the site), this link is for subcontractors who want to see a list of projects available for bidding. It's confusing that this link is sandwiched between two links intended for customers. Better to clearly separate links intended for different user groups. One possibility is to link to an "Information for Subcontractors" page, or just simplify this link to "Projects Available for Bidding."

12 No, it's not a poorly named link to a privacy policy—**online e-policy** goes to Slusser's internal corporate policy that warns employees about the appropriate and inappropriate use of company computer resources, including email, Internet, and other network services. Like most such policies, it contains warnings about how such computer use is monitored and how viewing certain content, such as pornography, is strictly prohibited. This information belongs only on Slusser's intranet—not on the public site. The impact on customers could be severe, in this case. It's not clear that the document is for employees only. A novice Internet user might think that Slusser's is monitoring his or her email and Internet usage, and leave immediately.

13 This category should be called something more specific, such as "Resources," since it goes to a list of websites related to transportation and landscaping.

14 There should be no need to indicate that the bidding list is up-to-date, because the assumption for a professionally managed business site is that all information is current. However, depending on how often new projects are put up for bidding, it might be useful to indicate when the bidding list was last updated. This would allow potential subcontractors to see whether the content has changed since their last visit to the site.

15 These logos are too small and detailed to be legible. They also look like they belong to the title **links** above them. These logos should be explained with a heading like "Membership Affiliations," and each should link to the group's website, if it has one. Also, these logos should not appear in a navigation area, but in a place on the main body of the page where they complement, instead of detract from, the main content.

continues

www.slussers.com

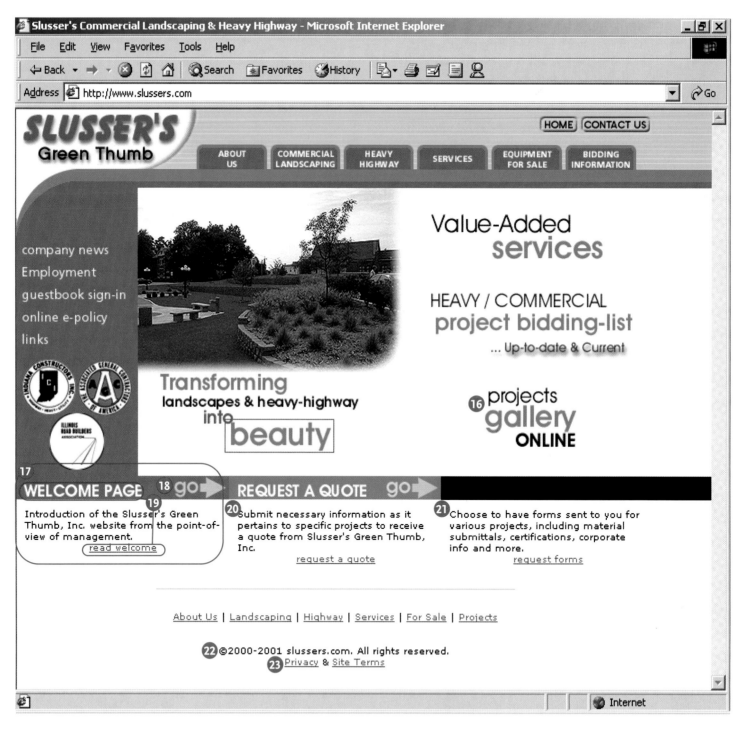

16 The **projects gallery online**, which shows photos of Slusser's work, should be incorporated with, or at least placed next to, the link to services. If the homepage featured a few photos from the gallery, this link could be replaced by a simple link underneath them to "More Project Photos."

17 It's not necessary to welcome users to your website, but it's especially unnecessary to do so anywhere but the homepage. The homepage *is* the place to introduce users to your site— give users any critical information up front. Also, no need to provide descriptions for simple links. Here the description borders on parody and seems like fodder for Dilbert—there's no value in attributing content to the generic "point-of-view of management."

18 Even though the color coding indicates what **go** button belongs to what headline, the placement of the arrow makes it seem like this **go** button is more closely associated with the **Request a Quote** headline.

19 Don't provide redundant links, especially right next to each other. They clutter the screen and confuse users. There's no need for the graphically intense strip of links on the **Welcome** bar. The links don't look particularly clickable, all uppercase letters aren't as readable as mixed case, and the arrows connect these three separate links in a misleading way—they look like they are steps in a process or have a hierarchical relationship. Better to just stick with simple links and add a brief explanation of **request forms**.

20 This description does nothing to clarify the simple **Request a Quote** link—it merely takes up space and complicates the uncomplicated. Any time you feel the urge to include the phrase "as it pertains to" on a web page, stop and yell for an editor.

21 This description of the forms request needs a rewrite. Currently the emphasis is on "Choose to have forms sent to you" (sounds dreadful), with no explanation of the service or its benefits. Is this for existing customers who need documentation of completed work? Or is Slusser's providing a resource area where users can download or request local and state government forms relating to landscaping?

22 The company is referred to under three names: **Slusser's Green Thumb**, **Slusser's Green Thumb, Inc.**, and **slussers.com**. Elsewhere on the site, the abbreviated name, **Slusser's** is used as well. It would be preferable to have as few variations on the name as possible, and one obvious candidate for elimination is slussers.com. It would be just as good to state that the site is copyright by Slusser's Green Thumb, Inc. In fact, it would be better because it would avoid an artificial distinction between the company and its website.

23 These links don't go to a privacy policy or site terms. Like the link to **online e-policy**, both go to Slusser's policies for employees regarding use of company computer resources.

www.southwest.com

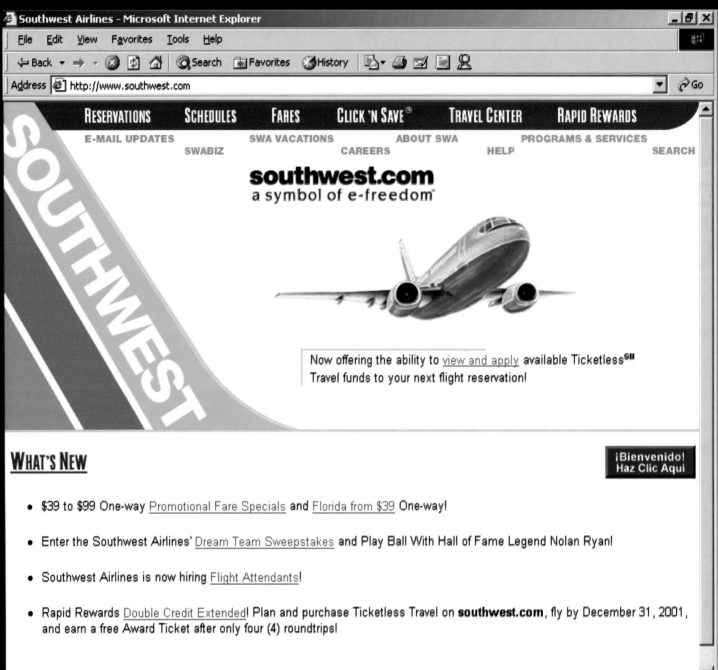

Southwest.com is the corporate homepage and e-commerce site for Southwest Airlines. Users can learn about Southwest, reserve and purchase airline tickets, and check air schedules and fares at this site.

This homepage successfully incorporates the Southwest look for customers familiar with the airline. It has a fairly clean appearance and doesn't overwhelm users with too many options. On the other hand, a downside to the site is that users have to click down to access what is probably the most frequent task—finding and/or purchasing a flight. It would be nice if Southwest included a simple tool for this on the homepage, as many airline sites do. Other good candidates for homepage tools would be one to check a flight's status and one to access a frequent-flier account summary. Another improvement area for Southwest would be to better communicate its value proposition over other airlines on the site. Southwest has long positioned itself as a low-fare airline, but this message doesn't come through on the homepage.

Window Title
This window title will bookmark in the appropriate alphabetical order.

Tag Line
A symbol of e-freedom could mean many things, but is not easily connected with an airline site. Better to simply tell what makes Southwest and its website different from the rest.

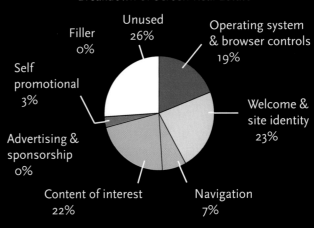

Breakdown of Screen Real Estate

Filler 0%
Unused 26%
Operating system & browser controls 19%
Self promotional 3%
Welcome & site identity 23%
Advertising & sponsorship 0%
Content of interest 22%
Navigation 7%

www.southwest.com

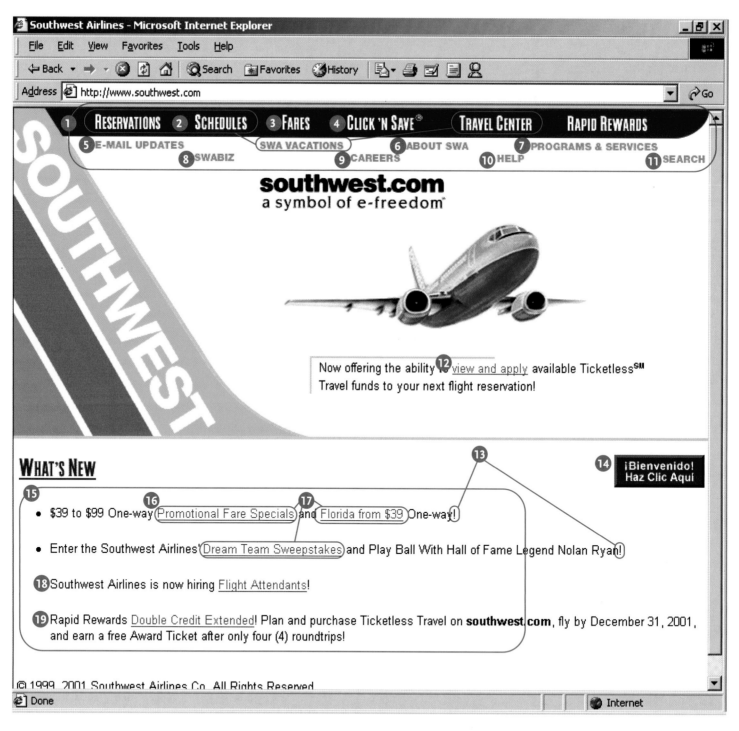

1 The difference between these two navigation rows is not completely clear. At first glance, it seems like the top row is for travel-related tasks, whereas the second row goes to pages about Southwest Airlines, such as **About SWA**. However, this isn't consistently implemented. Why isn't **SWA Vacations** or **SWABIZ** part of the first line?

2 To book a flight on Southwest, do you go to **Reservations**, **Schedules**, **SWA Vacations**, or **Travel Center**? These choices have some overlap and ambiguity. Is **Reservations** the place to *make* reservations, or make *changes to* them? Can't you book flights directly from the schedule, or must you go to another part of the site? It would be better to word these in a task-oriented way, or to at least differentiate the choices.

3 Separating **Fares** from the links that let you book a ticket, such as **Reservations** and **Travel Center**, doesn't make sense from a user's perspective. Southwest offers many fare types for each trip, but nearly all are contingent on availability. Although this link delivers some useful information about the rules governing fare types for a chosen combination of cities, it doesn't directly help users search for them. It would be great if users could choose a fare special, and have Southwest search for available seats at that fare close to the user's desired travel times.

4 It's not clear from the name what **Click 'N Save** means. When we checked it, the page just told us that Click 'N Save offers were expired for the week; it didn't describe it. **Click 'N Save** is actually, a list of weekly Internet specials—why not just say so?

5 **E-Mail Updates** is an unclear and unappealing option. Users have quickly become overwhelmed by and resistant to blithely signing up for emails from companies they patronize. Because this service is part of the Click 'N Save service, no need to give a separate homepage link for it. Better to explain the value of this service within the **Click 'N Save** section and give users a chance to sign up or manage their membership there.

6 This site frequently abbreviates the company name to **SWA** in navigation links. If you're going to use initials, use them in one instance with the full name spelled out—a good place to do this on this page would be in one of the logo areas.

7 **Programs & Services** is a vague label that implies comprehensive information, doesn't deliver. When we checked, this seemingly broad category contained only four unrelated "programs," which ranged from special deals on flights a to a means of getting rush shipment of tickets. If this category usually has only a few items, it's better to reconsider the information architecture than offer users this type of "miscellaneous" category.

8 It takes a few clicks to find out what **SWABIZ** means. Avoid made-up words if possible; if not, define them up front. All the more reason to cut to the chase in this case, since **SWABIZ** is Southwest's attempt to cater to business travelers, who are even more likely to want to get on with the transaction and not waste time puzzling over cutesy marketing terms.

9 **Careers** isn't as direct as "Employment" or "Jobs at Southwest."

10 **Help** is typically found on the far right, rather than toward the center of the page, as it is here.

11 **Search** should have an input box. Users now expect this and often overlook text links to search functions.

12 **View and apply** isn't a meaningful hyperlink—it would be better in this case to make "Ticketless Travel Funds" the link and then define the term and program when the user clicks it. More importantly, when you spotlight a new feature such as this, it's critical to continue offering access to the information once you have stopped featuring it. When we returned to this homepage, this link was no longer there, and there was no clear way on the homepage to access ticketless travel credits.

13 Avoid exclamation marks in business writing—they don't come across as professional and seem like you're yelling at the user. Also, when you emphasize every sentence by ending it in an exclamation point nothing gets emphasis.

14 While Southwest, like many companies, doesn't offer a translated or localized (to Spanish, in this case) version of the site, it's great that it addresses the needs of Spanish-speaking customers. This button leads to a letter in Spanish that gives a phone number for reservations assistance in Spanish from Southwest. Because users often have "banner blindness" even for small boxed-off text areas, however, we recommend linking to the letter from the main navigation area with a simple link, such as "Reservaciones en Español."

15 Inconsistent capitalization in these headlines—some use initial caps and some use sentence capitalization. Although these inconsistencies may seem petty, they make the UI look busy. Users often notice such inconsistencies and feel less confident about the website as a whole.

16 The difference between different discounted fares, such as **Promotional Fare Specials** and **Click 'N Save** is unclear. Better to have a single entry point for special price fares, which led to a description and listing of all available fares by city.

17 These hyperlinks are effective because they convey the content of what lies beneath in a simple, clear way.

18 This enthusiastic message is rather humorous, if read literally. It sounds as if Southwest finally caved in and decided to include flight attendants in the price of its famously low-priced tickets. Was Southwest self-service before? Also, it's odd that the link is merely **Flight Attendants**, as if you'll get a definition of a flight attendant here. It's important to phrase your links as clearly as possible to avoid confusion. A better headline would be something like, "Southwest Has Job Openings for Flight Attendant."

19 This headline is difficult to read. It's randomly riddled with capital letters ("Award Ticket") and no need to explain the word four (4).

www.ticketmaster.com

File   Edit   View   Favorites   Tools   Help

⇐ Back   ⇒   ⊗   ⊚   ⌂ | ⊙ Search   ⊞ Favorites   ⊙ History | ⊟▾   ⊜   ⊠   ⊟   ⊠

Address ⊜ http://www.ticketmaster.com   ▾   ⟳ Go

Thank you for visiting ticketmaster.com. Use of this site is subject to the express **terms and conditions**.
By continuing past this page, you expressly agree to be bound by those terms and conditions
which prohibit commercial use of this site.

ticketmaster.com

Privacy | Help | Check My Order

••••● **SEARCH**   ◉ **EVENTS** or ○ **VENUES** for   [   ]   **GO**

ticketmaster.com Card of Choice — AMERICAN EXPRESS Cards

browse by **STATE** or **VENUE**   •   check **TICKET ALERT**   •   go to **MY ACCOUNT**

MUSIC

Country/Folk
Jazz/Blues
Oldies
Rock/Popular
Urban
World Music

SPORTS

Baseball
Basketball
Boxing
Football
Golf
Hockey
Motorsports
Soccer
Tennis
Wrestling

ARTS

Ballet/Dance
Classical/Opera
Museums
Theatre

FAMILY

popular MUSIC events

Backstreet Boys
Barenaked Ladies
Janet Jackson
Radiohead
Tom Petty
more...

popular SPORTS events

Houston Astros
Los Angeles Lakers
New York Yankees
Seattle Mariners
WWF World Wrestling Federation
more...

popular ARTS events

Cabaret
Disney Presents: The Lion King (CA)
Disney Presents: The Lion King (NY)
Elton John & Tim Rice's Aida
Feet Of Flames
more...

in the SPOTLIGHT

Barenaked Ladies Pre-Sale
Register for our exclusive pre-sale now. See the Barenaked Ladies on tour this summer and get their new album, Maroon.

blink-182 Pre-Sale
Get your tickets for blink-182's summer tour. Register now and get yours before everyone else.

LA via Toyota RAV4
Toyota RAV4 is giving away trips and tickets this summer. Enter the Toyota RAV4 Cross-Country Concert Sweepstakes now.

Deal of the Week
Save $20 on tickets to select performances The Phantom of the Opera in Indianapolis and Louisville.

⊜   🌐 Internet

Ticketmaster.com offers online ticket sales to museums, concerts, and sporting, cultural, and other entertainment events. Ticketmaster claims that this site, combined with its real-world locations, make it the largest ticket-selling company in the world.

This homepage's greatest strength is that it categorizes information better than many homepages, mostly because it offers simple, realistic category names. It also gives several good examples of content on the homepage. On the other hand, the visual design of this homepage causes usability problems. Currently, this page screams like a loud concert—the many combinations of uppercase, bold, italic, and underline fonts aren't as readable as simple, mixed-case fonts.

This homepage could also do a much better job of selling the benefits of the site over equivalent real-world services. The online version of Ticketmaster saves users long lines and busy phone lines, and with its capability to print tickets from a PDF file, it saves users from waiting later at the Will Call window.

Window Title
Ticketmaster's **Welcome To** salutation makes this page useless for bookmarking because it will appear under "W" instead of "T."

Tag Line
A tag line that describes the site's purpose and highlights its advantages over Ticketmaster's real-world locations would be beneficial.

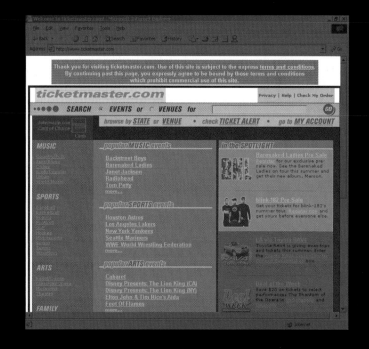

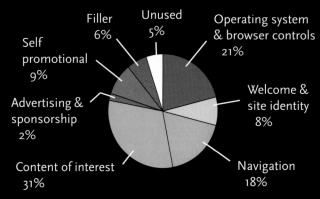

Breakdown of Screen Real Estate

- Filler 6%
- Unused 5%
- Operating system & browser controls 21%
- Self promotional 9%
- Advertising & sponsorship 2%
- Welcome & site identity 8%
- Content of interest 31%
- Navigation 18%

www.ticketmaster.com

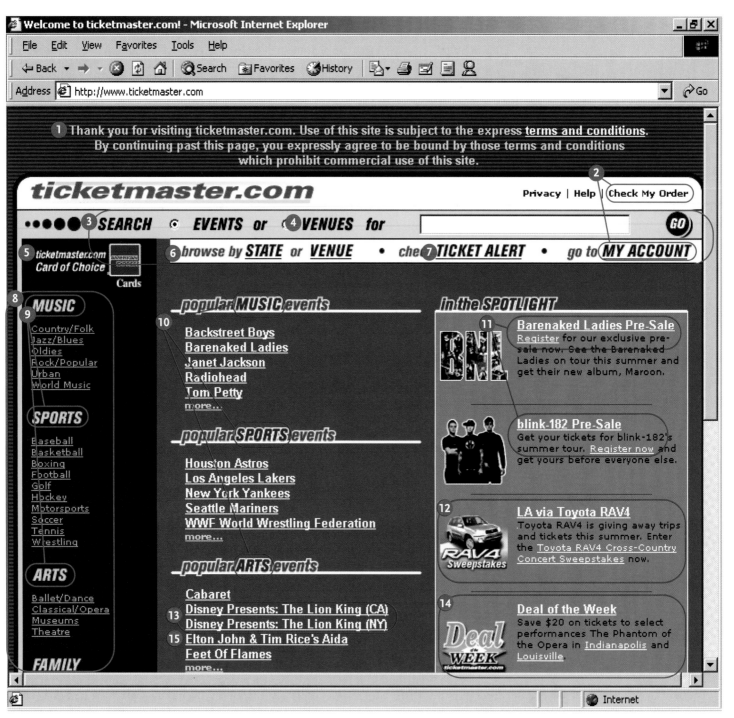

1 Besides sounding rude and scary, this is an odd placement and strange way of getting users to agree to the terms and conditions agreement. Users often assume that banners like this are ads, so they ignore them. Although a lawyer certainly approved this, it doesn't seem fair to bind people to rules that they might have never seen. Too, what does "continuing past this page" mean? (Does leaving the site count?) Better to include a simple link to terms and conditions at the bottom of the page, as most sites do, and incorporate any critical elements that require explicit user agreement, such as ticket purchase, into the relevant transaction.

2 What's the difference between **Check My Order** and **My Account**? Wouldn't users be able to check their orders from their account information?

3 This **Search** area gets points for including a wide input box, but it could be more usable. The uppercase, bold, italic fonts are not very readable—simpler fonts would be better, at least for the radio button choices. Right now, the search label and these choices have equal weight and are so visually busy, they look more like an ad than a search area. Also, although the individual elements are spaced evenly, they aren't grouped well. The entire search area should be closer together, instead of stretched across the width of the page. The radio buttons should be right next to their labels, and the **Go** button should be closer to the input box.

4 Too, if the search options were simplified to search the entire site as a default, the **browse by**, **Ticket Alert**, and **My Account** options could fit on the same line as **Search** and would simplify this entire area.

A scoped search by **Venue** seems like overkill here because there is a **browse by Venue** option directly below it. Browsing by venue should give users the option to enter a specific venue and view all upcoming events.

5 This ad for American Express keeps users from seeing several lines of navigation choices and doesn't compel users to use this credit card over any other card.

6 These browsing options don't reflect a user-oriented organization. Browsing by **State** seems very inexact. How common is it for users to shop for tickets within an area as broad as an entire state? Wouldn't users prefer to view local listings or listings for an area they planned to visit? Browsing by **Venue** is also not ideal when the user's local area has more than one popular venue. From a user's perspective, it's best to have the option of browsing all events within a defined area. It's more precise to let users enter a ZIP code, specify a distance limit from that area's code, and then browse events within that radius.

7 It's unclear what **Ticket Alert** does or how this differs from the presales that users can register for in the **Spotlight** area.

8 Users will likely struggle with the UI of this navigation area. The typeface is not very legible—it's small, and there isn't nearly enough contrast between the blue text and the dark blue background. The links are also very close together, forcing users to do some precise mousing to hit the right target.

9 These simple, straightforward category names and links can be easily differentiated from one another, although it's not clear whether they are clickable (they are).

10 The red typeface for the keywords in these names makes them stand out, but this might not be necessary if the typeface wasn't so busy to begin with and if the keywords weren't buried in the middle of the redundant phrase **popular events**.

11 No need to have two links next to each other that go to the same place. In each of these two concert listings, the links to the pre-sale go to the same place as the link to register. Better to make the heading links a bit more descriptive, such as "blink-182 Presale Tickets" and eliminate the "Register" links—not only are they redundant, they're not compelling from a user's perspective. Users don't like to register, especially when they don't know why they have to do it.

12 **LA via Toyota RAV4** is an awkward and unclear headline. Instead, be more direct about the user benefit for clicking through here: "Win a Trip to LA from Toyota." No need to offer both links to the same page—just improve the heading and have that link to the contest. Why this contest mentions and shows a photo of the Toyota RAV4 car model is a mystery.

13 Better to list these as "Lion King," with the location, and eliminate **Disney Presents**. Not only will this be more scannable, users looking for this alphabetically will surely look for "Lion King" under "L," not "D."

14 Who cares whether this is the **Deal of the Week** if it's not easy figure out *what* the deal *is*? The most noticeable parts of this area, the heading and the graphic, give the same useless information. It's not clear that deal of the week is offered by city, and the deal for these cities is totally lost among meaningless hyperlinks. Use the graphic area and the heading to showcase the deal city, the title of the event, and the savings. Then offer a clear link to view deals in other cities.

15 Although Elton John's and Tim Rice's contributions might make this production of Aida special, it's still more likely that users will look for this event under "Aida" first—not "Elton John." The link should begin with "Aida" and be listed alphabetically under "A."

www.travelocity.com

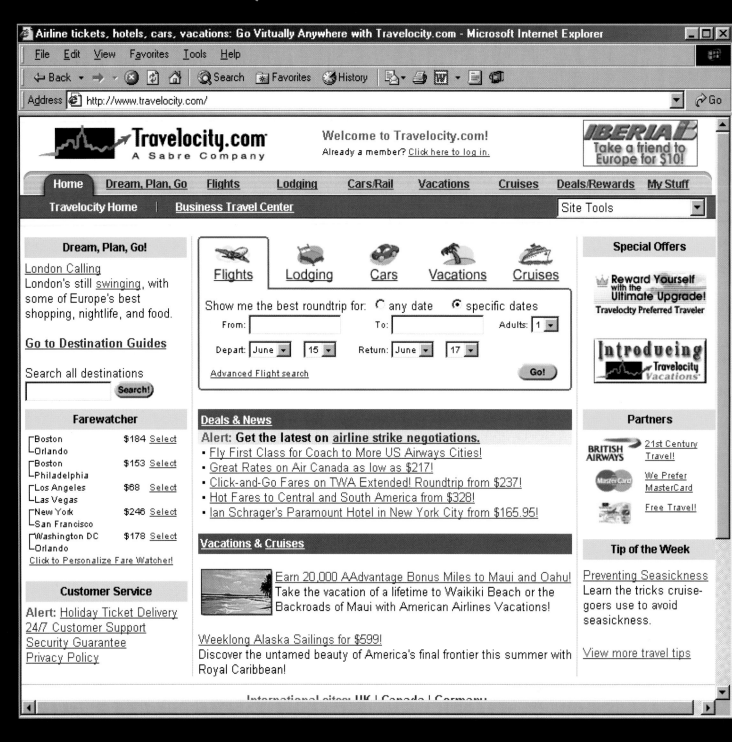

Travelocity.com is an online travel research and booking service. Users can make reservations and purchase tickets for air, rail, and boat travel, as well as reserve rental cars and hotel rooms. Users can also get travel tips and information about places they want to visit.

One of the best things about this homepage is that it shows many examples of the site's content, from specific travel bargains to travel tips. However, this homepage is cluttered with redundant navigation options and repetitious or inexact information categories. Reorganizing the content into dedicated areas and eliminating duplications would help users find what they are looking for and would allow more space to show travel content in each area.

It seems Travelocity wanted this homepage to convey a feeling of fun and instill a sense of urgency to book travel specials while they are available. Exclamation points and cartoon graphics abound. The net effect is that the site feels hectic and overwhelming. Wouldn't it be nice if the site could instead make users feel relaxed, like vacations are supposed to?

Although Travelocity has done a good deal to shed its nerdy ties to the Sabre travel agent software and has become popular with ordinary folks, it still has some residual travel speak that adds complexity to the site.

Window Title

Although it's good that this window title gives information about what users can do at the website, it should begin with "Travelocity," so that users can find it in bookmark lists and searches, and then describe the services offered. The **Go Virtually Anywhere** isn't necessary.

Tag Line

It would be more meaningful to non-travel agents to provide a brief tag line that explains what Travelocity offers, rather than its affiliation with Sabre.

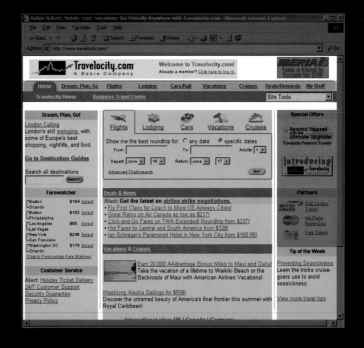

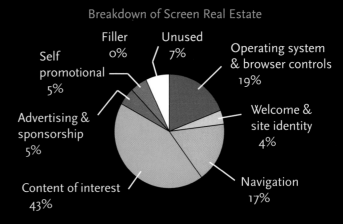

Breakdown of Screen Real Estate

Filler 0%
Unused 7%
Self promotional 5%
Operating system & browser controls 19%
Advertising & sponsorship 5%
Welcome & site identity 4%
Content of interest 43%
Navigation 17%

www.travelocity.com

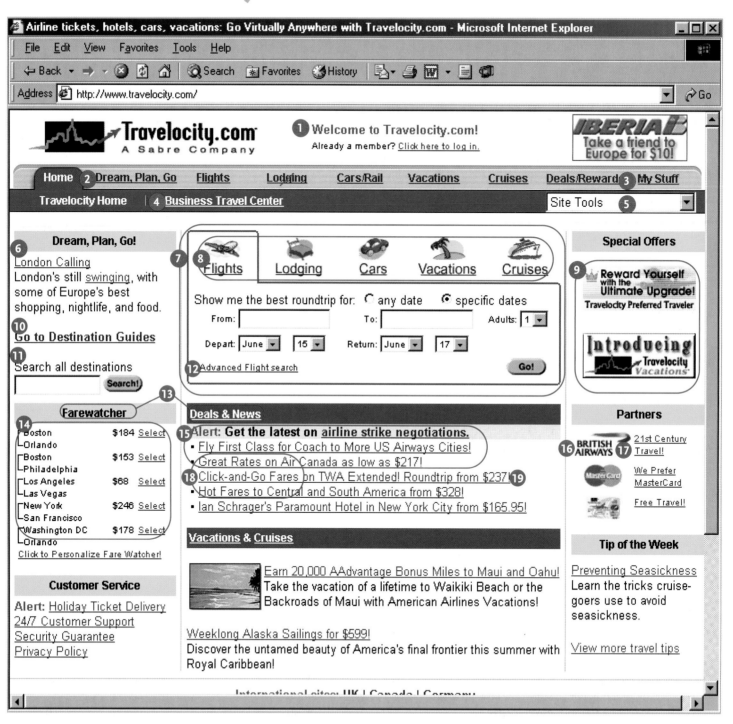

1. It's unnecessary to welcome users to your site. Here, **Welcome** uses prime real estate that would be better devoted to a site essential, such as search.

2. **Dream, Plan, Go** is a cutesy name that doesn't fit well with the other, more straightforward categories on the site. It's also not clear how it is different from **Vacations**.

3. **My Stuff** is vague and inelegant. Users can view their reservations and their traveler profiles from this area. Better to be more specific about what users can do in this area.

4. Although it's good to offer special benefits for business travelers, this link to the specialized site isn't very noticeable on the homepage. Nowhere on the rest of the page does it say that the default options are for leisure travel. It would be clearer if **Travelocity Home** were called "Leisure Travel" and **Business Travel Center** were "Business Travel."

5. This dropdown menu adds a level of complexity to the homepage without providing much value. Because a dropdown can list only the names of tools, users have to guess what the tools actually do. For example, what is **Team up to Travel**? Many of the items aren't even tools, such as **About Travelocity**, and many menu items, such as **Rail**, repeat items listed elsewhere on the homepage. Better to eliminate the dropdown and include the most critical and popular tools on the homepage, with a link to more travel tools.

6. This section is very confusing. Since they are listed under **Dream, Plan, Go**, one would assume these links would go to a London travel guide—and one can only guess what special London sights would appear under the **swinging** link. In fact, both **London Calling** and **swinging** just go to a travel article on London.

7. It's good to offer users the opportunity to start searching for these different travel options right on the homepage. However, these links are misleading because they stay active for the current selection (in this example, **Flights**) but they don't take the user to a more comprehensive flights section—they just link to the current page.

8. Great to highlight the most-frequently used feature (finding flights) by placing it in the part of the page where most users will look first.

9. These special offers don't give users any useful information. The introduction to Travelocity vacations is especially vapid. It would be much better to showcase some real deals here and include a link to more travel bargains.

10. It's great that this site compiles so much data for many cities in these guides. However, **Go to Destination Guides** is a term that is more common among travel planners than ordinary users. Why not just call these "City Guides?"

11. This search is too limited and confusing, especially from the homepage. Users expect to be able to search the whole site from the homepage and often get frustrated by this type of search because they don't realize it is scoped. Here, the scoping isn't explicit enough—**Search all destinations** doesn't adequately convey that users can search only for places here, and apparently only for cities. For example, a search on Disney World doesn't get any results.

12. **Advanced Flight search** works very well for a basic search UI. However, since many users will likely need to put in more criteria, this wording might scare off some users, since it implies some level of required user knowledge. Better to call it something less ominous, such as "Specify more flight information." Also, no need to capitalize "flight."

13. It's confusing that some of these headings are links and some are not. Also, why center some of the headings and left align others. Too many different formatting styles make the page look busy.

14. Great to deliver specific content like this on the homepage, especially good to include prices.

15. This homepage uses inconsistent capitalization styles, which detract from a professional appearance and add clutter. For example, these three links, all of which are sentences, use different formats. The first is sentence-style capitalization, the second is all keywords in initial caps, and the third is a hybrid (keywords in initial caps, but "low" in lowercase).

16. Having British Airways as a featured partner can lower the users' trust in the site and make them question whether they will be shown the best deals and cheaper tickets on other airlines.

17. One would assume that *all* travel options on this site would be for **21st Century Travel**. Did British Airways forget to change a slogan post-millennium?

18. Headlines grouped like this need to each reflect something unique, so users can easily and quickly differentiate them from each other. These headlines aren't easily scannable because they all begin with extraneous words about fares. In this case, better to start with the airline or the destination, then give the price, and eliminate phrases, such as **Click-and-Go Fares** and **Great Rates**.

19. Dark blue links are not as standard as medium blue to show an unvisited state. It's even more confusing on this site because the visited links show as medium blue, so they look unvisited.

continues

www.travelocity.com

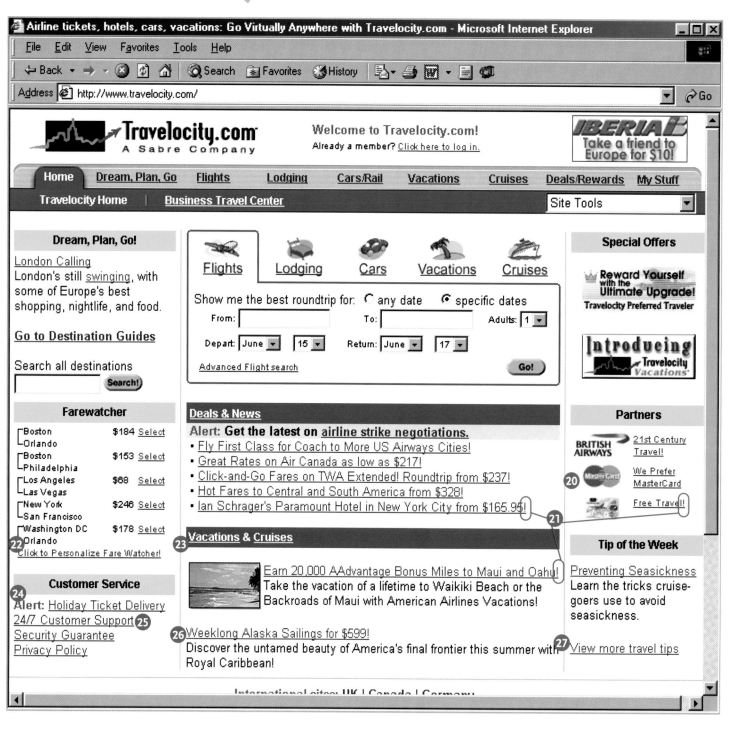

20 Although this **We Prefer MasterCard** option is a bit odd, as these credit card alliances always are, at least this one is listed under **Partners**, so it's more clear to users why Travelocity is listing this preference. It also gives links to benefits of using MasterCard. Like all these plugs, though, it makes users wonder if they can use any credit card, or just the one listed.

21 Exclamation points should rarely, if ever, be used in professional communication. When overused, they look especially unprofessional and make the headlines shout at the user. This homepage has at least 17! That's a lot of yelling.

22 Very good to let users customize this tool to show travel deals for their city. The words **Click to** in this link are unnecessary and make it more difficult to quickly comprehend the benefit of this feature (personalization).

23 This headline doesn't match the description that follows it. As written, the description belongs under **Special Offers**, not **Vacations** and **Cruises**.

24 Good to have alerts for critical travel news, but it would be nice to have all alerts listed in one section of the homepage.

25 **24/7** makes this link confusing. This phrase is too colloquial and not generally used in print. Users expect web services to be available 24 hours a day, so just calling the area "Customer Support" should suffice. Also, European users might think that "24/7" refers to something happening on the 24th of July. If Travelocity really wants to stress that customer support is always available, it should say "24 hour support."

26 This awkwardly worded headline would be much better as simply "Alaska One-Week Cruises for $599."

27 Great to include travel tips here. However, this description would better draw in users if it actually gave one of the tips and then had a link to more tips. Better to use descriptions of the actual content than promises of content to follow.

www.usatoday.com

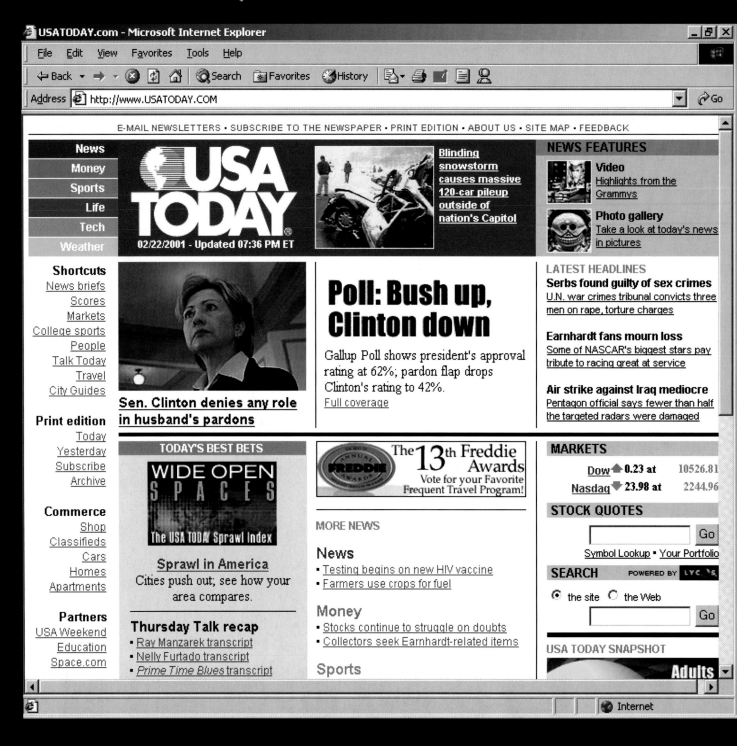

USA Today is a news website that offers headline news stories, as well as financial, sports, entertainment, travel, and other news departments. The site also offers subscription and archive-searching services for the print edition of *USA Today*.

USA Today's homepage does a good job overall of offering well-prioritized content. In fact, this homepage shows admirable restraint in promoting only top stories rather than trying to be comprehensive at this top level. The categories in the main area show just enough of their content to make clear what is in the category, without overwhelming readers. USA Today is one of the rare homepages that employs concise headline writing. One potential weakness of this homepage is the navigation support to nonheadline areas. The usability of this homepage suffers a bit from some redundant and unintuitive navigation devices.

Window Title

The window title is appropriate for bookmarking, and the company name is likely recognizable enough to stand on its own without a description.

Tag Line

USA Today can probably survive without a tag line because it demonstrates its content by example. Still, a tag line is a good way to give first-time visitors a quick taste of the site.

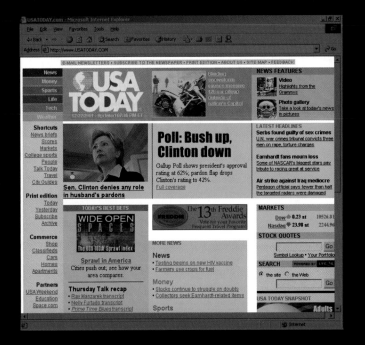

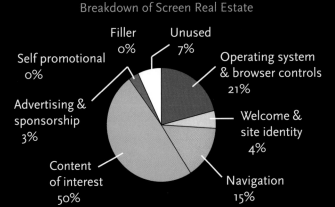

Breakdown of Screen Real Estate

- Filler 0%
- Unused 7%
- Operating system & browser controls 21%
- Self promotional 0%
- Advertising & sponsorship 3%
- Welcome & site identity 4%
- Content of interest 50%
- Navigation 15%

www.usatoday.com

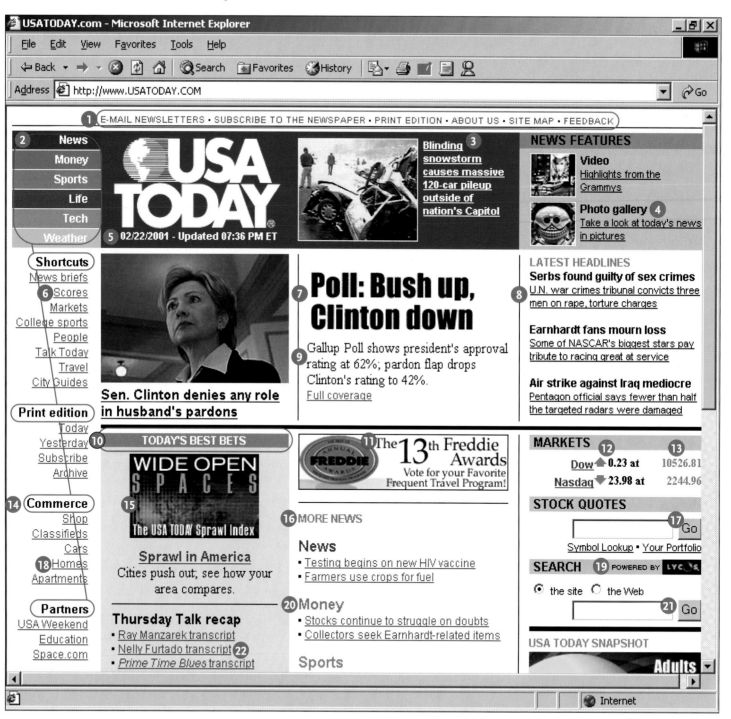

1 These links look inactive because of the gray color. Even if the color changed, though, they still would be more visible if they were incorporated into the navigation area on the left. Users don't look above big banners and horizontal lines; moving them would allow for more news content in the main areas of the site.

2 This navigation area doesn't give any visual cues that these buttons expand to show subcategories when you click them. It's also not clear how this area relates to the topic categories below it. Better to integrate these two areas or clearly separate them.

3 The combination of a wordy headline and placement within what looks to be a large promotional banner makes this top news story fade to obscurity. Users tend to dismiss or ignore graphical banner areas because they look like ads.

4 The **Photo gallery** is oddly named and described in a way that suggests comprehensiveness instead of selectiveness. Why would users want to view *all* of the day's news in pictures? Instead, emphasize that these photos are more *interesting* than others, in a title such as "Today's Best Photos."

5 The date and time stamp are essential on a news site so that users can know when the stories were last updated. These are well placed in a clearly visible area.

6 **Scores** doesn't make clear that this goes to scores from today's games. Also, this link should be next to **College sports**.

7 Good use of the main headline area. This headline conveys maximum information in minimal word count.

8 **Latest Headlines** should have links on each main headline, not on the decks. The current hyperlinks are too long for users to scan and comprehend.

9 This number comparison gets lost in the prose. It would be more noticeable if it was formatted in a more visual way, such as a table.

10 **Today's Best Bets** isn't a meaningful heading, especially because these are not the most prominently featured content links on the site. In addition, all uppercase small fonts are not very readable.

11 It's risky to place an ad in the middle of the page. Not only does this graphic lessen the impact of more useful graphics, but it also trains users to ignore a prime real estate area that USA Today uses for real content.

12 The **Markets** area needs some usability improvements. A percentage change, rather than points up or down, would facilitate better comparison between Dow and Nasdaq changes.

The size of the arrows could also proportionally show the magnitude of change.

Numbers should be consistently aligned at decimal points. Also, carrying the number out to two digits after the decimal point is probably overly precise and makes the numbers less scannable.

13 Because this site uses color coding to show up and down trends, why doesn't it do so consistently? Why are both numbers red here?

Comma separators would make these numbers more readable. Use them for numbers that have five digits or more, and do so consistently.

14 **Commerce** is a strange content category. Only **Classifieds** fits the model of a traditional newspaper. **Shop** seems like a desperate attempt to garner revenue through advertising kickbacks, somewhat akin to lifting every sofa cushion in hopes of finding a quarter.

15 This **Wide Open Spaces** graphic is a waste of space. It would be much more compelling to use the space to show some of the details of the story, such as listing statistics on how urban sprawl has affected top U.S. cities.

16 **More News** is an unnecessary heading and takes up space that could be used to show more actual news headlines. Better to move **Markets** into this area and expand the **Latest Headlines** area.

17 Having two search boxes, especially right next to each other, is confusing and problematic. Users will likely enter site search strings into the **Stock Quotes** lookup.

18 The distinction between **Homes** and **Apartments** is unclear. Is this rental properties versus homes to buy? **Homes** doesn't convey where this link actually goes—to a site exclusively for *new* homes.

19 Don't list who powers the search engine. Who cares?

20 Although it's a nice concept to use color coding (green for money here and in the upper-left navigation area), the site shouldn't use the same color for different purposes. For example, if red means sports, don't also use red for the latest headlines.

21 **Search** is not visible enough this far down on the page; it should be right at the top of the page.

22 Repeating the word **transcript** is a waste of space. Better to rename the whole area "Thursday Talk Transcripts" and then give a better description of what these people were talking about—for example, "Ray Manzarek Talks about The Doors," for people who don't recognize the name alone.

www.victoriassecret.com

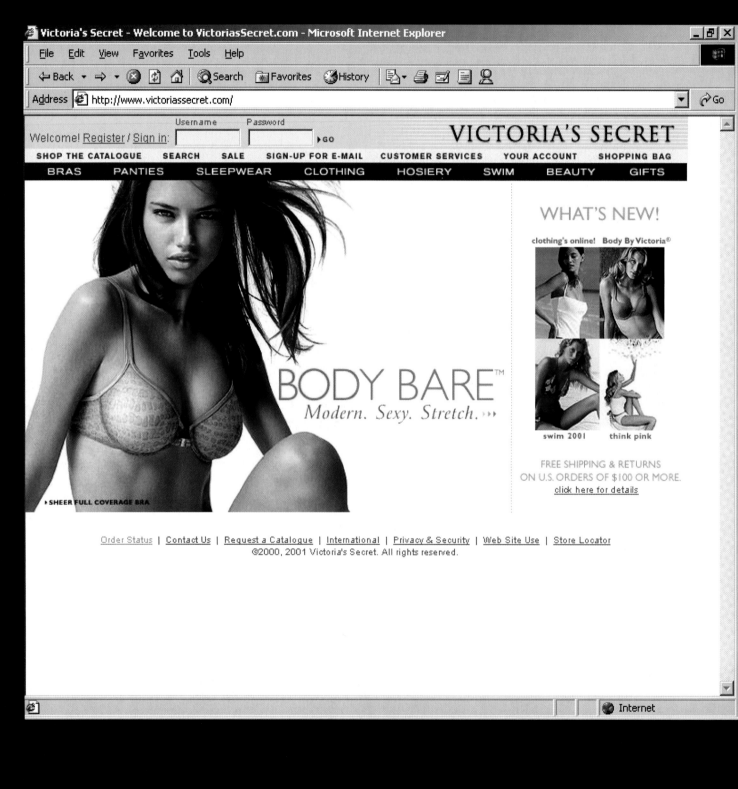

Victoriassecret.com is the online version of the lingerie company, which also has brick-and-mortar stores and a catalogue business. Besides lingerie, Victoriassecret.com sells clothing, swimwear, and beauty items. The site helps users find the appropriate styles and sizes of lingerie and clothing, and it offers advice on lingerie-relevant topics, such as how to launder delicate items.

This homepage does a good job of representing the Victoria's Secret brand in clearly identifiable ways, and it uses a simple page layout to do so. From the use of the trademark pink color to the choice of one large product photo, the homepage quickly establishes what this site is famous for selling. The homepage does not as effectively show the breadth of content that Victoria's Secret offers, though. The site actually contains some items that would be difficult to locate in the categories shown. Where would you look to find the bedding this site sells? Answer: under **Sleepwear**. The site could make better use of the **What's New** area to show some of these different products. And while the page's navigation looks fairly simple, some rather tricky dropdown menus lurk behind the simple category names at the top of the page.

Window Title

Good that the window title will bookmark alphabetically, but the additional "Welcome..." text makes it unnecessarily long.

URL

Users often have difficulties entering domain names that have concatenated words, like this one does, correctly. Victoria's Secret wisely registered **www.victoriasecret.com** as well (with only one "s").

Tag Line

Perhaps a tag line is unnecessary on a site that reveals its main content so adeptly on the homepage. However, Victoria's Secret could use a tag line to convey the message that it's not just about lingerie anymore.

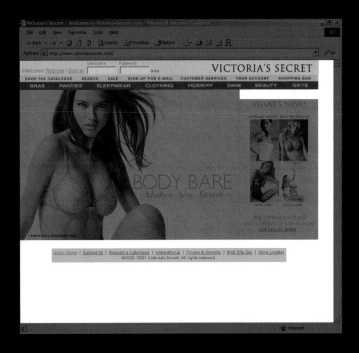

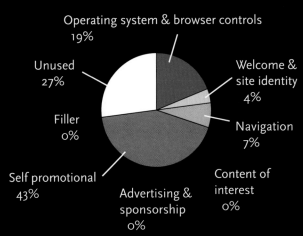

Breakdown of Screen Real Estate

Operating system & browser controls 19%

Unused 27%

Welcome & site identity 4%

Filler 0%

Navigation 7%

Self promotional 43%

Advertising & sponsorship 0%

Content of interest 0%

www.victoriassecret.com

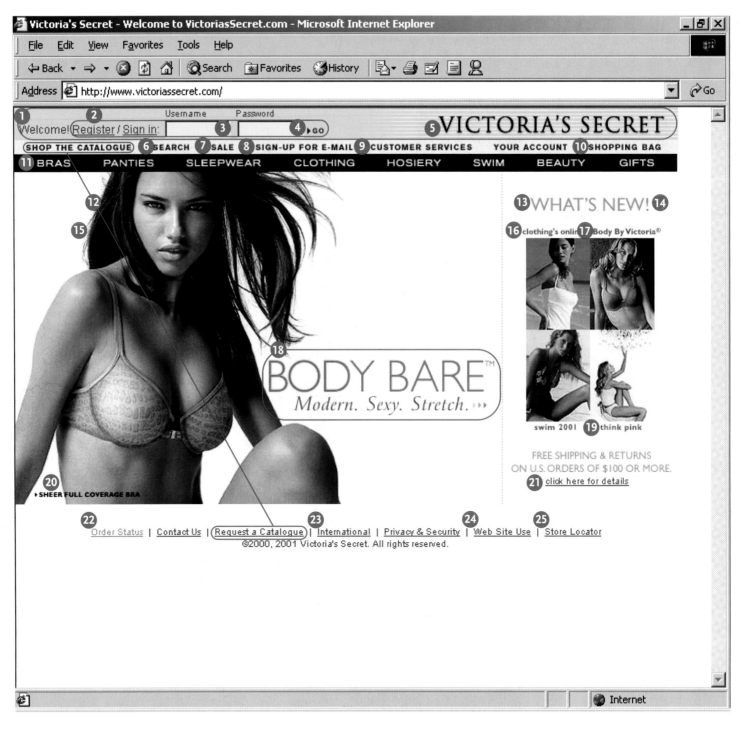

1. Good use of the Victoria's Secret signature pink color to bring the brand identity to the website.

2. Odd to devote such prime homepage real estate to registration and sign-in on a site where users don't get obvious benefits, such as homepage customization, for doing so. In fact, the only benefit that users get for registering before purchasing is the ability save their shopping bag for 48 hours. Why not just list that benefit for unregistered users and then prompt them for the necessary information?

3. These input boxes look like search boxes, which might confuse users trying to find search.

4. This button should be "Sign in," not "Go."

5. It's unusual to see the company logo in the upper-right like this—logos are most commonly in the upper-left corner. Because the logo is one of the most critical homepage elements, it's best to put it where users most expect it. Also, this logo is clickable on the homepage—pages shouldn't contain links back to the current page.

6. **Search** should have an input box on the homepage. Users frequently overlook links to search, and this one is especially small.

7. This link to **Sale** items is very small. Worse, it's not noticeable in this location. Why is **Sale** mixed in among these customer service options? Better to include it as a category in the black navigation area, or feature a sale item in the main body of the page and offer a link to more sale items.

8. This forthright and prominent offer to get spam is amusing, but it's likely not too compelling for most users. At least sell users on the benefit they'll get, such as early notification of sales and special discounts. People like sales—they don't like getting lots of junk email. This particular wording actually sounds like Victoria's Secret now offers email accounts.

9. Good to have a link to customer service right on the homepage. However, no need to make "Service" plural, as done here.

10. **Shopping Bag** is not as standard as "Shopping Cart." While this probably won't cause any real problems, users are likely to have a slightly easier time recognizing and understanding the more standard term.

11. These simple and straightforward category names mask a tricky UI. When you hover over each category, you get a single or cascading drop-down menu, which requires precise mousing to manipulate. Often the menus appear when you *don't* want them—it's difficult to click on any of the links in the navigation menu directly above this one without popping up one of these menus. The choices on the dropdowns are difficult to differentiate from, especially without pictures. Under **Bras**, how can a user choose between **Dream Angels Desire** and **Dream Angels Divine**? And is this a style or a collection? It would be better to either reveal more of the category hierarchy on the homepage or take users straight to a category page and skip the menus.

12. **Catalogue** options should be grouped.

13. This entire **What's New** area doesn't give users much information about these different product categories. It's also not clear whether this area showcases whole categories of products or a specific product line.

14. Avoid exclamation points! Let users get excited about the products, not the punctuation.

15. This product photo works well to instantly show users how this site differs from ordinary clothing sites. Users already familiar with the Victoria's Secret brand name will know that they've found the right site—users who don't know the name will quickly get an idea of what it's all about. The photo also shows good detail of the product itself.

16. Does this photo caption mean that users couldn't view or buy items from the **Clothing** category before now? Also, this product photo, especially with the ocean backdrop, isn't the best choice to differentiate these items from swimwear or lingerie. Victoria's Secret isn't known for its clothing, so it would be better to actually show some of it here.

17. **Body By Victoria** is a confusing caption. What exactly is the site selling here? In fact, this is the name of a lingerie line, but it's too vague and cutesy to work well as a headline—it sounds like a link to a fitness or plastic surgery area.

18. This bold heading works well to introduce and promote this particular product line; however, it needs a meaningful subheading to explain it a bit. The current subheading is rather insipid.

19. It's not clear what you'll find under **think pink**.

20. This typeface is so small that it's virtually unreadable, and users who can read it might be confused. Is this the product name or the description? Can a product simultaneously be "sheer" and "full coverage?" How does this relate to **Body Bare**, so prominently featured in the middle of the page? If they're both part of the product name, put this information in the same place.

21. No need for the separate **click here for details** link. This link means nothing on its own and takes up extra space. Better to make **Free Shipping & Returns on U.S. Orders of $100 or More** the hyperlink, and underline it, so users know it's clickable.

22. This link to **Order Status** seems unnecessary because users should be able to get this information from the more prominent **Your Account** link at the top. At least these items should be grouped together.

23. Good to provide a link to international shipping information right on the homepage.

24. **Web Site Use** is a rather obscure link. In fact, this goes to legal and copyright information and would be better as "Terms and Conditions."

25. This is a very low-visibility link for the **Store Locator**. It would make more sense to locate this next to **Shop the Catalogue** and, thus, group the two alternatives.

www.walmart.com

Walmart.com is an e-commerce counterpart to the famous, low-cost department store in the physical world. Walmart.com offers a subset of the merchandise one can find in Wal-Mart stores.

Bravo to the supergiant Wal-Mart for a well-organized homepage. For the most part, the categories are easy to differentiate and navigate. This homepage would be even simpler and cleaner if the redundant navigation was eliminated. This homepage joins the ranks of Drugstore.com and Amazon.com for successfully revealing its product content, here through the extensive categories. It's interesting to note how much of this site is dedicated to pure navigation, instead of internal promotions that are the signature of so many e-commerce sites. This is most likely because of the strength of the Wal-Mart name—the design seems to assume that the user wants to be on the site, and tries to get them to the products as quickly as possible, rather than selling them on how great the site is.

Window Title
This window title will bookmark in the appropriate alphabetical order. It's also good that the title includes a tag line of sorts, which mentions what Wal-Mart is famous for: low prices. We could have done without the exclamation mark.

URL
The company's official name is Wal-Mart, not Walmart, and since hyphens are legal characters in domain names, it would have been possible to give this site the URL www.wal-mart.com. Hyphenated domain names are rare, however, and it is much more common for websites to simply run the words together if they have compound names. Thus, it was the correct decision to name this site www.walmart.com and not www.wal-mart.com. Wal-Mart was also smart enough to buy the wal-mart.com domain and have it redirect the user's browser to walmart.com. Even better, the server redirects the request in a way that does not break the Back button.

Tag Line
Although the Wal-Mart brand is well known, it would still be good to include a brief tag line that tells what this site is all about. A good tag line for Wal-Mart would emphasize its

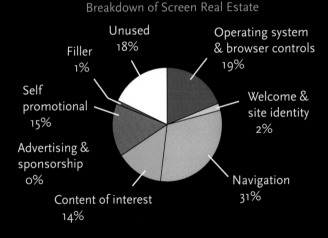

Breakdown of Screen Real Estate

- Operating system & browser controls 19%
- Welcome & site identity 2%
- Navigation 31%
- Content of interest 14%
- Advertising & sponsorship 0%
- Self promotional 15%
- Filler 1%
- Unused 18%

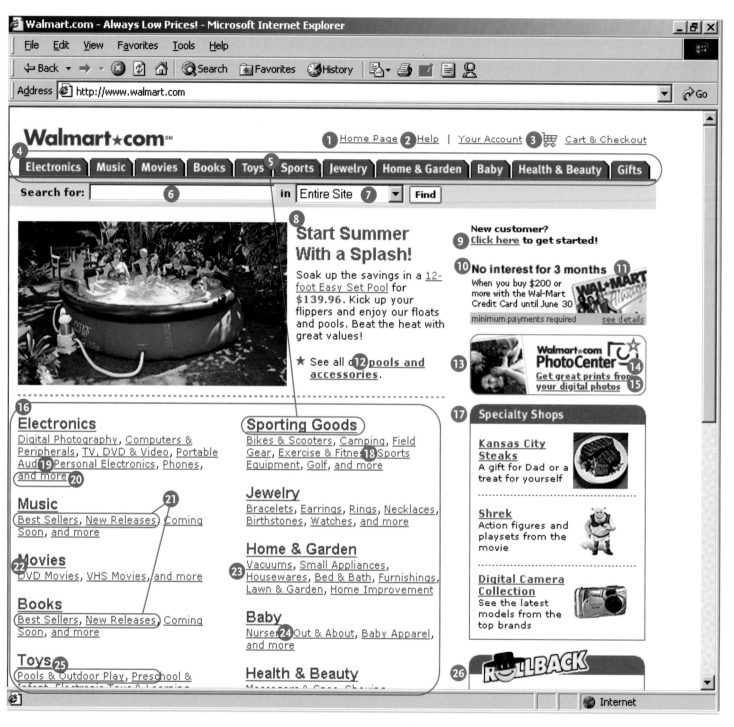

1 It's always bad to link to the current page—it's especially bad here because **Home Page** is spelled out, leaving users to wonder what page they're currently on. It's more standard to link to the homepage from the company logo on other pages on the site.

2 The most standard placement of **Help** is in the far-right corner.

3 Good to use the standard shopping cart icon—it's still more standard, however, to say "shopping cart," rather than just "cart."

4 Since users can access all these categories from category links lower on the page, these tabs are unnecessary and clutter the interface. The links give users more information about the categories, because they list some of the content below the link.

5 Inconsistent labels: **Sports** versus **Sporting Goods**.

6 Good to have a wide search input box, so users have room to enter and review their queries.

7 If you're going to offer a scoped search, it's good to default it to search the entire site, as is done here.

8 Great to feature one seasonal item prominently on the homepage. Although the description has some inspirational marketese, which can sometimes decrease readability, here the overall effect works because there are plenty of pertinent facts included, such as product name, price, size, and a photo.

9 Why include this area at all? First, it implies that new customers must follow the links before doing anything on the site. Second, the actual link should tell what's in it, for example, **Click here** should be "New Customer Registration." Last, this area leads users to an unfriendly registration area, which *isn't* mandatory before shopping on the site. Better to greet a new customer with good product offerings and do the paperwork later.

10 This is a well-written promotion for a Wal-Mart credit card. The headline quickly conveys the consumer value, and the small print gives an honorable amount of disclosure about the terms of the offer with a link to more details.

11 This picture doesn't look much like a credit card. The photo of the store card might be recognized by current cardholders, so if the promotion does not aim to sign up new customers, the illustration might work. To attract new customers who have not seen the Wal-Mart store card before, consider using a more stylized drawing of a card or a completely different type of illustration that communicates the main value proposition of saving money for an entire quarter.

12 Very good to have a clearly visible link to the broader category (**pools and accessories**) from the specific product description (12-foot pool).

13 Cute photo, but too much detail for its (appropriately) small size. Crop to leave only one puppy in the shot.

14 This graphic looks more like the Turkish flag than the little camera it's supposed to be.

15 Good that this link tells users precisely what they can do in the photo center. However, it might be a bit too specific, since users can also build photo albums and order digital copies of their photo prints from here as well.

16 These main categories are simple and clearly differentiable. The Yahoo-style navigation of links to subcategories works well to reveal some of the content in each category.

17 **Specialty Shops** is a nice way to showcase certain product categories that relate to current events or popular products (steaks for Father's Day and toys from the movie *Shrek*). Good to include a simple representative photo of the category to draw attention to this area and illustrate by example.

18 **Sports Equipment** doesn't help to subcategorize **Sporting Goods**. Too, it's not good to break up a phrase like **Sports Equipment**.

19 **Personal Electronics** is a rather vague and misleading name for a subcategory that is a hodgepodge of electronics dominated by radios with a few puzzling entries, such as **Flashlights**, thrown in. Better to specifically list two of the best-selling categories and let the link to more cover the rest. **Portable Audio** and **Phones** both seem like highly personal types of electronics, confirming that **Personal Electronics** is a poor name for a neighboring subcategory.

20 **And more** is a bit vague—better to just repeat the category name, such as "More Electronics."

21 The subcategories for music and books—**Best Sellers** and **New Releases**—are not easily differentiable categories for music and books. Which would you choose to find a new popular CD? It might be better to eliminate the subcategories for music and books and take the user directly to the main category pages, which could include both best-sellers and new releases, as well as a more meaningful list of genre-based subcategories (science fiction books, travel books, and so on).

22 Because Wal-Mart carries a different selection of movies on DVD and VHS, this is a good top-level distinction to make—akin to shopping for only the size clothes that fit you and are in stock. This way, users won't find the perfect movie, only to discover it's not available in their preferred format.

23 These subcategories under **Home & Garden** are just as confusing as they are in physical stores. What exactly is the difference between **Housewares**, **Furnishings**, and **Home Improvement**. If you need a decorative curtain rod, where do you go? Where do you find candleholders?

24 **Out & About**, although catchy, isn't very helpful. Better to follow the model of the rest of the links and list actual product names, such as "Strollers" and "Car Seats."

25 **Pools & Outdoor Play** should also be in **Sporting Goods**. This would be especially important if they weren't featured so prominently on the homepage.

26 Good to incorporate the **Rollback** smiley face that marks discounted prices, which Wal-Mart shoppers will recognize from the physical store (or at least from the commercials).

www.yahoo.com

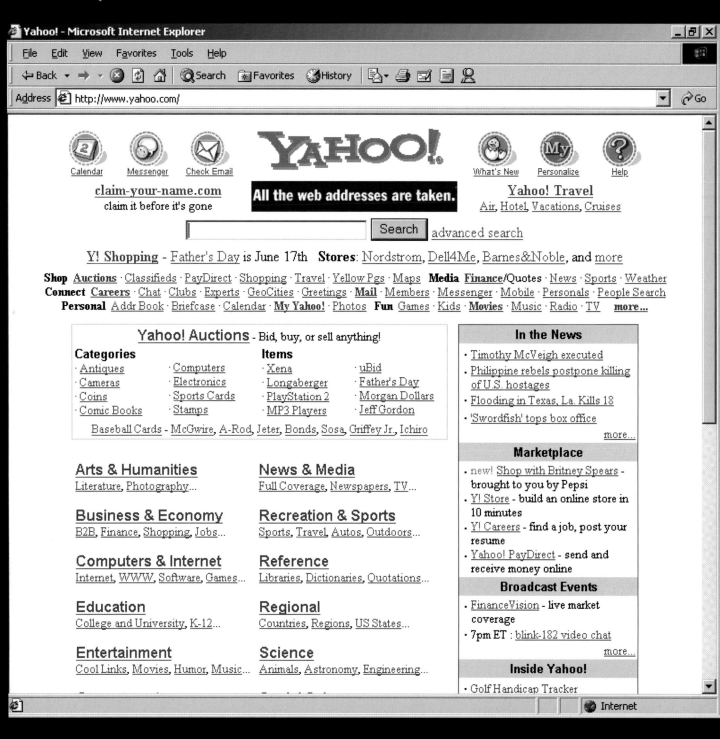

Yahoo is the most popular site on the Internet. It combines a directory service to find external resources with a large number of online tools and services.

Yahoo has kept a stable design style since the beginning, mainly by adding elements but doing so sufficiently slow enough that experienced users never felt jarred. Now the page is so crammed with features, however, that new users likely will feel overwhelmed. The page needs a more clearly defined starting place, which should probably be the topic hierarchy. In the original Yahoo design, the topic hierarchy was almost the only thing on the page other than the search box and the logo. Now this crucial feature is drowned out by all the surrounding boxes. Yahoo earns kudos for its very simple pages: plain and simple text links that stick to the Web standards in terms of link colors, typefaces, and other design elements. Also, this page downloads very quickly because of the minimal use of graphics.

Window Title

This window title will bookmark well. Better if it had a brief tag line for Yahoo as well.

Tag Line

Despite its fame, it would still be helpful if Yahoo had a tag line to briefly describe the purpose of the site and how it is different from the competitors.

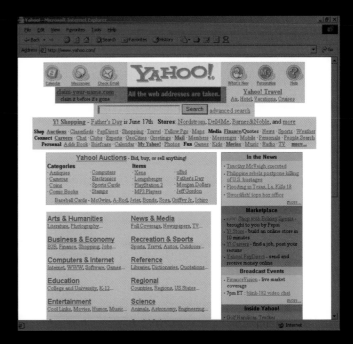

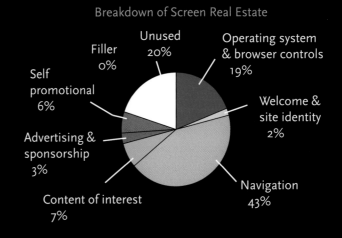

Breakdown of Screen Real Estate

Filler 0%

Unused 20%

Operating system & browser controls 19%

Self promotional 6%

Welcome & site identity 2%

Advertising & sponsorship 3%

Content of interest 7%

Navigation 43%

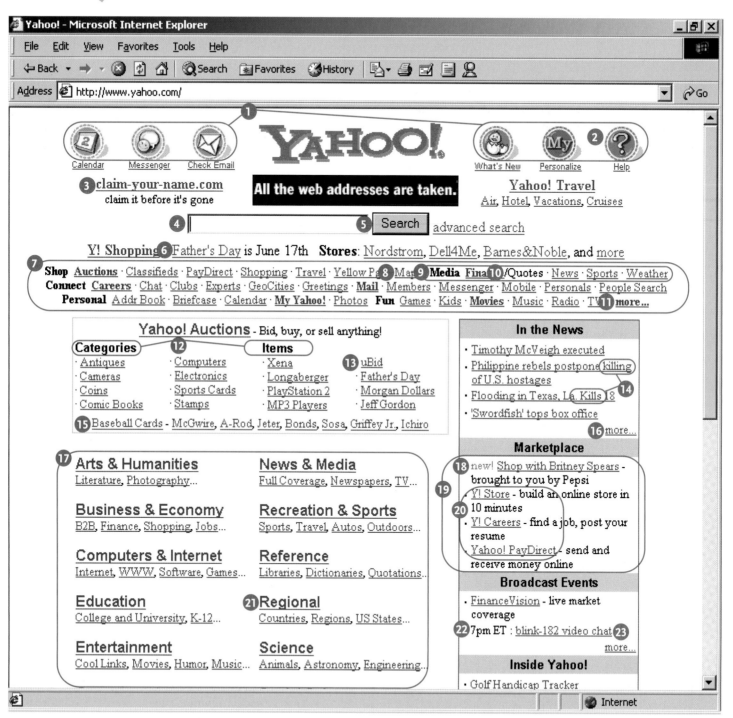

1. These cartoonish and weird icons for **Messenger** and **What's New** seem out of place. Given their small size, it's particularly hard to even recognize what the **Messenger** icon is supposed to depict.

2. **Help** is in a logical spot, is easy to find, and has an appropriate icon.

3. It's sneaky to disguise an ad as a Yahoo editorial category.

4. **Search** box is prominent and easy to find. Great to have a sufficiently wide input field to allow a multiword query.

5. Good to have an actual button for the **Search** action on this homepage. This button stands out on a page that has so many text links.

6. Good to promote seasonal events in a prominent place with simple links to more information. It's helpful to remind users about the specific date, as done here, and not just the name of the event.

7. This entire area is too dense and could use better categories. For example, the difference between **Connect** and **Personal** is not clear. To many users, their email *is* a personal service.

8. **Maps** do not belong in the shopping category. If anything,—out of the three categories available—they fit better under **Connect**.

9. The entire **Media** category makes no sense, except possibly for the **News** link. The other items are only media in the internal thinking of an Internet executive, not in the way they are perceived by users. In contrast, many of the items under **Fun** might be thought of as media (for example, movies, radio, and TV).

10. **Quotes** should be a link as well because the word stands out and feels different from the rest of this area—it is the only word in black, except for the category names.

11. It is not clear how much **more** you get by clicking this link, and it's not clear whether it's simply more **Fun** or more of all the categories. In fact, the link leads to a page with several additional services that are grouped in a much more logical manner than the listings on the homepage.

12. The difference between categories and items is somewhat vague, but it seems to be that **Items** are more specific, narrow sets, whereas **Categories** are broader, more generic sets. If this is so, **Father's Day** should be a category and not an item because it doesn't denote a specific set of products.

13. **uBid** does not belong in this list because it links to a different auction service. It would be better to integrate all the items sold by uBid into the main Yahoo **Auctions** topic classification.

14. The inconsistent capitalization of "K" in **killing** and **Kills** was probably inserted by Microsoft Word's AutoCorrect feature because the letter follows a period. This example shows the need to look carefully before posting.

15. Good to highlight an interesting subcategory and provide direct links to some high-profile items. This gives users a straightforward path to something concrete, thus giving them a fast, successful experience and direct exposure to the guts of the auction service.

16. Good to have links to more news and more events. The page might be more scannable with links named "More News" and "More Events," respectively, although the boxed areas of these categories help to identify these "more" links with their appropriate categories.

17. It is hard to look at this area with fresh eyes since it has become the canonical way to present a topic hierarchy in web design. The fact that this design is so commonplace makes it great from a usability perspective, since users will be accustomed to it. But even if this design were not a standard, we would praise it for being a good way of defining the categories.

18. Drop the exclamation point after **new**, especially since this page has so many other exclamation points. Making the word red is enough to make it stand out. No need to yell.

19. These good, clear feature explanations clarify what might have been hard to understand based on the names alone.

20. It's odd to abbreviate **Yahoo!** to **Y!** in these links, especially since **Yahoo! PayDirect** spells out the company name. Unless you introduce and consistently implement a standard like this on your site, better to just use the full name.

21. **Regional** is not an intuitive name. In particular, what's the difference between **Regional** and **Regions**?

22. When we checked this page at 7:10 P.M. eastern time, this listing did not have any special symbol to indicate that the event was currently in progress. For fans of blink-182, it would be a disaster to miss this live event, since you only get one chance for anything to be live.

23. Usually it's best to explain a concept like **blink-182**, which many people will not know. In this case, the minimal link may work, because people who don't know this rock group probably won't want to waste time on the video chat anyway. Users are good at ignoring page elements they don't understand. Don't have too many obscure items on your pages, however, or the entire site will feel unwelcoming.

Appendix

Throughout this project, we frequently had the pictures of all 50 homepages spread out on our office floor. We found it quite powerful and visually stunning to be able to see all of the sites side-by-side. We found ourselves wanting to zoom in and do more side-by-side comparisons of different aspects of the homepages, such as search, logos, and so forth. With the help of our editor and the talented graphic artists at New Riders, we were able to do so. We include some of these compilations here for your analysis and enjoyment.

Site	Window Title	Tag Line
About	About—The Human Internet	The Human Internet
Accenture	Accenture Home	Now It Gets Interesting
Amazon	Amazon.com—Earth's Biggest Selection	None
The Art Institute of Chicago	The Art Institute of Chicago Museum	None
Asia Cuisine	AsiaCuisine: New Asia Cuisine Website	Asia's Leading Food and Beverage Portal
Barnes & Noble	Barnes & Noble.com (www.bn.com)	None
BBC Online	BBC Online Homepage—Welcome	Welcome to the UK's Favourite Website
Boeing	The Boeing Company	Forever New Frontiers
CDNOW	CDNOW	Never Miss a Beat
Citigroup	Citigroup	Citigroup We Are Citigroup
CNET	Welcome to CNET!—CNET.com	The Source for Computing and Technology
CNNfn	CNNfn—The Financial Network	The Financial Network
Coles	Coles	Serving You Better
DIRECTV	DIRECTV: DIRECTV Is the #1 Digital Satellite Entertainment Service!	America's Leader in Digital Home Entertainment
Disney	Disney.com—Where the Magic Lives Online!	Where the Magic Lives Online!
Drugstore	Drugstore.com—Online Pharmacy & Drugstore, Prescriptions Filled	A Very Healthy Way to Shop, Plus Advice and Information from Drugstore.com
eBay	eBay—The World's Online Marketplace	The World's Online Marketplace
eMagazineshop	eMagazineshop.com—Magazine Subscriptions	Magazine Subscriptions on the Internet
ESPN	ESPN.com	None
ExxonMobil	ExxonMobil	ExxonMobil, the World's Premier Petroleum and Petrochemical Company
FedEx	FedEx|United States	None
Federal Highway Administration	Federal Highway Administration Home Page	None
Florida Department of Revenue	Florida Department of Revenue—Homepage	None
Ford Motor Company	Ford Motor Company Home Page	Striving to Make the World a Better Place

Site	Window Title	Tag Line
Gateway	Gateway Homepage	You've Got a Friend in the Business
General Electric	GE	We Bring Good Things to Life
General Motors	Home	None
Global Sources	Global Sources: Enabling Global Merchandise Trade	Product and Trade Information for Volume Buyers
IBM	ibm.com	None
James Devaney Fuel Co.	James Devaney Fuel Company—Greater Boston's Home Oil Heart Services Provider	The Greater Boston Area's Premier Home Oil Heat Service for more than 65 years
JobMagic	UK Jobs and Recruitment at JobMagic—Find UK Job Vacancies, Direct from Employers and Companies	JobMagic Online Recruitment Service
Learn2	Welcome to Learn2.com: The New Way to Learn	The New Way to Learn
Microsoft	Welcome to Microsoft's Homepage	Where Do You Want to Go Today?
MotherNature	MotherNature.com—Natural Products. Healthy Advice.	MotherNature Natural Products. Healthy Advice.
MTV	MTV.com	None
NewsNow	NewsNow: 17:17 12-Jul-01: Quality News Headlines Updated Every Five Minutes, Every Day—C	NewsNow Brings You Breaking News from Around the World
NewScientist	NewScientist.com—The World's No. 1 Science and Technology News Service	
PBS	PSB Online	None
Petsmart	PETsMART.com—The Smarter Way to Shop for Your Pet	None
Philip Morris	Philip Morris Home	Working to Make a Difference. The People of Philip Morris and Makers of the World's Finest Products
PlanetRx	PlanetRx|Online Pharmacy & Drugstore	Life Is Better on PlanetRx
Red Herring	RedHerring.com|The Business of Innovation	The Business of Innovation
Slusser's Green Thumb	Slusser's Commercial Landscaping & Heavy Highway	Transforming Landscapes and Heavy-Highway into Beauty
Southwest	Southwest Airlines	A Symbol of E-Freedom
Ticketmaster	Welcome to Ticketmaster.com!	None
Travelocity	Airline Tickets, Hotels, Cars, Vacations: Go Virtually Anywhere with Travelocity.com	None
USA Today	USATODAY.com	None
Victoria's Secret	Victoria's Secret—Welcome to VictoriasSecret.com	None
Wal-Mart	Walmart.com—Always Low Prices!	None
Yahoo!	Yahoo!	None

Breakdown of Screen Real Estate

About

Accenture

Amazon

The Art Institute of Chicago

Asia Cuisine

Barnes & Noble

BBC Online

Boeing

CDNOW

Citigroup

CNET

CNNfn

Coles

DIRECTV

Disney

Drugstore

eBay

eMagazineshop

ESPN

ExxonMobil

FedEx

Federal Highway Administration

Florida Department of Revenue

Ford Motor Company

Gateway

General Electric

General Motors

Global Sources

IBM

James Devaney Fuel Co.

obMagic

Learn2

Microsoft

MotherNature

MTV

NewScientist

NewsNow

PBS

Petsmart

Philip Morris

PlanetRx

Red Herring

Slusser's Green Thumb

Southwest

Ticketmaster

Logos

About

Accenture

Amazon

The Art Institute of Chicago

Asia Cuisine

Barnes & Noble

BBC Online

Boeing

CDNOW

Citigroup

CNET

CNNfn

Coles

DIRECTV

Disney

Drugstore

eBay

eMagazineshop

ESPN

ExxonMobil

FedEx

Federal Highway Administration

Florida Department of Revenue

Ford Motor Company

Gateway

General Electric

General Motors

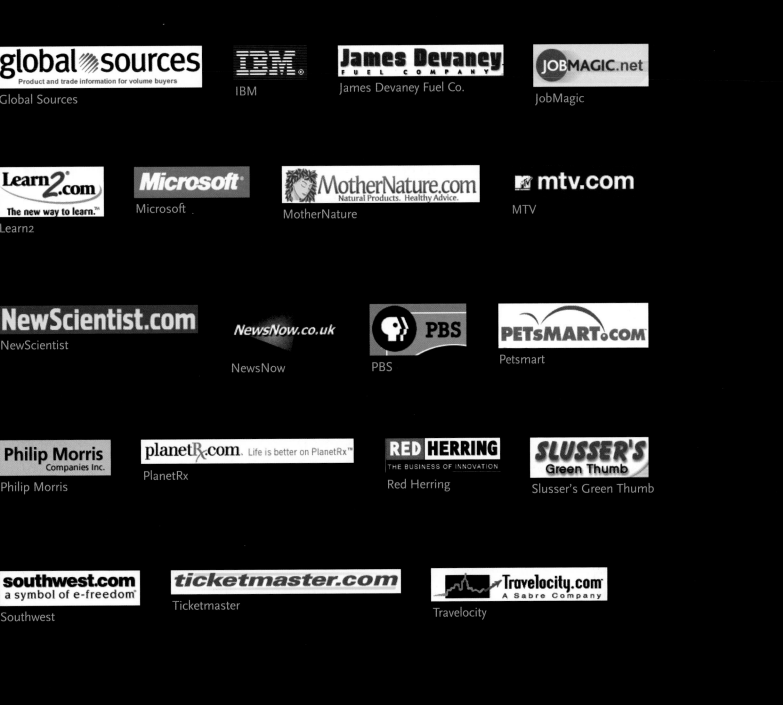

Global Sources

IBM

James Devaney Fuel Co.

JobMagic

Learn2

Microsoft

MotherNature

MTV

NewScientist

NewsNow

PBS

Petsmart

Philip Morris

PlanetRx

Red Herring

Slusser's Green Thumb

Southwest

Ticketmaster

Travelocity

USA Today

Victoria's Secret

Wal-Mart

Yahoo!

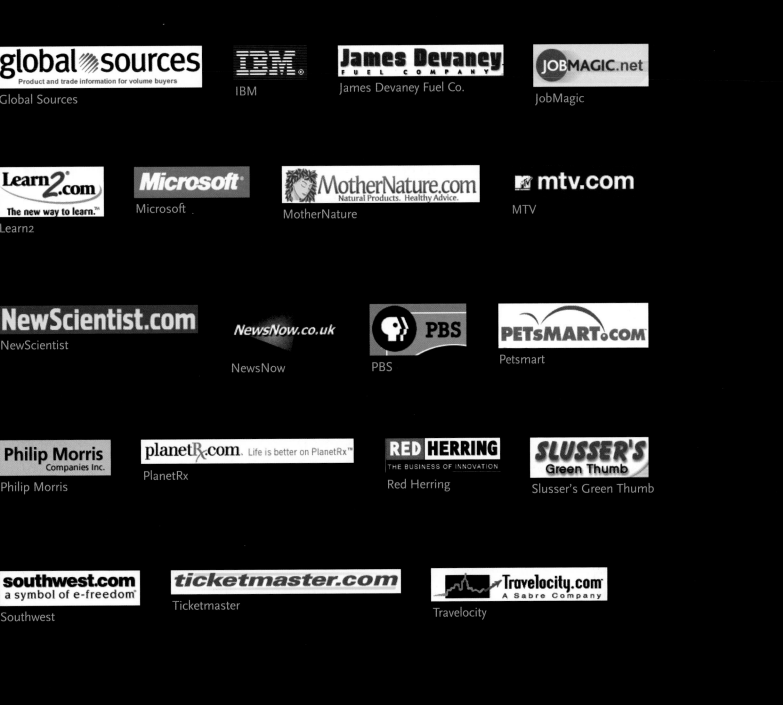

Search Features

About

Accenture

Amazon

The Art Institute of Chicago

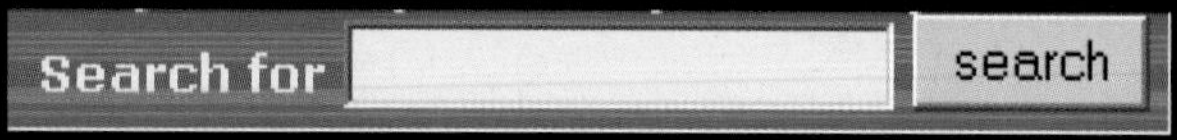

Asia Cuisine

Barnes & Noble

Boeing

CDNOW

CNET

CNNfn

Coles

DIRECTV

Disney

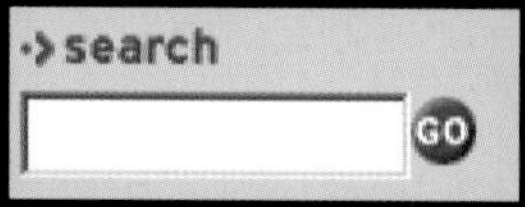

Drugstore

eBay

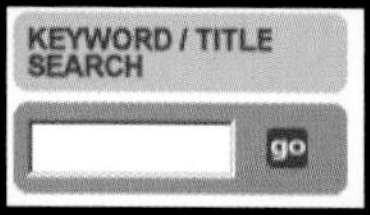

eMagazineshop

ESPN

ExxonMobil

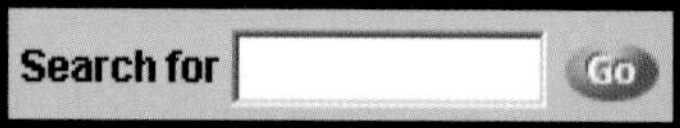

FedEx

Federal Highway Administration

Florida Department of Revenue

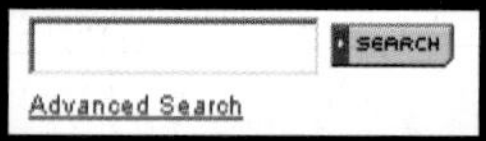

Ford Motor Company

General Electric

General Motors

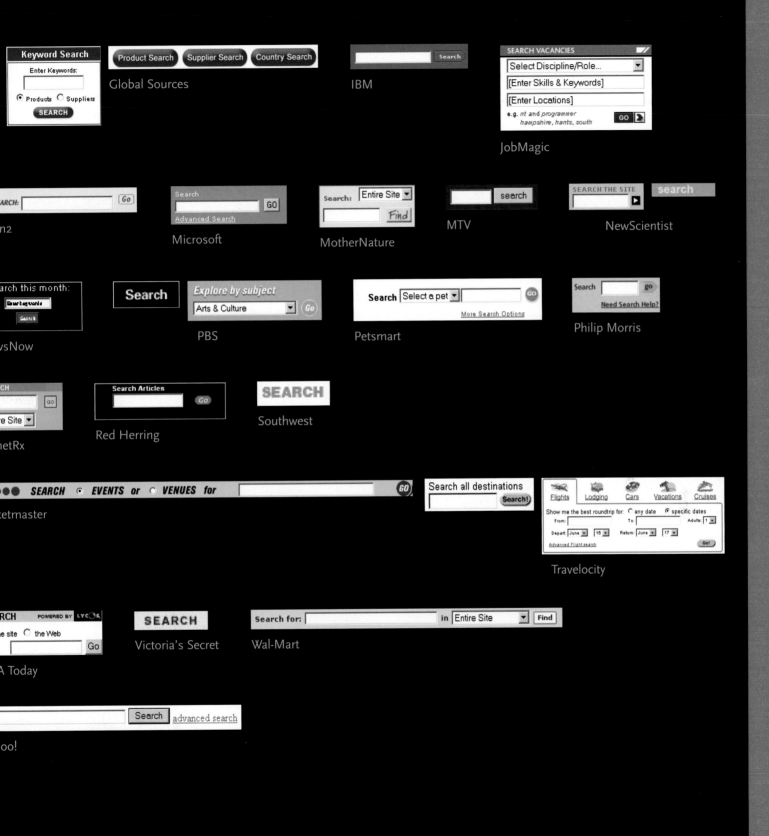

Keyword Search
Enter Keywords:
◉ Products ○ Suppliers
SEARCH

Global Sources

Product Search Supplier Search Country Search

IBM
Search

SEARCH VACANCIES
Select Discipline/Role...
[Enter Skills & Keywords]
[Enter Locations]
e.g. *nt* and *programmer*
   hampshire, hants, south
GO ▶

JobMagic

...ARCH: Go

n2

Search
GO
Advanced Search

Microsoft

Search: Entire Site ▾
Find

MotherNature

search

MTV

SEARCH THE SITE
▶

search

NewScientist

...arch this month:
Saurbegunia
Search

...vsNow

Search

Explore by subject
Arts & Culture Go

PBS

Search Select a pet ▾ GO
More Search Options

Petsmart

Search go
Need Search Help?

Philip Morris

...CH
Go
...e Site ▾

...etRx

Search Articles Go

Red Herring

SEARCH

Southwest

●●● SEARCH ◉ EVENTS or ○ VENUES for GO

...ketmaster

Search all destinations
Search!

Flights Lodging Cars Vacations Cruises
Show me the best roundtrip for: ○ any date ◉ specific dates
From: To: Adults: 1 ▾
Depart: June ▾ 16 ▾ Return: June ▾ 17 ▾
Advanced Flight search Go!

Travelocity

...RCH POWERED BY LYCOS
...e site ○ the Web
Go

...A Today

SEARCH

Victoria's Secret

Search for: in Entire Site ▾ Find

Wal-Mart

Search advanced search

...oo!

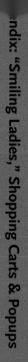

Accenture

Asia Cuisine

BBC Online

Citigroup

FedEx

Federal Highway Administration

IBM

Learn2

James Devaney Fuel Co.

MTV

Shopping Carts

VIEW CART

Amazon

cart

Barnes & Noble

Shopping Cart
contains 0 items

CDNOW

BASKET

eMagazineshop

Cart & Checkout

Walmart

SHOPPING CART

MotherNature

Petsmart

Popups

Barnes & Noble

eMagazineshop

JobMagic

Petsmart

Index

VOICES THAT MATTER

VISIT OUR WEB SITE

WWW.NEWRIDERS.COM

On our web site, you'll find information about our other books, authors, tables of contents, and book errata. You will also find information about book registration and how to purchase our books, both domestically and internationally.

EMAIL US

Contact us at: **nrfeedback@newriders.com**

- If you have comments or questions about this book
- To report errors that you have found in this book
- If you have a book proposal to submit or are interested in writing for New Riders
- If you are an expert in a computer topic or technology and are interested in being a technical editor who reviews manuscripts for technical accuracy

Contact us at: **nreducation@newriders.com**

- If you are an instructor from an educational institution who wants to preview New Riders books for classroom use. Email should include your name, title, school, department, address, phone number, office days/hours, text in use, and enrollment, along with your request for desk/examination copies and/or additional information.

Contact us at: **nrmedia@newriders.com**

- If you are a member of the media who is interested in reviewing copies of New Riders books. Send your name, mailing address, and email address, along with the name of the publication or web site you work for.

BULK PURCHASES/CORPORATE SALES

If you are interested in buying 10 or more copies of a title or want to set up an account for your company to purchase directly from the publisher at a substantial discount, contact us at 800-382-3419 or email your contact information to corpsales@pearsontechgroup.com. A sales representative will contact you with more information.

WRITE TO US

New Riders Publishing
1249 Eighth Street
Berkeley, California 94710

CALL/FAX US

Toll-free (800) 571-5840
If outside U.S. (317) 581-3500
Ask for New Riders

New Riders

Visit Peachpit on the Web at www.peachpit.com

- Read the latest articles and download timesaving tipsheets from best-selling authors such as Scott Kelby, Robin Williams, Lynda Weinman, Ted Landau, and more!

- Join the Peachpit Club and save 25% off all your online purchases at peachpit.com every time you shop—plus enjoy free UPS ground shipping within the United States.

- Search through our entire collection of new and upcoming titles by author, ISBN, title, or topic. There's no easier way to find just the book you need.

- Sign up for newsletters offering special Peachpit savings and new book announcements so you're always the first to know about our newest books and killer deals.

- Did you know that Peachpit also publishes books by Apple, New Riders, Adobe Press, Macromedia Press, palmOne Press, and TechTV press? Swing by the Peachpit family section of the site and learn about all our partners and series.

- Got a great idea for a book? Check out our About section to find out how to submit a proposal. You could write our next best-seller!

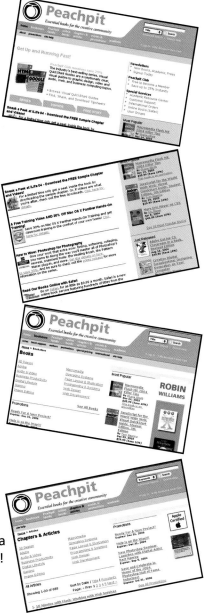

You'll find all this and more at www.peachpit.com. Stop by and take a look today!

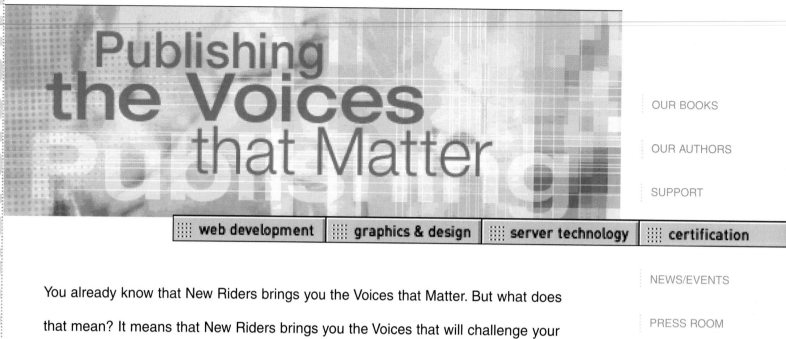

Publishing the Voices that Matter

OUR BOOKS

OUR AUTHORS

SUPPORT

| web development | graphics & design | server technology | certification |

You already know that New Riders brings you the Voices that Matter. But what does that mean? It means that New Riders brings you the Voices that will challenge your assumptions, take your talents to the next level, or simply help you better understand the complex technical world we're all navigating.

NEWS/EVENTS

PRESS ROOM

EDUCATORS

ABOUT US

CONTACT US

WRITE/REVIEW

Visit **www.newriders.com** to find:

▶ Previously unpublished chapters

▶ Sample chapters/excerpts

▶ Author bios

▶ Contests

▶ Up-to-date industry event information

▶ Book reviews

▶ Special offers

▶ Info on how to join our User Group program

▶ Inspirational galleries where you can submit
   your own masterpieces

▶ Ways to have your Voice heard

New Riders

WWW.NEWRIDERS.COM

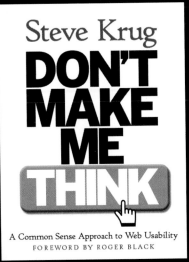

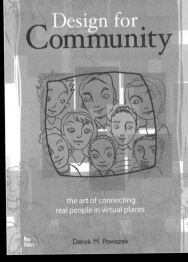
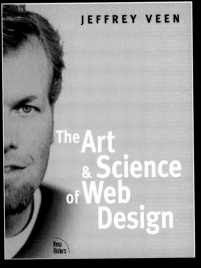
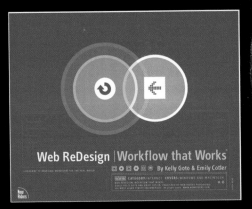

Read What the World Is Reading

In 2000, the world's leading expert on getting the most out of the Web published a book that changed how people think about the Web. Many applauded. A few jeered. Everyone listened. Love him or hate him, people pay attention. See what the debate is about, and decide for yourself.

English
ISBN 1-56205-810-X

Japanese
ISBN 4-8443-5562-7

German
ISBN 3-8272-5779-4

French
ISBN 2-7440-0887-7

Spanish
ISBN 84-205-3008-5

Russian
ISBN 5-93286-004-9

Chinese
ISBN 7-115-08726-1